MASTERING OHIO'S GRADE 4 SOCIAL STUDIES TEST

STUART ZIMMER

MARK JARRETT, PH.D.

JAMES KILLORAN

JARRETT PUBLISHING COMPANY

EAST COAST OFFICE
P.O. Box 1460
Ronkonkoma, NY 11779
631-981-4248

SOUTHERN OFFICE
50 Nettles Boulevard
Jensen Beach, FL 34957

WEST COAST OFFICE
10 Folin Lane
Lafayette, CA 94549
925-906-9742

www.jarrettpub.com
1-800-859-7679   Fax: 631-588-4722

The authors wish to thank the following educator for her comments, suggestions, and recommendations which proved invaluable to this manuscript.

Corbin Moore
Instructional Specialist, Social Studies, Hamilton City School District
President of the Ohio Council for the Social Studies, 2013–2014

Adam Motter
Instructional Specialist, Social Studies, Akron Public Schools
Vice President of the Ohio Council for the Social Studies, 2013–2014

Layout, maps, graphics, and typesetting: Burmar Technical Corporation, Sea Cliff, N.Y.

This book is dedicated...

to Joan, Todd, and Ronald,
and my grandchildren Jared and Katie   — *Stuart Zimmer*

to Malgorzata, Alexander, and Julia   — *Mark Jarrett*

to Donna, Christian, Carrie, and the memory of Jesse,
and to my grandchildren Aiden, Christian, Olivia,
Rutland, Shannon, and James   — *James Killoran*

ISBN 1-935022-24-5   [978-1-935022-24-4]
Printed in the United States of America
First Edition
10 9 8 7 6 5 4 3 2 1   17 16 15

TABLE OF CONTENTS

UNIT 3: GOVERNMENT   191

UNIT 4: ECONOMICS   272

UNIT 5: PRACTICE TEST   308

INTRODUCTION

This year, you will be taking Ohio's Grade 4 Social Studies Summative Assessment. An **assessment** is a test. This test will see what you have learned this year in social studies. The **Grade 4 Social Studies Test** actually has two parts:

PERFORMANCE BASED ASSESSMENT (PBA)

The first part of the test is the Performance-Based Assessment, or "PBA." This part of the test is taken first. Performance-Based Assessment items will ask you to do more than you would in answering a multiple-choice question. Each task requires you to create an answer, rather than select one from a group of choices.

This part of the test consists of both constructed-response and graphic-response questions. The Performance-Based Assessment will cover the first three-quarters of your course in social studies. It is worth a total of 20 points.

END-OF-YEAR TEST (EOY)

The second part of the test is the End-of-Year test, or "EOY." You will take this part of the test as close as possible to the end of the school year. It will cover all of the topics you will study this year in social studies. Where Performance-Based Assessment items are scored by your teachers, these questions will be scored by a computer.

This part of the test will have several different kinds of questions. There will be multiple-choice, short-answer, graphic-response and simulation questions. The End-of-Year test is worth a total of 44 points.

Both parts of the test will be taken "online" on a school computer.

PBA AND EOY QUESTION-TYPES

Let's look more closely at each of the types of questions that will appear on the **Grade 4 Social Studies Test**:

- **Multiple-Choice.** In these questions, you are asked to select the best answer from four choices.
- **Short-Answer.** In these questions, you are asked to type a short answer. Usually, your answer will be from one word to a sentence or two in length.
- **Graphic-Response.** In these questions, you are asked to move objects on the computer screen from one location to another. For example, you might have to sort items into different categories or match items.

- **Short Constructed-Response.** These questions include short reading passages, maps, graphs, diagrams or some other type of information. These sources will be followed by a question or a series of questions. You are then asked to type your answer to each part of the question. Your answer should be longer here than a response to a short-answer question.

- **Extended Constructed-Response.** This type of question is similar to a short con-structed- response question. However, it is different in that it has more documents or other data. It will also ask a longer and more detailed question. Your answer should be longer than for a short constructed-response question.

- **Simulation.** In this last type of question, you are provided with documents and other materials, and asked to interpret them. You may have an opportunity to change something in the documents or data you are provided with. You may also be asked to compare several different sources dealing with the same event or topic.

HOW THIS BOOK CAN HELP YOU ON THE TEST

While the Grade 4 Social Studies Summative Assessment is a test that is taken online, this book is on paper. You may be asking yourself: How can this "paper" book help me to do well on an online test?

In fact, every chapter of this book is designed to help you perform your very best on the test. You can better understand this by looking at each of the special learning features you will find in this book.

CONTENT STATEMENTS

Each of the 24 chapters in this book begins by identifying one of the tested social studies standards, also known as "Content Statements." The Content Statement spe-cifically indicates what the Ohio Department of Education wants you to know.

KEY NAMES, WORDS, AND PHRASES

Imagine playing a sport without knowing the rules, or playing a musical instrument without knowing how to read music. It is important that you are able to recognize the specialized vocabulary of social studies. This section of the chapter identifies those key names, words, and phrases that you should know.

WHAT YOU ARE EXPECTED TO ACHIEVE

Here you will find the core or essential information and skills that you should try to achieve after you have completed that chapter.

THE MAIN IDEAS

The key names, words and phrases are followed by the "main ideas" of the content statement. Here you will find a student-friendly text with plentiful illustrations to guide you through what you need to know. Each of these sections briefly reviews the main ideas necessary to understand the content statement.

Name _____ Date _____ **UNLAWFUL TO PHOTOCOPY OR PROJECT WITHOUT PERMISSION**

CHAPTER 1

MAP SCALE AND DIRECTIONS

CONTENT STATEMENT

TOPIC: SPATIAL THINKING SKILLS

What is "spatial thinking"? It means thinking about where things are located in space. You should be able to read, interpret and create maps and other geographic representations that show where things are located.

Geography 1 *A map scale and cardinal and intermediate directions can be used to describe the relative location of physical and human characteristics of Ohio and the United States.*

After reading this chapter, you should be able to:

★ Define the following terms:
- Relative location
- Scale of miles
- Cardinal directions
- Intermediate directions

★ Use a map scale and cardinal and intermediate directions to describe the relative locations of both physical and human characteristics.

MAIN IDEAS OF THIS CONTENT STATEMENT

Relative location is where something is located in relation to other things. It describes a place using reference points. For example, your school might be located next to a [park]. It could be one mile northeast of your town's [fire] station.

  Physical characteristics have to do with the [geogra]phy of a place. Physical characteristics of a [pla]ch things as its land forms, nearness to bod [altitu]**tude** (*height*) above sea level, and **climate** (*average* [temperatu]*res and rainfall*).

10

KEY NAMES, WORDS, AND PHRASES

MAIN IDEA

WHAT YOU ARE EXPECTED TO ACHIEVE

UNLAWFUL TO PHOTOCOPY OR PROJECT WITHOUT PERMISSION Name _____ Date _____

Chapter 1: Map Scale and Directions   **15**

STUDY CARDS

Maps

1. Map Scale: _____
_____
_____

2. Cardinal Directions: _____
_____

3. Intermediate Directions: _____
_____

Relative Location

1. What is relative location? _____
_____
_____
_____

2. Provide two examples of relative location:
A. _____
_____

B. _____
_____

STUDY CARDS

Next you will find a series of study cards. These are study cards you fill out yourself. The information you use on these cards is based on the content found in the chapter. By filling out these cards, you will learn this information better. You should cut out the study cards and use them to practice with. In Chapter 1, you will learn more about how to use them.

CONTENT-AREA VOCABULARY

The Content-Area Vocabulary consists of a mix of different vocabulary exercises. The focus of these vocabulary exercises is to familiarize you with the key vocabulary of the content statements in social studies.

In addition, these exercises use proven strategies that can help you to learn difficult terms, names and concepts used in fourth grade social studies.

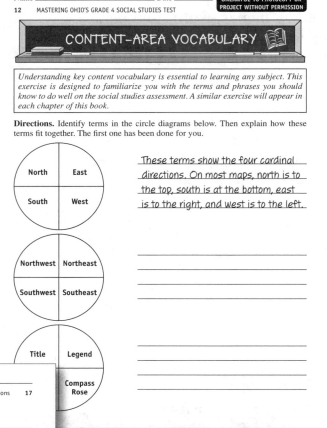

Name _____ Date _____

12   MASTERING OHIO'S GRADE 4 SOCIAL STUDIES TEST

CONTENT-AREA VOCABULARY

Understanding key content vocabulary is essential to learning any subject. This exercise is designed to familiarize you with the terms and phrases you should know to do well on the social studies assessment. A similar exercise will appear in each chapter of this book.

Directions. Identify terms in the circle diagrams below. Then explain how these terms fit together. The first one has been done for you.

| North | East |
| South | West |

These terms show the four cardinal directions. On most maps, north is to the top, south is at the bottom, east is to the right, and west is to the left.

| Northwest | Northeast |
| Southwest | Southeast |

_____
_____
_____
_____

| Title | Legend |
| Compass Rose | |

_____
_____
_____
_____

Name _____ Date _____

Chapter 1: Map Scale and Directions   **17**

INTERPRETING MAPS

SKILL BUILDER

*Skill Builders will show you how to answer questions dealing with different types of data. A similar **SKILL BUILDER** section, will appear in many chapters of this book.*

Many questions on **Ohio's Grade 4 Social Studies Test** will be based on maps. Let's look at how to "read" a map. A map is a drawing of a geographic area. Most maps show the political divisions or major physical characteristics of an area. However, there is almost no limit to the kinds of information that can be shown on a map.

STEPS TO UNDERSTANDING A MAP

LOOK AT THE TITLE

The title of the map identifies the information found on the map. For example, the title of the map to the right indicates that it shows Ohio's main cities and rivers.

EXAMINE THE LEGEND

The **legend** lists the symbols used. It identifies what each symbol represents. This map uses three symbols:

- The dark curved lines (⌒) show the locations of the major rivers in Ohio.
- Each • shows the location of a major city in Ohio.
- The ⊙ is the **symbol** used to show the location of Ohio's capital city.

CHECK THE COMPASS ROSE

The **compass rose** shows the four basic directions — north, south, east, and west. If there is no compass rose, you can usually assume north is at the top of the map.

OHIO'S MAJOR CITIES AND RIVERS

Toledo, LAKE ERIE, Sandusky, Cleveland, Warren, Findlay, Akron, Youngstown, Lima, Marion, Mansfield, Canton, Springfield, Columbus, Steubenville, Dayton, Zanesville, Cincinnati, Chillicothe, Athens, Portsmouth, OHIO RIVER

SCALE OF MILES 50

~ Rivers
• Cities
⊙ Capital City

SKILL BUILDERS

Some questions you will need to answer on the actual test, will ask you to interpret a piece of data. Throughout this book, you will find sections that explain how to read, understand and interpret different types of data. These types of data include diagrams, charts, tables, circle graphs, pictographs, line and bar graphs, and pictures.

PBA AND EOY QUESTIONS

The last part of each chapter asks you to answer a variety of PBA and EOY questions similar to those that you will find on the real **Grade 4 Social Studies Test**.

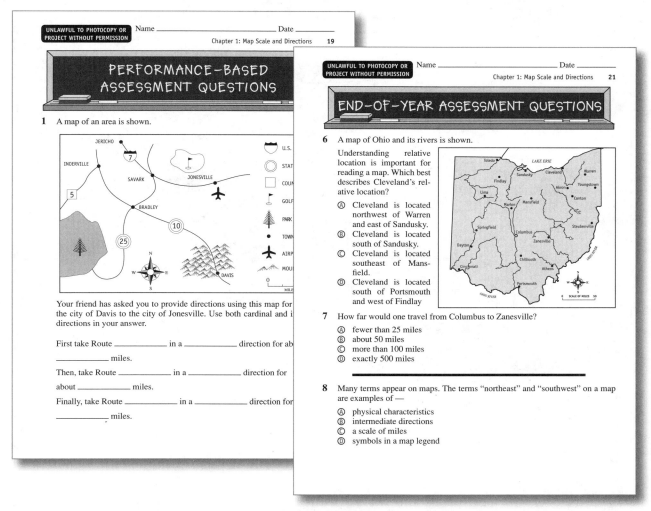

Of course, unlike the actual test that you will take online, this book is made of paper. There are two main differences between the online test and this book:

1. The actual test will ask you to move items on your computer screen when answering a "graphic-response" question. In the book, we ask you to **rewrite** information in the proper box or column, or to indicate where information should go by **drawing an arrow**.
2. The actual test will ask you to **type** your answers. In this book, you are asked to **write** those answers in the spaces provided.,

Apart from these two differences, the form of the practice questions is the same. By studying this book and listening to your teacher, you should be sure to perform your very best when the day of each part of the real test arrives.

UNIT 1

GEOGRAPHY

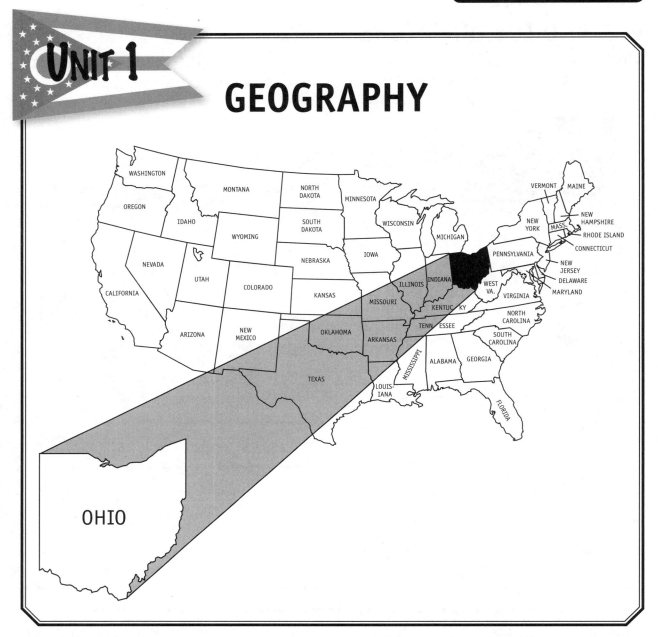

Geography is the study of the world's surface. It shows where things are located, what different places are like, and how people interact with their physical environment.

The following topics are examined in this unit:

1. **SPATIAL THINKING SKILLS**

2. **PLACES AND REGIONS**

3. **HUMAN SYSTEMS**

GEOGRAPHY PRE-TEST

This school year you will take a test in fourth grade social studies. All units will open with a pre-test. These pre-tests will show you some of the kinds of questions you can expect on the actual test. At the end of each unit, you will take another test. This second test will show you how much you have learned in the unit. Good luck on this first pre-test.

1 How did the Erie Canal play a role in the economic development of Ohio?

Ⓐ Ohio settlers grew wealthy by selling land along the Erie Canal.
Ⓑ The Erie Canal directly connected Eastern states with the West Coast.
Ⓒ Southern cotton was sent over the Eire Canal to British factories.
Ⓓ Goods from Ohio could more easily be shipped to New York City and the Atlantic Ocean.

2 Which statement best describes the South during the early 1800s?

Ⓐ It was a leading manufacturing center in the United States.
Ⓑ Its soils provided the nation with such crops as cotton, rice, and tobacco.
Ⓒ Known as the nation's "bread basket" it grew wheat and other food crops.
Ⓓ The South's location made it a center for shipbuilding.

3 A concept map is shown.

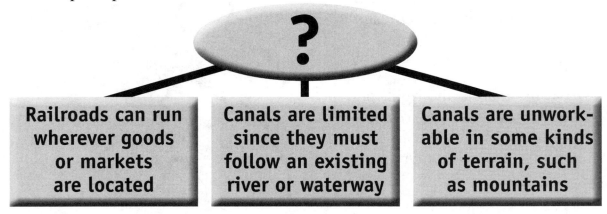

?

| Railroads can run wherever goods or markets are located | Canals are limited since they must follow an existing river or waterway | Canals are unworkable in some kinds of terrain, such as mountains |

Which is the best title for this concept map?

Ⓐ Why Canals Replaced Railroads in Ohio
Ⓑ Ohio's Growing Canal System
Ⓒ Why Railroads Replaced Canals in Ohio
Ⓓ Ohio's Canal System: The Ideal Way to Ship Goods

4   A photograph with several children is shown.

What concept is this photograph an expression of?

[   ]

5   The following question has two parts. First, answer part A. Then, answer part B.

Kroger, a retail supermarket chain, has its headquarters in Cincinnati, Ohio. It has received a large order from a store in New Orleans, Louisiana.

Part A.

On the map to the right, put an X on an all-water route the company could use to ship their goods to New Orleans.

Part B.

Identify the major waterways used:

● _____

● _____

6   The following question has two parts. First, answer part A. Then, answer part B.

You have just been elected to your town's Planning Board. A builder has submitted this artist's drawing for a proposed dam to be built across the main river in the town. The Planning Board cannot decide whether or not to approve this change to the environment. They have asked you

Artist's rendering of the proposed dam.

to analyze the situation. You are to report to them with a suggested course of action. You decide to present the Planning Board with **one** positive and **one** negative consequence of this change to the environment.

Part A. Positive consequence of building the dam:

_____

_____

_____

_____

_____

Part B. Negative consequence of building the dam:

_____

_____

_____

_____

_____

END OF PRE-TEST

CHAPTER 1

MAP SCALE AND DIRECTIONS

TOPIC: SPATIAL THINKING SKILLS

What is "spatial thinking"? It means thinking about where things are located in space. You should be able to read, interpret and create maps and other geographic representations that show where things are located.

Geography 1	*A map scale and cardinal and intermediate directions can be used to describe the relative location of physical and human characteristics of Ohio and the United States.*

After reading this chapter, you should be able to:

★ Define the following terms:
  • Relative location
  • Scale of miles
  • Cardinal directions
  • Intermediate directions

★ Use a map scale and cardinal and intermediate directions to describe the relative locations of both physical and human characteristics.

MAIN IDEAS OF THIS CONTENT STATEMENT

Relative location is where something is located in relation to other things. It describes a place using reference points. For example, your school might be located next to a public park. It could be one mile northeast of your town's police station.

Physical characteristics have to do with the physical geography of a place. Physical characteristics of a place include such things as its land forms, nearness to bodies of water, **altitude** (*height*) above sea level, and **climate** (*average temperatures and rainfall*).

Human characteristics refer to things put in place by humans rather than by nature. For example, human-made features include buildings, roads, dams, cities and farms. You can locate human features — such as Ohio's capital city of Columbus — on a map.

The state capital at Columbus, Ohio — an example of a human-made feature.

FEATURES OF A MAP

The **scale** on a map shows what the distances on the map represent in real life. One inch on a map, for example, might represent one mile in real life. Usually, the smaller the number used on the map scale, the more detailed the map will be.

Using a map's scale has certain benefits. First, it provides us with a simple and easy way to determine distances between places. Secondly, if the size of the map is made larger or smaller, the scale is also enlarged or reduced. This allows a map's scale to remain accurate even when the size of the map changes.

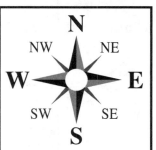

We use cardinal and intermediate directions to make it easier to find places, both in real life and on a map. The **cardinal directions** are *north*, *south*, *east* and *west*. Usually, the top of the map is north.

Intermediate directions lie between the four cardinal directions. They include *northeast*, *northwest*, *southeast*, and *southwest*. Mapmakers often indicate directions on their maps by adding a **compass rose** similar to the ones shown above.

CONTENT-AREA VOCABULARY

Understanding key content vocabulary is essential to learning any subject. This exercise is designed to familiarize you with the terms and phrases you should know to do well on the social studies assessment. A similar exercise will appear in each chapter of this book.

Directions. Identify terms in the circle diagrams below. Then explain how these terms fit together. The first one has been done for you.

North	East
South	West

These terms show the four cardinal directions. On most maps, north is to the top, south is at the bottom, east is to the right, and west is to the left.

Northwest	Northeast
Southwest	Southeast

_____
_____
_____
_____

Title	Legend
Scale	Compass Rose

_____
_____
_____
_____

HOW TO USE YOUR STUDY CARDS

During this school year, you will learn about important events and the many people who have influenced the development of Ohio and the United States. With such a large amount of information, it is sometimes difficult to remember what is important. Learning how to use **Study Cards** will help you to do that.

Just after the content summary in every chapter, you will find two or more **Study Cards**. These **Study Cards** identify the most essential information you should know about a term or concept in the chapter. You are asked to fill in the front of the **Study Card** yourself. You should add a drawing or diagram to help you to remember the information in the **Study Card**. Turning written information into a picture can help you to better understand the term or concept. Many students learn better when they visualize something. By "seeing" the term or concept, you create an impression in your mind that helps you to remember it better. In drawing these illustrations, do not be concerned with your artistic ability. That is not important. What is important is that your illustration captures the main idea of the term or concept.

You should make a habit of building a collection of these **Study Cards** by cutting them out. You will notice that the reverse of each card already contains a printed **prompt**. When you review these cards, you should look at the prompt to test your memory. See if you can recall the information it asks. Then flip the card over. Compare what you have written down with what you were able to remember.

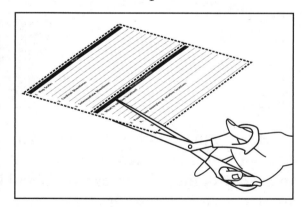

Maps
1 Map Scale: _____
_____
_____
_____
2 Cardinal Directions: _____
_____
_____
3 Intermediate Directions: _____
_____
_____

Maps
1 Map Scale: _A map scale shows what distances on a map represent in real life. For example, one inch might equal 100 miles._
2 Cardinal Directions: _These are the four basic directions — north, south, east and west._
3 Intermediate Directions: _These are between the cardinal directions — northeast, southeast, northwest, and southwest._

There are many ways to use these *Study Cards* to recall information when it comes to a class quiz or test. One method is to sort your cards into two stacks, based on how well you recall the information on each card.

First, gather your *Study Cards* into one pile. Try to recall the information on the card at the top of the stack. If you can recall it, place the card in the "Know It" stack. If you have trouble recalling the information, place the card in the "Don't Know It" stack.

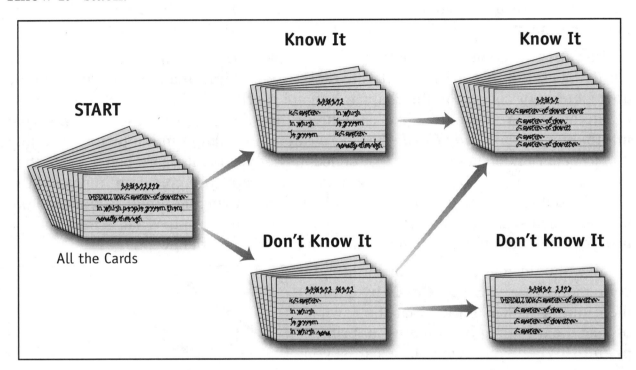

Review the cards in the "Don't Know It" stack every time you study. Review the *Study Cards* in the "Know It" stack every other time you study. As you move closer to the day of the quiz or test, you should see the number of cards in the "Don't Know It" stack start to grow less. This will give you even more time to study the ones you know the least.

This book will provide you with a summary of what you will need to know about *history*, *geography*, *government*, and *economics*. With this book as your guide, you should be well prepared to face the challenges presented by the *Fourth Grade Ohio Achievement Test in Social Studies*. It also provides you with practice questions and other learning features. For more details about your learning standards, we recommend you use our activity book, *Ohio in the United States*.

STUDY CARDS

Maps

1. Map Scale: _____

_____

_____

_____

2. Cardinal Directions: _____

_____

_____

3. Intermediate Directions: _____

_____

_____

Relative Location

1. What is relative location? _____

_____

_____

_____

_____

2. Provide two examples of relative location:

    A. _____

_____

    B. _____

_____

STUDY CARD PROMPTS

Timeline

1. **What is a map scale?**

2. **What are cardinal directions?**

3. **What are intermediate directions?**

To check your answers to these questions, turn the card over and review the information you have written on the other side.

Relative Location

1. **What is relative location?**

2. **Provide two examples of relative location.**

To check your answers to these questions, turn the card over and review the information you have written on the other side.

INTERPRETING MAPS

SKILL BUILDER

> *Skill Builders* *will show you how to answer questions dealing with different types of data. A similar* ***SKILL BUILDER*** *section, will appear in many chapters of this book.*

Many questions on **Ohio's Grade 4 Social Studies Test** will be based on maps. Let's look at how to "read" a map. A map is a drawing of a geographic area. Most maps show the political divisions or major physical characteristics of an area. However, there is almost no limit to the kinds of information that can be shown on a map.

STEPS TO UNDERSTANDING A MAP

LOOK AT THE TITLE

The title of the map identifies the information found on the map. For example, the title of the map to the right indicates that it shows Ohio's main cities and rivers.

EXAMINE THE LEGEND

The **legend** lists the symbols used. It identifies what each symbol represents. This map uses three symbols:

- The dark curved lines (⌇) show the locations of the major rivers in Ohio.

- Each • shows the location of a major city in Ohio.

OHIO'S MAJOR CITIES AND RIVERS

Toledo, Lake Erie, Sandusky, Cleveland, Warren, Findlay, Youngstown, Akron, Lima, Canton, Marion, Mansfield, Springfield, Columbus, Steubenville, Zanesville, Dayton, Chillicoth, Cincinnati, Athens, Ohio River, Portsmouth

Legend: Rivers, Cities, Capital City

SCALE OF MILES 0 — 50

- The ✪ is the **symbol** used to show the location of Ohio's capital city.

CHECK THE COMPASS ROSE

The **compass rose** shows the four basic directions — north, south, east, and west. If there is no compass rose, you can usually assume north is at the top of the map.

EXAMINE THE SCALE

A map would be impossible to use if it were the same size as the area it shows. Mapmakers reduce the size of the map so that it can fit onto a page. The **scale** shows what the distances on the map represent. Map scales are often shown as a line marked: "**Miles**" or "**Scale of Miles**." On the map above, about three-quarters of one inch equals 50 miles.

FINDING SPECIFIC INFORMATION

If you wanted to find all the cities about 50 miles from the capital of Ohio, here is what you would have to do:

- Examine the map to find where Columbus, the capital of Ohio, is located.

- Next, using the *Scale of Miles*, place the start of a piece of paper at the 0 on the scale. Mark the paper exactly where 50 miles is. Then, place the start of the piece of paper at Columbus.

- Lastly, with the paper at Columbus, move it around to see the cities that surround Columbus — Springfield, Marion, Zanesville, Mansfield, and Chillicothe. You will discover that Zanesville is actually closest to the 50-mile mark from Columbus.

Now that you have learned how to use a scale to find distances on a map, let's see how well you can apply this skill.

ANSWERING MAP-BASED QUESTIONS

Look at the map on the previous page to answer the following questions. Write your answers in the boxes below:

A   What is the distance between the cities of Cleveland and Canton?

B   What is the distance between the cities of Dayton and Mansfield?

C   Which Ohio city is precisely 50 miles away from the Ohio River?

PERFORMANCE-BASED ASSESSMENT QUESTIONS

1 A map of an area is shown.

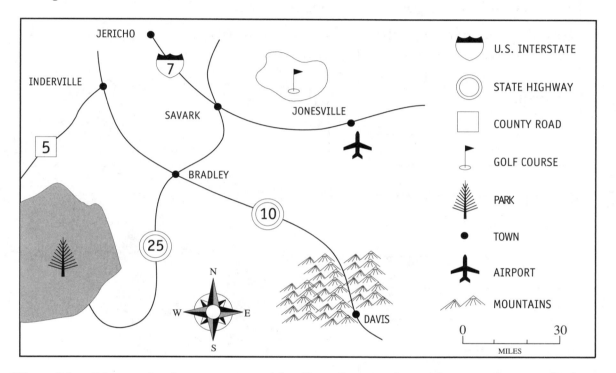

Your friend has asked you to provide directions using this map for travel from the city of Davis to the city of Jonesville. Use both cardinal and intermediate directions in your answer.

First take Route _____ in a _____ direction for about

_____ miles.

Then, take Route _____ in a _____ direction for

about _____ miles.

Finally, take Route _____ in a _____ direction for

_____ miles.

2   **A**   According to this map, Bradley is _____ miles from Davis.

    B   Jonesville is _____ miles _____ (direction) of Savark.

    C   Jericho is _____ miles _____ (direction) of Savark.

    D   Bradley is _____ miles _____ (direction) of Savark.

---

3   A map of Ohio's major land regions is shown.

Based on the map, describe the relative location in Ohio of the Appalachian Plateau.

_____

_____

_____

_____

_____

_____

_____

_____

_____

OHIO'S REGIONS

LAKE ERIE

GREAT LAKES PLAINS

TILL PLAINS

APPALACHIAN PLATEAU

OHIO RIVER

BLUEGRASS REGION

OHIO RIVER

4   Based on the map, describe the relative location of the Great Lakes Plains in Ohio.

_____

_____

_____

5   Based on the map, what is the relative location of the Bluegrass Region in Ohio?

_____

_____

_____

Name _____ Date _____

END-OF-YEAR ASSESSMENT QUESTIONS

6 A map of Ohio and its rivers is shown.

Understanding relative location is important for reading a map. Which best describes Cleveland's relative location?

Ⓐ Cleveland is located northwest of Warren and east of Sandusky.

Ⓑ Cleveland is located south of Sandusky.

Ⓒ Cleveland is located southeast of Mansfield.

Ⓓ Cleveland is located south of Portsmouth and west of Findlay

7 How far would one travel from Columbus to Zanesville?

Ⓐ fewer than 25 miles

Ⓑ about 50 miles

Ⓒ more than 100 miles

Ⓓ exactly 500 miles

8 Many terms appear on maps. The terms "northeast" and "southwest" on a map are examples of —

Ⓐ physical characteristics

Ⓑ intermediate directions

Ⓒ a scale of miles

Ⓓ symbols in a map legend

9   What is the "Scale of Miles" primarily used for on a map?

Ⓐ   to locate cardinal and intermediate directions

Ⓑ   to describe relative locations

Ⓒ   to indicate the distances between places

Ⓓ   to discover the location of physical features

10   A map of the northeastern United States is shown.

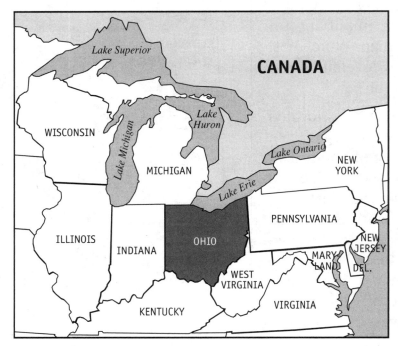

In the box below, write the name of the state that is located directly west of Ohio.

11   If you were to travel southwest of Ohio, write the name of the state which you would come to first.

12   Write the name of the state located northwest of Ohio and southwest of Lake Huron.

Name _____ Date _____

CHAPTER 2

OHIO'S IMPACT ON OUR NATION'S ECONOMIC DEVELOPMENT

TOPIC: PLACES AND REGIONS

A **place** is a location with its own unique characteristics. These characteristics give a place its meaning and character, and separate it from other locations. A **region** is an area with one or more common characteristics that make it different from surrounding areas.

Geography 2	*The economic development of the United States continues to influence and be influenced by agriculture, industry and natural resources in Ohio.*

After reading this chapter, you should be able to:

★ Define the following terms: • Economic development • Erie Canal • Natural resources • Industry	★ Describe connections between the agriculture, industry, and natural resources of Ohio and the economic development of our nation.

MAIN IDEAS OF THIS CONTENT STATEMENT

Economic development refers to how a region's ways of producing goods and services improves over time. Economic development often takes place when people apply new technologies to develop their resources. The economic development of the United States has been greatly influenced by Ohio.

NATURAL RESOURCES

Ohio has many **natural resources**. These include water resources, such as the **Ohio River, Lake Erie** and other rivers flowing into Lake Erie or the Ohio River.

Aerial view of the Ohio River

The Ohio River flows southwards into the Mississippi River, providing an important shipping route for farmers and manufacturers. Ohioans also ship goods into Lake Erie, eastward to the **Erie Canal** in New York State, and down the Hudson River to New York City. This method of shipment allows many Ohio companies to connect to important markets along the east coast of the United States.

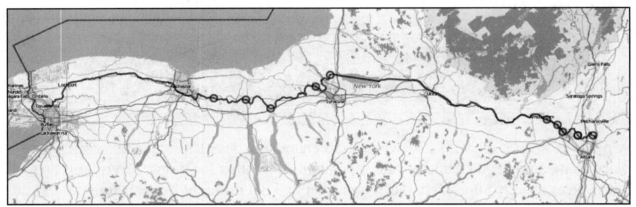

Ariel view of the Erie Canal to the Great Lakes

Mineral Resources are minerals found in nature that can be used by humans. Unlike some resources, mineral resources cannot be renewed once they are used. Ohio has many valuable mineral resources, including coal, natural gas, iron ore and gypsum. Ohio's coal deposits once fueled early American industries. Ohio also once had important oil reserves. John D. Rockefeller first developed his oil refining operations in Ohio. He refined crude oil to make kerosene for lamps. Later, he developed gasoline to fuel automobiles.

Coal mining began in Ohio around 1800. When the United States developed into an industrial giant in the late-1800s, Ohio became one of the nation's largest coal-producing states. Since then, billions of tons of coal have been mined in Ohio. Coal was used to heat iron ore to make

The coal industry in Ohio has witnessed great changes in the nation's demand for coal.

steel. In more recent times, Ohio's coal industry has faced great instability. Today, it has seen a sharp decline. This is due to technological advances, rising transportation costs, and evidence that burning coal has a negative impact on the environment.

Lumber is another valuable natural resource. In Ohio, lumber and other forest products are important to such manufacturing sectors as those providing wood and wood products, furniture and paper. At one time, Ohio was covered by plentiful forests, which provided lumber for houses and fences. Today, many of Ohio's forests have been restored in the eastern part of the state.

AGRICULTURE AND FISHING

Farming has always been important to Ohio. Early settlers to Ohio grew wheat, corn and other crops. Their activities helped the United States to expand westward. Ohio farmers continue to grow soybeans, corn, and other crops today.

Corn is used in cereal, cooking oil, gasoline, glue, ice cream, and even ink. Over 3,000 grocery products include some corn ingredient. About half of Ohio's corn is used to feed livestock, while a quarter of it is exported. Approximately 5% is used to make **biofuels** — fuels made from biological materials such as corn, soybeans, tree trimmings and grass.

Corn is one of Ohio's main crops.

Biodiesel, commonly made from soybeans, is Ohio's leading alternative fuel. Biodiesel can be used in diesel engines without changing a car's engine. It is a favorite fuel since it burns cleaner, acts as a better engine lubricant, creates jobs in Ohio, and reduces the nation's dependence on foreign oil.

Fishing in the Great Lakes and Ohio's rivers provides an important source of protein to Ohioans and other Americans.

TRANSPORTATION

Ohio's location and transportation systems greatly contributed to the state's economic importance. The location of Lake Erie, the Ohio River and other rivers greatly influenced Ohio's settlement patterns. Many early settlers first came to Ohio by traveling along the Ohio River by flat boat.

A railroad yard in the early 1900s in Lima, Ohio

After 1825, the addition of the **Erie Canal** made it possible for Ohio farmers and manufacturers to ship their goods to the East. Later, railroads and highways connected Ohio to the rest of the country.

INDUSTRY

Manufacturing is one of Ohio's most important economic activities. Ohio's many rivers helped to provide needed water and energy to power factory machines. Manufacturers learned to produce more goods for less money. Goods then became cheaper. This increased demand for goods. It also led to the creation of more jobs. Ohio's mineral and water resources made the state an early center of American manufacturing.

An early steel plant in Youngstown, Ohio.

The nation's growing demand for manufactured goods led to the rise of many new industries in Ohio. Ohioans refined oil into kerosene and other products. Ohioans made iron, steel, and rubber products. The Goodyear Tire and Rubber Company began in Akron in 1898. It treated natural rubber to make rubber for car tires. Today, Ohio still remains one of our nation's leading states for manufacturing. Ohioans continue to make car and aircraft parts. One out of four jobs in Ohio continues to be in manufacturing.

In 1947, the United States was the world's factory. Half of all global manufacturing took place in the United States. However, Ohioans and other Americans now face greater competition from foreign manufacturers. Many goods can be more cheaply produced abroad and shipped to the United States. Many of these are no longer produced here. These include many high-tech goods like computer parts, as well as textiles.

Foreign competition is challenging many industries in the United States.

Several factors influence which economic activities are conducted abroad. Many activities, for example, can only be conducted in the place where they are used. Housing construction, treating medical patients, and selling retail goods typically remain in the place where goods and services are used.

STUDY CARDS

Economic Development

1. Define "economic development." _____

_____

_____

_____

_____

2. How does an area's natural resources promote its economic development?

_____

_____

_____

_____

Ohio's Influence on American Economic Development

1. What were Ohio's advantages in location and natural resources?

_____

_____

2. What has been the influence of Ohio's agriculture on American development?

_____

_____

3. What has been the influence of Ohio's manufacturing on American development? _____

_____

_____

STUDY CARD PROMPTS

Economic Development

1. **What is "economic development"?**

2. **How does an area's natural resources promote its economic development?**

To check your answers to these questions, turn the card over and review the information you have written on the other side.

Ohio's Influence on American Economic Development

1. **What were Ohio's advantages in location and natural resources?**

2. **What has been the influence of Ohio's agriculture on American development?**

3. **What has been the influence of Ohio's manufacturing on American development?**

To check your answers to these questions, turn the card over and review the information you have written on the other side.

Name _____ Date _____

CONTENT-AREA VOCABULARY

Directions. Make a question for each of the following clusters of names and terms. Then define or identify any of these names and terms that you cannot recall.

| Ohio River
Lake Erie
Erie Canal | _____
_____
_____
_____ |

| Coal
Natural gas
Iron ore
Gypsum | _____
_____
_____
_____ |

| Corn
Wheat
Soybeans
Biofuels | _____
_____
_____
_____ |

| Oil
Iron
Steel
Rubber | _____
_____
_____
_____ |

PERFORMANCE-BASED ASSESSMENT QUESTIONS

13 A map of the northeastern United States in the early 1800s is shown.

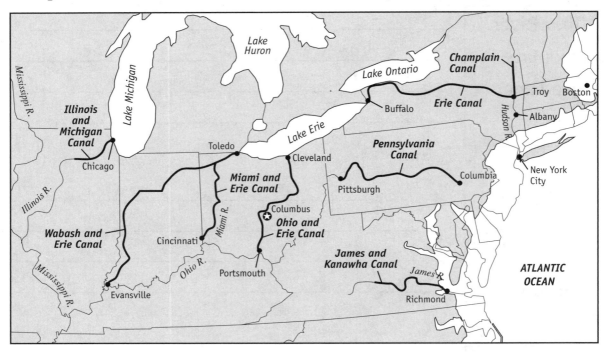

Ohio's plentiful water resources have played an important role in the economic development of the United States. Using the map above:

Describe how goods from Columbus, Ohio, were once shipped by water routes to New York City.

_____

_____

14 Explain how settlers from areas in eastern Pennsylvania were able to reach the Mississippi River by using waterways.

_____

_____

_____

15 The following lists economic activities in Ohio and the rest of the United States. Review the list. Then classify each item by placing it in the proper column of the T-Chart below, based on whether it is less affected or more highly affected by global competition.

ECONOMIC ACTIVITIES IN OHIO AND THE UNITED STATES	
A Home construction	**F** Manufacture of computer parts
B Health care services	**G** Providing police and security services
C Fast food restaurants	**H** Manufacture of shoes
D Manufacture of chemicals	**I** Manufacture of clothing
E Manufacture of television sets	**J** Farming of corn and other grains

LESS AFFECTED BY GLOBAL COMPETITION	HIGHLY AFFECTED BY GLOBAL COMPETITION

16 Why has corn production become an important source of energy for transportation in recent years?

_____

_____

_____

_____

17 Identify **two** industries that were powered by Ohio's coal resources.

A.	B.

18 Listed below are four major industries in Ohio.

Steel Industry (SI)	Rubber Industry (RI)	Food Process-ing Industry (FPI)	Oil Refining Industry (ORI)

Place the letters (*shown in parenthesis*) that represents that industry into the second column, which shows the industry that uses that resource. A natural resource or raw material can be used by more than one industry. The first one has been done for you.

Natural Resources / Raw Materials	The Industry that Uses that Natural Resource / Raw Material
Oats	FPI
Petroleum	
Corn	
Water	
Wheat	
Coal	
Latex (natural rubber)	
Iron ore	

19 Explain how two of the industries listed in Question 18 above contributed to the growth of the U.S. economy in the 19th and 20th centuries.

A. _____

_____

B. _____

_____

END-OF-YEAR ASSESSMENT QUESTIONS

20 A map of canals in the northeastern United States is shown.

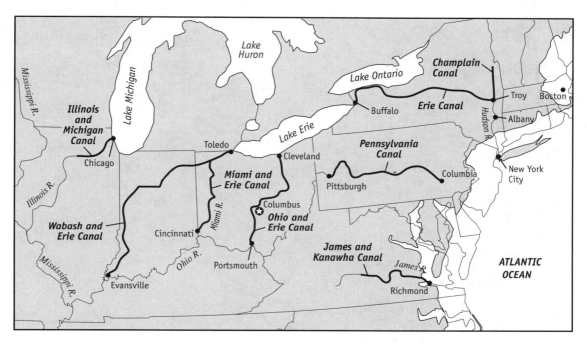

Based on the map, how did the completion of the Ohio and Erie Canal affect Ohio?

Ⓐ It slowed travel from Toledo, Ohio, to Boston, Massachusetts.
Ⓑ Trade decreased between Ohio and Canada.
Ⓒ Goods could now travel by water from new parts of Ohio to Canada.
Ⓓ People moved away from cities in Ohio to the countryside.

21 Based on the map, which city along the Great Lakes became a major trading center after the completion of the Erie Canal?

Ⓐ Richmond
Ⓑ Portsmouth
Ⓒ Boston
Ⓓ Cleveland

22 Name **two** cities that the Miami and Erie Canal helped to connect:

A.	B.

23 A product map based on Ohio's economic activities is shown.

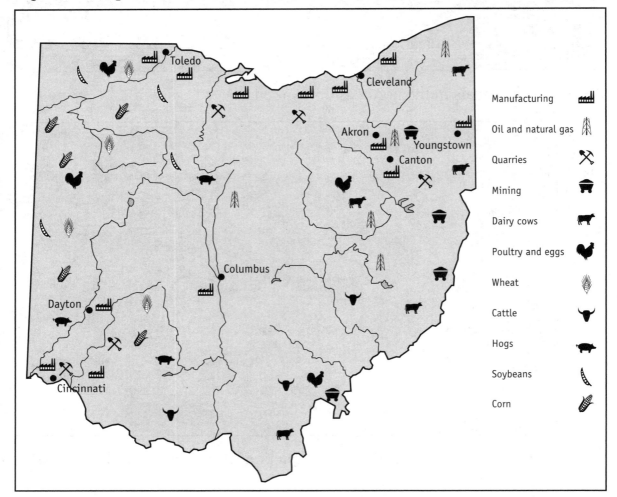

Based on the map, which part of Ohio has the most centers for manufacturing?

Ⓐ   Northeast
Ⓑ   Southeast
Ⓒ   Northwest
Ⓓ   Southwest

24 Fishing is important to the economy of some cities in Ohio. Based on the map, in which two cities is fishing most likely a major industry?

Ⓐ   Cincinnati and Akron
Ⓑ   Cleveland and Toledo
Ⓒ   Dayton and Youngstown
Ⓓ   Canton and Cleveland

25 A list of sections in the table of contents of a pamphlet about Ohio is shown.

> Chapter 1: Ohio's Natural Resources
>
> Chapter 2: Ohio's Central Location
>
> Chapter 3: Ohio's Skilled and Educated Workforce

What would be the best title for this pamphlet?

Ⓐ Ohio: A Great State For Vacationing
Ⓑ Water Transportation in Ohio
Ⓒ The Economy of Ohio
Ⓓ A Brief History of the State of Ohio

26 Which headline illustrates how Ohio is seeking to expand its economy?

CINCINNATI HERALD

**Doctors from Ohio Volunteer
to Treat Patients in Africa**

Ⓐ

Akron Beacon

*Ohio Governor Meets Chinese
Leaders to Sell Ohio Goods*

Ⓒ

CLEVELAND PLAIN DEALER

**The Voters of Ohio
Elect a New Governor**

Ⓑ

COLUMBUS DISPATCH

**Student Enrollment Grows
At Ohio Colleges**

Ⓓ

27 A passage about the economy of Ohio is shown.

> Ohio's economy went through difficult times in the 1970s and 1980s. The automobile, steel, and coal industries went into decline. Since then, Ohio has expanded its service sector. With the Cleveland Clinic, Ohio is now an important center for health care. Industrial research in Ohio is still important: Nela Park (Cleveland) and Battelle Memorial Institute (Columbus) are two centers for industrial research. In addition, important laboratories continue to conduct research on rubber in Akron.

Which conclusion about Ohio's economy can be reached from this passage?

Ⓐ It no longer plays a role in the nation's economy.
Ⓑ It continues to influence the nation's economy.
Ⓒ It has ended all growth in the service sector.
Ⓓ It is no longer able to expand.

CHAPTER 3

REGIONS OF THE UNITED STATES IN THE EARLY 1800s

TOPIC: PLACES AND REGIONS

| Geography 3 | *The regions which became known as the North, South, and West of the United States developed in the early 1800s largely based on their physical environments and economies.* |

After reading this chapter, you should be able to:

★ Define the following terms:
  • Regions
  • North
  • South
  • West

★ Identify the early regions of the United States based on their physical environments and economies.

MAIN IDEAS OF THIS CONTENT STATEMENT

In the early 1800s, three regions of the United States developed differently based on their physical environments and responses to the rise of industry.

Two of these sections had already emerged by the early 1800s — the North and the South. An imaginary line, known as the **Mason-Dixon line**, was seen by many to be the dividing line between the North and South in the first half of the 1800s. The Mason-Dixon line was created in the mid-1700s by two surveyors, Charles Mason and Jeremiah Dixon. They mapped the line to settle a border dispute between several of the colonies.

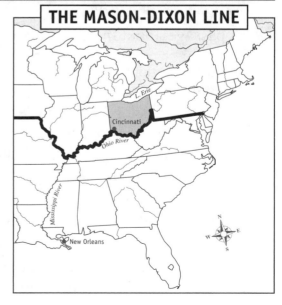

THE MASON-DIXON LINE

L. Erie

Cincinnati

Ohio River

Mississippi River

New Orleans

The **North** was the first part of the United States to industrialize. It had mostly rocky soil, long winters, and a cold climate. These factors made the region unsuited for many forms of agriculture. The North was located along the Atlantic Ocean, providing it with excellent harbors. As a result, many people became merchants or fishermen. It became the country's center of manufacturing, shipbuilding, logging and small farms. **Manufacturers** built textile (*clothing*) mills and other factories using steam power. As the number of workers in factories grew, Northern cities increased in size. By the mid-1800s, the North had more factories, textile mills, and railroads than any other section. Coal was the major fuel used by factories to power their steam engines.

The **South** had long, hot summers and fertile soil. Its coastal marshes and long growing season provided excellent conditions for growing cotton, rice and tobacco. During the Industrial Revolution, cotton became the economic backbone of the Southern economy. Southern plantations used slave labor to grow cotton crops for sale to manufacturers in Great Britain and the Northeast. Plantation owners relied more and more on slave labor. As cotton production grew, the South failed to develop as many cities or factories as in the North.

Slaves were made to pick cotton to satisfy the growing demand of textile factories.

A third section, the **West**, was the region covered by the Northwest Territory. With its flat lands and rich, fertile soil, the West focused on growing wheat and other crops. By the 1830s, this region replaced the North as the country's "**bread basket**" — growing corn and wheat and milling flour. Crops were shipped by river, canal, road and train to the North and South. Wagon trains carried migrants to the West in growing numbers. Its inexpensive farmland attracted farmers and settlers. All

along its major rivers, cities such as Pittsburgh, Chicago, and St. Louis sprang up. The attraction of the West was more than just farmland. An important motive for many settlers was the appeal of timber, gold, silver and grazing lands. Settlers poured across the Mississippi River to establish ranches, dig mines, and farm the land.

CONTENT-AREA VOCABULARY

Directions. Which term or phrase does not belong with the others in the same box? In the space to the right of each box, identify the term or phrase that does not fit. Then use the same term or phrase in a sentence.

Mason-Dixon Line
Plantation system
Slavery
"Bread basket"

_____

_____

_____

_____

Manufacturing
Rocky soil
Short-growing season
Crops of cotton and rice

_____

_____

_____

_____

Wheat and corn
Cheap farmland
Flat landscape
Use of slave labor

_____

_____

_____

_____

Industry
Factories
Railroads
Plantations

_____

_____

_____

_____

STUDY CARDS

The North

1. Describe the North's physical environment: _____

_____

_____

2. Describe the economy of the North in the early 1800s: _____

_____

_____

The South

1. Describe the South's physical environment: _____

_____

_____

2. Describe the economy of the South in the early 1800s: _____

_____

_____

The West

1. Describe the West's physical environment: _____

_____

_____

2. Describe the economy of the West in the early 1800s: _____

_____

_____

STUDY CARD PROMPTS

The North

1. **Describe the North's physical environment.**

2. **Describe the economy of the North in the early 1800s.**

To check your answers to these questions, turn the card over and review the information you have written on the other side.

The South

1. **Describe the South's physical environment.**

2. **Describe the economy of the South in the early 1800s.**

To check your answers to these questions, turn the card over and review the information you have written on the other side.

The West

1. **Describe the West's physical environment.**

2. **Describe the economy of the West in the early 1800s.**

To check your answers to these questions, turn the card over and review the information you have written on the other side.

Name _____ Date _____

Chapter 3: Regions of the United States in the Early 1800s   **41**

PERFORMANCE–BASED ASSESSMENT QUESTIONS

28 A graphic organizer of the United States in the early 1800s is shown.

Select **two** of the regions shown in the graphic organizer. For each region selected, describe the region's physical and economic characteristics.

Region Selected: _____

Physical Characteristics: _____

_____

Economic Characteristics: _____

_____

_____

Region Selected: _____

Physical Characteristics: _____

_____

Economic Characteristics: _____

_____

_____

29 Complete the chart below. Rewrite or draw a line from each of the statements to the economic characteristic that describes that region:

Statements

- Use of slave labor to grow cash crops.
- A center of U.S. manufacturing and industry.
- Served as the "Bread Basket" of the early United States.

THE UNITED STATES IN THE EARLY 1800s

Region	Economic Characteristic that Describes Region
North	
South	
West	

The following question has three parts. First, answer part A. Then, answer part B. Finally, answer part C.

30

My name is Henry Hill. I am a farmer in the West. I grow wheat and corn, which I ship to Lake Erie.

Part A. In the space provided, explain how the physical and economic characteristics of the West help Henry at his occupation.

_____

_____

_____

_____

_____

Name _____ Date _____

Chapter 3: Regions of the United States in the Early 1800s   **43**

Part B. In the space provided, explain how the physical and economic characteristics of the North help Sam at his occupation.

_____

_____

_____

_____

_____

_____

Part C. In the space provided, explain how the physical and economic characteristics of the South help John at his occupation.

_____

_____

_____

_____

_____

_____

INTERPRETING TABLES

SKILL BUILDER

In this section, you'll learn to answer questions about finding information in a table.

A **table** is an arrangement of information in columns and rows. It is used to organize large amounts of information so that individual facts can be easily compared.

PROPORTIONS OF FOREIGN-BORN IN OHIO BY GEOGRAPHIC AREA

Geographic Areas	2000	2010	% Change
Rural Areas	1.0%	1.6%	+60%
Urban Areas	3.6%	4.9%	+36%
Cleveland Suburbs	5.3%	5.9%	+13%
Columbus Suburbs	4.5%	7.2%	+60%
Cincinnati Suburbs	2.6%	4.3%	+65%

Source: The Chicago Council on Global Affairs, 2012

STEPS TO UNDERSTANDING A TABLE

EXAMINE THE TITLE AND CATEGORIES

The title of this table tells you what kind of information is shown. Here the title is: *Proportion of Foreign-Born in Ohio by Geographic Area.*

There are four categories in the headings: *Geographic Areas, 2000, 2010,* and *% Change.* The information is also broken down by rows. The left column identifies the rows: *Rural Areas, Urban Areas, Cleveland Suburbs, Columbus Suburbs, Cincinnati Suburbs.*

FINDING SPECIFIC INFORMATION

Suppose you wanted to find out how the foreign-born population in the Columbus suburbs has changed from 2000 to 2010.

- First, put your finger on the row marked *Columbus Suburbs.* Then slide your finger across that row until you reach *2000.* You can see that in *2000,* foreign-born residents made up *4.5%* of the population living in Columbus suburbs.
- Next, continue sliding your finger across the row until the column for *2010.* By 2010, the foreign-born population of Columbus suburbs had risen to *7.2%.*
- In the final column, you will see the foreign-born population of Columbus suburbs increased by *60%* between *2000* and *2010.* (4.5% + 2.7% = 7.2%)

END-OF-YEAR ASSESSMENT QUESTIONS

31 A table about the economies of the North and South is shown.

THE ECONOMIES OF THE NORTH AND SOUTH IN THE EARLY 1800s

Item	North	South
Railroad Mileage	72% of the nation's track	28% of the nation's track
Value of Exports	68% of the nation's exports	32% of the nation's exports
Factories	85% of the nation's factories	15% of the nation's factories
Farms	16% of the nation's farms	84% of the nation's farms
Iron/Steel Production	92% of iron/steel production	8% of iron/steel production

Which statement is supported by evidence from this table?

Ⓐ The South became the nation's major manufacturing section.
Ⓑ Regions of the United States developed differently.
Ⓒ The value of foreign imports to the United States increased over time.
Ⓓ Each region in the United States developed in a similar manner.

32 Which conclusion can be drawn by looking at this table?

Ⓐ The South's economy was mostly based on agriculture.
Ⓑ The North's construction of railroads was behind that of the South.
Ⓒ Most of the nation's factories were located in the West.
Ⓓ The South exported more goods than the North.

33 In the box below, write **one** physical or economic characteristic of the West that describes that region during the early 1800s:

34 A passage describing the United States in the early 1800s in shown.

> "During the early 1800s, settlers traveled over the Appalachian Mountains into new territories. Many of these pioneers established settlements. They pushed the frontier across the Mississippi into lands soon admitted into the Union as states."

Which area of the United States in the early 1800s is described by this statement?

(A) the North
(B) the South
(C) the West
(D) the Northeast

35 A graphic organizer describing physical and economic characteristics is shown.

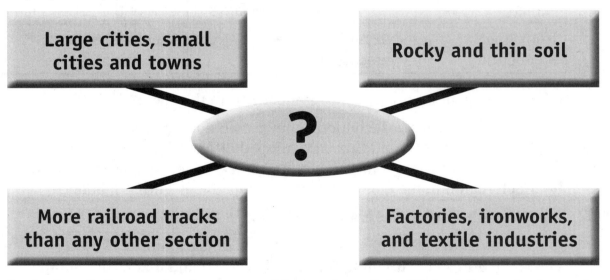

In the box below, write the name of the region of the United States in the early 1800s that is most closely associated with the characteristics described above:

36 What effect did the South's long growing season and coastal marshes have on the region in the early 1800s?

(A) It allowed the South to become a center for growing cotton and rice.
(B) It helped Southern farmers to ship their wheat to Europe.
(C) It forced Southerners to end the practice of slavery.
(D) It aided the development of large-scale manufacturing in the South.

Three pictures of different regions in the United States are shown.

Each illustration characterizes a region of the United States in the early 1800s. Write the name of each region in one of the boxes below based on the characteristics shown in the image:

37

38

39

CHAPTER 4

MODIFYING THE ENVIRONMENT

TOPIC: HUMAN SYSTEMS

> **Geography 4**
>
> *People have modified the environment since prehistoric times. There are both positive and negative consequences for modifying the environment in Ohio and the United States.*

After reading this chapter, you should be able to:

★ Define the following terms:
  • Positive consequences
  • Negative consequences
  • Environment
  • Wetlands

★ Describe some of the benefits and risks involved in modifying or making changes to the environment.

MAIN IDEAS OF THIS CONTENT STATEMENT

People **modify** (*change*) the **environment** (*the air, land, and water around us*) for a variety of reasons. Such modifications can have both positive and negative **consequences** (*effects*).

Some Ohioans have modified the environment by draining large areas of shallow water and soggy soil known as **wetlands**. These wetlands were drained by settlers to increase the amount of land they could farm. The destruction of wetlands has had a positive impact by creating new farmland.

However, the wetlands act to filter water and to stop pollutants from entering large bodies of water. A negative consequence of destroying wetlands is that this wetlands filter is removed and no longer acts to trap pollutants.

Wetlands in Ohio.

People have also modified the environment of Ohio by cutting down forests and building dams. These changes have had both a positive and negative effects on the environment.

Forests. Cutting down forests provides needed lumber for building homes. It also creates more farmland. Yet these changes to the environment can have negative consequences. Cutting down forests can cause soil erosion. This often leads to the **extinction** (*death*) of some forms of animal and plant life. Forests also provide recreational areas, which are lost when forests are cut down.

Dams. Building dams has many positive consequences. A dam can help generate low-cost electricity, prevent floods, and store water for a time when it is needed. On the negative side, dams often require the creation of an artificial lake on one side. This sometimes leads to the flooding of homes and forces people in an affected area to have to relocate (*move*).

Chemicals. Ohio's farmers have further modified the environment by using fertilizers, pesticides and herbicides. Farmers use these chemicals to increase and protect the amount of crops grown in the soil.

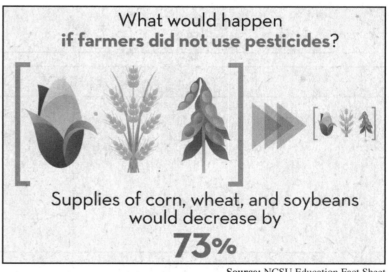

Source: NCSU Education Fact Sheet

- **Fertilizers** are chemicals that are added to the soil to help crops grow.

- **Pesticides** are poisons sprayed on plants to kill insects and other pests that eat the crop.

- **Herbicides** are poisons used to kill unwanted plants, like weeds.

Fertilizers, pesticides and herbicides can help farmers to grow more food. However, they can also have negative consequences. Use of fertilizers, pesticides and herbicides can lead to increased pollution of the environment. We may eat small amounts of these chemicals when we eat foods that have been sprayed by them.

CONTENT-AREA VOCABULARY

ENVIRONMENT	
Define "environment."	Provide some examples of physical environments in Ohio.
Use "environment" in a sentence.	Provide an example that is not a physical environment.

MODIFY	
Define "modify."	Provide an example of successfully modifying the environment.
What are some of the positive and negative consequences of modifying the environment?	Give an example of something that is not modifying the environment.

Name _____ Date _____

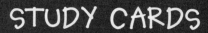

STUDY CARDS

Positive Consequences

Suppose Ohioans wished to build a new dam across a major river. What might be some of the positive effects of building this dam to the environment?

- _____
  _____

- _____
  _____

- _____
  _____

- _____
  _____

Negative Consequences

What might be some of the negative consequences of building this dam to the environment?

- _____
  _____

- _____
  _____

- _____
  _____

- _____
  _____

STUDY CARD PROMPTS

Positive Consequences

Suppose Ohioans wished to build a new dam across a major river. What might be some of the positive effects of building this dam to the environment?

For the answer to this question, turn the card over and review the information you have written on the other side.

Negative Consequences

What might be some of the negative consequences of building this dam to the environment?

For the answer to this question, turn the card over and review the information you have written on the other side.

PERFORMANCE-BASED ASSESSMENT QUESTIONS

40 The following question has two parts. First, answer part A. Then, answer part B.

In the past 75 years, Ohio farmers increased their crop yields by using chemicals such as fertilizers, herbicides, and pesticides.

Part A.
Describe one positive consequence of the use of fertilizers, herbicides, and pesticides.

_____

_____

Part B.
Describe one negative consequence of the use of fertilizers, herbicides, and pesticides.

_____

_____

41 The following question has two parts. First, answer part A. Then, answer part B.

Part A.
Humans often modify their physical environment to meet their needs. Describe how dams modify the environment.

_____

_____

Part B.
Explain either **one** positive or **one** negative consequence of that modification to the environment.

_____

_____

42 People often modify their physical environment to improve transportation routes. Such modifications include building bridges, draining swamps, widening roads, and constructing paved highways. Describe **one** positive and **one** negative consequence of modifications to the physical environment to improve transportation.

_____

_____

_____

_____

_____

_____

43 The following question has two parts. First, answer part A. Then, answer part B.

Part A.
Describe **one** positive consequence of clearing forest areas for farm land.

_____

_____

_____

_____

_____

Part B.
Describe **one** negative consequence of clearing forest areas.

_____

_____

_____

_____

_____

Name _____ Date _____

44 The following question has two parts. First, answer part A. Then, answer part B.

Part A.

Describe **one** positive consequences of converting wetlands to other uses.

_____

_____

_____

_____

_____

_____

_____

_____

_____

_____

Part B.

Describe **one** negative consequence of converting wetlands to other uses, such as constructing homes, building highways, or increasing farm land.

_____

_____

_____

_____

_____

_____

_____

_____

_____

_____

END-OF-YEAR ASSESSMENT QUESTIONS

45 A graphic organizer on the destruction of Ohio's wetlands is shown.

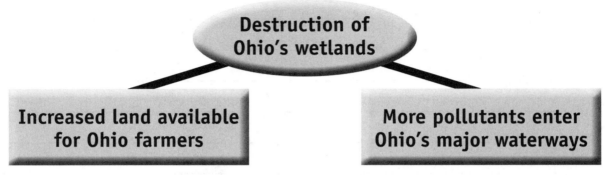

Which statement is best supported by the information in this graphic organizer?

Ⓐ   Changing the environment can have both positive and negative results.
Ⓑ   Ohio's wetlands are its most valuable natural resource.
Ⓒ   Where one lives determines how one earns a living.
Ⓓ   A major need for Ohio is to sell its natural resources.

46 Which conclusion can be drawn from these two photographs?

A dam in Ohio.

A forest in Ohio.

Ⓐ   People sometimes modify the physical environment for their benefit.
Ⓑ   Most human changes to the environment have positive consequences.
Ⓒ   People bring about negative consequences when they alter the environment.
Ⓓ   Ohioans are more destructive to the environment than people in other states.

47 A graphic organizer dealing with dams is shown.

What would be the best title for this graphic organizer?

Ⓐ The History of Dams in Ohio
Ⓑ The Positive Consequences of Dams
Ⓒ Ohio's Most Important Dams
Ⓓ The Negative Consequences of Dams

---

48 A partial outline dealing with forests is shown.

I. _____

    A. Farmers cut down forests to clear land for planting crops
    B. Forests are cut down to provide space for cities to expand
    C. Cutting down forests destroys the habitat for many animal and plant species

Which heading best completes this outline?

Ⓐ How Humans Modify the Environment
Ⓑ The Advantages of Cutting Down Forests
Ⓒ Major Threats to Ohio's Animal and Plant Species
Ⓓ Positive and Negative Consequences of Cutting Down Forests

Name _____ Date _____

CHAPTER 5

THE CHANGING POPULATION OF OHIO AND THE NATION

TOPIC: HUMAN SYSTEMS

> **Geography 5**
>
> *The population of the United States has changed over time, becoming more diverse (e.g., racial, ethnic, linguistic, religious characteristics). Ohio's population has become increasingly reflective of the cultural diversity of the United States.*

After reading this chapter, you should be able to:

★ Define the following terms:
- Cultural diversity
- Ethnic groups
- Racial
- Linguistic

★ Describe how the United States has become more diverse.
★ Describe how Ohio reflects the greater cultural diversity of the United States.

MAIN IDEAS OF CONTENT STATEMENT

Diversity refers to a variety or to differences. **Culture** refers to a people's way of life and includes language, traditions, customs, and beliefs. Merging these two terms, **cultural diversity** exists when people from different cultures live together. These cultural groups may have different racial, ethnic, linguistic, and religious backgrounds.

Linguistic refers to language. A linguistic group is a group of people who speak their own language. **Ethnic groups** are groups of people with common traditions and customs. Often they share ancestors from the same country. Ethnicity and language are frequently tied together. For example, Arab Americans and French Americans are both linguistic as well as ethnic groups.

Early Immigration to Ohio. Both Ohio and the United States have become more diverse over time. Ohio was first populated mainly by white settlers from Northeastern states. These settlers included the descendants of English and Scottish colonists. **Amish** settlers, a Protestant religious group, moved from Europe to Pennsylvania and Ohio to establish their own religious communities. German immigrants were also among the first settlers to Ohio. They came for economic opportunities and political freedom. Irish immigrants came to Ohio to escape the **Great Potato Famine** of 1845–1846 in Ireland.

African Americans. In the late nineteenth and early twentieth century, many African Americans moved from Southern states to Ohio. They came to escape poverty and racial discrimination. They came seeking jobs in Ohio's industries. During the **Great Migration** following World War I, African Americans came to Ohio in even greater numbers. Many settled in Ohio's cities.

The Great Migration saw many African Americans leave the South for Ohio.

Recent Immigration to Ohio. More recently, immigrants from Mexico, India and China have settled in Ohio. Like the nation as a whole, the numbers of Hispanic Americans and Asian Americans in Ohio have been growing.

Immigration continues to be a major source of new residents for Ohio. By 2011, the foreign-born population of Ohio had grown to 456,000 out of Ohio's total population of 11,500,000 — or 4% of the state's population. For the United States as a whole, the percentage of foreign-born residents is even higher — about 13 out of every 100 people.

Today, Ohio's population reflects great cultural diversity, as does the nation as a whole. For example, 13% of the nation and 12% of Ohioans are African Americans; 5% of the nation and 2% of Ohioans are Asian Americans; while 17% of the nation and 3% of Ohioans are Hispanic Americans. From this

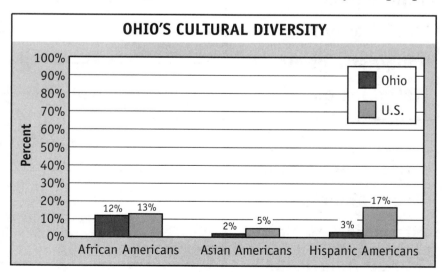

evidence we can see that the great mix of different cultures and ethnic groups that exists throughout the United States exists in Ohio as well.

CONTENT–AREA VOCABULARY

Directions. Each box below contains four terms. Use the cluster of terms to create a question that shows how the terms are related to each other.

Amish settlers	_____
German immigrants	_____
Great Migration	_____
Mexican immigrants	_____

Diverse	_____
Diversity	_____
Culture	_____
Cultural diversity	_____

Ethnic group	_____
Racial group	_____
Linguistic group	_____
Religious group	_____

African Americans	_____
Asian Americans	_____
Hispanic Americans	_____
Indian Americans	_____

Name _____ Date _____

Chapter 5: The Changing Population of Ohio and the Nation   **61**

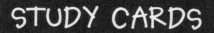

STUDY CARDS

The Diversity of the United States

How has the nation's population changed and become more diverse?

- _____
  _____
  _____

- _____
  _____
  _____

- _____
  _____
  _____

- _____
  _____

The Diversity of Ohio

How does Ohio's population reflect the growing cultural diversity of the United States?

- _____
  _____
  _____

- _____
  _____
  _____

- _____
  _____
  _____

- _____
  _____

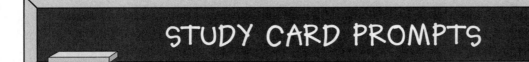

STUDY CARD PROMPTS

Maps

How has the nation's population changed and become more diverse?

For the answer to this question, turn the card over and review the information you have written on the other side.

Relative Location

How does Ohio's population reflect the growing cultural diversity of the United States?

For the answer to this question, turn the card over and review the information you have written on the other side.

INTERPRETING PICTOGRAPHS

SKILL BUILDER

In a **pictograph**, a symbol or illustration is used to represent a number of something, such as money or people.

THE AVERAGE PERSONAL INCOME IN OHIO: 2005–2012	
YEAR	**AMOUNT OF INCOME**
2005	$ $ $ $ $ $ $ $ $ $ $
2006	$ $ $ $ $ $ $ $ $ $ $ (
2007	$ $ $ $ $ $ $ $ $ $ $ (
2008	$ $ $ $ $ $ $ $ $ $ $ $ (
2009	$ $ $ $ $ $ $ $ $ $ $
2010	$ $ $ $ $ $ $ $ $ $ $
2011	$ $ $ $ $ $ $ $ $ $ $ $ (
2012	$ $ $ $ $ $ $ $ $ $ $ $ (

LEGEND
Each $ = $3,000

In this pictograph, we see from the title that it shows the average yearly income of an Ohioan in the years 2007 to 2012. The legend shows what each symbol or picture in the pictograph represents. In this pictograph, we learn that each dollar sign ($) equals $3,000 in yearly income. Thus, two and a half dollar symbols ($$$) represent $7,500 in yearly income:

$$ \$ \quad + \quad \$ \quad + \quad \$ $$
$$ \$3,000 \quad + \quad \$3,000 \quad + \quad \$1,500 \quad = \quad \$7,500 $$

INTERPRETING THE INFORMATION IN A PICTOGRAPH

If you want to find the average yearly personal income in Ohio in 2008, here is what you need to do:

● Look at the years listed on the left side of the pictograph. Find the year "2008." Slide your finger along the "2008" row. As you do, count the number of $ symbols on that line.

● The year "2008" has 12 complete $ and a small part of another $ symbol. Recall that each full $ symbol represents $3,000 in yearly income. Thus, in 2008, the average person in Ohio earned about $36,400 in income.

PERFORMANCE–BASED
ASSESSMENT QUESTIONS

49 A pictograph showing the foreign-born population of Ohio is shown.

THE FOREIGN-BORN POPULATION OF OHIO, BY CONTINENT OF ORIGIN		
	2000	**2010**
Europe	👤👤👤👤👤👤👤👤👤👤👤👤👤👤👤	👤👤👤👤👤👤👤👤👤👤👤👤👤👤
Asia	👤👤👤👤👤👤👤👤👤👤👤👤👤👤👤	👤👤👤👤👤👤👤👤👤👤👤👤👤👤👤👤👤👤👤👤
Africa	👤👤👤👤👤	👤👤👤👤👤👤
Latin America	👤👤👤👤👤👤👤👤👤	👤👤👤👤👤👤👤👤👤👤

Each 👤 = 10,000 people

Source: U.S. Bureau of the Census

Based on the information in the pictograph, identify one change that has taken place in the origins of foreign-born residents coming to Ohio between 2000 and 2010.

_____

_____

_____

_____

_____

50 Describe one way in which the cultural diversity of Ohio has changed over time.

_____

_____

_____

_____

_____

_____

51 A table of the nation's changing population is shown.

THE CHANGING FACE OF AMERICA, 1950 TO 2020

	1950	1960	1970	1980	1990	2000	2006	2010	2020
White	87%	85%	86%	80%	76%	70%	67%	65%	60%
African American	10%	11%	11%	12%	12%	13%	13%	13%	13%
Hispanic	3%	4%	5%	6%	9%	13%	14%	16%	19%
Asian	1%	1%	1%	2%	3%	4%	5%	5%	6%

Source: U.S. Bureau of the Census

The following question has three parts. First, answer part A. Then, answer part B. Finally, answer part C.

Part A. Based on the table, describe one change that has already taken place or that will take place in the population of the United States from 1950 to 2020.

_____

_____

_____

Part B. Based on the table, describe a second change that has already taken place or that will take place in the population of the United States from 1950 to 2020.

_____

_____

_____

Part C. Based on the table, describe a third change that has already taken place or that will take place in the population of the United States from 1950 to 2020.

_____

_____

_____

_____

END-OF-YEAR ASSESSMENT QUESTIONS

52 Which have been the two most recent ethnic groups to migrate to Ohio?

Ⓐ German and Irish
Ⓑ Hispanic and Asian
Ⓒ African Americans and Amish
Ⓓ Swedish and Italian

53 Which concept is illustrated by the menu to the right?

Ⓐ "Bread Basket"
Ⓑ natural resources
Ⓒ cultural diversity
Ⓓ new immigrants

> ✳ MENU BOARD ✳
> **LUNCH SPECIALS**
> ✳ Spanish Omelet   ✳ Greek Gyro
> ✳ French Fries   ✳ Mexican Taco
> ✳ Hungarian Goulash   ✳ Italian Pizza

54 A table comparing the Asian-American populations of Ohio and the United States is shown.

ASIAN-AMERICAN POPULATIONS OF OHIO AND THE UNITED STATES

	2010 Census	July 2011	July 2012	Percent Change 2011 to 2012
Ohio	249,440	249,747	257,584	3.1%
United States	17,676,507	18,325,193	18,855,104	2.9%

Source: U.S. Census Bureau

Based on the chart, which statement is most accurate?

Ⓐ Ohio's Asian-American population is increasing at a rate faster than that of the United States.
Ⓑ The Asian-American populations of both Ohio and the United States have remained unchanged from 2010 to 2012.
Ⓒ Most Asian-Americans moving to Ohio were born in China or Japan.
Ⓓ More Asian-Americans moved to Ohio in 2010–2011 than in 2011–2012.

55 A table showing the foreign-born population of Ohio is shown.

FOREIGN-BORN POPULATION OF OHIO, 1990–2012

Place of Birth	1990		2000		2012	
	Number	Percent	Number	Percent	Number	Percent
Africa	7,059	2.8%	22,034	6.5%	57,788	12.8%
Asia	73,547	29.0%	120,213	35.4%	178,378	39.5%
Europe	138,877	54.8%	131,683	38.8%	111,110	24.6%
South & Central America	18,154	7.2%	47,124	13.9%	89,365	19.8%

Source: Migration Policy Institute

According to the table, which area in the world saw the largest growth of immigrants living in Ohio in 2012?

56 According to the table, which area saw a decrease in the number of immigrants living in Ohio since 1990?

57 Which statement supports the view that Ohio's population is becoming more culturally diverse?

Ⓐ Many people are leaving Ohio and moving to the southwest.
Ⓑ Ohio's location makes it a major transportation center for the United States.
Ⓒ Senior citizens in Ohio are among the fastest growing age groups today.
Ⓓ More foreign-born immigrants are moving to Ohio than in past years.

CHAPTER 6

THE IMPACT OF OHIO'S LOCATION AND TRANSPORTATION SYSTEMS

TOPIC: HUMAN SYSTEMS

Geography 6	*Ohio's location in the United States and its transportation systems continue to influence the movement of people, products and ideas.*

After reading this chapter, you should be able to:

★ Define the following terms: • Movement • Products • Ideas	★ Explain how Ohio's location plays a role in influencing the movement of people, products and ideas in the nation.

MAIN IDEAS OF THIS CONTENT STATEMENT

Ohio was once considered the "**Gateway to the West**" because of its location. Ohio's location served to connect the eastern and western regions of our nation. Ohio's unique location continues to promote the state's economic growth. Ohio is within 600 miles of 60% of all U.S. and Canadian manufacturing. The state continues to link the Northeast to the Midwestern part of the nation.

Ohio borders one of the **Great Lakes** and is just west of the Appalachian Mountains. It borders the **Ohio River** to the south, which flows into the Mississippi River. This connects Ohio to the American South and the Gulf of Mexico.

In the 19th century, the Ohio River served as a major route into the interior of much of North America. **Lake Erie**, to the north, connects Ohio to New York, the other states of the Northeast and the Atlantic Ocean.

Ohio's Canals. In the early nineteenth century, Americans built the Erie Canal and other canals. A **canal** is a human-made water route. The Erie Canal was a path measuring 50 feet wide and 4 feet deep, stretching for 360-miles. The importance of the canal was that it allowed Ohioans and others to ship goods by water across Lake Erie. Goods then traveled along the Erie Canal to the Hudson River, down the Hudson River to New York City, and out to the Atlantic Ocean. From there, ships could travel carrying goods made in Ohio to anywhere in the world.

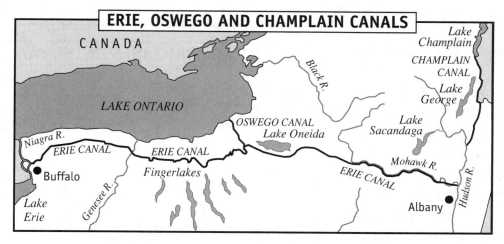

In Ohio, the **Ohio and Erie Canal** ran from Portsmouth to Cleveland, and the **Miami and Erie Canal** ran from Toledo to Cincinnati. In the twentieth century, the St. Lawrence River was widened to allow ocean-going ships to travel. Ships could then carry goods from the Great Lakes over the St. Lawrence Seaway to the Atlantic Ocean.

The National Road. In addition to these water routes, Ohioans built roads — such as the **National Road** in the early nineteenth century. This road greatly advanced transportation by linking the frontier with the East Coast.

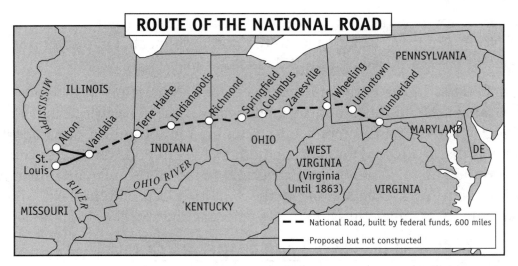

ROUTE OF THE NATIONAL ROAD

- - - National Road, built by federal funds, 600 miles
——— Proposed but not constructed

Railways and Highways. Later, Ohioans built railroads and highways. By the late nineteenth century, railroads like the Baltimore and Ohio Railroad and the New York Central crisscrossed Ohio. Canals had been especially useful in the days when goods were carried over land by animals or horse-drawn carriages. With the development of the steam engine, and later, the internal combustion engine, travel on land by railroads and highways became faster, cheaper, and more direct than canals. They were also less expensive and easier to build.

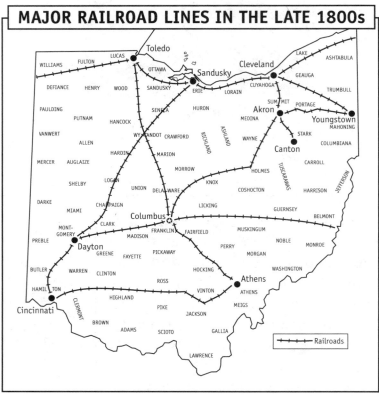

MAJOR RAILROAD LINES IN THE LATE 1800s

Air Travel. Ohio is also called the birthplace of air travel. It was two brothers from Dayton, Ohio — **Orville and Wilbur Wright** — who invented the world's first airplane. Air travel remains an important part of Ohio's transportation system. Ohio has major airports in Cleveland, Columbus, Dayton, Akron-Canton, and many smaller airports.

The state's rivers, roads, canals, railroads, highways and airports continue to move people, products and ideas across the state of Ohio. Those transportation routes connect Ohioans with the wider world.

STUDY CARDS

How Ohio's Location Promotes the Movement of Goods

1. Connections to Major Waterways: _____

_____

_____

_____

_____

2. Links to Other Regions of the United States: _____

_____

_____

_____

_____

How Ohio's Transportation System Influence People, Products, and Ideas

1. Waterways and Canals: _____

_____

_____

2. Railroads: _____

_____

3. Roads and Highways: _____

_____

_____

4. Airports and Air Travel: _____

_____

STUDY CARD PROMPTS

How Ohio's Location Promotes the Movement of Goods

1. **Connections to Major Waterways**

2. **Links to Other Regions of the United States**

To check your answers to these questions, turn the card over and review the information you have written on the other side.

How Ohio's Transportation System Influence People, Products, and Ideas

1. **Waterways and Canals**

2. **Railroads**

3. **Roads and Highways**

4. **Airports and Air Travel**

To check your answers to these questions, turn the card over and review the information you have written on the other side.

CONTENT-AREA VOCABULARY

Directions. Make a statement for each of the following clusters of names and terms that explains how they are connected to each other.

River **Road** **Canal** **Railroad** **Highway** **Airport**	_____ _____ _____ _____ _____ _____

Highway 70 **Columbus International Airport** **Miami and Erie Canal** **Columbus-Ohio River Railroad**	_____ _____ _____ _____ _____ _____

Cincinnati: **Home of Proctor & Gamble** **Columbus:** **Home of Nationwide Insurance** **Dublin:** **Home of Wendy's Hamburgers** **Cleveland:** **Home of Key Bank**	_____ _____ _____ _____ _____ _____

PERFORMANCE-BASED ASSESSMENT QUESTIONS

58 A map of part of the United States is shown.

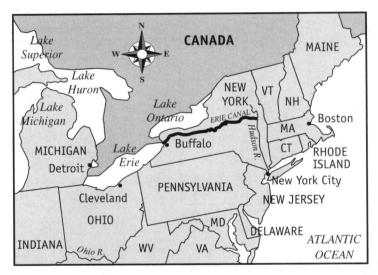

The American Greetings Corporation is headquartered in Cleveland, Ohio. It has received an order from a store in Boston, Massachusetts, for its party goods and gift wrappings. On the map above, trace an all-water route the company might use from Cleveland to ship their products to the Boston store.

59 A reading passage on the Ohio and Erie Canal is shown.

> "Work began on the Ohio and Erie Canal in 1825. By 1832, 309 miles of the canal linked Lake Erie with the Ohio River. The canal led to settlement and development all along its banks. It became a spark for economic growth. Barges now were able to cross the state in only eighty to ninety hours. The canal transported grain and coal to eastern states and finished goods to Western settlers.

Based on the passage, describe **two** positive consequences of building the Ohio and Erie Canal in the space below.

_____

_____

_____

60 A chart about Ohio transportation is shown.

METHODS OF TRANSPORTATION IN OHIO IN THE MID-1800s

Method of Transportation	Average Speed	Cost of Shipping Goods
Roads	Wagon: 2 miles per hour; Stagecoach: 6–8 miles per hour	15 cents per ton per mile
Canals	2–5 miles per hour	1.1 cents per ton per mile
Railroads	10–20 miles per hour	3.4 cents per ton per mile

Source: The Transportation Revolution by George Rogers Taylor

Based on the information in the chart, explain why shipping goods by canal in Ohio was replaced by railroads. Answer on the lines below.

_____

_____

61 In the 1800s, Ohio began on a program to build canals that would link the southern part of the state with the northern part.

Each box describes a situation either before or after canals were built in Ohio. Draw an arrow from each statement to the correct column in the chart.

BEFORE CANALS WERE BUILT IN OHIO	AFTER CANALS WERE BUILT IN OHIO

Goods from northern Ohio had to be sent overland to reach southern Ohio.

Ohio was now able to compete shipping goods with the more established Atlantic states.

The cost of shipping goods from Ohio dropped sharply.

Goods could now move by water from Lake Erie to the Ohio River.

The cost of shipping goods overland in Ohio were very high.

Ohio could not compete economically with states along the Atlantic coast.

62 A map of Ohio and its surrounding states is shown.

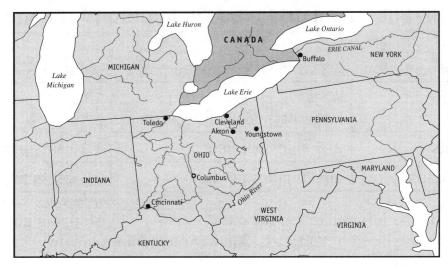

This question has two parts. First answer part A. Then, answer part B.

Part A. Complete the map above by placing an industry on the map of Ohio. The industry can be one that already exists in Ohio or an imaginary one taking advantage of Ohio's resources.

Part B. Then explain why that location would allow that industry easy transportation of goods.

_____

_____

_____

_____

63 Why have canals become less important today in Ohio than they were in the 1830s and 1840s? Write your answer on the lines below.

_____

_____

_____

_____

END-OF-YEAR ASSESSMENT QUESTIONS

64 A list of statements about Dubai, a city in the Middle East, is shown.

> • Dubai's airport in the United Arab Emirates is now the world's busiest international air travel center.
> • Dubai's location in the Middle East serves as a crossroads connecting Europe, Asia, and Africa.
> • Dubai's location places it within 8-hours flying time of two-thirds of the world's population.

What similarity does Ohio's location in the United States share with Dubai?

Ⓐ Both Dubai and Ohio lack a busy airport.

Ⓑ Both Dubai and Ohio serve as important links to other areas.

Ⓒ Both Dubai and Ohio are close to large desert areas.

Ⓓ Both Dubai and Ohio are located very near each other.

65 Ohio's location played an important role in the economic development of the United States. Why was Ohio once considered to be the "Gateway to the West"?

Ⓐ The state bordered both Lake Erie and Lake Michigan.

Ⓑ The Wright brothers' invention permitted easier travel to the West.

Ⓒ Journey down the Mississippi River led travelers to Ohio.

Ⓓ Most travelers passed through Ohio on their journey westwards.

66 Which would be an accurate statement about the Ohio River and Lake Erie?

Ⓐ Both bodies of water are shipping routes for farmers and manufacturers.

Ⓑ Both bodies of water flow directly into the Atlantic Ocean.

Ⓒ Both bodies of water are directly linked to the Erie Canal.

Ⓓ Both bodies of water are located along the southern border of Ohio.

67 Identify **two** major water routes in or near Ohio that are important for national transportation. Write your answer on the lines below.

1. _____

2. _____

68 A map of the National Road, the first major highway in the United States built by the federal government, is shown.

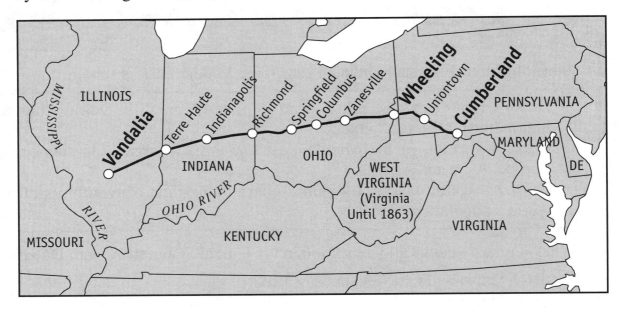

In which general direction did the national road follow as it left Ohio?

Ⓐ Northeast
Ⓑ Northwest
Ⓒ Southeast
Ⓓ Southwest

69 Which statement describes the impact of the National Road on Ohio's economy?

Ⓐ It linked Ohio with the eastern and western regions of the United States.
Ⓑ It cut off Ohioans in the North from those in the southern part of the state.
Ⓒ It prevented people in Ohio from traveling northwards to Canada.
Ⓓ It slowed down the future growth of Ohio's economy and transportation systems.

70 After the Miami and Erie and Ohio and Erie canals opened, the cost of shipping freight in Ohio fell from about $100 per ton to under $10 per ton. What was the result of those lowered freight rates on Ohio's economy?

Ⓐ The canals became the most popular way to ship goods in Ohio.
Ⓑ Passenger travel to the West through Ohio was discouraged.
Ⓒ Ohio farmers continued to ship their crops by horse and wagon.
Ⓓ Ohioans lost most of their business to farmers in other states.

71 A chart listing the names of Ohio companies is shown.

Ohio Banks	Fifth Third Bank	Huntington Bank	Key Bank
Ohio Insurance	Grange Insurance	Nationwide Insurance	Progressive Insurance
Ohio Manufacturers	Owens Corning	Procter and Gamble	Sherwin Williams Paints
Ohio Restaurants	Bob Evans Farms	Wendy's Hamburgers	
Ohio Retailers	Kroger Supermarkets	Limited Brands	Macys Department Stores
Ohio Utilities	American Electric Power	First Energy Corporation	

Which would be the best title for this chart?

Ⓐ Leading Ohio Manufacturing Companies
Ⓑ Major American Companies Headquartered in Ohio
Ⓒ Businesses about to Move to Ohio
Ⓓ Important Retailers in the United States

72 Which is the best explanation for the location of the businesses listed in the chart above?

Ⓐ Ohio requires all companies doing business in Ohio to be located there.
Ⓑ Ohio's workers are more skilled than workers in other states.
Ⓒ Most companies want to locate in Ohio because of its natural resources.
Ⓓ Ohio's location and transportation systems have attracted major companies.

73 Describe **one** reason why canals were replaced by railroad and highway travel as the main means of transporting goods to market. Write your answer below.

_____

_____

_____

_____

_____

GEOGRAPHY UNIT TEST

1   A table is shown.

HISPANICS AND NON-HISPANICS AS A PERCENTAGE OF THE U.S. POPULATION, 2000–2050

	2000	2010	2020	2030	2040	2050
Hispanic	11%	15%	20%	22%	28%	30%
Non-Hispanic	89%	85%	80%	78%	72%	70%

Source: U.S. Bureau of the Census

Based on the table, describe **one** change to the Hispanic population of the United States compared to the non-Hispanic population from 2000 to 2050. Write your answer below.

_____

_____

_____

2   A passage on canals and railroads in Ohio is shown.

Before the growth of our highway system, most transportation was by railways and canals. "Canal fever" hit Ohio in the early 1820s. Between 1810 and 1840, U.S. canal mileage grew from 100 to over 3,300 miles. Canals benefited businesses and helped many cities to growth. Canals began to decline because of their high construction costs and slower speed compared to railroads. As a result, Ohio focused more on building railroads as a cheaper form of transportation. Railways began to replace canals in the early 1880s.

Source: H.B. Paul, *America and Her Problems*

What is the main idea of this passage? Write your answer below.

_____

_____

_____

_____

3   A map of an imaginary island nation is shown.

In which cardinal direction would a person travel in going from City A to City C?

Ⓐ north

Ⓑ east

Ⓒ south

Ⓓ west

4   In which city of Islandia would you expect to find fishing as a major occupation?

Ⓐ City A

Ⓑ City B

Ⓒ City C

Ⓓ City D

5   If you lived at City B and wished to visit City D, in which direction would you have to travel?

Ⓐ northeast

Ⓑ southeast

Ⓒ northwest

Ⓓ southwest

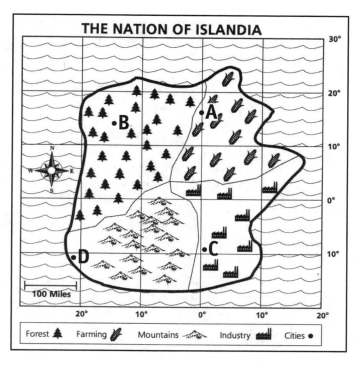

THE NATION OF ISLANDIA

Forest 🌲   Farming   Mountains   Industry   Cities ●

6   Each box below identifies a person from a region of the United Sates in the mid-1800s. Rewrite or draw a line from each person to the correct column in the chart.

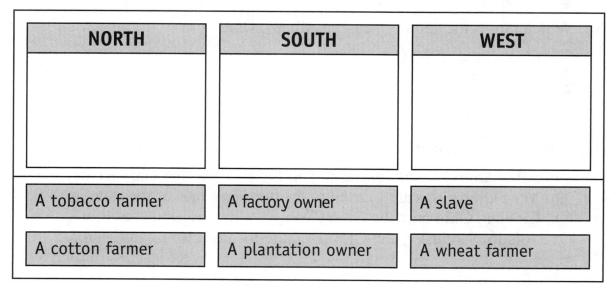

NORTH	SOUTH	WEST

A tobacco farmer	A factory owner	A slave
A cotton farmer	A plantation owner	A wheat farmer

7   A map of Ohio and its major rivers is shown.

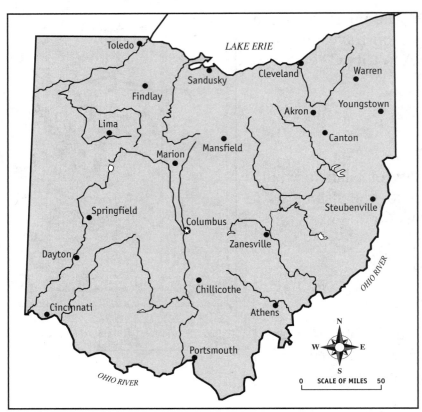

Using the map scale, what is the distance from Columbus to Chillicothe?

Ⓐ   less than 30 miles
Ⓑ   about 50 miles
Ⓒ   exactly 100 miles
Ⓓ   it cannot be determined

8   Which city is located northeast of Athens, Ohio?

Ⓐ   Chillicothe
Ⓑ   Steubenville
Ⓒ   Zanesville
Ⓓ   Portsmouth

9   What conclusion can be drawn from the information on this map?

Ⓐ   All of Ohio's cities are located on Lake Erie or the Ohio River.
Ⓑ   Most Ohio cities are located in the northeast part of the state.
Ⓒ   Cities in Ohio near the Ohio River have the largest populations.
Ⓓ   Toledo, Sandusky, and Cleveland are located closest to Canada.

10 A map of an imaginary community is shown.

The map shows a few blocks of a section of an imaginary community. Which statement identifies the relative location of the bank?

Ⓐ The bank acts as a place to store for money.

Ⓑ The bank is at the corner behind the house on 20 Main Street.

Ⓒ The bank is located at the intersection of Washington Place and Main Street.

Ⓓ The bank is located in Columbus, Ohio.

11 In which general direction would a person travel when going from the bank to 17 Main Street?

Ⓐ North

Ⓑ Northeast

Ⓒ West

Ⓓ South

12 Which house is located southeast of the bank?

Ⓐ 312 Washington Place

Ⓑ 21 Main Street

Ⓒ 302 Washington Place

Ⓓ 23 Main Street

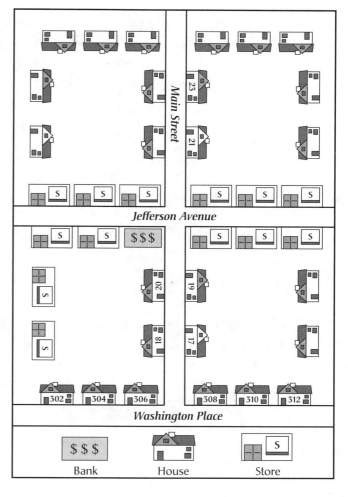

13 Which statement identifies a negative consequence of clearing the wilderness for farms?

Ⓐ It provides lumber for building homes.

Ⓑ It allows for the creation of hydro-electricity.

Ⓒ It permits the storing of water.

Ⓓ It leads to the loss of some forms of animal life.

14 A map of Ohio's canals and railroads are shown.

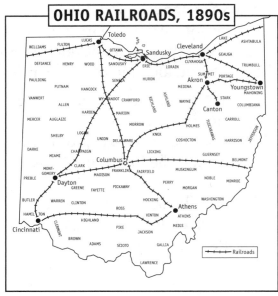

Each statement below describes something about the canals and railroads of Ohio. Some of these statements are accurate. Some of them are inaccurate. Rewrite or draw a line from the statement to the correct column below.

ACCURATE STATEMENT	INACCURATE STATEMENT

Ohio's canal system connected more parts of the state than railroads did.	Ohio's railroads connected more parts of the state than the canals did.	There was a direct connection by rail travel from Cincinnati to Cleveland.
Canals were more popular in Ohio before railroads came along.	Canals were mainly used for shipping goods from eastern to western Ohio.	There was a direct connection by water from the city of Akron to Cincinnati.

15 A map of Ohio's cities and major roadways is shown.

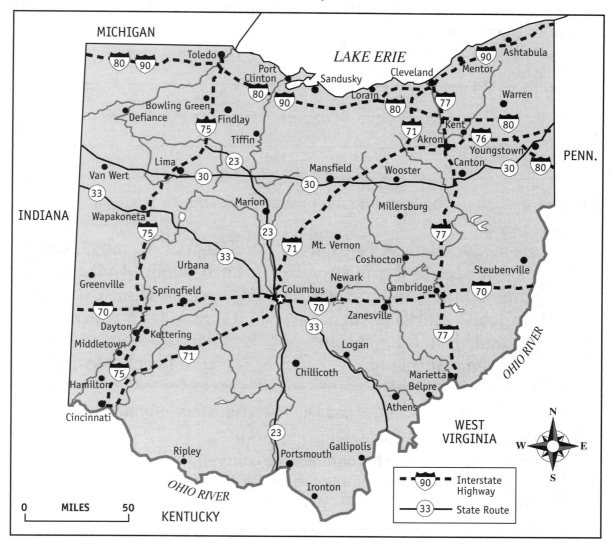

Using the map's scale of miles, which city would you arrive at if you traveled from Cincinnati north for 100 miles along Route 75, and then southeast for 60 miles?

16 Using the scale of miles on the map, how many miles along Route 70 is Springfield, Ohio, from the Indiana border?

17 Cutting down forests for lumber has many benefits for the people and economy of Ohio. At the same time, cutting down forests can also have damaging effects. Describe **one** positive and **one** negative consequence of cutting down forests in Ohio. Write your answer below.

_____

_____

_____

_____

18 Two statements about immigration patterns are shown.

| Before 1900, most foreign-born people living in Ohio came from Western European countries such as England, Ireland, Scotland and Germany. | After 1950, most foreign-born people living in Ohio came from Eastern European countries such as Poland, Hungary and Czechoslovakia. |

What conclusion about Ohio can be drawn from this information?

Ⓐ   Ohio is becoming less popular to Europeans.
Ⓑ   Ohio's population is becoming more culturally diverse.
Ⓒ   Ohio tends to lack the cultural diversity of other states.
Ⓓ   Ohio's population is made up of only European immigrants.

19 Ohio has many important waterways. Which are **two** important waterways adjoining Ohio that helped move goods and people across the nation?

Ⓐ   the Pacific Ocean and the Ohio River
Ⓑ   Lake Erie and the Ohio River
Ⓒ   the Atlantic Ocean and the Mississippi River
Ⓓ   the Gulf of Mexico and the Ohio River

20 In which general direction would you need to travel starting from Columbus to reach the Great Lakes?

Ⓐ   north
Ⓑ   south
Ⓒ   east
Ⓓ   west

21 Read the names and terms listed below. Then decide in which column each name or term belongs. Move or draw a line from the term to its correct column.

Natural Waterways	Human-made Waterways	Land Transportation	Air Transportation

National Road	Railroads	St. Lawrence River	Ohio River
Orville & Wilbur Wright	Baltimore and Ohio Railroad	Erie Canal	Ohio and Erie Canal
Mississippi River	Airports	Miami and Erie Canal	St. Lawrence Seaway

22 Which statement best explains why the North, South, and West of the United States developed differently in the early 1800s?

Ⓐ The people of each region did not get along with each other
Ⓑ They had different physical and economic characteristics.
Ⓒ The South and West refused to allow slavery in their region.
Ⓓ Transporting factory machinery to the South and West was too difficult.

23 Which best explains why railroads replaced canals as a better way to ship goods in Ohio?

Ⓐ Canals were easier to rob than railroads.
Ⓑ Railroads were faster and cheaper than shipping by canal.
Ⓒ There was no room on a canal boat to carry goods.
Ⓓ Railroads could be operated with computers, while canals could not.

UNIT 2

HISTORY

*General Washington crossing the Delaware River
during the American Revolution.*

The Battle of Lake Erie during the War of 1812.

History is all about the past. It refers both to past events and to the study of those events. Just as your own life would be confusing if you had no memory of what you had done in the past, each society looks to its history for its sense of identity. History allows a society to remember where it has been and where it is going.

The following topics are examined in this unit:

1. HISTORICAL THINKING SKILLS

2. HERITAGE

HISTORY PRE-TEST

1   A timeline of key events is shown.

The Northwest Ordinance prohibits slavery in Ohio	The Ohio Constitution prohibits slavery in Ohio	Cincinnati's Levi Coffin helps thousands of slaves escape to Canada	Cincinnati's Harriet Beecher Stowe writes *Uncle Tom's Cabin*
↓	↓	↓	↓
1787	**1802**	**1840s**	**1852**

Which conclusion can be drawn from this timeline?

Ⓐ   Most Ohioans supported the continuation of slavery.

Ⓑ   Ohioans were active in the antislavery movement.

Ⓒ   Slavery was banned in the United States.

Ⓓ   Most Ohioans were members of antislavery organizations.

2   A chart of early battles in Ohio is shown.

Name of Battle	Year	War	Participants
Battle at Fort Sandusky	1763	Pontiac's Rebellion	Wyandot Tribe vs. Great Britain
Battle of Chillicothe	1779	American Revolution	Colonial Militia vs. Shawnee tribe
Big Bottom Massacre	1791	Northwest Indian War	Lenape and Wyandot Tribes vs. Ohio Settlers
Siege at Dunlap's Station	1791	Northwest Indian War	Several Ohio tribes vs. Ohio Settlers

Which conclusion can be drawn from the chart?

Ⓐ   Most Indian dealings with settlers were peaceful.

Ⓑ   Settlers and Indians sometimes were in conflict.

Ⓒ   The Battle of Chillicothe occurred after the American Revolution.

Ⓓ   The Battle at Fort Sandusky occurred before the French and Indian War.

3   An outline of British colonial policies is shown.

> **I. British Colonial Policies**
> A. Sugar Act of 1764
> B. Stamp Act of 1765
> C. Tea Act of 1773

What was the main goal of the policies in this outline?

Ⓐ   To permit American colonists greater self-government
Ⓑ   To help the British raise money in the colonies
Ⓒ   To encourage increased immigration to the colonies
Ⓓ   To support the colonists' desire for independence

4   Why did many colonists feel that British tax laws were unfair?

Ⓐ   The colonists did not have their own representatives in Parliament.
Ⓑ   Taxes were already higher in the colonies than in Britain.
Ⓒ   The new tax laws excused American Indians from paying.
Ⓓ   The British treasury already had a large surplus of money.

5   A concept map is shown.

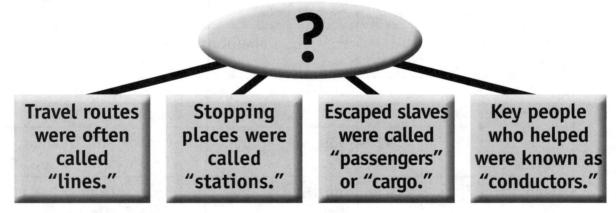

Which term or phrase best completes this concept map?

Ⓐ   Fugitive Slave Laws
Ⓑ   Abolitionists
Ⓒ   Underground Railroad
Ⓓ   Free-born African Americans

6   A map of the United States is shown.

What do the two shaded states on this map represent?

Ⓐ   States that were two of the original thirteen states
Ⓑ   States with major battles during the American Revolution
Ⓒ   States whose representatives signed the Declaration of Independence
Ⓓ   States created out of the Northwest Territory

7   A concept map is shown.

Which title belongs in place of the question mark?

Ⓐ   Ohio Inventors Who Benefited the United States
Ⓑ   Leading Ohio Political Leaders
Ⓒ   Innovators Who Worked at Ohio State University
Ⓓ   Ohio Chemists Develop New Medicines and Drugs

END OF THE HISTORY PRE-TEST

CHAPTER 7

CREATING A TIMELINE

TOPIC: HISTORICAL THINKING SKILLS

Historical thinking begins with a clear sense of time — past, present and future. Historical thinking also includes the skills of locating, researching, and interpreting primary and secondary sources. A good historian must be able to see relationships between events and draw conclusions.

History 1	*The order of significant events in Ohio and the United States can be shown on a timeline.*

After reading this chapter, you should be able to:

★ Define the following terms:
  • Timeline
  • Chronological order
  • B.C. / Before the Common Era
  • A.D. / Common Era
  • Decade / Century

★ Arrange different events in chronological order.
★ Create a timeline that shows significant events in the history of Ohio and the United States.

MAIN IDEAS OF THIS CONTENT STATEMENT

A **timeline** shows the order in which events have occurred. This is called **chronological order**. Events on a timeline are spread out to show how much time actually passed between those events in real life. A longer space on the timeline indicates the passage of a longer period of time. For example, a hundred years on a timeline should be twice the length of 50 years. This is because 100 years is twice as long as 50 years in real life.

These pictures of a child, arranged in chronological order, trace the child's development.

The Title. In the timeline below, the **title** indicates that all of these events are connected in some way to the history of Ohio.

Events. As on most timelines, the earliest event is shown on the far left. Other events are placed to the right of this in the order in which they occurred. The space between events shows the amount of time that has passed between those events.

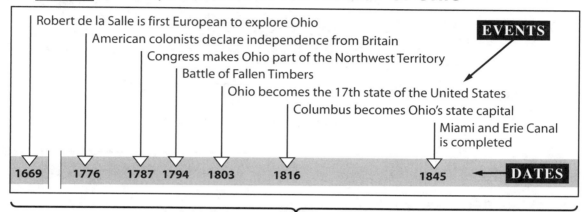

TITLE ➝ **MAJOR EVENTS IN THE HISTORY OF OHIO**

Robert de la Salle is first European to explore Ohio
American colonists declare independence from Britain
Congress makes Ohio part of the Northwest Territory
Battle of Fallen Timbers
Ohio becomes the 17th state of the United States
Columbus becomes Ohio's state capital
Miami and Erie Canal is completed

EVENTS

1669   1776   1787 1794   1803   1816   1845   ← DATES

DATES IN CHRONOLOGICAL ORDER

As you can see, each event on this timeline is clearly related to the title. An event such as "Christopher Columbus lands in Haiti" would not appear because this event was not a major event related to the history of Ohio.

Periods of Time. A timeline can represent any length of time. For shorter periods of time, a timeline may be divided into one-year intervals. For a longer period of time, a timeline might be divided into decades. A **decade** is a period of ten years. A period of time of 100 years is known as a **century**.

B.C. and A.D. Dates in many parts of the world are based on when it is believed that Jesus was born. These dates are divided into BC and AD. BC refers to "Before Christ," while AD refers to *Anno Domini*, Latin for "in the year of our Lord." Sometimes

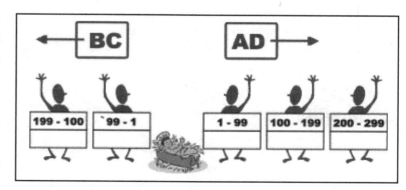

BC is shown as BCE — **Before the Common Era.** AD may be shown as CE — the **Common Era.** As time passes, BC dates go from higher numbers (900 BC) to lower numbers (500 BC), while AD dates go from lower numbers (100) to higher numbers (2015).

CONTENT-AREA VOCABULARY

Directions. Fill in the boxes in the concept ladder below by adding your own explanations of each term along the ladder.

CONCEPT: TIMELINES

Century

Decade

B.C./A.D.

Chronological Order

Timeline

Name _____ Date _____

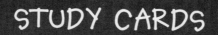

STUDY CARDS

Timeline

1. What is a timeline? _____

_____

_____

_____

_____

2. What is the major purpose of a timeline? _____

_____

_____

_____

_____

_____

Parts of a Timeline

Describe each part of a timeline and the role it plays.

1. What role does the *title* of the timeline play? _____

_____

_____

2. What is *chronological order*? _____

_____

_____

3. What are the *events* that are placed on a timeline? _____

_____

_____

STUDY CARD PROMPTS

Timeline

1. What is a timeline?

2. What is the major purpose of a timeline?

To check your answers to these questions, turn the card over and review the information you have written on the other side.

Parts of a Timeline

Describe each part of a timeline and the role it plays.

1. What role does the *title* of the timeline play?

2. What is *chronological order*?

3. What are the *events* that are placed on a timeline?

To check your answers to these questions, turn the card over and review the information you have written on the other side.

Name _____ Date _____

PERFORMANCE–BASED ASSESSMENT QUESTIONS

1 The following question has two parts. First answer part A. Then, answer part B.

Use the list of events in United States history below to create a timeline.

Part A.

Place or rewrite **each** event on the timeline in correct chronological order in the boxes below. Also add the date for each event.

The British Parliament passes the Stamp Act (1765)	The French and Indian War ends (1763)	Thomas Jefferson writes the Declaration of Independence (1776)	The Boston Tea Party takes place (1773)

Part B.

Then, provide an appropriate title for your timeline.

Title: _____

EVENTS

DATES

END-OF-YEAR ASSESSMENT QUESTIONS

2   A timeline of some events in United States history is shown.

What would be the best title for this timeline?

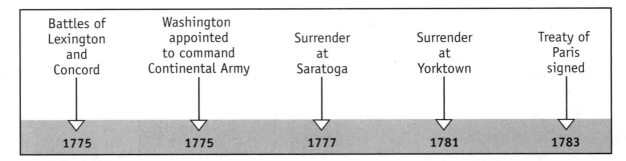

Battles of Lexington and Concord	Washington appointed to command Continental Army	Surrender at Saratoga	Surrender at Yorktown	Treaty of Paris signed
1775	1775	1777	1781	1783

Ⓐ   The French and Indian War
Ⓑ   The American Revolutionary War
Ⓒ   War with Chief Tecumseh
Ⓓ   The War of 1812

3   Where should the Treaty of Alliance with France (1778) be placed on the timeline?

Ⓐ   To the left of the battles of Lexington and Concord
Ⓑ   Between the surrender at Saratoga and the Surrender at Yorktown
Ⓒ   Between the battles of Lexington and Concord and surrender at Saratoga
Ⓓ   To the right of the Treaty of Paris

4   Which event occurred after the Surrender at Yorktown?

Ⓐ   British soldiers fired on colonists in Boston.
Ⓑ   Thomas Paine published *Common Sense*.
Ⓒ   The Declaration of Independence was signed.
Ⓓ   The Treaty of Paris was signed.

5   Which statement about a timeline is most accurate?

Ⓐ   Events on a timeline are usually not presented in chronological order.
Ⓑ   The earliest historical event is always shown on the right.
Ⓒ   A timeline can be shown to represent any period of time.
Ⓓ   The space between any two events on a timeline is always the same.

6   A timeline is shown.

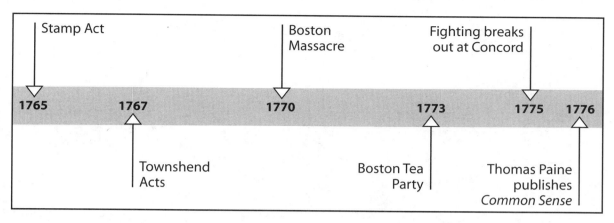

Which development do the events on this timeline explain?

Ⓐ   How Prehistoric Indian tribes once lived in Ohio.
Ⓑ   Why settlers entered the Ohio River Valley.
Ⓒ   Why the Declaration of Independence was issued in 1776.
Ⓓ   Why Ohio became a state in 1803.

7   Which two events on this timeline are separated by a decade?

Ⓐ   The Stamp Act and Townshend Acts
Ⓑ   The Boston Massacre and Fighting breaks out at Concord
Ⓒ   The Stamp Act and Fighting breaks out at Concord
Ⓓ   The Boston Tea Party and Thomas Paine publishes *Common Sense*

8   How much time is represented on this timeline?

Ⓐ   Exactly one year
Ⓑ   Less than a decade
Ⓒ   Just over a decade
Ⓓ   More than a century

9   Which of these groups of items is arranged in order from the shortest to the longest?

Ⓐ   A year, a century, a decade.
Ⓑ   A year, a decade, a century
Ⓒ   A century, a decade, a year
Ⓓ   A decade, a year, a century

10 A timeline of historical events is shown.

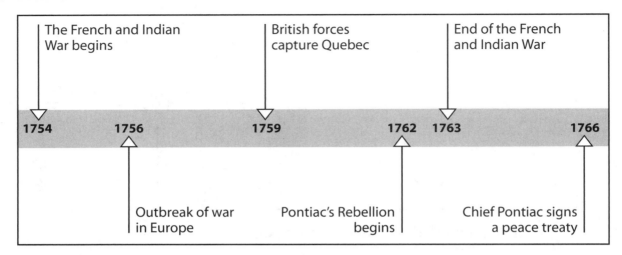

What would be the best title for this timeline?

Ⓐ Events in the French and Indian War and Pontiac's Rebellion
Ⓑ Key Events of the French and Indian War
Ⓒ Key Events of the Seven Years' War in Europe
Ⓓ Events leading up to the French and Indian War

11 Which event happened within two years of Pontiac's Rebellion?

Ⓐ Chief Pontiac signs a peace treaty
Ⓑ Outbreak of war in Europe
Ⓒ British forces capture Quebec
Ⓓ End of the French and Indian War

12 Which two events on the timeline are separated by more than a decade?

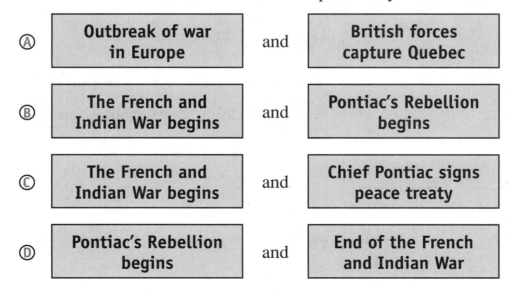

Name _____ Date _____

CHAPTER 8

HISTORICAL NARRATIVE

TOPIC: HISTORICAL THINKING SKILLS

| History 2 | *Primary and secondary sources can be used to create historical narratives.* |

After reading this chapter, you should be able to:

★ Define the following terms:
  • History
  • Primary sources
  • Secondary sources
  • Historical narrative

★ Understand the difference between a primary and secondary source.
★ Create a historical narrative using primary and secondary sources.

MAIN IDEAS OF THIS CONTENT STATEMENT

As you know, **history** is the study of the past. A knowledge of history gives us insight and provides us with a guide for future action.

To learn about the past, historians use different sources.

● **Primary sources** are the original records of an event. These include eyewitness reports, letters sent by people directly involved in the event, diaries, drawings and photographs, newspaper reports written at the time, and **artifacts** (*objects*) from the event.

● **Secondary sources** are the writings, interpretations and viewpoints of later writers who have reviewed the information in primary sources. Textbooks, encyclopedias, and Internet sources like Wikipedia are considered secondary sources.

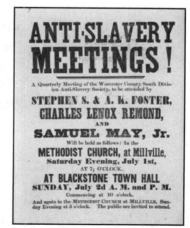

An Abolitionist broadside is a primary source.

WRITING A HISTORICAL NARRATIVE

A **historical narrative** tells the story of a historical event. The **narrator** is the person telling the story. The people, places, and events in the narrative are true, but the account is told in the form of a story.

When you write a historical narrative, you combine the skills of a fiction and nonfiction writer. Like all nonfiction, a historical narrative describes people who actually lived and events that actually happened. However, when you write an historical narrative, you must also use your "historical imagination." You must put the evidence together to imagine what those people and events were really like. Of course, you never actually met George Washington. However, you can surely imagine what he might have been like. If you wrote a historical narrative about the American Revolutionary War, Washington would be one of your main characters.

A historical narrative should include **who** was involved, **where** the events took place, **what** happened, **why** it happened, and the **effects** of the event. The concept map below shows the important points your historical narrative should include.

In writing a historical narrative, events are usually told in the order in which they occurred. Your narrative may also provide a central idea or lesson to be learned from the experience.

Name _____ Date _____

STUDY CARDS

Sources

1. What is a primary source? _____

_____

_____

2. Provide one example of a primary source: _____

_____

3. What is a secondary source? _____

_____

_____

4. Provide one example of a secondary source: _____

_____

Historical Narrative

1. What is a historical narrative? _____

_____

_____

2. How does a historical narrative differ from other types of writing?

_____

_____

3. What does a historical narrative have in common with other types of writing?

_____

_____

_____

_____

STUDY CARD PROMPTS

Sources

1. **What is a primary source?**

2. **What is an example of a primary source?**

3. **What is a secondary source?**

4. **What is an example of a secondary source?**

To check your answers to these questions, turn the card over and review the information you have written on the other side.

Historical Narrative

1. **What is a historical narrative?**

2. **How does a historical narrative differ from other types of writing?**

3. **What does a historical narrative have in common with other types of writing?**

To check your answers to these questions, turn the card over and review the information you have written on the other side.

Name _____ Date _____

CONTENT-AREA VOCABULARY

Directions. Fill in the boxes below.

PRIMARY SOURCE	
Define "primary source."	How does a primary source differ from other sources?
Give an example of a primary source.	Give an example of a source that is **not** a primary source.

SECONDARY SOURCE	
Define "secondary source."	How does a secondary source differ from other sources?
Give an example of a secondary source.	Give an example of a source that is **not** a secondary source.

HISTORICAL NARRATIVE	
Define "historical narrative."	How does a historical narrative differ from other types of writing?
Give an example of a historical narrative.	Give an example of a type of writing that is **not** a historical narrative.

PERFORMANCE-BASED ASSESSMENT QUESTIONS

13 Which of these two sources would be considered a primary source on the American Revolution?

Actual examples of the stamp that the Stamp Act required to be on all legal documents.

A book by H.S. Commager and R. Morris.

---

14 This is a powder horn used to hold gunpowder. Carved on it is: "Robert Holmes, Ft. Edward, 1758." Mr. Holmes was an American colonist, who fought in the French and Indian War.

Is this artifact a primary or a secondary source? _____

Explain your response on the lines below.

_____

_____

_____

Name _____ Date _____

END-OF-YEAR ASSESSMENT QUESTIONS

15 A diagram is shown.

Which phrase best completes the diagram?

Ⓐ Artifacts and Artworks
Ⓑ Primary Sources
Ⓒ Secondary Sources
Ⓓ Oral Histories

16 A timeline is shown.

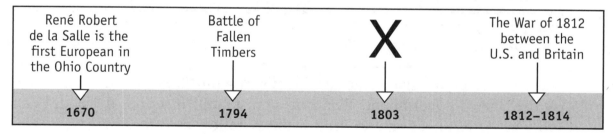

Which event should be placed where the **X** is located?

Ⓐ Pontiac's War
Ⓑ King George III issues the Proclamation Line
Ⓒ Publication of Harriet Beecher Stowe's book *Uncle Tom's Cabin*
Ⓓ Ohio becomes the seventeenth state of the Union

17 Which is a primary source about the Indian tribes who once lived in Ohio?

Ⓐ A history book on Indians of the United States.
Ⓑ A television show about the history of Ohio's Indians.
Ⓒ A bow and arrow from a Prehistoric Indian tribe in Ohio.
Ⓓ An interview with a historian about the Indian tribes of Ohio.

18 Two passages are shown.

Decide whether each passage is a primary or a secondary source.

Place an **X** in the correct box under each passage.

PASSAGE 1	PASSAGE 2
Article II. Each state retains its [supreme power], freedom and every power, and right, which is not given to the United States …. **Article III.** The States enter into a league of friendship with each other, for their defense, the security of their liberties, and their general welfare, binding them to assist each other against all attacks upon them …. — Articles of Confederation	Americans recognized the need for a national government. The Continental Congress was weak as a national government. Because of their recent experiences in living under British rule, the former colonists were afraid of creating a central government that would be too powerful. As a result, the Continental Congress decided to create the Articles of Confederation in 1776. They hoped that this would solve the problem. — A U.S. history textbook
Primary Source **Secondary Source**	**Primary Source** **Secondary Source**

19 A passage about colonial times is shown.

> "As a merchant living in America, I feel we colonists are being unfairly treated by the British government. This abuse must stop! If it does not end, I cannot tell where this situation may lead with my fellow colonists."

Why is this passage considered a primary source?

Ⓐ It was taken from a textbook in American History.
Ⓑ It is words from a movie script about the American Revolution.
Ⓒ It was spoken by someone who lived during the colonial period.
Ⓓ It is from a recent letter written by a historian.

20 Which of the following documents would be considered a primary source?

Ⓐ An encyclopedia article about George Washington
Ⓑ A textbook with a chapter on Colonial America
Ⓒ A biography about George Washington
Ⓓ A letter written by George Washington

Name _____ Date _____

CHAPTER 9

GROUPS OF OHIOANS INTERACT

TOPIC: HERITAGE

Ideas and events from the past have shaped the world we live in today. The actions of past individuals and groups have made a difference in the lives of later generations.

> **History 3** *Various groups of people have lived in Ohio over time including prehistoric and historic American Indians, migrating settlers and immigrants. Interactions among these groups have resulted in both cooperation and conflict.*

After reading this chapter, you should be able to:

★ Define the following terms:
  • Prehistoric Indians
  • Ohio's Historic Indian Tribes
  • Hunter gatherers
  • Mound Builders
  • Longhouses / wigwams
  • Conflict
  • Cooperation

★ Identify the various groups that have lived in Ohio over time.
★ Describe the interactions of these groups and how they resulted in both cooperation and conflict.

MAIN IDEAS OF THIS CONTENT STATEMENT

OHIO'S PREHISTORIC INDIANS

Prehistory is the period of time before the rise of written records. More than 20,000 years ago, hunters from Asia crossed a narrow band of land that once connected Asia and North America. This band of land stretched for several hundreds of square miles. These hunters followed the movements of animal herds and spread throughout the Americas.

The first humans to settle in the region of present-day Ohio were the **Paleo-Indians**. They arrived in Ohio between 15,000 and 12,000 years ago. They were **hunter-gatherers**. The Paleo-Indians obtained their food by gathering wild plants and hunting animals. They were constantly on the move seeking new animals and plants.

Paleo-Indians were hunter-gatherers.

A second group of prehistoric Indians were known as the **Archaic Indians**. They arrived in Ohio around 10,000 years ago. They, too, were hunter-gatherers. The Archaic Indians made baskets, pottery, and copper objects.

A third wave of prehistoric Indians, the **Mound Builders**, came to Ohio sometime after the **Archaic Indians**. They are also known as the **Woodland Indians**. The **Adena** and **Hopewell** peoples were both Woodland Indians. Historians believe that the Adena actually later developed into the Hopewell culture. The Adena were mainly hunters and gatherers, but also lived by growing sunflowers, squash and other plants. The Adena were master craftsmen who made jewelry and objects out of copper.

The **Hopewell** Indians appeared around 2,000 years ago. They lived in the Ohio and Mississippi Valleys. Like the Adena, the Hopewell planted squash and other plants. But like other tribes before them, they mainly relied on hunting and gathering for their food.

Mound builders began with the burial of one important person, often the tribal leader. As time passed, more individuals were buried at the same place.

The Adena and the Hopewell were both **mound-builders**. One purpose of their mounds was to allow families to bury their dead. However, historians have found that this was not their only purpose. Mounds were also used for ceremonies, such as for a marriage or a young person's "coming of age" as an adult.

Name _____ Date _____

LATER PRE-HISTORIC INDIANS

The planting of corn (also known as **maize**) first developed in Mexico. From Mexico, techniques for growing corn spread among American Indian peoples throughout much of North America. It is believed that the knowledge of how to grow corn came to Ohio about 1,000 years ago.

The Great Serpent Mound.

The **Fort Ancient Indians** adopted these techniques for growing corn, while also continuing to create great mounds of earth, wood and shells, such as the Great Serpent Mound. The **Great Serpent Mound** is the largest of these mounds. This mound does not contain any human remains. It was not built for burial purposes. The Fort Ancient Indians also used bows and arrows for hunting and warfare.

OHIO'S HISTORIC INDIANS

A large number of historic Indians lived in Ohio before the voyages of Christopher Columbus. These historic "tribes" (*peoples*) included the Shawnee, Delaware, Ottawa, Miami, Ohio Seneca, and Wyandot.

Four of these historic tribes — the Shawnee, Delaware, Ottawa, and Miami — spoke **Algonquian** languages and shared similar traditions and lifestyles. They lived in **wigwams**, an Indian word for "house." Their wigwams were made by bending tree branches into dome-shaped frames. The dome was then covered by the bark of birch trees. They built canoes with wood frames covered by bark.

The **Shawnee** lived in southern Ohio. The **Delaware** (*also known as the Lenape*) lived in eastern Ohio. Both the Shawnee and the Delaware planted corn, beans, squash, and tobacco. Their clothing was made from the skin of deer. They continued to hunt, catching ducks and turkeys, as well as to plant their own food.

Their public meetings were usually held in a **longhouse** or similar public buildings. The Delaware had steam baths, where their members could relax and cleanse themselves.

The **Ottawa** had once lived in Canada but moved southward to Ohio in the 1740s. They lived in longhouses that were up to 100 feet long. The Ottawa acted as traders

A typical Indian longhouse.

between other Indian tribes and European explorers. They traded furs and food in exchange for European guns and cooking utensils.

The **Miami** were another Algonquian people. They lived in villages in wigwams, surrounded by their fields. The Miami hunted, fished and farmed. They decorated their bodies with tattoos and pierced their noses and ears. The Miami often traded with different tribes in the Great Lakes region. Often they buried their dead under piles of logs.

Two groups of historic Indians in Ohio spoke **Iroquoian** languages: the Ohio **Seneca** and the **Wyandots** (*also known as the Hurons*). These groups followed many Iroquoian customs. For example, they lived in longhouses. They traveled along rivers and streams, and fished in lakes, in their birch-bark canoes. They grew corn, squash and beans. They wore clothes made up of deer skin (*buckskin*). Like the Ottawa, they engaged in trade, especially in the fur trade.

COOPERATION AMONG OHIO'S INDIAN TRIBES

Cooperation within each tribe was essential to everyday life. The interests of the tribe were more important than the interests of any individual. Tribal members cooperated with each other when hunting, building settlements, and growing crops. The remains of massive burial mounds still exist throughout Ohio. These are further evidence that hundreds of tribal members cooperated with one another to construct these massive mounds. Tribes also cooperated with other tribes — including distant ones — to conduct trade.

Name _____ Date _____

CONFLICT AMONG OHIO'S INDIAN TRIBES

There is also evidence that Indian tribes sometimes came into **conflict**. Because tribes sometimes fought one another, settlements were often surrounded by wooden fences made of sharpened sticks. To prepare for manhood, boys might even have to prove themselves by participating in a raid against another tribe.

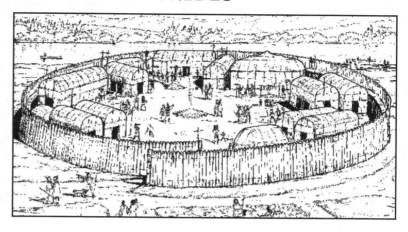

Although tribes generally lived in a one area, they sometimes fought each other over hunting rights.

MIGRATING SETTLERS AND IMMIGRANTS

European explorers and settlers came to North America after Columbus' voyage in 1492. **René Robert de la Salle** was the first European explorer to come to Ohio. He arrived in 1669. La Salle claimed the region for France.

The French and Indian War. French and British colonists both became interested in Ohio by the 1750s. French colonists were fur trappers and traded with the Indians to obtain furs to sell in Europe. The French built forts along the Great Lakes, including in the region of Ohio. British colonists were interested in moving into this region from the British colonies further east. The conflicting claims of British and French settlers in the Ohio River Valley was one reason for the outbreak of the French and Indian War (1755–1763).

Pontiac's Rebellion. British settlers and the Indians in this territory got along well at first. The Indians welcomed trade with the colonists. They were eager to receive European guns, gunpowder, rum and cloth. However, British settlers wanted to farm the land. Their desire to own the land soon brought the settlers and Indians in Ohio into conflict. In 1762, **Chief Pontiac** organized an uprising

Indians prepare to attack Fort Detroit.

with other warriors against the British colonists. **Pontiac's Rebellion** was finally put down and peace was restored.

The Proclamation Line of 1763. The British eventually won the French and Indian War. The territory between Lake Erie and the Ohio River now came under British rule. However, in 1763 **King George III** issued a proclamation that forbade the colonists from settling west of the Appalachian Mountains. The purpose of this "**Proclamation Line**" was to protect the Indians and prevent future conflicts. This proclamation greatly angered the colonists. It closed the frontier to further colonial expansion. The proclamation contributed to bad feelings between the colonists and the British government.

Eventually, the colonists rebelled against Great Britain. You will learn more about the causes of this conflict, known as the American Revolution, in the next chapter. In 1776, the colonists declared their independence. By 1783, the American Revolutionary War was over.

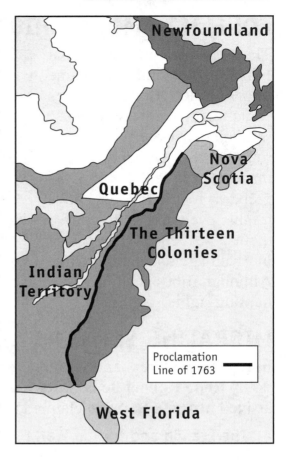

Settlers from other parts of the United States and Europe began to pour into Ohio in the years after the American Revolution (1775–1783). They built the town of **Marietta**, which became the first capital of the Ohio Territory. During this period, most of Ohio was still covered with thick forests. Often, settlers cut down some of the forest to build a cabin and prepare the land for planting crops. Increasing numbers of settlers led to new conflicts with the Indians.

The Battle of Fallen Timbers. In 1792, President George Washington sent General **Anthony Wayne** and a group of soldiers to Ohio to protect the settlers. In 1794, General Wayne defeated the Indians in the **Battle of Fallen Timbers**. Several Indian tribes agreed to give up their claims to Ohio in the **Treaty of Greenville**. This treaty prepared the way for even more settlers to move to Ohio.

After the United States achieved its independence, Europeans continued coming to America. These newcomers from other countries were known as **immigrants**. In the early 1800s, many immigrants chose to live in Ohio. They came from Germany, Ireland and other parts of Europe. They were attracted to Ohio by its available farm land and a desire to build a new life.

Name _____ Date _____

STUDY CARDS

American Indians in Ohio

Identify and describe these two groups of Indian tribes in Ohio.

1. Prehistoric Indians: _____

_____

_____

_____

2. Historic Indians: _____

_____

_____

_____

_____

Settlers and Early Immigrants in Ohio

Describe the settlers and immigrant groups that came to Ohio:

_____

_____

_____

_____

_____

_____

_____

_____

_____

_____

STUDY CARD PROMPTS

American Indians in Ohio

Identify and describe these two groups of Indian tribes in Ohio.

1. Prehistoric Indians

2. Historic Indians

To check your answers to these questions, turn the card over and review the information you have written on the other side.

Settlers and Early Immigrants in Ohio

Describe the settlers and immigrant groups that came to Ohio.

To check your answers to these questions, turn the card over and review the information you have written on the other side.

Name _____ Date _____

STUDY CARDS

Cooperation Among Ohio's American Indians

Describe some of the ways in which Indians cooperated with each other.

1. _____

_____

_____

2. _____

_____

_____

3. _____

_____

_____

Conflict Among Ohio's American Indians

1. Describe some of the ways in which Indians were in conflict with each other.

_____

_____

_____

_____

2. Describe some of the ways Indians and settlers were sometimes in conflict.

_____

_____

_____

_____

STUDY CARD PROMPTS

Cooperation Among Ohio's American Indians

Describe some of the ways in which Indians cooperated with each other.

To check your answers to these questions, turn the card over and review the information you have written on the other side.

Conflict Among Ohio's American Indians

1. **Describe some of the ways in which Indians were in conflict with each other.**

2. **Describe some of the ways Indians and settlers were sometimes in conflict.**

To check your answers to these questions, turn the card over and review the information you have written on the other side.

Name _____ Date _____

CONTENT-AREA VOCABULARY

Directions. Review the following names and terms.

Hopewell	Proclamation Line	Buckskin	Canoes
Shawnee	Germans	Anthony Wayne	Longhouses
Delaware	Adena	French and Indian War	René Robert de la Salle
Ohio Seneca	Irish	Wigwams	King George III
Mound Builders	Ottawa	Great Serpent Mounds	Battle of Fallen Timbers
Paleo-Indians	Wyandot	Miami	Treaty of Greenville
Pontiac's War	Maize (*corn*)	Fort Ancient Indians	European Immigrants

Then rewrite or draw a line from each of these terms to one of the following categories.

Prehistoric Indian Tribes	Historic Indian Tribes	Immigrants	Indian Lifestyles	Conflict Between Settlers and Indians

PERFORMANCE–BASED ASSESSMENT QUESTIONS

21 Two passages about Indians in Ohio are shown.

INDIAN VIEW OF LAND OWNERSHIP	SETTLERS VIEW OF LAND OWNERSHIP
Indians in Ohio had no idea of "private property." Indian tribes shared land ownership. "Mother Earth" was a part of the universe. This meant that the community shared the land on which they lived and hunted. As Black Hawk explained, "My reason teaches me that land cannot be sold. The Great Spirit gave it to all his children to live on." When Indians "gave" land to settlers, they did not mean to give up their own rights to use the land. They thought they would all continue to share hunting rights and live on the land together.	Under European law, land was a product to be bought and sold. European settlers to Ohio believed they were entitled to the lands they needed. The settlers believed that to own land it had to be enclosed. Land in Ohio was not enclosed. Thus, Ohio settlers believed this was free land just waiting to be claimed by them. When settlers purchased land from the Indians, they believed they had paid for the exclusive use of the land. They also believed that they had a right to forbid trespassers.

Explain how these two views of land ownership led to conflicts between American Indians and Ohio settlers.

_____

_____

_____

_____

_____

_____

_____

Name _____ Date _____

END-OF-YEAR ASSESSMENT QUESTIONS

22 A cause-and-effect diagram is shown.

Below are statements about cooperation and conflict among Indian tribes that lived in Ohio. Draw a line from the box to the correct column in the chart.

SHOWED COOPERATION AMONG INDIAN TRIBES	SHOWED CONFLICT AMONG INDIAN TRIBES

Massive burial mounds provided evidence of this.	Tribes raided other tribes over hunting rights in certain areas.
Indian villages had fences with sharpened sticks at their top.	Trade existed among different Indian tribes.

23 Two statements about Ohio's historic Indians are shown.

- Many historic Indian tribes in Ohio traded with one another.
- Members of Indian tribes often hunted and farmed together.

Which conclusion can be drawn from this information?

Ⓐ Indian tribes were often in conflict.
Ⓑ War between tribes groups led to raids and killing.
Ⓒ Most tribes practiced various types of rituals.
Ⓓ Cooperation among Indians was a common behavior.

24 How were the Shawnee and Delaware tribes of Ohio similar?

Ⓐ Both spoke the Iroquoian language.
Ⓑ Both left no evidence to help us understand their cultures.
Ⓒ Both settled in different regions of Central America.
Ⓓ Both used enslaved Africans to perform their farm work.

25 The arrival of new settlers in Ohio after the American Revolution led to conflicts between which two groups?

Ⓐ   Indian tribes and American settlers
Ⓑ   American colonists and the British government
Ⓒ   British soldiers and Indian tribes
Ⓓ   Southern slaves and Northern colonists

26 A picture of the interior of a longhouse is shown.

This longhouse was similar to ones used by Indian tribes in many parts of Ohio. What conclusion can be drawn from the picture?

Ⓐ   Most Indian families did not live under one roof.
Ⓑ   Tribal members often cooperated in their everyday life.
Ⓒ   Most Indian families enjoyed modern conveniences.
Ⓓ   Indian tribes in Ohio were highly industrialized.

27 An early Indian village is shown.

What conclusion can be drawn from this picture about Indians living in Ohio?

Ⓐ   Indians always cooperated with nearby tribes.
Ⓑ   Indians often built their villages along the Ohio River.
Ⓒ   Indians were sometimes in conflict with other tribes.
Ⓓ   Indians often built their villages close to Canada.

28 A chart about the first prehistoric Indians of Ohio is shown.

Paleo-Indians	Archaic Indians
Worked together to hunt animals	Worked together to hunt animals
Formed small groups to hunt animals	Formed small groups to hunt animals
Ate a wide variety of plants	Ate a wide variety of plants
Lacked permanent settlements	Lacked permanent settlements

What can be concluded from this chart about the characteristics of the Paleo Indians and Archaic Indians of Ohio?

Ⓐ These prehistoric Indians were primarily mound builders.
Ⓑ Cooperation and teamwork were central features in daily life.
Ⓒ These Indian tribes grew corn and squash to increase their food supply.
Ⓓ Most Prehistoric Indians were master craftsmen and traders.

29 How did the Paleo-Indians and the Archaic Indians of Ohio demonstrate cooperation among tribe members?

Ⓐ Both tribes hunted and gathered plants in groups.
Ⓑ Both tribes lived in large villages and towns.
Ⓒ Both tribes used primitive machines to make pottery.
Ⓓ Both tribes used tools made from metal.

30 What was the most common cause of conflict between the Indians and settlers moving into Ohio?

Ⓐ American Indians wanted money from the settlers.
Ⓑ Settlers wanted lands occupied by the Indians.
Ⓒ American Indians were copying settlers' lifestyles.
Ⓓ Ohio settlers were unwilling to pay Indian workers good wages.

31 Which is an accurate statement about the Indian tribes that lived in Ohio before settlers came?

Ⓐ Indian tribes never went to war with other Ohio tribes.
Ⓑ Indian tribes were unable to cooperate with other Indian tribes.
Ⓒ The method to grow corn spread among all Indian tribes in Ohio.
Ⓓ All Indian tribes that settled in Ohio lived in wigwams.

CHAPTER 10

AMERICAN COLONISTS FIGHT FOR INDEPENDENCE

TOPIC: HERITAGE

History 4	*The 13 colonies came together around a common cause of liberty and justice, uniting to fight for independence during the American Revolution and to form a new nation.*

After reading this chapter, you should be able to:

★ Define the following terms:
- Boston Massacre
- Lexington / Concord
- Thomas Paine's *Common Sense*
- American Revolution
- Declaration of Independence

★ Describe how the thirteen American colonists were able to come together to fight the British for their independence.
★ Describe the importance of the Declaration of Independence.

MAIN IDEAS OF THIS CONTENT STATEMENT

THE BRITISH COLONIES

By the end of the French and Indian War, there were 13 British colonies in North America. The **New England colonies** — Massachusetts, New Hampshire, Connecticut and Rhode Island — had colder climates, rocky soil and a short growing season. New England colonists specialized in shipbuilding, lumbering, whaling and carrying goods on ships.

A typical colonial town in New England.

The **Middle Atlantic colonies** consisted of New York, New Jersey, Delaware and Pennsylvania. These colonies enjoyed longer growing seasons and more fertile soil. Their farmers grew wheat, barley, rye, corn and fruits for the colonies on their small farms. The fertile soil of the area permitted a large amount of grain to be sold in Europe. The Middle Atlantic colonies consisted of large forested lands which attracted many settlers to this area. Its plentiful forests gave birth to an active lumbering and shipbuilding industry. The Middle Atlantic colonies also had a greater mix of religions and ethnic groups than the other colonies.

The **Southern colonies** — Virginia, Maryland, North Carolina, South Carolina and Georgia — were mainly rural settlements. They had warmer climates and longer growing seasons. Some Southerners, part of the planter class, owned large **plantations** supported by slave labor. They grew cotton, tobacco, rice and indigo (*a plant used to produce blue dye*) for shipment to Britain in exchange for manufactured goods.

DIFFERENCES BETWEEN BRITAIN AND HER COLONIES

After the French and Indian War, the British government was in debt. The British government decided to tax the colonists more in order to pay off its debts. The British felt it was only fair that the colonists should pay some of the costs of their own defense against France, Spain and the American Indians.

Stamp Act. The first new tax that the British introduced was the **Stamp Act**. This act required a government stamp on all newspapers, pamphlets and legal documents. The colonists objected that they had not been consulted (*asked for their opinion*) about the Stamp Act. The colonists cried out that "**taxation without representation**" was unjust. The colonists demonstrated, **boycotted** (*refused to buy*) British goods, sent petitions to London, and even attacked some British tax collectors in protest.

Colonists protesting against the British Stamp Act.

Townshend Duties. These protests by the colonists took the British government by surprise. In response to the protests, the British dropped the Stamp Act but insisted on their right to tax the colonists. To gain needed **revenue** (*money*), the British Parliament next passed the **Townshend duties**. The Townshend duties taxed glass, paper, lead, and other goods imported from Britain. Again the colonists were not consulted before the Townshend duties were passed. The British felt the colonists were just too far away to be represented in Parliament.

Colonial Unrest Grows. The British sent more troops to the colonies to prevent further unrest. In 1770, British troops reacted to a protest by colonists by firing on a hostile crowd in Boston. This event became known as the "**Boston Massacre**."

The Boston Massacre.

Once again, the British government cancelled the taxes to please the colonists. But the British still needed more revenue from the colonists. This time, the British introduced a new tax on tea. The colonists again protested. In 1773, a group of colonists dressed as Indians threw chests of tea off a ship in Boston Harbor.

OUTBREAK OF THE AMERICAN REVOLUTION

The British government and Parliament were shocked by this protest. They passed a series of acts closing Boston Harbor and suspending (*temporarily shutting down*) the colonial legislature of Massachusetts until the tea was paid for. Because these acts were so unbearable, the colonists called them the "**Intolerable Acts**."

Continental Congress Meets. Twelve of the thirteen colonies sent representatives to a **Continental Congress** in Philadelphia to discuss relations with Britain. Some colonists also began organizing for a possible conflict. The Massachusetts Governor sent British troops to arrest colonial leaders and take away their weapons. During this mission, British troops and colonists fired on one another at **Lexington and Concord** in 1775.

American colonists battle British soldiers at Concord Bridge in 1775.

The fighting here marked the start of the American Revolution.

Washington Takes Commands of the Continental Army. A Second Continental Congress met shortly after the fighting began. The other colonies agreed to join Massachusetts in fighting for their liberty and justice. The Continental Congress created the **Continental Army**. They appointed **George Washington** as their commander.

Name _____ Date _____

The Continental Army that Washington commanded was described as "a mixed group of people with little discipline, order or government."

Washington led his forces to victory in Boston. He then moved to New York to fight the British there. However, after a series of defeats Washington had to retreat behind the Delaware River.

The great distance of the American colonies from Great Britain meant the colonies were in many ways independent of the King and Parliament.	**The French and Indian War ended with a British victory over the French, making the colonies less dependent on Britain for protection.**	**The Proclamation of 1763 prohibited the colonists from settling beyond the Appalachian Mountains. This greatly offended many colonists.**

A SUMMARY OF THE CAUSES FOR THE OUTBREAK OF THE AMERICAN REVOLUTION

The British ordered the colonists to house and feed British soldiers in the colonies, which angered many colonists.	**The British required the colonists to pay new taxes, which were passed without their consent. Most colonists saw this as a violation of their rights.**

Many colonists were shocked at the steps taken by the British to defeat them. The British sent troops and mercenaries (*hired soldiers*). The fighting took lives and destroyed property. Early in 1776, **Thomas Paine** published his pamphlet, ***Common Sense***. Paine argued that it was "common sense" for American colonists to break free from British rule. He argued that a whole continent should not be governed by a tiny island thousands of miles away.

The question of independence was debated in the Second Continental Congress. In June 1776, the delegates passed a resolution in favor of independence. Members sought to obtain the help of France and Spain, but could only do so once they had declared their independence. **John Adams**, a leader for breaking away from Britain, led the debate in favor of independence at the Continental Congress.

John Adams

THE DECLARATION OF INDEPENDENCE

After the resolution was passed in favor of independence, a small committee was appointed to write an explanation telling the world of this decision. **Thomas Jefferson** was the main author of the **Declaration of Independence**.

Members of the Second Continental Congress gather to sign the Declaration of Independence.

The Declaration of Independence stated the basis for America's theory of government:

- All people are endowed (*born with*) with certain **unalienable** (*basic*) rights, including life, liberty and the pursuit of happiness.

- Governments are created to protect these rights.

- Citizens have the right to change their government if it fails to protect these rights.

A List of Grievances. The Declaration also listed the **grievances** (*complaints*) that the colonists had against **King George III**. These grievances claimed that the King was a dictator who taxed the colonists without their consent, and who kept standing armies in the colonies in times of peace.

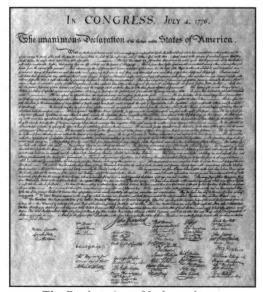
The Declaration of Independence.

Independence. Finally, the Declaration announced that the colonists had given up their loyalty to the King. The former colonies now formed a new, independent country capable of forming its own alliances.

STUDY CARDS

Causes of the American Revolution

Describe the issues that turned colonists against the British government:

1. Proclamation Line: _____

_____

_____

2. British Taxes: _____

_____

_____

3. British Abuses of Power: _____

_____

_____

_____

Steps that Led to American Independence

Describe the role played by each of the following events:

1. The Battles at Lexington and Concord: _____

_____

_____

2. Formation of the Continental Army: _____

_____

3. Thomas Paine's Pamphlet: _____

_____

4. Debate in the Second Continental Congress: _____

_____

STUDY CARD PROMPTS

Causes of the American Revolution

Describe the issues that turned many colonists against the British government:

1. **Proclamation Line**

2. **British Taxes**

3. **British Abuses of Power**

To check your answers to these questions, turn the card over and review the information you have written on the other side.

Steps that Led to American Independence

Describe the role played by each of the following events:

1. **The Battles at Lexington and Concord**

2. **Formation of the Continental Army**

3. **Thomas Paine's Pamphlet**

4. **Debate in the Second Continental Congress**

To check your answers to these questions, turn the card over and review the information you have written on the other side.

Name _____ Date _____

CONTENT-AREA VOCABULARY

Directions. Which name or term does **not** belong with the other names and terms in the same box? Write your answer on the lines to the right of the box. Then use the same name or term in a sentence.

New England Colonies
Mid Atlantic Colonies
Southern Colonies
French and Indian War

_____
_____
_____
_____
_____

Proclamation Line of 1763
Declaration of Independence
Townshend Duties
Stamp Act

_____
_____
_____
_____
_____

Second Continental Congress
British Parliament
Thomas Paine's *Common Sense*
Declaration of Independence

_____
_____
_____
_____
_____

PERFORMANCE-BASED ASSESSMENT QUESTIONS

32 A chart of conflicting viewpoints is shown.

Fill in the two empty boxes in the chart.

CONFLICTING ISSUES IN THE AMERICAN REVOLUTION

British Viewpoint	American Colonists' Viewpoint
Stamp Act: The colonists need to pay this tax to repay our government for the cost of protecting them during the French and Indian War.	
	The Proclamation of 1763 is very unfair. It prohibits us from settling in areas in the Western frontier, beyond the Appalachian Mountains.

33 A passage from Samuel Adams is shown.

"The acts passed by Parliament placing taxes on newspapers, pamphlets and legal documents, to raise money are threats to our natural and constitutional rights. Since the colonists are not represented in the British Parliament, the Parliament cannot lawfully tax our property without our consent."

— Samuel Adams, *A Letter against Taxation* (1767)

Which tax was Samuel Adams protesting against in this passage?

34 A concept map is shown.

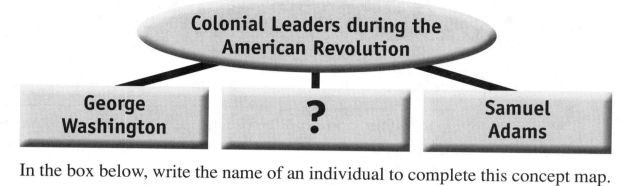

In the box below, write the name of an individual to complete this concept map.

35 American colonists fought against the British to achieve their independence.

Select **two** causes of the American Revolution from the boxes provided. Rewrite or draw an arrow from your two answers to the blank boxes.

CAUSES OF THE AMERICAN REVOLUTION

First Cause	Second Cause

| Great Britain had successfully defeated France in the French and Indian War. | The colonists felt that "taxation without representation" violated their rights as Englishmen. |
| The Continental Congress appointed George Washington to lead the Continental Army. | The British imposed a new taxes on the colonists to help pay for the costs of their defense. |

END-OF-YEAR ASSESSMENT QUESTIONS

36 A passage about the American Revolution is shown.

> "We have grown accustomed to little interference from the British government. We see the new regulations from Parliament as a challenge. We believe that each person has a natural right to life, liberty, and property. Such new tax laws should only be passed when we are represented in Parliament."

Identify one colonial leader who might have made this statement in the period before the American Revolution. Write your answer in the box below.

37 A list of items is shown.

- A list of grievances committed by King George III against the colonists.
- A statement that the right to life, liberty, and the pursuit of happiness are natural rights.
- An announcement that people have the right to change their government if that government fails to protect the people it is governing.

Which document includes all three of these items?

38 In the Declaration of Independence, the colonists listed their grievances. Which grievance resulted from the lack of colonial representation in Parliament?

- Ⓐ   "For quartering large bodies of armed troops among us."
- Ⓑ   "For cutting off our trade with all parts of the world."
- Ⓒ   "For imposing taxes on us without our consent."
- Ⓓ   "For depriving us, in many cases, of the benefits of trial by jury."

39 Which event is correctly matched with its description?

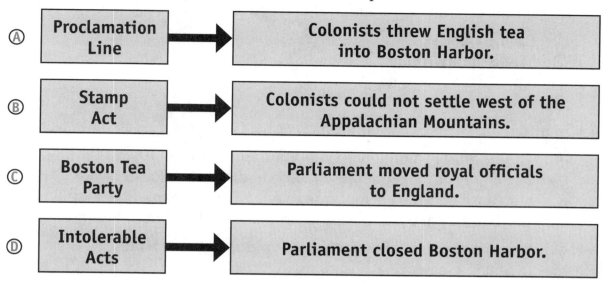

Ⓐ | Proclamation Line → Colonists threw English tea into Boston Harbor.

Ⓑ | Stamp Act → Colonists could not settle west of the Appalachian Mountains.

Ⓒ | Boston Tea Party → Parliament moved royal officials to England.

Ⓓ | Intolerable Acts → Parliament closed Boston Harbor.

40 A passage is shown.

> "I have heard some say that America has thrived from her connection with Britain, and this connection is necessary for its future happiness. We may as well say that because a child has had milk, that it is never to have meat. I challenge any supporter of Great Britain to show me a single advantage that America can gain by being connected with Great Britain."

Which leader made this statement?

Ⓐ King George III
Ⓑ Thomas Paine
Ⓒ Oliver Perry
Ⓓ Harriet Beecher Stowe

41 Why were many colonists angered by the Proclamation of 1763?

Ⓐ It took large amounts of land from Canada.
Ⓑ It gave a part of the territory of Louisiana to France.
Ⓒ It limited the colonists' freedom to move westward.
Ⓓ It provided guns to American Indians living in Ohio.

42 Which physical feature acted as the western boundary for settlements by American colonists in the period prior to the American Revolution?

- Ⓐ Pacific Ocean
- Ⓑ Mississippi River
- Ⓒ Appalachian Mountains
- Ⓓ Great Plains

43 Why did many American colonists feel that Great Britain's tax laws were unfair?

- Ⓐ The colonists paid higher taxes than people living in Great Britain.
- Ⓑ The colonists lacked representation in the British Parliament.
- Ⓒ Indian tribes were exempt from paying British taxes.
- Ⓓ The British government had a surplus and did not need the money.

44 Which event supports the view that people sometimes protest government policies to obtain greater liberty and justice?

- Ⓐ The start of the French and Indian War
- Ⓑ The issuance of the Proclamation of 1763
- Ⓒ The Boston Tea Party
- Ⓓ The founding of the state of Ohio

45 Below are statements about the Declaration of Independence. Draw a line from the boxed statements to the correct column of the chart.

PART OF THE DECLARATION OF INDEPENDENCE	NOT PART OF THE DECLARATION OF INDEPENDENCE

The Second Continental Congress passes a resolution in favor of independence from Great Britain.	All people are born with certain basic rights, such as life, liberty, and the pursuit of happiness.
All enslaved Africans brought to the United States shall now be set free.	Governments are created to protect the people's rights.
Listed various grievances that King George III committed.	A government has a right to tax its people without their consent.

Name _____ Date _____

CHAPTER 11

THE NORTHWEST ORDINANCE

TOPIC: HERITAGE

History 5	*The Northwest Ordinance established a process for the creation of new states and specified democratic ideals to be incorporated in the states of the Northwest Territory.*

After reading this chapter, you should be able to:

★ Define the following terms:
  • Northwest Ordinance
  • Democratic ideals
  • Freedom of religion
  • Right to a trial by a jury

★ Describe the key provisions of the Northwest Ordinance.
★ Describe the democratic ideals that were promoted by the Northwest Ordinance.

MAIN IDEAS OF THIS CONTENT STATEMENT

After declaring independence from Great Britain, each colony became an independent state and adopted its own state constitution. In addition, the **Second Continental Congress** created a new national government in a document known as the **Articles of Confederation**.

Members of the Second Continental Congress meet to discuss forming a new national government.

The Articles of Confederation. Members of the Continental Congress feared that individual freedom might be threatened if the national government had too much power. Therefore, they created only a loose **confederation** of states. They left most power in the hands of the individual states, making the new national government weak. Under the Articles of Confederation, each state had one vote in the Confederation Congress, and nine states were needed to pass any law. The Confederation Congress was unable to raise its own army or collect taxes. The national government depended on the state governments for support.

The Northwest Ordinance. One of the most important achievements of the Confederation Congress was passing the **Northwest Ordinance** in 1787. An **ordinance** is a type of law. The Northwest Ordinance was a law dealing with government of the Northwest Territory. The Northwest Ordinance divided this immense area into several smaller "territories."

The Northwest Ordinance then established a series of steps for each of these territories to become new states.

● First, a group of leaders would be appointed by Congress to govern each territory.

● Once a territory reached a population of 5,000 adults, its citizens would elect their own representatives to govern themselves.

● Finally, once the population of the territory reached 60,000 people, it could apply for admission as a state. Once admitted, the new state would be on an equal footing with all the existing states.

Equality of States. It declared that all territories could come into the Union as equal states with the same status and privileges as the original states.

Slavery. It abolished slavery in the Northwest Territory, although it did provide for the return of "fugitive" or escaped slaves to their owners in the South.

DEMOCRATIC IDEALS IN THE NORTHWEST ORDINANCE

Voting Rights. It guaranteed voting rights to every adult male who owned 50 acres of land.

Education. A related law in 1785 established a system in which a portion of land in each township would pay for public education.

Individual Rights. It included guarantees of individual rights, such as freedom of religion, the right to a trial by jury, and the right to reasonable bail.

Indian Affairs. It stated that new lands should not be taken from the Indians without their consent. Settlers were forbidden to unjustly harm Indians living in surrounding areas.

Name _____ Date _____

STUDY CARDS

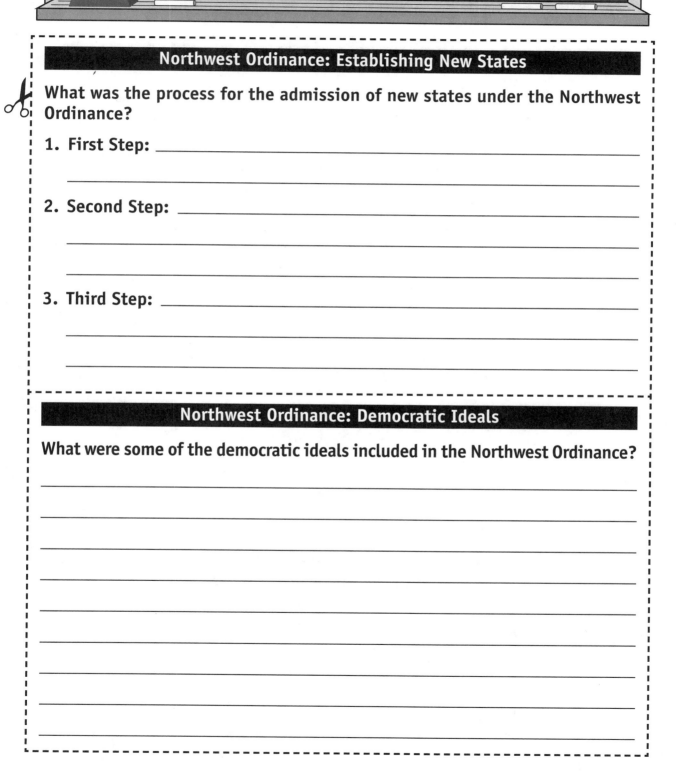

Northwest Ordinance: Establishing New States

What was the process for the admission of new states under the Northwest Ordinance?

1. **First Step:** _____

_____

2. **Second Step:** _____

_____

_____

3. **Third Step:** _____

_____

_____

Northwest Ordinance: Democratic Ideals

What were some of the democratic ideals included in the Northwest Ordinance?

_____

_____

_____

_____

_____

_____

_____

_____

_____

_____

_____

STUDY CARD PROMPTS

Northwest Ordinance: Establishing New States

What was the process for the admission of new states under the Northwest Ordinance?

1.

2.

3.

To check your answers to these questions, turn the card over and review the information you have written on the other side.

Northwest Ordinance: Democratic Ideals

What were some of the democratic ideals included in the Northwest Ordinance?

To check your answers to these questions, turn the card over and review the information you have written on the other side.

CONTENT-AREA VOCABULARY

Directions. Identify the terms and phrases in each of the concept circles below. Then explain how these four terms and phrases are connected to each other.

Articles of Confederation	Unable to raise an army
Confederation Congress	Fear of powerful government

_____

_____

_____

_____

Northwest Territory	Three Step Process
Northwest Ordinance	A State of the Union

_____

_____

_____

_____

Banned slavery	Freedom of religion
Funded public education	Right to a trial by jury

_____

_____

_____

_____

PERFORMANCE-BASED ASSESSMENT QUESTIONS

46 A list of statements dealing with the Northwest Ordinance is shown.

Classify each item in the T-Chart below as a statement that either deals with admission of a territory as a new state or as a right guaranteed under the Northwest Ordinance. Write each statement in the appropriate column below or indicate where it goes by drawing an arrow.

- All males who own 50 acres of property must be allowed to vote.
- Congress will appoint a group of leaders to govern the territory.
- Public education should be encouraged.
- Freedom of religion is guaranteed.
- Slavery is banned in all parts of the Northwest Territory.
- Citizens living in the territory are granted the right to a trial by jury.
- When 5,000 adults live in a territory, they can elect representatives to govern themselves.
- Indian lands will not be taken without their consent.
- People will have the right to enter into private contracts

GUARANTEE OF INDIVIDUAL RIGHTS	ADMISSION TO STATEHOOD

47 A passage in the Northwest Ordinance is shown.

> "There shall be neither slavery nor involuntary servitude in the territory. Any person escaping into the territory, from whom labor or service is lawfully claimed in any of the states, that fugitive may lawfully be reclaimed and returned to the person claiming his or her labor or service …."
>
> — Article 6, Northwest Ordinance, 1787

Summarize two provisions found in this article of the Northwest Ordinance?

A. _____

_____

B. _____

_____

48 A three-step plan for the admission of new states was established by the Northwest Ordinance.

Rearrange the three steps for admitting states from the Northwest Ordinance. Rewrite or indicate where each goes by drawing an arrow to a step in the blank boxes below.

| When a territory reaches a population of 5,000 adults, its citizens should elect their own representatives to govern themselves. | When the population of a territory reaches 60,000 people, and its citizens write a state constitution, it can apply for admission as a state. | A group of leaders are appointed by Congress to govern the territory. |

PROCESS ESTABLISHED BY THE NORTHWEST ORDINANCE FOR THE ADMISSION OF NEW STATES

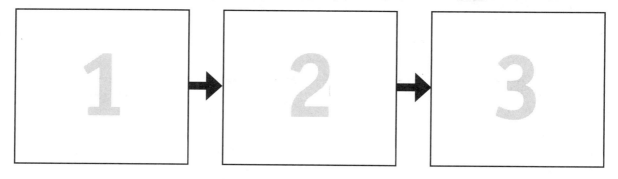

END-OF-YEAR ASSESSMENT QUESTIONS

49 A group of statements is shown.

> - Slavery is prohibited.
> - Citizens have a right to a trial by a jury
> - Citizens have the right to practice their own religion.

In which document can these three democratic ideals be found?

Ⓐ Declaration of Independence
Ⓑ Articles of Confederation
Ⓒ Northwest Ordinance of 1787
Ⓓ The Bill of Rights

50 What was the main reason why most settlers moved to the Northwest Territory?

Ⓐ To escape from crowded city slums
Ⓑ To be near American Indian tribes
Ⓒ To acquire inexpensive farm land
Ⓓ To have a better chance at getting a job

51 A timeline of historical events is shown.

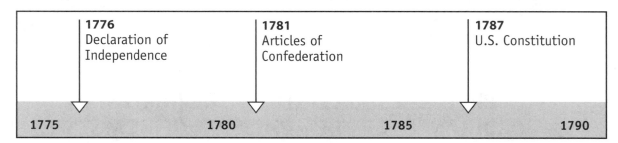

| 1776 Declaration of Independence | 1781 Articles of Confederation | 1787 U.S. Constitution |

1775   1780   1785   1790

What would be the best title for this timeline? Write your answer in the box.

Name _____ Date _____

52 A concept map is shown.

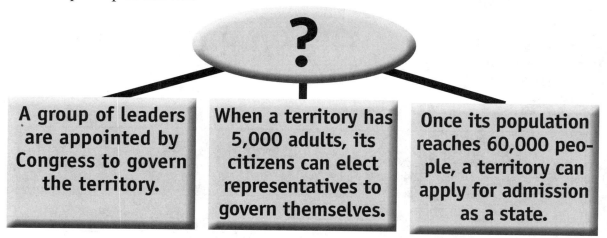

A group of leaders are appointed by Congress to govern the territory.

When a territory has 5,000 adults, its citizens can elect representatives to govern themselves.

Once its population reaches 60,000 people, a territory can apply for admission as a state.

Which item best completes the concept map?

Ⓐ Articles of Confederation (1781)
Ⓑ Treaty of Paris of 1783
Ⓒ Northwest Ordinance of 1787
Ⓓ Treaty of Ghent of 1814

53 A passage is shown.

Article 5. There shall be formed in the territory, not less than three nor more than five States. When any of the States shall have sixty thousand free inhabitants, such State shall be admitted into the Congress of the United States on an equal footing with the original States in all respects.

From which document does this passage come?

Ⓐ Declaration of Independence
Ⓑ Thomas Paine's Pamphlet, *Common Sense*
Ⓒ Northwest Ordinance of 1787
Ⓓ United States Constitution

54 What was the significance of the Northwest Ordinance?

Ⓐ It established procedures to limit westward expansion
Ⓑ It sought to limit the individual rights of people living in the territory.
Ⓒ It established a three-step plan for admitting new states.
Ⓓ It was supported by most of the Indian tribes living in Ohio.

CHAPTER 12

THE WAR OF 1812

TOPIC: HERITAGE

History 6	*The inability to resolve standing issues with Great Britain and ongoing conflicts with American Indians led the United States into the War of 1812. Victory in the Battle of Lake Erie contributed to American success in the war.*

After reading this chapter, you should be able to:

★ Identify these terms and people:
- General Anthony Wayne
- Battle of Fallen Timbers
- War of 1812
- Battle of Lake Erie
- Admiral Oliver Perry

★ Describe the issues that led the United States into the War of 1812.
★ Describe how the Battle of Lake Erie contributed to American success in the War of 1812.

MAIN IDEAS OF THIS CONTENT STATEMENT

CONFLICTS BETWEEN SETTLERS AND INDIANS

During the American Revolution, many American Indian tribes sided with the British because they did not trust the colonists. After the Revolution, the British continued to supply many of these Indians with guns. Some British agents even wanted to create an Indian nation between the United States and Canada.

Many Indians sided with the British during the American Revolution.

The British were also interested in continuing their profitable fur trade in the Northwest Territory. Most Americans felt that the British traders and their Indian allies had lost all rights to the Northwest Territory after the American Revolution.

THE BATTLE OF FALLEN TIMBERS

The **Northwest Ordinance** had recognized tribal rights. It stated that all future purchases of Indian lands had to be made by treaty. But many American Indian leaders still did not trust the Americans. Led by **Little Turtle** and his Shawnee ally **Blue Jacket**, Indian warriors attacked settlers in Ohio in 1790 and 1791.

President George Washington sent **General Anthony Wayne** to Ohio in 1792 to protect the settlers. In 1794, General Wayne defeated the Indians in the **Battle of Fallen Timbers**. This turned out to be the final battle for control of the Northwest Territory. A year later, many Indian tribes agreed to leave Ohio in the **Treaty of Greenville**.

The Battle of Fallen Timbers

The **Treaty of Greenville** was signed in late 1795. It became a major turning point in relations between Indians and Americans in Ohio.

Peace. The treaty brought about peace. It also brought a final end to the Northwest Indian Wars.	**Opened the West.** The treaty opened up Western lands to white settlers. This greatly increased westward migration and speeded up the settlement of frontier areas.

TERMS OF THE TREATY OF GREENVILLE (1795)

Surrender of Lands. These Indian tribes agreed to give up a large portion of their lands. These amounted to almost two-thirds of present-day Ohio. In addition, many Indian tribes were required to move west of the Mississippi River.	**Payment to the Indians.** As payment, the U.S. government agreed to give the Indian tribes $20,000 in goods — blankets, utensils, and domestic animals. The government also agreed to pay $9,500 in goods each year.

Chief Tecumseh. In 1806, Shawnee chief **Tecumseh** and his brother, known as the **Prophet**, began to unite all the Indian tribes in the region. They argued that the tribes should band together against the growing numbers of settlers.

They also believed that they should refuse to give up any more lands. In 1811, American soldiers fought Tecumseh's brother in the **Battle of Tippecanoe** and burned a Shawnee village.

THE WAR OF 1812

Meanwhile, the British and Americans began having new disagreements. Britain was already at war with France. The British navy began stopping U.S. ships at sea and seizing many American sailors. The British claimed that these sailors were **deserters** from the British navy. They were taken and forced to serve in the British navy. This practice of seizing sailors was known as **impressment**.

Many sailors who were impressed, were not British but Americans.

Americans were also angry because they believed that the British were still supplying Indians in the Northwest Territory with guns. These guns were sometimes used to attack American settlers.

Finally, several U.S. Congressmen believed the time was right for the United States to seize Canada from the British. For all of these reasons, a new conflict broke out between the United States and Britain — known as the **War of 1812**. Much of the fighting took place on the Great Lakes. **Fort Meigs**, on Ohio's Naumee River, was attacked twice by the British army.

An American victory in 1813 in the **Battle of Lake Erie** greatly contributed to America's success in the war. **Admiral Oliver Perry** led a fleet of American ships to victory over British warships. The victory gave the United States control of Lake Erie. It also blocked the British from supplying their fort in Detroit.

Commodore Perry at the Battle of Lake Erie

In Ohio, many Indians refused to accept the Treaty of Greenville. Leaders like Chief Tecumseh struggled to regain their lost lands. Tecumseh was later wounded and died in 1813, during the war.

Name _____ Date _____

STUDY CARDS

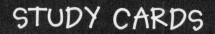

Conflicts with American Indians

Describe what occurred in each of these cases:

1. Alliance between Little Turtle and Blue Jacket: _____

_____

_____

2. Attempts by Tecumseh and the Prophet to unite the Indians: _____

_____

_____

3. The role of the Indians in the War of 1812: _____

_____

_____

The Treaty of Greenville

What were the most important provisions of the treaty regarding:

1. Surrender of lands: _____

_____

_____

2. Payment to the Indians: _____

_____

_____

3. Opening the West: _____

_____

_____

STUDY CARD PROMPTS

Conflicts with American Indians

Describe what occurred in each of these cases:

1. Alliance between Little Turtle and Blue Jacket

2. Attempts by Tecumseh and the Prophet to unite the Indians

3. The role of the Indians in the War of 1812

To check your answers to these questions, turn the card over and review the information you have written on the other side.

The Treaty of Greenville

What were the most important provisions of the treaty regarding:

1. Surrender of Lands

2. Payment to the Indians

3. Opening the West

To check your answers to these questions, turn the card over and review the information you have written on the other side.

Name _____ Date _____

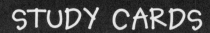

STUDY CARDS

Causes of the War of 1812

Describe the issues that led to the War of 1812:

1. Impressment of U.S. sailors: _____

_____

_____

2. British cooperation with American Indians: _____

_____

_____

3. American desire to seize Canada: _____

_____

_____

Important Battles

Describe the significance of each of these battles:

1. Battle of Fallen Timbers: _____

_____

_____

2. Battle of Tippecanoe: _____

_____

_____

3. Battle of Lake Erie: _____

_____

_____

STUDY CARD PROMPTS

Causes of the War of 1812

What were the issues that led to the War of 1812:

1. **Impressment of U.S. sailors.**

2. **British cooperation with American Indians.**

3. **American desire to seize Canada.**

To check your answers to these questions, turn the card over and review the information you have written on the other side.

Important Battles

Describe the significance of each of these battles:

1. **Battle of Fallen Timbers.**

2. **Battle of Tippecanoe.**

3. **Battle of Lake Erie.**

To check your answers to these questions, turn the card over and review the information you have written on the other side.

CONTENT-AREA VOCABULARY

Directions. Create a sentence using the names and terms in each of the boxes below.

Little Turtle

Blue Jacket

General Anthony Wayne

Battle of Fallen Timbers

_____

_____

_____

_____

Tecumseh

The Prophet

Battle of Tippecanoe

Treaty of Greenville

_____

_____

_____

_____

Impressment

Canada

War of 1812

**Supplying Indians
with weapons**

_____

_____

_____

_____

Fort Meigs

Battle of Lake Erie

Admiral Oliver Perry

British warships

_____

_____

_____

_____

PERFORMANCE-BASED ASSESSMENT QUESTIONS

55 During the War of 1812, Americans fought against Great Britain for a second time in less than three decades after the end of the American Revolution.

Complete the chart below by selecting two causes of the War of 1812 from the boxes below the chart. Write your answers in the blank spaces in the chart.

CAUSES OF THE WAR OF 1812

First Cause	Second Cause

The seizing of American sailors on the high seas from U.S. naval ships by British warships.	The British navy began a blockade of the European coast to prevent the shipping of goods.
Some Americans sought to force the British out of Canada and make Canada part of the United States.	President Washington ordered General Wayne to attack the Indians in the Battle of Fallen Timbers.

56 In 1813, American and British ships fought in Lake Erie. The battle took place on the side of the lake closest to Ohio. Admiral Oliver Perry led a fleet of U.S. ships to victory over British warships. Describe **one** effect of the U.S. victory at the Battle of Lake Erie.

_____

_____

_____

_____

57 One important development in Ohio's early history was the conflict between local Indian tribes and the U.S. Army. Equally important to Ohio's early history was the War of 1812.

Below are boxed statements about both conflicts. Rewrite or draw a line from the boxed statements to the correct column in the chart.

OHIO'S EARLY HISTORY

Indian Wars and the U.S. Army	The War of 1812

The Battle of Fallen Timbers was the final battle for control of the Northwest Territory.	President George Washington orders General Anthony Wayne to the region to protect settlers.
The Treaty of Greenville was a major turning point in Ohio's history.	Much of the fighting in this war took place on the Great Lakes.
The British seized these sailors claiming that they were deserters from the British navy.	The American victory in the Battle of Lake Erie greatly contributed to America's success in the war.

END-OF-YEAR ASSESSMENT QUESTIONS

58 A passage about American Indians is shown.

> In this treaty, several Indian tribes gave up their claims to lands south and east of the Cuyahoga River. A new boundary ran southward to Fort Laurens and westward to Fort Laramie and Fort Recovery. It then turned southward to the Ohio River. The treaty opened Western lands to white settlers.

Which treaty is described in this passage?

59 A newspaper headline is shown.

> ❖ **THE OHIO WESTERN JOURNAL** ❖
>
> ### General Wayne Defeats
> ### Indians At Fallen Timbers

What was one effect of the event in this headline?

Ⓐ Britain established colonies in North America.
Ⓑ The United States declared its independence from Great Britain.
Ⓒ American Indians moved into Ohio.
Ⓓ Ohio was opened to settlement by U.S. citizens

60 How did the Battle of Lake Erie contribute to the victory of the United States in the War of 1812?

Ⓐ It led to the passage of the Northwest Ordinance.
Ⓑ It gave the United States control of Lake Erie.
Ⓒ It improved relations with the Indians living along Lake Erie.
Ⓓ It outlawed future slavery in the state of Ohio.

61 A concept map is shown.

Which phrase correctly completes this concept map?

- Ⓐ American Revolutionary War
- Ⓑ Battle of Fallen Timbers
- Ⓒ Battle of Lake Erie
- Ⓓ American Civil War

62 Which event in United States history does this concept map refer to?

- Ⓐ French and Indian War
- Ⓑ American Revolutionary War
- Ⓒ Indian Wars in Ohio
- Ⓓ War of 1812

63 A list of statements is shown.

- This naval battle boosted the confidence of American troops.
- Victory in this battle gave the United States control of the Great Lakes.
- The battle helped Americans to rid themselves of British interference.

Which battle does this information describe?

- Ⓐ Battle of Tippecanoe
- Ⓑ Battle at Lexington
- Ⓒ Battle of Fallen Timbers
- Ⓓ Battle of Lake Erie

64 Why is the Battle of Fallen Timbers important?

- Ⓐ It led to a major victory for the American Indians.
- Ⓑ It was the first naval battle in the War of 1812.
- Ⓒ It marked the final battle of the Indian Wars in Ohio.
- Ⓓ It prevented settlers from entering Ohio.

CHAPTER
13

SECTIONALISM
AND SLAVERY

TOPIC: HERITAGE

History 7	*Sectional issues divided the United States after the War of 1812. Ohio played a key role in these issues, particularly with the antislavery movement and the Underground Railroad.*

After reading this chapter, you should be able to:

★ Identify these terms and people:
  • Sectionalism
  • Slavery
  • Abolitionists
  • Underground Railroad
  • Levi Coffin
  • Harriet Beecher Stowe

★ Identify the sectional issues that divided the nation after the War of 1812.
★ Describe the role played by Ohio in the antislavery movement and the Underground Railroad.

MAIN IDEAS OF THIS CONTENT STATEMENT

THE RISE OF SECTIONALISM

Sectionalism refers to the loyalty that many people feel to their "section," or region of the country, rather than to the nation as a whole. By the 1830s, the United States had developed into three distinct sections. Each of these sections had its own characteristics.

The **North** was the country's manufacturing center. Workers made thread and cloth in Northern textile factories. The North had more factories, railroads, and cities than any other part of the nation. The North also attracted immigrants. A growing portion of this population worked in industry and lived in cities. Farmers in the North sold dairy products and fruits and vegetables to nearby cities.

Name _____ Date _____

In the **West**, farmers grew wheat and corn to ship to the rest of the nation. By the mid-1800s, the number of settlers moving to the West increased greatly. The desire for land and new opportunities continued to attract settlers. In addition, the West's fertile soil attracted many farmers.

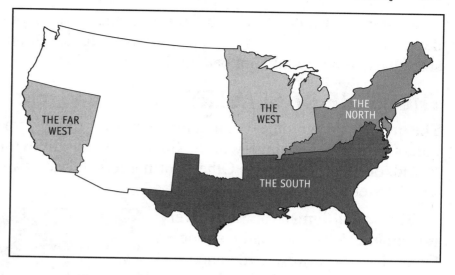

The **South** remained largely agricultural. The plantation system had spread throughout much of the South. The slave population steadily grew larger. Plantations grew more dependent on slave labor to grow cotton, rice, tobacco and other cash crops to sell to the North and to the British overseas.

THE TARIFF ISSUE

Each of these sections had different ideas on what should be the policies of the national government. Manufacturers in the North wanted special taxes, known as tariffs. A **tariff** is a tax placed on manufactured goods imported from abroad. Such taxes would make it easier for American manufacturers to compete with British manufacturers by increasing the cost of British imported goods.

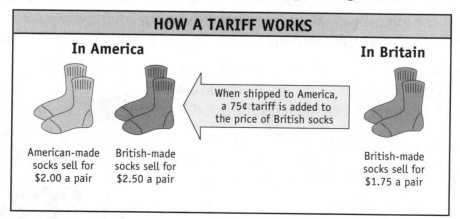

Southerners, however, strongly opposed such tariffs. The South was shipping large amounts of cotton to Britain. Southerners wanted to be able to buy cheap British manufactured goods. They feared that if tariffs were in place against the British, it might lead the British to tax the South's raw cotton.

Westerners wanted to use the money from tariffs to build national roads linking the East and West. Southerners opposed using federal money to build national roads since these roads would not benefit the South.

THE ISSUE OF SLAVERY

The greatest disagreement at that time was over the system of **slavery**. Many Northerners believed that slavery in the South was morally wrong. **Abolitionists** wanted to end, or *abolish*, slavery. Other Northerners did not want to see slavery spread to new Western territories.

The **abolitionist** or antislavery, **movement**, was especially strong in Ohio. The Northwest Ordinance and the Ohio Constitution had both banned slavery in Ohio. Quakers and other groups in Ohio organized to bring an end to slavery in the rest of the country. The seeds of the antislavery movement in Ohio were planted by local antislavery newspapers. By the 1830s, there were more than 200 antislavery societies in Ohio.

Ohio abolitionists pose for a photograph.

After the passage of the **Fugitive Slave Law of 1850**, Ohio became one of the routes along the **Underground Railroad**. This was not an actual railroad. Instead, its was a network of people who helped slaves escape from the South to freedom in Canada. They led escaped slaves along secret routes, with safe houses and resting places known as "stations." Several Ohioans helped guide Ohio's abolitionist movement:

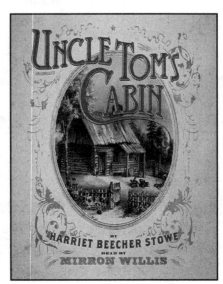

- **Levi Coffin**, lived in Cincinnati. He helped lead so many slaves to freedom that he became known as the "President of the Underground Railroad."

- **John Rankin**, an Ohio minister, was also a conductor on the Underground Railroad. It is believed that Rankin helped 2,000 slaves to escape to freedom. Many of the escaping slaves fled to Canada. Some settled in Ohio.

- **Harriet Beecher Stowe**, another Cincinnati resident, published *Uncle Tom's Cabin* in 1852. Her novel focused public attention on slavery's injustices. It also showed the horrors of the Fugitive Slave Law.

Name _____ Date _____

STUDY CARDS

Sectionalism

Which three issues divided Americans in the mid-1800s?

1. _____
   _____
   _____
   _____

2. _____
   _____
   _____
   _____

3. _____
   _____
   _____
   _____

Ohio's Antislavery Documents

What did each of these documents say about slavery?

1. Northwest Ordinance: _____
_____
_____
_____

2. Ohio Constitution: _____
_____
_____
_____
_____

STUDY CARD PROMPTS

Sectionalism

Which three issues divided the nation in the mid-1800s?

1.

2.

3.

To check your answers to these questions, turn the card over and review the information you have written on the other side.

Ohio's Antislavery Documents

What did each of these documents say about slavery?

1. **Northwest Ordinance**

2. **Ohio Constitution**

To check your answers to these questions, turn the card over and review the information you have written on the other side.

Name _____ Date _____

STUDY CARDS

Ohio's Role in the Antislavery Movement

What role did each of these play in Ohio's antislavery movement?

1. Antislavery Societies: _____

_____

_____

_____

2. Underground Railroad: _____

_____

_____

_____

_____

_____

Ohio's Abolitionist Leaders

What role did each of these individuals play in the antislavery movement?

1. Levi Coffin. _____

_____

_____

2. John Rankin. _____

_____

_____

3. Harriet Beecher Stowe. _____

_____

_____

STUDY CARD PROMPTS

Ohio's Role in the Antislavery Movement

What role did each of these play in Ohio's antislavery movement?

1. **Antislavery Societies**

2. **Underground Railroad**

To check your answers to these questions, turn the card over and review the information you have written on the other side.

Ohio's Abolitionist Leaders

What role did each of these individuals play in the antislavery movement?

1. **Levi Coffin**

2. **John Rankin**

3. **Harriet Beecher Stowe**

To check your answers to these questions, turn the card over and review the information you have written on the other side.

Name _____ Date _____

CONTENT-AREA VOCABULARY

Directions. Fill in the concept ladders below.

CONCEPT: SECTIONALISM

Tariffs

The West

The South

The North

CONCEPT: ANTISLAVERY MOVEMENT

Harriet Beecher Stowe

John Rankin

Levi Coffin

Underground Railroad

Antislavery Movement

PERFORMANCE-BASED
ASSESSMENT QUESTIONS

65 A passage written by a runaway slave is shown.

"I travelled until I had arrived at the place where I was to call on an abolitionist, but I did not stop. My fear was so great of being captured by pro-slavery hunting dogs of the South. I journeyed for the next forty-eight hours without food or rest. I struggled against all difficulties such as no one can imagine. I feared being captured while traveling. I moved through cold and fear, against the winds, thinly clothed, hit by snow storms in the night hours, and not a house could I enter to shelter myself from the storm."

— *The Story of Henry Bib*

A. What hardships did Henry Bib, a runaway slave, face on his trip northwards to freedom? Write your answer on the lines below.

_____

_____

_____

_____

_____

_____

_____

_____

B. Explain what Henry Bib hoped to achieve by his escape.

_____

_____

_____

_____

Name _____ Date _____

66 The following question has two parts. First answer part A. Then answer part B.

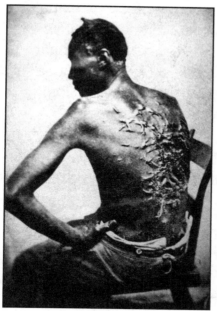

*Scars of a slave who was
whipped by his slaveholding master.*

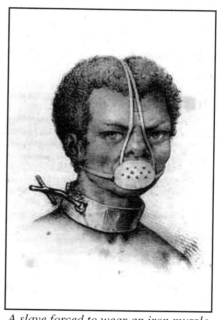

*A slave forced to wear an iron muzzle
for trying to escape.*

Part A.
Based on these two pictures, explain why most abolitionists believed that slavery was evil and immoral (*wrong; against accepted standards*). Write your answer on the lines below.

_____

_____

_____

_____

_____

Part B.
If you lived in Ohio during the early 1800s, would you have joined the antislavery movement? Explain your answer.

_____

_____

_____

_____

_____

67 A passage describing the fugitive slave law is shown.

> Slave owners were an important social class in Southern states. In 1740, North Carolina made it a crime to help escaped slaves. A national Fugitive Slave Law was first passed by the U.S. Congress in 1793. In 1850, a stricter fugitive slave law was passed. It required law enforcement officers in free states to help capture and return runaway slaves to their owners.

Explain why runaway slaves were not safe in Ohio after 1850, even though slavery had been outlawed by the Ohio Constitution. Write your answer on the lines below.

_____

_____

_____

68 In this excerpt from Harriet Beecher Stowe's book *Uncle Tom's Cabin*, Simon Legree, a plantation owner, orders his slave Tom to beat another slave. Tom refuses.

> "Now jest take this gal and whip her; you've seen enough to know how."
> "I beg Mas'r's [master's] pardon," said Tom, "hopes mas'r won't set me at that. It's what I ain't used to — never did — and can't do it, no way possible."
> "Ye'll learn many things ye never did before. I'm done with ye!" said Legree, taking up a cowhide and striking Tom a heavy blow across his cheek, and following up the hit with a shower of blows.
> "There!" he said, as he stopped to rest. "Now will ye tell me ye can't do it?"
> "Yes, mas'r" said Tom, raising his hand to wipe the blood that trickled down his face. "I'm willin' to work night and day, and work while there's still life and breath in me; but I can't feel it right to do this; and mas'r, I never shall do it — *never*!"

Explain how the publication of *Uncle Tom's Cabin* helped promote the antislavery movement. Write your answer on the lines below.

_____

_____

_____

_____

INTERPRETING A LINE GRAPH

SKILL BUILDER

A **line graph** is a graph made up of points connected by a line. It is used to show how something has increased, decreased, or stayed the same over a period of time.

UNDERSTANDING A LINE GRAPH

LOOK AT THE TITLE

The **title** states the overall topic of the line graph. In this graph, the title is *Regional Population Growth: 1800–1830*.

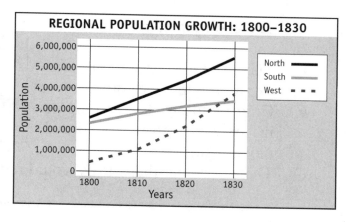

EXAMINE THE VERTICAL AND HORIZONTAL AXES

Line graphs include both a **vertical axis** and a **horizontal axis**. These axes identify what items are being compared. In this graph, the vertical axis, which runs from the bottom to the top, shows the size of the population. The horizontal axis, which runs from left to right, shows the years being displayed.

LOOKING FOR TRENDS

One helpful thing about a line graph is its ability to identify a **trend** — a general direction or movement. We can often generalize a trend by looking at the direction of several points on the line. For example, one trend in this graph is that the population of the North was growing faster than the other regions.

FINDING SPECIFIC INFORMATION

To find specific information, you need to examine the lines on the graph. For example, if you wished to find the population of the South in 1810, you would:

- First, run your finger across the horizontal axis (*years*) until you reach 1810. Then, move your finger up until you reach the line showing the population size of the South. In this case, it is the light gray line.

- Next, slide your finger to the left to the population numbers along the vertical axis. The line for 1810 crosses the population line at 2.8 million people. Thus, the population of the South in 1810 was 2.8 million people.

END-OF-YEAR ASSESSMENT QUESTIONS

69 A line graph is shown.

This line graph shows a development that divided the nation in the period following the War of 1812. What was that development?

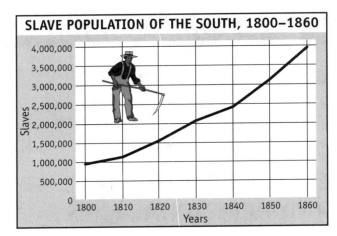

SLAVE POPULATION OF THE SOUTH, 1800–1860

Ⓐ The abolitionist movement had ended.

Ⓑ The slave population was expanding in the South.

Ⓒ Ohio refused to participate in the Underground Railroad movement.

Ⓓ There was fear that slaves would replace factory workers in Ohio.

70 A chart about the movement against slavery is shown.

Person or Group	Year	Purpose
Antislavery Society	1820s	Their lecturers traveled around Ohio to convince people to abolish slavery.
Underground Railroad	1830s	A method used to help runaway slaves to escape to Canada.
Ohioan Levi Coffin	1840s	He helped more than 3,000 slaves to escape their Southern masters.
Ohioan Harriet Beecher Stowe	1852	She wrote a popular novel describing a slave's life, showing the horrors of slavery.

Which conclusion can be drawn from the chart?

Ⓐ Ohio played a key role in the antislavery movement.

Ⓑ Most Ohioans supported the abolitionist cause.

Ⓒ Ohio was more opposed to slavery than other states were.

Ⓓ Ohio sought slave labor to replace its factory workers.

71 A passage about slavery is shown.

> "[Slavery is] something so opposed to humanity, that I am ashamed of my country whenever I hear of it. If ever I leave the South, it will be because of that alone."
>
> — Southerner Thomas Roderick Dew, 1832

What name was given to people who believed as Thomas Roderick Dew did?

72 What horrors did the publication of Harriet Beecher Stowe's book, *Uncle Tom's Cabin*, help to expose?

73 A list of activities is shown.

- They provided a secret network to help people escape to freedom.
- They offered hiding places, food, and sometimes transportation.
- They guided escaped slaves along the safest way to flee further north.
- They were sympathetic to the cause and often provided "safe houses."

Whose activities are described by these statements?

- Ⓐ Leaders of several American Indian tribes
- Ⓑ People active in the Underground Railroad
- Ⓒ Slaveholders living on Southern plantations
- Ⓓ Inventors and innovators living in Ohio

74 During the first part of the 19th century, differences arose between the North, South, and West. What did these differences lead to?

- Ⓐ The rise of sectionalism
- Ⓑ The War of 1812
- Ⓒ The first Continental Congress
- Ⓓ The French and Indian War

75 Below are statements concerning the antislavery movement in Ohio. Move or draw a line from each statement to the column on the chart indicating whether it was in favor of Ohio's antislavery movement or opposed to it.

FAVORED OHIO'S ANTISLAVERY MOVEMENT	OPPOSED TO OHIO'S ANTISLAVERY MOVEMENT
Uncle Tom's Cabin focused public attention on the issue of slavery.	The law provided that an escaped slave had to be returned to his owner.
The Ohio Constitution of 1802 banned slavery in the state.	Abolitionists saw the South's plantation system as morally wrong and evil.
Anyone helping a slave to escape would face a fine of $1,000.	John Rankin served as a conductor on the Underground Railroad in Ohio.

76 Why did the Southern plantation system expand in the early 1800s?

    Ⓐ The U.S. Congress passed laws supporting slavery.
    Ⓑ The South was well-suited for growing the cotton needed by factories.
    Ⓒ Most early factories were built on Southern plantations.
    Ⓓ The South became the nation's "bread basket."

77 Which factor was most important in the economic development of the North in the early 1800s?

    Ⓐ Its rise as a manufacturing center.
    Ⓑ The availability of slave labor.
    Ⓒ The discovery of gold mines.
    Ⓓ The exploration of the Appalachian Mountains.

78 In the early to mid-1800s, which factor most contributed to the growth of the plantation system in the South?

    Ⓐ The falling price of cotton, tobacco and rice
    Ⓑ The growing demand for more cotton
    Ⓒ The new methods of manufacturing that demanded more cotton
    Ⓓ The switch from planting cotton to raising wheat

Name _____ Date _____

CHAPTER 14

OHIO'S INVENTORS

TOPIC: HERITAGE

| History 8 | *Many technological innovations that originated in Ohio benefited the United States.* |

After reading this chapter, you should be able to:

★ Identify the following individuals:
  • Thomas Edison
  • Garrett Morgan
  • James Ritty
  • Wilbur and Orville Wright
  • Charles Kettering
  • Thomas Midgley, Jr.

★ Describe some of the technological innovations that began in Ohio.
★ Describe how these technological innovations have benefitted the United States.

MAIN IDEAS OF THIS CONTENT STATEMENT

Ohio has been the birthplace or home of many important inventors. Their technological innovations have greatly benefitted all Americans.

WHAT IS A TECHNOLOGICAL INNOVATION?

Technology consists of our tools, machines, and the ways we do things. An **innovation** is something new. A **technological innovation** is a new way of doing something that makes use of technology.

● **Thomas Edison** (1847–1931), was born in Milan, Ohio. He may have been the greatest inventor of all time. Edison invented the light bulb, the phonograph, motion pictures and electric batteries.

Edison received 1,093 patents for his many important inventions.

- **Garrett Morgan** (1877–1963) was the son of former slaves. He developed a hand-operated traffic signal. This invention has helped to prevent countless numbers of car accidents. He is also credited with inventing a safety-hood gas mask for firefighters.

- **James Ritty** (1836–1928) was from Dayton, Ohio. He invented the cash register, which recorded sales of a business. His invention helped business owners to keep track of their money. This prevented employees from taking money and putting it in their pockets.

- **Wilbur and Orville Wright** grew up in Dayton, Ohio, after the Civil War. They owned a bicycle shop. The Wright brothers built the first successful airplane on a wood frame covered with fabric. It was powered by an engine the brothers designed themselves. They conducted their first flight at Kitty Hawk, North Carolina in 1903. Their plane was able to stay in the air for almost a minute. Later, after they improved their design, their plane was able to fly 34 miles and remain in the air for 40 minutes.

- **Charles Kettering** (1876–1958) developed the first electric system to start car engines. He also developed automotive spark plugs, the automatic transmission, and four-wheel brakes. Kettering created a new high-octane gasoline, weather-proof paint for cars, and an incubator for infants born too early. Finally, Kettering co-founded the Sloan-Kettering Institute, a research center for cancer.

Model of Kettering torpedo plane on display at Dayton's Air Force Museum.

- **Thomas Midgley, Jr.** (1889–1944) was an Ohio chemist. He developed a lead-based gas that prevented car engines from making loud knocking noises. After 1975, lead-based fuels were phased out of gasoline because of the dangers they posed to the environment. Midgley also invented Freon, a chemical that made refrigerators possible in the average household. Freon was also used in air conditioners. This made it possible for people to live comfortably in areas once considered too hot, such as the Southwest.

Name _____ Date _____

STUDY CARDS

Ohio's Inventors

List and describe three Ohio inventors whose innovations helped to benefit the United States.

1. _____

_____

_____

2. _____

_____

_____

3. _____

_____

Ohio's Inventors

List and describe three other Ohio inventors whose innovations helped benefit the United States.

1. _____

_____

_____

2. _____

_____

_____

3. _____

_____

STUDY CARD PROMPTS

Ohio's Inventors

List and describe three Ohio inventors whose innovations helped to benefit the United States.

1.

2.

3.

To check your answers to these questions, turn the card over and review the information you have written on the other side.

Ohio's Inventors

List and describe three other Ohio inventors whose innovations helped to benefit the United States.

1.

2.

3.

To check your answers to these questions, turn the card over and review the information you have written on the other side.

Name _____ Date _____

Thomas Edison	James Ritty	Charles Kettering
Garrett Morgan	Wilbur & Orville Wright	Thomas Midgley, Jr.

A. Write one sentence for each of the names above.

1. _____

2. _____

3. _____

4. _____

5. _____

6. _____

B. Now find a sentence in this chapter similar to the sentence you created above.

	Sentence from the Chapter	Page
1.		
2.		
3.		
4.		
5.		
6.		

PERFORMANCE−BASED ASSESSMENT QUESTIONS

79 Illustrations of three inventions by Ohioans are shown.

In the box to the right of each picture, describe how that invention benefitted the United States.

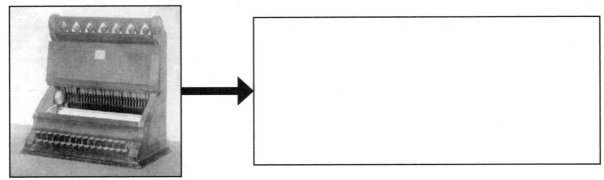

James Ritty's cash register

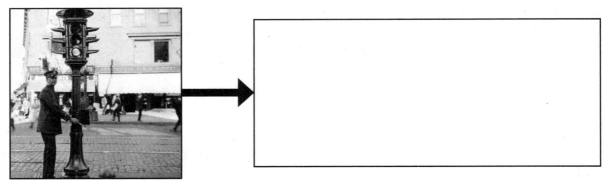

Garrett Morgan's early traffic signal

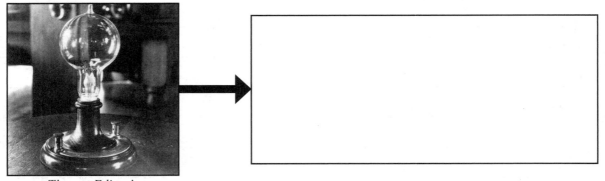

Thomas Edison's electric light bulb

80 A passage about Wilbur and Orville Wright is shown.

The invention of the airplane by Wilbur and Orville Wright had important effects on American society as well as the rest of the world.

Part A.

Explain how their invention changed the way Americans travel.

_____

_____

_____

_____

_____

_____

_____

_____

Part B.

Describe how their invention influenced the nation's economy.

_____

_____

_____

_____

_____

_____

_____

81 Identify **two** important inventions in either communications, technology, or transportation that began in Ohio. Write your answers on the lines below.

1. _____

2. _____

END-OF-YEAR ASSESSMENT QUESTIONS

82 A chart of four individuals is shown.

James Ritty (1836–1928)	Garrett Morgan (1877–1963)
Charles Kettering (1887–1958)	Thomas Midgley, Jr. (1889–1944)

In what way were these individuals similar?

Ⓐ They all found cures to dangerous diseases.
Ⓑ They all made inventions that benefitted the nation.
Ⓒ They all worked for Thomas Edison.
Ⓓ They all represented Ohio in the U.S. Congress.

83 A passage from a speech by an Ohio inventor is shown.

In 1878, I traveled by steamship to Europe. I became fascinated by a device that counted how many times the ship's propeller went around. This got me thinking. I came up with an idea for a machine that would count the sales at my saloon. I needed something to keep track of the money coming in and the amount of sales.

Who would most likely have made this statement?

Ⓐ Orville Wright
Ⓑ Thomas Edison
Ⓒ James Ritty
Ⓓ Charles Kettering

84 How were Thomas Edison, Garrett Morgan, and the Wright Brothers similar?

Ⓐ They persuaded colonists to declare independence from Great Britain.
Ⓑ They made innovations that benefitted all Americans.
Ⓒ They were active participants in the Underground Railroad.
Ⓓ They urged Congress to free slaves living in the South.

85 What is the name of the individual who invented the light bulb, phonograph, and electric batteries? Write your answer in the space provided.

86 A diagram about technological innovations is shown.

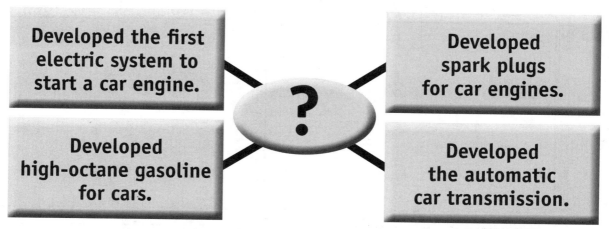

Which Ohio inventor completes this diagram?

Ⓐ Garrett Morgan
Ⓑ James Ritty
Ⓒ Orville Wright
Ⓓ Charles Kettering

87 Which Ohio inventor is correctly paired with his accomplishment?

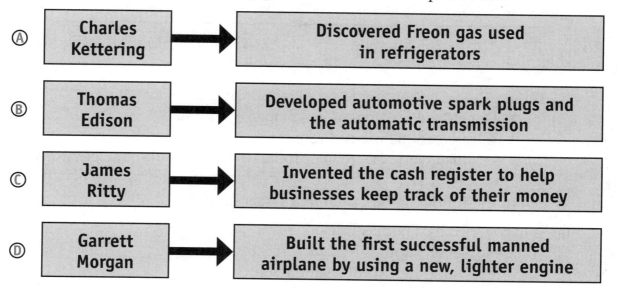

88 Innovators and inventors from Ohio have had an important impact on our nation. Below are six statements about two important inventors from Ohio.

Write or draw a line from the boxed statements about Charles Kettering or Garrett Morgan to the correct column in the chart indicating their name.

GARRETT MORGAN	CHARLES KETTERING

He developed the first electric system to start a car engine.	He is responsible for inventing a safety-hood mask used by firefighters.
He invented the hand-operated traffic signal.	He developed an incubator used for infants that were born prematurely.
He developed spark plugs so that car engines run more efficiently.	He was the first to develop the automatic car transmission.

89 A part of an outline is shown.

> I. _____
>   A. Developed lead-based gasoline
>   B. Introduced the use of Freon
>   C. His discoveries were later found to be harmful to the environment

Which of the following best completes the outline?

Ⓐ Discoveries by Thomas Edison
Ⓑ Innovations of Thomas Midgley, Jr.
Ⓒ Charles Kettering, Inventor and Scientist
Ⓓ The Advances Made by Garrett Morgan

HISTORY UNIT TEST

1 A timeline of events is shown.

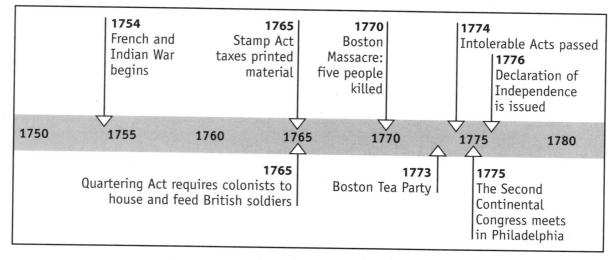

1754 French and Indian War begins

1765 Stamp Act taxes printed material

1770 Boston Massacre: five people killed

1774 Intolerable Acts passed

1776 Declaration of Independence is issued

1750   1755   1760   1765   1770   1775   1780

1765 Quartering Act requires colonists to house and feed British soldiers

1773 Boston Tea Party

1775 The Second Continental Congress meets in Philadelphia

Which pair of events were separated by the longest period of time?

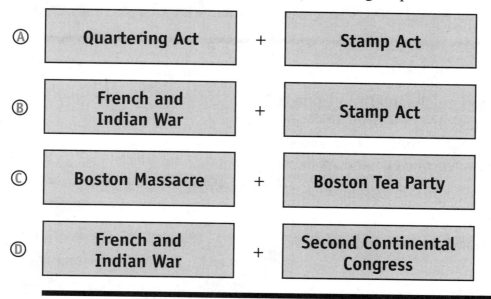

Ⓐ **Quartering Act** + **Stamp Act**

Ⓑ **French and Indian War** + **Stamp Act**

Ⓒ **Boston Massacre** + **Boston Tea Party**

Ⓓ **French and Indian War** + **Second Continental Congress**

2 In the early 1770s, many colonists cried "No taxation without representation!" What did these colonists demand?

Ⓐ Trade between Great Britain and the colonies.
Ⓑ Economic independence for the colonies.
Ⓒ Supremacy of the British Parliament.
Ⓓ No new taxes without the colonists' consent.

Name _____ Date _____

184 MASTERING OHIO'S GRADE 4 SOCIAL STUDIES TEST

3 A timeline of different events in United States history is shown.

Place **each** event on the timeline in chronological order in the boxes below.

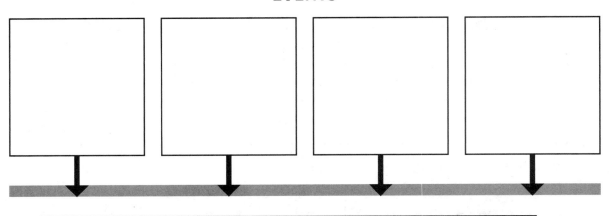

| The British Parliament passes the Stamp Act (1765) | The French and Indian War ends (1763) | Thomas Jefferson writes the Declaration of Independence (1776) | The Boston Tea Party takes place (1773) |

EVENTS

4 Why were many colonists unhappy with the Proclamation of 1763?

Ⓐ It took too much land from Canada.
Ⓑ It gave territory in Florida to France.
Ⓒ It limited the colonists' freedom to move west.
Ⓓ It encouraged raids by Indian tribes.

5 Three pieces of a puzzle are shown.

In which document are these three pieces identified as the main goals of government?

Ⓐ Declaration of Independence
Ⓑ Articles of Confederation
Ⓒ Northwest Ordinance of 1787
Ⓓ Bill of Rights

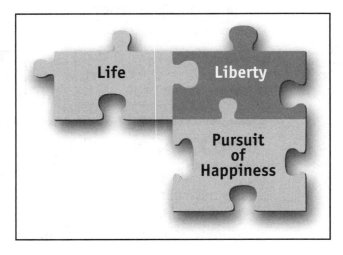

6 Two photographs are shown.

Mound City, Chillicothe, Ohio

Miamisburg Mound

Mound City is a large rectangular field with 23 mounds. Miamisburg Mound is the largest earthen mound in the United States. What conclusion can be drawn about the Hopewell and Adena Indians from these photographs?

Ⓐ These tribes used earth-moving equipment to build their mounds.

Ⓑ These tribes demonstrated a degree of cooperation among their members.

Ⓒ The Hopewell Indians were more advanced than the Adena Indians.

Ⓓ The Adena Indians were unable to build long-lasting burial mounds.

7 Below are two of the three steps the Northwest Ordinance established for a territory to become a state. One of the steps is missing. Write in the missing step in the box below:

> **3. Once the population reaches 60,000 people, the territory can apply for admission as a state.**

> **2.**

> **1. A group of leaders will be appointed by Congress to govern the territory.**

8 Why were more slaves found in Southern colonies than in New England colonies?

   Ⓐ Southern colonies were closer to Africa.

   Ⓑ Slaves were needed to work in factories in the South.

   Ⓒ Slaves had successfully rebelled in New England.

   Ⓓ The geography of the South encouraged the plantation system.

9 Which of the following was a major cause of the War of 1812?

   Ⓐ Impressing U.S. sailors into the British navy

   Ⓑ British attacks on Ohio settlers

   Ⓒ The Battle of Fallen Timbers

   Ⓓ The passage of the Northwest Ordinance

10 Two statements about slavery are shown.

"The first business of the antislavery men is to help the fugitives." — Theodore Parker, Boston minister

"I helped them through forests, mostly at night. Boys dressed as girls and girls as boys; on foot, on horseback, in wagons, in boats; and often on rafts." — Calvin Fairbanks, minister

Which term describes Theodore Parker and Calvin Fairbanks, the two individuals who made these statements?

   Ⓐ slave-owners

   Ⓑ abolitionists

   Ⓒ escaped slaves

   Ⓓ hunters of escaped slaves

11 Which set of events is in correct order from the earliest to latest?

   Ⓐ Articles of Confederation adopted → Northwest Ordinance passed → Ohio granted statehood

   Ⓑ Articles of Confederation adopted → Proclamation Line of 1763 issued → Ohio Territory created

   Ⓒ Ohio granted statehood → Ohio Territory created → American Revolution begins

   Ⓓ Ohio granted statehood → Boston Massacre occurs → Ohio Territory created

12 A painting by William Henry Powell is shown.

This painting is on display in the Ohio Statehouse. It was painted in honor of Admiral Oliver Perry's victory in 1813 over the British fleet.

Write the name of the battle which Perry achieved victory in the space below.

---

13 A newspaper advertisement is shown.

How would Ohio abolitionists most likely have reacted to such an advertisement?

Ⓐ They would support harsh treatment for runaway slaves.

Ⓑ They would assist the efforts of the Underground Railroad.

Ⓒ They would work to prevent freed slaves from settling in Ohio.

Ⓓ They would want to strengthen the provisions of the Fugitive Slave Law.

> **100 DOLLARS REWARD!**
>
> Ranaway from the subscriber on the 27th of July, my Black Woman, named **EMILY,** Seventeen years of age, well grown, black color, has a whining voice. She took with her one dark calico and one blue and white dress, a red corded gingham bonnet; a white striped shawl and slippers. I will pay the above reward if taken near the Ohio river on the Kentucky side, or THREE HUNDRED DOLLARS, if taken in the State of Ohio, and delivered to me near Lewisburg, Mason County, Ky.
> **THO'S H. WILLIAMS.**
> August 4, 1853.

---

14 Why were so many African Americans living in the South in the early to mid-1800s?

Ⓐ Their ancestors were forcibly brought to the United States as slaves.

Ⓑ They wanted farmland that was unavailable to them elsewhere.

Ⓒ Their ancestors came in search of religious freedom.

Ⓓ They wanted to live in a place that had a democracy.

15 A group of statements is shown.

Wilbur and Orville Wright, who both grew up in Dayton, Ohio, built the first manned flying machine.	**Thomas Midgley, Jr. an Ohio chemist, developed a lead-based gas for cars, and Freon — a gas that made possible refrigerators and air conditioners.**	**Charles Kettering, born in Loudonville, Ohio, created an ignition system to start an automobile by turning a key.**

Which conclusion can be draw from this information?

Ⓐ   Many inventions by Ohioans have benefited the nation.
Ⓑ   Most of our nation's technological innovations first began in Ohio.
Ⓒ   Ohio has had more technological innovators than any other state.
Ⓓ   Ohioans were the nation's leaders in creating new technologies.

16 A graph of colonial populations is shown.

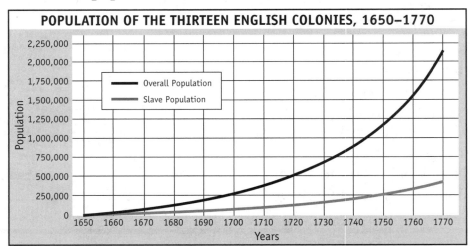

Which aspect of colonial life does this graph illustrate?

Ⓐ   The economic privileges of white colonists
Ⓑ   The decline in the number of colonists from disease
Ⓒ   The constant increase in the slave population
Ⓓ   Limits placed on the growth of colonial trade

17 What are the original records of an event, such as eyewitness reports, letters, and diaries called? Write your answer below.

Name _____ Date _____

18 What was a major goal of the Ohio abolitionist movement of the early 1800s? Write your answer in the space provided.

_____

19 A concept map is shown,

Which would be the best title for this concept map?

- Ⓐ Famous Ohio Inventors
- Ⓑ U.S. Presidents from Ohio
- Ⓒ Notable Ohio Abolitionists
- Ⓓ Popular Ohio Writers

20 An illustration of a modern traffic light is shown.

Garrett Morgan created the first version of a traffic signal with a yellow light. Before this, intersections had only a "stop and go" signal.

What effect did Morgan's invention have on Ohio and the United States?

- Ⓐ It prevented all future traffic accidents.
- Ⓑ It allowed drivers to rely more completely on their automobiles.
- Ⓒ It signaled to drivers that they would need to get ready to stop at an intersection.
- Ⓓ It eliminated the need for cars to stop at intersections.

21 The Declaration of Independence and the Northwest Ordinance are two of the most important documents in United States history.

Below are statements describing some of the democratic provisions in these documents. Rewrite or draw a line from each of these statements to the correct column in the chart.

DECLARATION OF INDEPENDENCE	NORTHWEST ORDINANCE

All people are born with certain basic rights, such as the right to life and liberty.	Pubic education should be encouraged.
Freedom of religion and the right to a trial by jury are guaranteed to citizens.	Governments are created to protect the rights of their citizens.
Slavery is banned although fugitive slaves are to be returned.	All territories granted statehood are to be equal to all of the original states.

22 From which region in the world did most foreign settlers to Ohio come from after Ohio became a state in 1803?

Ⓐ Europe
Ⓑ South America
Ⓒ Asia
Ⓓ Middle East

Name _____ Date _____

UNIT 3

GOVERNMENT

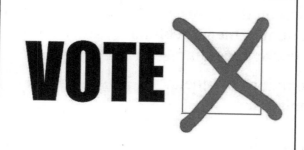

Voting is one way for citizens to make themselves heard by government.

Students demonstrate before entering school about an issue important to them.

The role of **government** is to protect and help its citizens. Government works best by setting up and enforcing rules for citizens to live by. When your teacher establishes classroom rules, he or she is acting as a kind of government. In this unit, you will learn about your national and state governments. You will also learn about the rights and responsibilities of citizenship in a democracy.

The following three topics will be examined in this unit:

1. CIVIC PARTICIPATION AND SKILLS

2. RULES AND LAWS

3. ROLES AND SYSTEMS OF GOVERNMENT

GOVERNMENT PRE-TEST

1 Below is a list of the rights and responsibilities of citizens of the United States. In the T-chart below, classify each item on the list as a right or a responsibility. If it is a right, place the letter of that item in the left column. If it is a responsibility, place the letter of that item in the right column.

A. Respect the rights, beliefs, and opinions of others.
B. Participate in your local community.
C. Express yourself freely.
D. Participate in the democratic process.
E. Obey federal, state, and local laws.
F. Be able to worship as you wish.
G. Serve on a jury when called upon.
H. Defend the country if the need should arise.
I. Have a prompt, fair trial by jury.
J. Be able to vote in elections for public officials.
K. Defend the U.S. Constitution.
L. Stay informed about issues affecting your community.
M. Pay taxes to federal, state, and local authorities.
N. Be able to run for elected office.
O. Seek "life, liberty, and the pursuit of happiness."

RIGHTS	RESPONSIBILITIES

2   A list of statements about early voting is shown.

> • Early voting by citizens will be limited to the weekend before the election.
> • Early voting for this election will begin at 8:00 AM and end at 10:00 AM.
> • Citizens who wish to vote early will be required to show three forms of identification.

Based on these statements, what conclusion can be made?

Ⓐ   These rules encourage more people to vote.
Ⓑ   These rules will make early voting difficult.
Ⓒ   Workers will be given the day off to vote early.
Ⓓ   These rules will encourage young people to vote.

3   Which statement describes something different from the others?

Ⓐ   Freedom to express oneself.
Ⓑ   Freedom to decide who to vote for on election day.
Ⓒ   Having to serve on a jury when called upon.
Ⓓ   Having the right to run for elected office.

4   Which of the following correctly lists three branches of Ohio's state government?

Ⓐ   Supreme Court, Governor, National Guard
Ⓑ   City Council, Mayor, Congress
Ⓒ   Governor, Congress, President
Ⓓ   Governor, General Assembly, State Supreme Court

5   Individuals are expected to act responsibly if they wish to enjoy a nation's rights and privileges. Which term is used to identify the national membership bringing these rights and responsibilities?

Ⓐ   freedom
Ⓑ   citizenship
Ⓒ   diversity
Ⓓ   immigration

6   A passage by U.S. Supreme Court Justice Brandeis is shown.

> Those who won our independence … believed that freedom to think as you wish and to speak as you think are [important] to the discovery of political truth. Without free speech and assembly, discussion would be [useless].

Which document is Justice Brandeis praising in this passage?

Ⓐ   Declaration of Independence
Ⓑ   Articles of Confederation
Ⓒ   Northwest Ordinance of 1787
Ⓓ   First Amendment of the U.S. Constitution

7   To which basic principle of American government does this passage refer?

Ⓐ   The rights of people who were once slaves should be protected.
Ⓑ   Settlers moving into the Ohio Territory deserve the right to vote.
Ⓒ   Citizens should be able to express their thoughts in a democratic society.
Ⓓ   Immigrants should find it easy to become American citizens.

8   In the United States today, how are the people who serve in government, such as legislators and governors, chosen?

Ⓐ   They are selected by the U.S. Supreme Court.
Ⓑ   They are voted into office by state legislatures.
Ⓒ   They are elected by ordinary citizens.
Ⓓ   They are selected at random by a computer.

9   What is the Ohio General Assembly most similar to?

Ⓐ   U.S. Congress
Ⓑ   Office of the Governor of Ohio
Ⓒ   U.S. Supreme Court
Ⓓ   U.S. House of Representatives

10   Which is an example of a citizen trying to influence the government?

Ⓐ   A citizen listens to news reports on the evening news.
Ⓑ   A citizen refuses to vote in local elections.
Ⓒ   A citizen writes letters to elected legislators advising them how to vote.
Ⓓ   A citizen searches the Internet to find an public official's email address.

END OF THE PRE-TEST

Name _____ Date _____

CHAPTER 15

CITIZEN RIGHTS AND RESPONSIBILITIES

TOPIC: CIVIC PARTICIPATION AND SKILLS

Civic participation means having citizens **participate**, or play a part, in government. It means that an individual can become involved in his or her community, state or nation for the **common good**. Good communication skills, including negotiation, compromise and collaboration, and skills in accessing and analyzing information are essential for citizens in a democracy.

Government 1	*Individuals have a variety of opportunities to participate in and influence their state and national government. Citizens have both rights and responsibilities in Ohio and the United States.*

After reading this chapter, you should be able to:

★ Define the following terms:
  • Citizen
  • Rights
  • Responsibilities
  • Bill of Rights

★ Describe how individuals participate in and influence their state and national government.
★ Identify the rights and responsibilities of citizens in Ohio and the United States.

MAIN IDEAS OF THIS CONTENT STATEMENT

A **citizen** is a member of a nation. Citizens have both **rights** and **responsibilities**.

In the United States, most citizens have U.S. citizenship at birth. A person born in the United States or whose parents are citizens becomes a U.S. citizen at birth.

Some immigrants to the United States also become U.S. citizens later in life. To become a U.S. citizen, a foreigner has to live five years in the United States. In addition, he or she needs to pass a citizenship test on U.S. history and government, and swear an oath of allegiance to the United States. This process is called **naturalization**.

A group takes the oath to become citizens.

THE RESPONSIBILITIES OF CITIZENSHIP

A U.S. citizen has many important **duties** (*or obligations*). These are things that a citizen *must* do. These obligations include obeying the law, paying taxes and attending school. If called upon, a citizen must also serve on a jury, defend the nation against foreign enemies, and give evidence in a court of law.

Serving on a jury is one the most important responsibilities of citizenship.

In addition to these duties, citizens also have several **responsibilities**, or things they *should* do. These responsibilities include voting in elections, becoming well-informed, participating in local events, joining a political party, running for political office, and serving in government.

To **participate** in an activity or in a group means to take an active role. An active participant asks questions, speaks up, and volunteers to help with tasks. In our country, we have a government of elected officials. As a result, these officials frequently consult public opinion. This creates many opportunities for citizens to partici-

pate in and to influence both their state and local government.

For example, a citizen might run for a government office or share political ideas in a discussion with neighbors. A citizen might also write to representatives in Congress or write a letter to the editor of a local newspaper.

Ordinary citizens have their strongest influence on local, state and national governments when they vote in elections. Citizens can also write to their representatives or send an email. They can even arrange a meeting with a representative or meet with staff members working for that representative.

THE RIGHTS OF CITIZENSHIP

Freedom of religion is one of the freedoms that Americans most value.

Citizens also have important rights. A **right** is something they are entitled to. It is something the law says they can do. The rights of American citizens are guaranteed by the U.S. Constitution and by the **Bill of Rights**. American citizens, for example, enjoy **freedom of religion** — they can worship God in their own way. Citizens also have **freedom of speech** — they can say or publish criticisms of government policies without fear of punishment. Citizens also enjoy the **right to assemble** (*to hold meetings*) and the right to petition the government. A **petition** is a request to ask government officials to change their policies. A petition is often signed by many other supporters besides its author.

THE RIGHTS OF CITIZENS ACCUSED OF A CRIME

In the United States, individuals accused of committing a crime also have rights, guaranteed by the U.S. Constitution. Here are some examples:

- The police cannot search a person's home or car without a **search warrant** or "**probable cause**."

- Citizens accused of a crime have the right to a **trial by jury**.

- Citizens have the **right to a lawyer** if they cannot afford one and they are accused of a serious crime.

The rights of Ohio citizens are further protected by the Ohio Constitution. This gives rights similar to those in the U.S. Constitution and Bill of Rights.

CONTENT-AREA VOCABULARY

Directions. Which phrase does **not** belong with the other phrases in the same box? In the space to the right of each box, identify the phrase that does not fit. Then use that phrase in a sentence.

Duties of citizenship

Obeying the law

Paying taxes

Becoming a naturalized citizen

_____

_____

_____

_____

Responsibilities of citizenship

Vote in elections

Volunteer in civic activities

Freedom of speech

_____

_____

_____

_____

Rights of citizenship

Trial by jury

Freedom of the press

Defending the nation

_____

_____

_____

_____

Give evidence in a courtroom

Petition government officials

Gather with others to demonstrate

Vote in elections

_____

_____

_____

_____

Name _____ Date _____

STUDY CARDS

Participating in Government

What are three ways that a citizen can participate in or influence government?

1. _____
   _____
   _____

2. _____
   _____
   _____

3. _____
   _____
   _____

Rights of a Citizen

What are three rights enjoyed by American citizens?

1. _____
   _____
   _____

2. _____
   _____
   _____

3. _____
   _____
   _____

STUDY CARD PROMPTS

Participating in Government

What are three ways that a citizen can participate in or influence government?

1.

2.

3.

To check your answers to these questions, turn the card over and review the information you have written on the other side.

Rights of a Citizen

What are three rights enjoyed by American citizens?

1.

2.

3.

To check your answers to these questions, turn the card over and review the information you have written on the other side.

Name _____ Date _____

PERFORMANCE-BASED ASSESSMENT QUESTIONS

1   Citizens in Ohio and the United States have both rights and responsibilities. List **one** right and **one** responsibility of citizens in Ohio and the United States.

RIGHT OF A CITIZEN	RESPONSIBILITY OF A CITIZEN

2   The following question has two parts. First, answer part A. Then, answer part B.

In the United States and Ohio, citizens can influence their state or national government by writing letters to elected officials. Letters let government officials know how citizens feel about an issue or problem. Letters encourage officials to vote for or against various proposed measures and laws.

Part A.
Describe **one** other way citizens can influence their state or national government.

_____

_____

_____

Part B.
Then, explain why your example of how citizens can influence their government is important in a democracy.

_____

_____

_____

END-OF-YEAR ASSESSMENT QUESTIONS

3   Three photographs are shown.

These photographs have something in common. Which concept is illustrated by all three of these photographs?

4   What role do citizens play in our national and state governments?

   Ⓐ   They elect government officials who make decisions for them.
   Ⓑ   They do not have any say in government choices.
   Ⓒ   They elect special judges to appoint government leaders.
   Ⓓ   They directly make most government decisions.

5   Which example is a right of citizenship?

   Ⓐ   Serve on a jury if called upon.
   Ⓑ   Express oneself freely.
   Ⓒ   Serve in the military if called upon.
   Ⓓ   Obey the laws.

6   A concept map is shown.

Write the concept below that belongs in the oval at the top of this concept map.

7   Which best illustrates civic participation?

(A)   Encouraging an immigrant to settle in the United States.
(B)   Learning to speak a foreign language.
(C)   Working during the weekend in a homeless shelter.
(D)   Obeying traffic laws in your community.

8   Each choice below describes a right or responsibility of a citizen of the United States. Move or draw a line from each box to the correct column in the chart.

CITIZENSHIP RIGHT	CITIZENSHIP RESPONSIBILITY

Free to express yourself.	Defend the country if called upon.	Serve on a jury when called upon.
Free to run for political office.	Get a fair and prompt trial by a jury.	Support and defend the U.S. Constitution.
Be informed and vote in elections.	Show respect for other people's opinions.	Pay taxes.

CHAPTER
16

CIVIC PARTICIPATION
AND DECISION-MAKING

TOPIC: CIVIC PARTICIPATION AND SKILLS

Government 2	*Civic participation requires individuals to make informed and reasoned decisions by accessing and using information effectively.*

After reading this chapter, you should be able to:

★ Define the following terms:
  • Citizen participation
  • Informed decisions
  • Reasoned decisions
  • Access information

★ Describe how citizens make informed and reasoned decisions when participating in government.

MAIN IDEAS OF THIS CONTENT STATEMENT

Democracy depends upon its citizens to participate in government. Citizens can vote, run for office, and serve in government. When participating in government — whether by voting or by serving in government — it is important for citizens to make informed and reasoned decisions. **Informed decisions** are based on the facts. A **reasoned decision** is one that is logical.

To become informed, citizens today have a variety of **print and electronic** (*or "digital"*) **sources** of information that they can use. These sources include newspapers, books, news magazines, television programs, radio programs, and Internet websites — such as Wikipedia, the online encyclopedia.

It is a good plan to first learn about the background to a problem or issue by using Wikipedia and other general sources. There is now so much information available on the Internet that one of the key problems is accessing it effectively. To **access** information is to find it.

Using a Search Engine. Usually you will access information by using a search engine like **Google**. A **search engine** is a system used to search for information on the Internet. You should enter words and phrases related to the information you are trying to find. For example, if you are looking for information on the rights of citizens, you might enter: "citizenship rights" and "United States." When you search these terms, you should find information about the rights of American citizens.

Google, Yahoo, and Bing are search engines.

Sometimes your search will bring up too many results. Then you need to narrow your search by including additional search terms or by adding more details. For example, you might add to the search above, "Freedom of the Press" or "Free Press." The search results that come up first on the screen are those most likely to include the information you are looking for.

Making an Informed Decision. Once a citizen becomes informed by finding useful and relevant information, he or she must make a reasoned decision based on the facts. Many public decisions concern solving problems faced by the community, state or nation. Often, a citizen will follow these steps to make a reasoned decision:

1. Identify the problem.

2. Gather information.

3. List and consider options. An **option** (*choice or alternative*) is any possible way of solving the problem.

4. Consider the advantages and disadvantages of each option.

5. Choose and implement a solution. When you **implement** a solution, you put that plan, agreement, or decision into effect.

6. Develop **criteria** to judge the solution's effectiveness. **Criteria** are standards used to judge or evaluate something. To **evaluate** a proposed solution, a citizen usually has to consider how well it will solve the problem, what it will cost, and whether it will create any new problems.

STUDY CARD PROMPTS

Informed Decisions

1. What is an informed decision?

2. What types of sources of information does a citizen have to make an informed decision? Identify two types.

   A.

   B.

To check your answers to these questions, turn the card over and review the information you have written on the other side.

Making a Reasoned Decision

Identify the various steps required to make a reasoned decision when solving a problem.

1.

2.

3.

4.

5.

6.

To check your answers to these questions, turn the card over and review the information you have written on the other side.

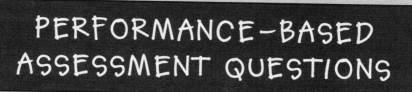

PERFORMANCE-BASED ASSESSMENT QUESTIONS

9 This question has two parts. First, answer part A. Then, answer part B.

Some Americans ask: Should additional limits be placed on senior citizens who drive cars? For example, senior citizens might be asked to take a new driving test when they renew their licenses after a certain age.

Part A.

Examine the chart below and the bar graph on the next page. Then present your informed decision on this topic based on this information.

ANNUAL CAR CRASHES BY AGE, 16 TO 75

Driver's Age	Crashes for Every 100 Licensed Drivers
16	58 crashes
17	45 crashes
18	36 crashes
19	32 crashes
20	27 crashes
25	15 crashes
35	14 crashes
45	12 crashes
55	10 crashes
65	10 crashes
75	10 crashes

Source: National Safety Council, Injury Facts, 2010

What information does this table provide about the number of automobile crashes involving senior drivers aged 65 and older? _____

_____

_____

_____

Part B.

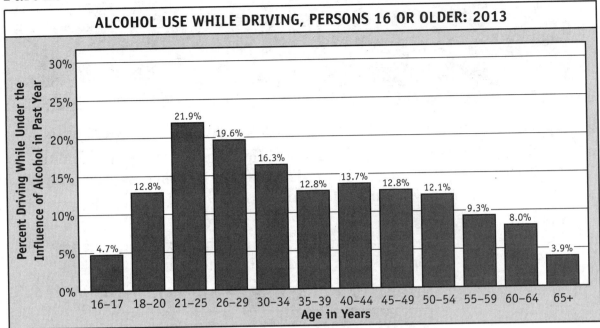

ALCOHOL USE WHILE DRIVING, PERSONS 16 OR OLDER: 2013

Source: U.S. Department of Health and Human Services

What information do we learn from the bar graph above about the use of excessive alcohol among various aged drivers in the last year? _____

_____

_____

_____

_____

_____

_____

_____

_____

_____

_____

_____

_____

Name _____ Date _____

Now based on this information, write a short response to the following question.

Should additional limits be placed on senior citizens who drive cars?

_____

_____

_____

_____

_____

_____

_____

_____

_____

10 Citizens often follow certain steps when they make an informed decision.

Each box below describes a correct or incorrect step in making an informed decision. Move or draw a line from each step to the correct column in the chart.

CORRECT STEP IN MAKING AN INFORMED DECISION	INCORRECT STEP IN MAKING AN INFORMED DECISION

Identify the problem that needs to be solved.

Don't bother with developing criteria.

Consider only the difficulty of each option.

Take the first option without considering others.

Choose and implement a solution.

Gather all information that is needed.

11 A line graph on the issue of lowering the drinking age is shown.

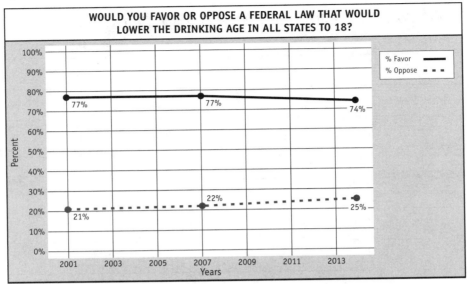

Source: Gallup Poll

Based on this graph, how have American views on lowering the drinking age changed between 2001 and 2013? Write your answer in the space below.

12 A poster from World War I (1917–1918) is shown.

Identify one way in which this World War I poster appeals to citizens to participate actively in their government. Write your answer in the box below.

DISTINGUISHING A FACTUAL STATEMENT FROM AN OPINION

SKILL BUILDER

In the next section, you will be asked to answer a fact-and-opinion question. This skill builder will help you to answer such questions.

FACTS

A **fact** is a statement that can be proven to be true. For example, the following is a factual statement:

"Abraham Lincoln was elected President on November 6, 1860."

To see if something is a fact, you should ask yourself if this statement can be proven. We can often check the accuracy of a factual statement by looking at different sources — such as textbooks, encyclopedias, and almanacs.

OPINIONS

An **opinion** is an expression of someone's belief. It cannot be checked for accuracy. To check for opinions, you should ask yourself if the statement would be true all of the time or if the statement tells a thought or feeling. Often, opinions have words expressing feelings, such as happy, best, or most. An example of an opinion would be:

"Abraham Lincoln was the best American President."

There is no way for someone to check the statement that Abraham Lincoln was "the best." This judgment is just a matter of personal preference. Therefore, it is an opinion not a fact. Other opinions make predictions about the future.

Questions that ask you to distinguish fact from opinion might appear as:

Which of these statements expresses a fact rather than an opinion?

Ⓐ Americans elect their President every four years.
Ⓑ Running for elective office is one of the greatest experiences of citizenship.
Ⓒ Freedom to worship is one of the least important rights of a citizen.
Ⓓ People should be happy to pay their income taxes.

The first choice above is the correct one. It is correct because it is the only one that can be checked by outside sources.

END–OF–YEAR ASSESSMENT QUESTIONS

13 Which of these statements expresses a fact rather than an opinion?

Ⓐ Ohio is the birthplace of the greatest Presidents in U.S. history.

Ⓑ In the Presidential election of 2012, a majority of Ohioans voted for Barack Obama.

Ⓒ Ohio's state capital is the most attractive capital in the nation.

Ⓓ The voters of Ohio are the best educated voters in the nation.

14 It is against the law to drive in a car and not to wear your seat belt. Explain how this law helps citizens. Write your answer in the box below.

15 Which of the following best illustrates civic participation?

Ⓐ A student cleans his room before his mother asks him to.

Ⓑ A student watches a film about United States history.

Ⓒ A student goes door-to-door helping elect a candidate to the school board.

Ⓓ A student mows lawns after school to earn money for college.

16 Which statement is an opinion rather than a fact?

Ⓐ American citizens elect a President every four years.

Ⓑ George Washington was the first President of the United States.

Ⓒ Presidential elections should be held more often than every 4 years.

Ⓓ All the U.S. Presidents from 1789 to 2015 have been males.

17 A bar graph on voting is shown.

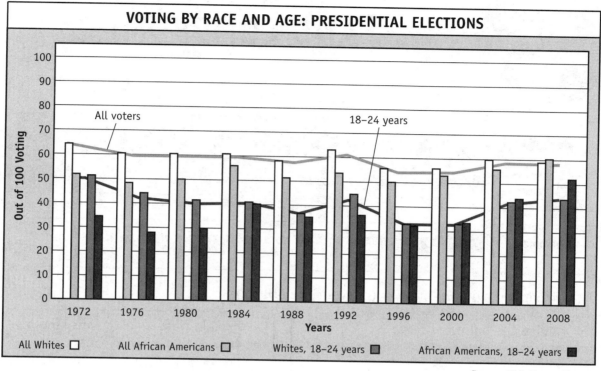

What proportion of African Americans, 18 to 24 years old, voted in the Presidential election of 2008?

Ⓐ   43 out of every 100 African Americans in that age group.
Ⓑ   53 out of every 100 African Americans in that age group.
Ⓒ   59 out of every 100 African Americans in that age group.
Ⓓ   61 out of every 100 African Americans in that age group.

18 What has been the trend in voting by African-American citizens between 1996 and 2008?

Ⓐ   It has remained about the same.
Ⓑ   It has gone up.
Ⓒ   It has fallen sharply.
Ⓓ   In 2008, fewer African Americans voted than ever before.

19 Which statement accurately describes the voting trend for 18-to-24 years old whites, between 1972 and 1988?

Ⓐ   It has remained about the same.
Ⓑ   It has gone up.
Ⓒ   It has fallen.
Ⓓ   It fell, then went up, then fell again.

Name _____ Date _____

CHAPTER 17

DISAGREEMENT AND COMPROMISE

TOPIC: CIVIC PARTICIPATION AND SKILLS

| Government 3 | *Effective participants in a democratic society engage in compromise.* |

After reading this chapter, you should be able to:

★ Define the following term:
  • Disagreement
  • Compromise

★ Explain what a compromise requires.
★ Describe how participants in a democracy often use compromise to settle differences.

MAIN IDEAS OF THIS CONTENT STATEMENT

Who should get to sit in the front seat on the drive home? Who gets to pick what the family eats for dinner tonight? Whose turn is it to clean up after dinner? In a **disagreement**, each side feels it should not give in. Both sides usually feel they have good reasons to support their point of view. However, when people disagree, they often resolve their disagreement through a compromise.

In a **compromise**, each side gives up something. Each side also gets something in return. Usually in a compromise, none of the parties

walk away from the agreement feeling they got everything they asked for. But both parties are willing to end their dispute because each gets some of what it wanted.

Name _____ Date _____

Several conditions are needed for people to be able to resolve a dispute through compromise:

Understand What Is at Stake	**Be Respectful of the Other Person**	**Be Open to Negotiate With the Other Party**
The first step is to make sure that both sides are really interested in reaching a solution. Each party needs to understand the other's viewpoint.	If someone thinks others are really listening thoughtfully, he or she is far more likely to respond positively.	Both parties in a dispute need to come up with creative compromise solutions that work for both parties.

Democratic societies depend on compromise. A democratic society like the United States has millions of individuals with different interests and viewpoints. Many times, these individuals will disagree. Resolving those disagreements peacefully through compromise is essential to making democracy work.

THE PROCESS OF COMPROMISE AT WORK

We can see an example of this process at work at the Constitutional Convention in 1787.

The Disagreement. Delegates from the small states wanted all states to have an equal number of representatives in Congress. Delegates from states with large populations demanded more representatives for themselves, based on their larger populations.

The compromise at the Constitutional Convention allowed the new nation to move ahead.

The Solution. In the end, a compromise was reached between these conflicting viewpoints. The new national Congress was created with two houses. In the Senate, each state was given two representatives regardless of its size. This pleased the smaller states. In the House of Representatives, the number of representatives a state was given was based on its population. This satisfied the larger states.

Why Was This a Compromise? This was a compromise because each side got something it wanted. However, neither the small nor large states got everything they wanted.

CONTENT-AREA VOCABULARY

Directions. Fill in the boxes below.

DISAGREEMENT	
Define a "disagreement."	How is a disagreement different from other relationships?
Provide an example of a disagreement.	Provide an example of a relationship between people that is **not** a disagreement.

COMPROMISE	
Define a "compromise."	How is a "compromise" different from other ways of resolving disagreements?
Provide an example of a compromise.	Provide an example of a way of dealing with a disagreement that is **not** a compromise.

STUDY CARDS

Compromise

1. Describe how people in a disagreement sometimes reach a compromise.

   A. What is a compromise? _____

   _____

   _____

   B. How is a compromise reached when two sides disagree? _____

   _____

   _____

   _____

   _____

   _____

Describing a Personal Compromise

Describe a time in your life when you were in a disagreement, and you and the other side were able to reach a compromise.

_____

_____

_____

_____

_____

_____

_____

_____

_____

STUDY CARD PROMPTS

Compromise

1. Describe how people in a disagreement sometimes reach a compromise.

   A. What is a compromise?

   B. How is a compromise reached when two sides disagree?

To check your answers to these questions, turn the card over and review the information you have written on the other side.

Describing a Personal Compromise

Describe a time in your life when you were in a disagreement, and you and the other side were able to reach a compromise.

To check your answers to these questions, turn the card over and review the information you have written on the other side.

Name _____ Date _____

PERFORMANCE-BASED ASSESSMENT QUESTIONS

20 Two passages are shown.

MR. SMITH	THE STUDENTS
Mr. Smith says that the local skateboarding park is too noisy. Sometimes teenagers sneak into the park late at night. They play loud music and leave cans and other garbage in the skateboard park. He wants to close the park.	The students from Ms. Dorado's class have written a letter to the town council. They say they enjoy the skateboard park. If the skateboard park is shut down all the time, they will not have a safe place to ride their skateboards.

This question has two parts. First answer Part A, then answer Part B.

Part A.
Imagine you are a member of the town council. You have been asked to propose a compromise between these two opposing points of view. Write your compromise on the lines below.

_____

_____

_____

_____

_____

Part B.
Explain why your compromise would be a good solution to the problem.

_____

_____

_____

_____

21 A passage about the Compromise of 1790 is shown.

THE COMPROMISE OF 1790

Differences between the Northern and Southern states threatened the unity of the United States shortly after the U.S. Constitution was approved. The first Congress faced two issues:

(1) Where should the nation's capital be located? A capital is the city where a country's national government is located.

(2) Who should pay the debts from fighting the American Revolutionary War?

A compromise was reached. Southerners agreed to let the national government take over paying the debts of the states. The North agreed to locate the nation's capital in the South in Washington, D.C. between two Southern states — Maryland and Virginia.

List the **two** main groups involved in the Compromise of 1790.

1. _____

2. _____

22 Which statement best summarizes the compromise they reached?

ⓐ The North would not have to pay debts from the American Revolution.

ⓑ Congress would decide at a later date who would pay debts from the American Revolution.

ⓒ The South agreed that the national government would pay the war debts, and the North agreed that the nation's capital would be built in the South.

ⓓ The nation's capital would be built between Maryland and Virginia.

Name _____ Date _____

23 Each box below describes a characteristic essential to reach a compromise. Move or draw an line from each box to the correct column in the chart.

A CHARACTERISTIC NEEDED FOR A COMPROMISE	A CHARACTERISTIC THAT PREVENTS A COMPROMISE

Someone needs to propose a solution that is acceptable to both sides.	Each side needs to show it will not yield unless the other side goes first.	Each side needs to stress why only its point of view should be accepted.
Both sides must stick to their positions and refuse to yield to the other side.	Both sides need to have an opportunity to explain their points of view.	Both sides must be interested in reaching a solution.

24 In a compromise, each side may not feel entirely happy with the outcome, but they are willing to accept it.

Why is this important to a compromise? Write your answer in the space provided.

25 A passage about censorship is shown.

> Censorship occurs when the government reviews writings to take out words, images, or ideas that are considered "offensive." Some governments believe it is necessary to censor citizens' writings at all times. They say censorship is needed to encourage patriotism and prevent disloyalty. Others oppose censorship. They argue that citizens should always have the right to say whatever they want, or to read whatever they want.

This passage identifies two different viewpoints on censorship.

Which of the following is a compromise between these two points of view?

Ⓐ The government should always censor all publications.
Ⓑ The government should never censor publications because this violates freedom of speech.
Ⓒ The government should only censor publications in a serious emergency, such as a war.
Ⓓ Censorship is always needed to protect children from unpatriotic views.

26 The governments of two countries have become involved in a major dispute over their common border. Which of the following would most likely prevent a war between the two countries?

Ⓐ Military leaders in each nation promise their governments an easy victory.
Ⓑ One of the nations refuses to honor a treaty it had previously signed.
Ⓒ Both countries refuse to participate in any peace-keeping organizations.
Ⓓ Both countries agree to enter into negotiations to reach a compromise.

27 Some Americans believe that certain television shows teach children poor values. They demand that the government remove these shows. The television stations, however, believe they should be free to show whatever television shows they want.

Which of the following actions would be a compromise?

Ⓐ Refuse to allow television stations to show any programs with questionable values.
Ⓑ Allow television stations to show any program they want.
Ⓒ Show programs with questionable values late at night when children are asleep and not watching television.
Ⓓ Ask children which programs they would like to see on television and only allow those shows.

Name _____ Date _____

CHAPTER 18

LAWS: RIGHTS, BENEFITS, AND RESPONSIBILITIES

TOPIC: RULES AND LAWS

Rules play an important role in establishing order in families, classrooms and organizations. Laws are made by governments to perform a similar role.

Government 4	*Laws can protect rights, provide benefits and assign responsibilities.*

After reading this chapter, you should be able to:

★ Define the following terms:
  • Laws
  • Rule of law
  • Rights
  • Benefits
  • Responsibilities

★ Show how laws help to protect people's rights.
★ Explain how laws provide benefits but also come with responsibilities.

MAIN IDEAS OF THIS CONTENT STATEMENT

A **law** is a written rule that is enforced by the government. Usually, there is a penalty of some kind for breaking the law.

Americans live under the "**rule of law**." This means that no one is above the law. Everyone is subject to written laws and not to the whims or impulses of a dictator or king. Every citizen is governed by the same set of laws. Even the government and its officials are required to obey the law.

There are many **sources of law**. Some laws are passed on the national level by Congress and approved by the President. Other laws are passed on the state level by state legislatures and signed by the Governor.

In addition to laws passed by legislatures, courts also help to develop the law. When a court reaches a decision in applying a law, other courts usually follow that court's example. They apply the same rule to their own cases. This makes the law more fair. It also means that the reasoning applied by courts provides another source of law.

LAWS FULFILL MANY IMPORTANT ROLES IN SOCIETY

- **Laws Protect Rights.** The rule of law allows us to live in a society in which everyone's rights are respected. One important role that law plays is to protect people who are too weak to protect themselves. Laws also protect our freedom of speech and freedom of religion. They further protect our safety and property by outlawing crimes.

- **Laws Provide Benefits.** Many laws provide **benefits** — things that help us. For example, Ohio state law guarantees children the right to a free public education. Other laws provide social security benefits to older Americans.

- **Laws Assign Responsibilities.** Some laws establish responsibilities. For example, local laws define responsibilities when we drive. We must obtain a driver's license before driving. We must obey the speed limit, and stop for stop signs and red lights. Other laws establish income taxes, sales taxes, and other taxes we must pay to support the services that our government provides. Still other laws require us to serve on juries and to register for selective service when we are 18 years old if we are male.

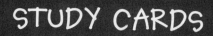

STUDY CARDS

The Rule of Law

1. What is a law? _____

_____

_____

_____

_____

2. What is the rule of law? _____

_____

_____

_____

_____

Roles Fulfilled by Laws in a Society

Identify and describe three roles that laws play in our society.

1. _____

_____

_____

2. _____

_____

_____

3. _____

_____

_____

STUDY CARD PROMPTS

The Rule of Law

1. What is a law?

2. What is the rule of law?

To check your answers to these questions, turn the card over and review the information you have written on the other side.

Roles Fulfilled by Laws in a Society

Identify and describe three roles that laws play in our society.

1.

2.

3.

To check your answers to these questions, turn the card over and review the information you have written on the other side.

Name _____ Date _____

Chapter 18: Laws: Rights, Benefits, and Responsibilities   **229**

CONTENT-AREA VOCABULARY

Directions. Write your own sentence in the right column using each of the following terms or phrases.

TERM OR PHRASE	YOUR SENTENCE
Law	
Rule of Law	
Benefits	
Rights	
Responsibilities	
Sources of Law	

PERFORMANCE-BASED
ASSESSMENT QUESTIONS

28 Give one reason why Ohio and our nation make laws. Write your answer on the lines provided.

_____

_____

_____

_____

_____

29 A passage about the Voting Rights Act of 2014 is shown.

> In January 2014, Congress passed the Voting Rights Act of 2014. This act has new protections to prevent discrimination against voters. The law states any change in a state's laws in voting has to be first approved by the national government. The law also requires local governments to provide public notice of proposed voting changes.

Identify **two** ways in which this law protected the voting rights of citizens.

1. _____

_____

_____

2. _____

_____

_____

Name _____ Date _____

END-OF-YEAR ASSESSMENT QUESTIONS

30 Three rights of American citizens are shown.

The right to contribute to political campaigns	**The right to state your own point of view**	**The right to wear campaign pins for the candidate you support**

How do laws protect these rights?

---

31 Which of the following illustrates a benefit of a law?

Ⓐ Laws against theft protect our private property.
Ⓑ Laws against theft lead some people to go to jail.
Ⓒ Laws against theft are expensive to enforce.
Ⓓ Laws against theft mean we should never steal.

32 Which of the following is an example of a law?

Ⓐ You must raise your hand in class before speaking.
Ⓑ You should eat three meals a day.
Ⓒ You cannot drive a car through a red light.
Ⓓ You should be respectful to your parents.

33 Why are laws necessary to a society?

Ⓐ They keep society running properly and prevent chaos.
Ⓑ They allow the government to control free speech.
Ⓒ They prevent citizens in society from acting lazily.
Ⓓ They encourage people to be themselves.

34 A passage about property rights is shown.

> A new law was just passed. It allows the government to take a person's private property for the public good. The person must be paid fairly for the property. An Ohio city has decided it wants private developers to build a shopping mall where fifty homeowners now live.

Which part of the law protects the homeowners in this case?

Ⓐ The government can take private property even without paying the owners.
Ⓑ Private property cannot be taken without paying the owners double what their property is worth.
Ⓒ No new shopping malls can be built in the state without first getting government permission.
Ⓓ Private property cannot be taken from a property-owner and used for private developers instead of the public good.

35 A concept map is shown.

Which term would best complete the concept map?

36 The United States and Ohio have each developed their own set of laws. How can these "laws" best be defined?

Ⓐ They are problems carried out by public officials.
Ⓑ They are rules that regulate the conduct of people in society.
Ⓒ They are techniques used by a government to raise money.
Ⓓ They are punishments passed by a government to punish criminals.

Name _____ Date _____

CHAPTER 19

LIMITED GOVERNMENT AND THE FIRST AMENDMENT

TOPIC: RULES AND LAWS

Government 5	*The U.S. Constitution establishes a system of limited government and protects citizens' rights; five of these rights are addressed in the First Amendment.*

After reading this chapter, you should be able to:

★ Define the following terms:
- U.S. Constitution
- Limited Government
- Bill of Rights
- First Amendment
- Freedom of Religion
- Freedom of the Press
- Freedom of Assembly

★ Describe how the U.S. Constitution establishes a system of limited government.
★ Describe how the First Amendment protects five important rights of citizens.

MAIN IDEAS OF THIS CONTENT STATEMENT

The authors of the **U.S. Constitution** were very afraid of creating a national government that would be too strong. They feared that a strong government might overpower or threaten individual rights.

At the same time, they knew that Americans needed a government strong enough to protect them and to promote cooperation. The authors of the U.S. Constitution therefore created a system of **limited government**.

> The government is the servant, not the master, of the people.

Authors of the Constitution strongly believed in this ideal.

233

LIMITED GOVERNMENT

A **written constitution** establishes a framework for government. One of the most important roles of a constitution is to limit government power. A constitution usually tells what a government can and cannot do.

Power Comes from the People. The most basic principle of the U.S. Constitution begins with the first words of the Preamble. The **Preamble** is the introduction to the U.S. Constitution. In its first three words, we learn that the government of the United States exists because "We the People" choose for it to exist.

Our government has only those limited powers that the people have chosen to give it. It has no right to do anything more than the people give it permission to do. Its powers and authority are therefore strictly limited.

Power is Divided. The U.S. Constitution divided powers among the three branches of government. The **legislative power** was given to **Congress**. The **executive power** was given to the Chief Executive (*the President*). Finally, the judicial power was given to the **federal courts**. Each branch was forbidden from using any powers beyond those it was given in the Constitution.

Powers were Spelled Out. The U.S. Constitution spelled out the precise powers of each branch of government. The authors of the Constitution limited power of our national government by giving it very specific powers. For example, Congress's lawmaking powers were listed in Article I. They include such powers as taxing, declaring war, and printing money. Congress can exercise those powers but no others. It is forbidden to use any other powers beyond those in the Constitution. The powers of Congress and of the two other branches of government are thus limited.

Individual Rights are Protected. Another reason our national government's powers were limited was to protect the rights of individuals. Even so, opponents of the new Constitution feared that this document would make the national government too strong. They worried that the new government might abuse people's rights and freedoms. As a result, before some states would support the new U.S. Constitution, they demanded a "**Bill of Rights**" to protect individual rights.

After the U.S. Constitution was adopted, the first Congress proposed a series of **amendments** (*changes*) to the Constitution. These became known as the "Bill of Rights." The **Bill of Rights** consists of the first ten amendments to the U.S. Constitution.

THE FIRST AMENDMENT

The **First Amendment** contains some of the most important of our rights. The amendment has been interpreted by the U.S. Supreme Court to apply to the states as well as to our national government.

> **THE FIRST AMENDMENT**
>
> Congress shall make no law respecting an establishment of religion, or prohibiting the free exercise thereof; or abridging the freedom of speech, or of the press; or the right of the people peaceably to assemble, and to petition the Government for a redress of grievances.

- **Freedom of Speech.** American citizens have the right to express themselves freely. Although there are some limits to this, freedom of speech gives individuals and groups the right to criticize the government.

- **Freedom of the Press.** American citizens have the right to express themselves freely in newspapers, journals, books and other published materials.

- **Freedom of Religion.** Americans have the right to follow their own religious beliefs.

- **Freedom of Assembly.** Americans have the right to hold public meetings to discuss, promote, criticize or defend ideas and policies.

- **The Right to Petition Government.** Americans have the right to send letters of complaint to government officials. These petitions, often with people's signatures, can demand that government right a wrong or correct a problem by changing a law.

Other amendments in the Bill of Rights guarantee citizens the right to a fair trial by jury, freedom from unreasonable searches and seizures, and the right to have a lawyer provided to them when they are accused of a serious crime.

CONTENT-AREA VOCABULARY

Directions. Fill in the boxes in the concept ladder below by writing your own description or explanation of each item.

CONCEPT: FIRST AMENDMENT

Right to Petition _____

Right of Assembly _____

Freedom of Religion _____

Freedom of the Press _____

Freedom of Speech _____

CONCEPT: LIMITED GOVERNMENT

Individual Rights Are Protected _____

Powers of Government Are Spelled Out _____

Government Power Is Divided _____

Power Comes from the People _____

STUDY CARDS

Limited Government

Identify four ways that the U.S. Constitution limits the power of our national government.

1. _____

_____

2. _____

_____

3. _____

_____

4. _____

_____

First Amendment

List and describe the five rights identified in the First Amendment.

1. _____

_____

2. _____

_____

3. _____

_____

4. _____

_____

5. _____

_____

STUDY CARD PROMPTS

Limited Government

Identify four ways that the U.S. Constitution limits the power of our national government.

1.

2.

3.

4.

To check your answers to these questions, turn the card over and review the information you have written on the other side.

First Amendment

List and describe the five rights identified in the First Amendment.

1.

2.

3.

4.

5.

To check your answers to these questions, turn the card over and review the information you have written on the other side.

PERFORMANCE-BASED ASSESSMENT QUESTIONS

37 The concept map below is missing four of the five freedoms found in the First Amendment. Rewrite or draw a line from each of the boxed descriptions to the blank boxes that show it is one of the freedoms in the First Amendment.

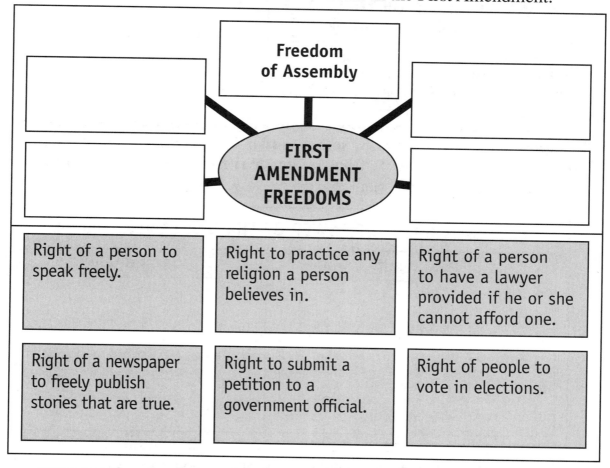

Freedom of Assembly

FIRST AMENDMENT FREEDOMS

Right of a person to speak freely.

Right to practice any religion a person believes in.

Right of a person to have a lawyer provided if he or she cannot afford one.

Right of a newspaper to freely publish stories that are true.

Right to submit a petition to a government official.

Right of people to vote in elections.

38 A Supreme Court Justice once said that "free speech would not protect a man who falsely shouted fire in a crowded theatre, causing panic."

What conclusion can be made from this statement about the limits of the First Amendment's right of free speech?

_____

_____

39 Which description correctly identifies the right of citizens to petition their government? Write the correct answer or draw an arrow to the box below.

Freely worship your God in the way you wish.

Vote in an election for the person you think will do the best job.

Gather with other people to hold a public demonstration against the government.

Send elected officials a list of signatures asking for a change in a law.

40 Complete the boxes below by selecting **two** limits on the power of the U.S. government found in the U.S. Constitution. Write or draw an arrow from each of your two answers to the blank boxes.

LIMITS ON THE POWER OF THE U.S. GOVERNMENT

First Limit	Second Limit

The government has only those powers given to it by the Constitution.

Some people feared the U.S. Constitution gave too much power to the national government.

Power is divided among the three branches of government.

The Bill of Rights consists of the first ten amendments to the U.S. Constitution.

Name _____ Date _____

Chapter 19: Limited Government and the First Amendment   **241**

END-OF-YEAR ASSESSMENT QUESTIONS

An illustration of individual freedoms in the United States Constitution is shown.

- **Freedom of religion:** The government cannot establish an official religion.
- **Freedom of speech:** The government is forbidden from making laws that stop us from saying what we think.
- **Freedom of the press:** The government cannot control what is printed in books or newspapers.
- **Freedom of assembly:** Citizens have the right to come together in private and public meetings.
- **Right to petition:** By gathering names on a petition and sending it to their representatives, citizens can ask for changes in the government.

41 Which freedom gives Americans the right to gather peacefully as part of a large crowd?

42 In what part of the Bill of Rights can these five freedoms be found?

43 A concept map is shown.

The people hold supreme power.

The national government was given only certain powers.

A Bill of Rights was created to protect citizens' individual liberties.

Which of the following belongs in the oval at the top of the concept map?

- Ⓐ First Amendment Rights
- Ⓑ The Declaration of Independence
- Ⓒ Limits on the Power of the U.S. Government
- Ⓓ The Writers of the U.S. Constitution

44 Which document guarantees the freedom of the press in the United States?

Ⓐ Declaration of Independence
Ⓑ Articles of Confederation
Ⓒ Northwest Ordinance of 1787
Ⓓ Bill of Rights

45 A group of statements about the U.S. Constitution is shown.

> • The U.S. Constitution specifically lists the powers of Congress in Article 1.
> • The U.S. Constitution specifically lists the powers of the executive branch in Article 2.
> • The U.S. Constitution specifically lists the powers of the judicial branch in Article 3.

Which best explains why the authors of the U.S. Constitution specifically listed the powers of each branch of government?

Ⓐ They believed that the government should be all-powerful.
Ⓑ They sought to limit the power of the government.
Ⓒ They felt that the government has a natural right to rule.
Ⓓ They wanted to limit the authority of the American people.

46 What was the main reason for adding the First Amendment to the U.S. Constitution?

Ⓐ To prevent an increase in crime in the nation.
Ⓑ To protect colonists from abuses by the British King.
Ⓒ To protect the rights of individuals.
Ⓓ To give men and women equal rights.

47 Which document guarantees Americans freedom of speech and religion?

Ⓐ Declaration of Independence
Ⓑ Articles of Confederation
Ⓒ First Amendment of the U.S. Constitution
Ⓓ Northwest Ordinance

48 Which best describes a characteristic of the national government established by the U.S. Constitution?

Ⓐ The powers of the national government were limited.
Ⓑ Its courts had less authority than the Ohio courts.
Ⓒ The President was placed in charge of all government powers.
Ⓓ States had more power than the national government.

49 The First Amendment is shown.

> "Congress shall make no law respecting an establishment of religion, or prohibiting the free exercise thereof; or abridging (*limiting*) the freedom of speech, or of the press; or the right of the people peaceably to assemble, and to petition the Government for a redress of grievances."

Which statement about this passage expresses an opinion?

Ⓐ Congress can make no law respecting an establishment of religion.
Ⓑ This amendment is part of the Bill of Rights.
Ⓒ This is the most important amendment in the Bill of Rights.
Ⓓ Congress can make no law limiting the freedom of speech.

50 Which would a supporter of limited national government most likely favor?

Ⓐ Putting all governmental powers in the hands of one branch.
Ⓑ Removing the list of powers given to our national government in the U.S. Constitution.
Ⓒ Protecting individual rights from abuses by government officials.
Ⓓ Eliminating some of the freedoms provided by in the First Amendment.

51 Which statement would be made by a person who supported a limited national government?

Ⓐ "Our national government is supposed to be our servant, not our master."
Ⓑ "Government at all levels needs to be doing many more things."
Ⓒ "Our federal government should be supreme over the people it rules."
Ⓓ "We can trust our government not to abuse the rights of individuals."

52 A part of the English Bill of Rights (1689) is shown.

> "It is the right of the (*people of Great Britain*) to petition the king, and all prosecutions (*putting people in prison*) for such petitioning are illegal."

A provision of which document later gave similar guarantees to Americans?

Ⓐ Proclamation Line of 1763
Ⓑ Northwest Ordinance
Ⓒ Treaty of Greenville
Ⓓ Bill of Rights

CHAPTER 20

THE OHIO AND U.S. CONSTITUTIONS

TOPIC: ROLES AND SYSTEMS OF GOVERNMENT

The purpose of our government is to establish order, protect the rights of individuals, and promote the common good. Governments may be organized in different ways. They can have limited or unlimited powers.

Government 6	*A constitution is a written plan for government. Democratic constitutions provide the framework for government in Ohio and the United States.*

After reading this chapter, you should be able to:

★ Define the following terms:
 • Constitution
 • Government
 • Ohio Constitution
 • U.S. Constitution

★ Identify the purpose of a constitution.
★ Show how both the U.S. and Ohio Constitutions provide the framework for their governments.

MAIN IDEAS OF THIS CONTENT STATEMENT

A **constitution** is a written plan for government. It "constitutes," or creates, the government. A constitution tells what the government can and cannot do. It also establishes a framework for government. A framework provides the structure and powers that make up the government.

For example, the U.S. Constitution established the Congress, the Presidency and the U.S. Supreme Court.

The center of our national government is in Washington, D.C.

Name _____ Date _____

The U.S. Constitution was written in 1787. It created the three branches of our national government. Ohio's plan of government is the Ohio Constitution. Like the U.S. Constitution, the **Ohio Constitution** also organized its government into three branches — a legislative, executive, and judicial branch. The main purpose of the Ohio Constitution is to establish a government that protects the rights and freedoms of its people.

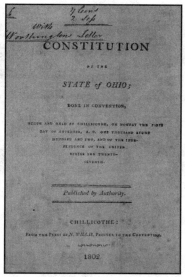

Both the U.S. Constitution and the Ohio Constitution are **democratic**. They are based on the belief that the source of all political power is the people. People are entitled to freely express their views. They use their political power by electing government officials.

Ohio's first Constitution (1802).

Because the source of all political power in our democracy is the people, the authors of the U.S. Constitution began that document with the same three words: "We the People."

Like the U.S. Constitution, the preamble (*introduction*) of the Ohio Constitution begins with the same three words "We, the people."

> *We, the people of the State of Ohio, grateful to Almighty God for our freedom, to secure its blessings and promote our general welfare, do establish this Constitution.*

Also like the U.S. Constitution, the Ohio Constitution is democratic. A **democracy** is a form of government in which its citizens, either directly or through elected representatives, make decisions. The Ohio Constitution establishes an executive (*the Governor*) and legislature that are elected by the people.

The center of Ohio's government is in Columbus.

CONTENT-AREA VOCABULARY

Directions. Fill in the boxes below.

CONSTITUTION	
Define the term "constitution."	How is a constitution different from other laws?
Give an example of a constitution.	Give an example of a law or government document that is **not** a constitution.

DEMOCRACY	
Define "democracy."	How is a "democratic" form of government different from other forms of government?
Give an example of a democratic government.	Give an example of a government that is **not** democratic.

Name _____ Date _____

STUDY CARDS

The U.S. Constitution

1. What is a constitution? _____

_____

_____

2. How many branches of government are established by the U.S. Constitution? _____

3. In what ways is the U.S. Constitution democratic? _____

_____

_____

_____

_____

_____

A Comparison of the U.S. and Ohio Constitutions

1. How many branches of government are established by the Ohio Constitution? _____

2. In what ways is the Ohio Constitution democratic? _____

_____

_____

_____

_____

_____

_____

_____

STUDY CARD PROMPTS

The U.S. Constitution

1. What is a constitution?

2. How many branches of government are established by the U.S. Constitution?

3. In what ways is the U.S. Constitution democratic?

To check your answers to these questions, turn the card over and review the information you have written on the other side.

A Comparison of the U.S. and Ohio Constitutions

1. How many branches of government are established by the Ohio Constitution?

2. In what ways is the Ohio Constitution democratic?

To check your answers to these questions, turn the card over and review the information you have written on the other side.

PERFORMANCE-BASED ASSESSMENT QUESTIONS

53 What is the main purpose of the Ohio Constitution?

_____

_____

_____

_____

_____

54 What is the role of each of the three branches of Ohio's government?

A. _____

_____

B. _____

_____

C. _____

_____

55 This question has two parts. First, answer part A. Then, answer part B.

Ohio's Constitution is similar to the U.S. Constitution in that both established democratic systems of government.

Part A.
Identify one way in which the Ohio Constitution is democratic.

_____

_____

Part B.
Identify one way in which the U.S. Constitution is democratic.

_____

_____

END-OF-YEAR ASSESSMENT QUESTIONS

56 A diagram of legislative, executive, and judicial powers is shown.

Legislative Power
(to the make laws)

Executive Power
(to carry out the laws)

Judicial Power
(to apply the laws to
specific situations)

Which title would be most appropriate for the diagram above?

Ⓐ Powers of Government
Ⓑ Bill of Rights
Ⓒ Duties of a U.S. Citizen
Ⓓ First Amendment Rights

57 What is the name given to a written plan for the organization of a government?

58 In a democracy such as Ohio, who runs the government?

Ⓐ Its leaders who are elected by the people
Ⓑ The people who own the most property
Ⓒ Its officials who are appointed for life
Ⓓ The U.S. President and the General Assembly

59 Which documents provided the specific framework for democratic government in both the United States and Ohio?

Ⓐ The Proclamation Line of 1763 and the Northwest Ordinance
Ⓑ The U.S. Constitution and the Ohio Constitution
Ⓒ The Declaration of Independence and the Northwest Ordinance
Ⓓ The Articles of Confederation and the U.S. Constitution

60 Which is the best definition of government?

Ⓐ   A group of rules used by judges to settle disputes
Ⓑ   A political organization with authority over people in a particular area
Ⓒ   A group of people who act to protect their neighbors from harm
Ⓓ   An effort by people from several nations to protect human rights

61 The U.S. Constitution and the Ohio Constitution both established a framework for government. What is meant by a "framework" for government?

Ⓐ   It lists all of the obligations of its citizens.
Ⓑ   It establishes the structures and powers of the government.
Ⓒ   It provides information citizens need to contact their officials.
Ⓓ   It lays out the rules for changing the constitution.

62 What do the U.S. Congress and the Ohio General Assembly have in common?

Ⓐ   They are both appointed by the executive branch.
Ⓑ   The members of each are elected for six-year terms.
Ⓒ   They are both law-making bodies of government.
Ⓓ   They both meet in Washington, D.C.

63 Which principle of government is found in both the U.S. Constitution and the Ohio Constitution?

Ⓐ   Governing power is best in the hands of a strong executive.
Ⓑ   Political power comes from the people.
Ⓒ   Only the President and Governor of Ohio can declare war.
Ⓓ   The right to vote is guaranteed to both citizens and non-citizens.

64 In both the U.S. Constitution and the Ohio Constitution, how are government leaders, such members of the U.S. Congress and General Assembly, chosen?

Ⓐ   They are appointed by the U.S. Supreme Court.
Ⓑ   They are elected by ordinary citizens.
Ⓒ   They are selected by a panel of business leaders.
Ⓓ   They are picked by state legislators.

65 What is the name given to a document that tells a government what it can and cannot do, and establishes a framework for the operation of government?

Ⓐ   A right
Ⓑ   A law
Ⓒ   An amendment
Ⓓ   A constitution

66 Two important documents to the people of Ohio are the U.S. Constitution and the Ohio Constitution.

Below are statements about one or both of these documents. Write or draw a line from the boxed statements to the correct column in the chart.

APPLIES TO BOTH THE OHIO AND U.S. CONSTITUTIONS	APPLIES ONLY TO THE OHIO CONSTITUTION

The source of all political power rests in the hands of the people.	The government is organized into a legislative, executive and judicial branch.
This establishes the framework for Ohio's state government.	Begin with the three words, "We the people."
This is based on democratic principles of government.	The chief executive of the government is the Governor.

67 Which statement describes a basic feature of democratic government?

Ⓐ Government leaders do what they think is best for the people.
Ⓑ Everyone pays an equal amount of taxes to the government.
Ⓒ Citizens elect the government leaders they want to represent them.
Ⓓ People must announce who they voted for in an election.

68 In a democracy such as Ohio, where do government leaders get their power?

Ⓐ Their powers come from being born into the families of leaders.
Ⓑ Their powers are given to them by the President of the United States.
Ⓒ Their powers come from being elected by the citizens of Ohio.
Ⓓ Their powers come from their wealth and influence in Ohio.

CHAPTER
21

THE SEPARATION OF POWERS

TOPIC: ROLES AND SYSTEMS OF GOVERNMENT

| Government 7 | *The Ohio Constitution and the U.S. Constitution separate the major responsibilities of government among three branches.* |

After reading this chapter, you should be able to:

★ Define the following terms:
- Separation of Powers
- Legislative Power
- Executive Power
- Judicial Power
- General Assembly

★ Describe how the Ohio and U.S. Constitutions applied the idea of separation of powers in government.

MAIN IDEAS OF THIS CONTENT STATEMENT

The U.S. Constitution was not our first national government. After the thirteen colonies declared their independence from Britain in 1776, each colony became a separate state.

The thirteen new states then joined together in a loose confederation. They sent their representatives to a common assembly, known as "Congress." In this Congress, each state was given only one vote. Although there was now a Congress to make laws, the new national government still faced many problems.

Delegates from the new states met in Philadelphia to plan a new government.

Limits of the New Government. This new national government lacked the power to enforce its laws. It lacked both a national executive or any national courts. It soon became obvious that this government would be unsuccessful. It was unable to deal with many of the challenges facing the nation. This new government had no national army to put down rebellions or to defend the nation against foreign enemies. It could not collect its own taxes, so it had very little money. Meanwhile, states were able to tax each other's goods.

LIMITS ON THE NATIONAL GOVERNMENT

- **No power to enforce laws**
- **No national courts to settle disputes between the states**
- **No power to tax**
- **No power to regulate trade: could not place tariffs on foreign goods**

Delegates Meet in Philadelphia. Faced with such problems, twelve of the 13 states sent representatives to Philadelphia in 1787 to revise the national government. They soon came to realize that it would be easier to write a whole new **constitution** — or written plan of government.

WHY POWER WAS SEPARATED AMONG THE BRANCHES

The representatives in Philadelphia set about writing the U.S. Constitution. They wanted a strong national government. They also wanted to protect people's individual freedoms. They feared giving the new government too much power. They were afraid that if they did, the government would abuse its powers.

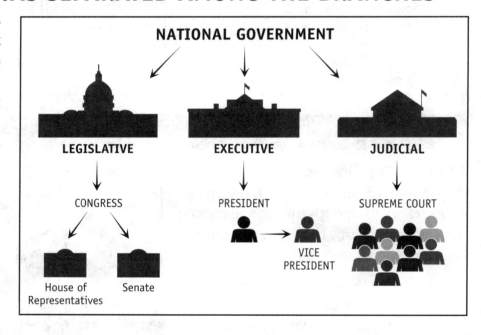

The authors of the U.S. Constitution believed they could prevent such abuse by separating the powers of government among three branches of government. Each branch was given a different power.

| The **legislative branch** makes the laws. This branch is known as the **U.S. Congress.** | The **executive branch** enforces the laws. This branch is known as the **President.** | The **judicial branch** interprets and applies the laws. This branch is known as the **Supreme Court.** |

The purpose of this separation was to make sure that no one branch of our national government — also known as the "federal government" — became so powerful that it would be tempted to challenge the people's liberties.

THE OHIO CONSTITUTION

The **Ohio Constitution** also separates government power among three branches, just like the U.S. Constitution. The Ohio Constitution was first passed in 1802, but it has changed several times. The Ohio Constitution of 1851 provides the main basis for the state's constitution today.

The three separate branches of Ohio's state government are the following:

- The **Ohio General Assembly** is the state's legislative, or law-making, branch. It consists of two houses: the **Ohio Senate** and the **Ohio House of Representatives**.

The two houses of the Ohio General Assembly meet in different rooms of the state capitol.

- Ohio's **Governor** serves as the state's executive branch.

- The **Ohio Supreme Court** serves as the state's highest court. It is part of Ohio's judicial branch.

CONTENT-AREA VOCABULARY

General Assembly	Congress	Separation of Powers
President	U.S. Supreme Court	Governor
Ohio Supreme Court	Executive Power	Legislative Power
	Judicial Power	

Directions. Classify these terms and phrases into the categories below. Then identify or define each term and phrase.

Constitutional Principles

1. _____

Powers of Government

1. _____

2. _____

3. _____

Branch of the U.S. Government

1. _____

2. _____

3. _____

Branches of the Ohio State Government

1. _____

2. _____

3. _____

Name _____ Date _____

STUDY CARDS

The Three Branches of Government

1. What are the three branches of the U.S. government? What is the function of each?

   A. _____

   B. _____

   C. _____

2. What are the three branches of Ohio's state government? What function is each branch responsible for?

   A. _____

   B. _____

   C. _____

The Separation of Powers

Explain why the powers of government were separated among three branches in the U.S. Constitution.

_____

_____

_____

_____

_____

_____

_____

_____

_____

STUDY CARD PROMPTS

The Three Branches of Government

1. **What are the three branches of Ohio's state government?**

   A.

   B.

   C.

2. **What function is each branch responsible for?**

   A.

   B.

   C.

To check your answers to these questions, turn the card over and review the information you have written on the other side.

The Separation of Powers

Explain why the powers of government are separated.

To check your answers to these questions, turn the card over and review the information you have written on the other side.

Name _____ Date _____

INTERPRETING DIAGRAMS

SKILL BUILDER

In this section, you will learn how to interpret diagrams. A **diagram** is a simplified picture that shows how something is organized, how several things are related, or how the different parts of something work together. Parts of a diagram are often identified with labels. Arrows and lines in a diagram often indicate important relationships.

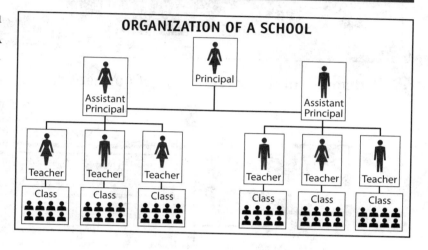

ORGANIZATION OF A SCHOOL

STEPS TO UNDERSTANDING DIAGRAMS

LOOK AT THE TITLE

The title usually tells you what kind of information is presented. For example, the title of the diagram above is: "Organization of a School."

USING THE INFORMATION IN THE DIAGRAM

To find specific information you need to look at the diagram's labels. This diagram shows the main levels of a school's organization. The lines between the levels are important because they indicate each level's relationship with the other levels. In this diagram, a line from the principal shows that the principal has two assistant principals at a slightly lower level. This means that the principal has authority over the two assistant principals.

ANSWERING A DIAGRAM-BASED QUESTION

Look at the diagram above to answer the following questions:

A. Who is the immediate supervisor of a teacher? _____

B. Name three levels of school employees that run a school.

   1. _____ **2.** _____ **3.** _____

PERFORMANCE-BASED ASSESSMENT QUESTIONS

69 A diagram of the organization of our national and state governments is shown.

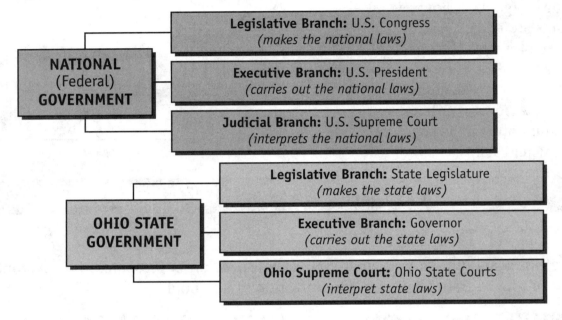

Identify the three branches of our national government shown in the chart above. Then describe the role played by each branch.

1. _____

_____

_____

2. _____

_____

_____

3. _____

_____

_____

Name _____ Date _____

70 Identify the three branches of the Ohio government shown in the chart above. Then describe the role played by each branch.

1. _____
   _____

2. _____
   _____

3. _____
   _____

71 The duties and responsibilities of the national government are divided among three branches of government.

Each box below lists a responsibility of one of the branches of our national government. Move or draw a line from each responsibility to the correct column in the chart.

LEGISLATIVE BRANCH	EXECUTIVE BRANCH	JUDICIAL BRANCH
It has the power to interpret the words of the Constitution.	It has the power to declare war and raise and support an army.	It rules on the constitutionality of laws passed by Congress.
Its chief executive directs the nation's foreign policy.	It has the power to review decisions of lower state courts.	It controls the spending of the national government.
It makes the laws for the entire nation.	It is in charge of the nation's armed forces.	Its powers are used to enforce the nation's laws.

INTERPRETING VENN DIAGRAMS

SKILL BUILDER

In the section that follows, you will find questions about Venn diagrams. This section will help you to interpret a Venn diagram.

The **Venn diagram** was first invented by an English mathematician named John Venn. A Venn diagram is a type of graphic organizer. It uses overlapping circles to show how two things are similar and different. Information that is the same for both things is represented in the space where the circles intersect. What is unique about each item is shown in the parts of the circles that do not intersect.

AN EXAMPLE OF A VENN DIAGRAM

A Venn diagram below compares whales and fish. The "unique" part of the circle for whales might include: (1) their bodies have hair; (2) they can breathe air; (3) they are often quite large.

The "unique" part of the circle for fish might include: (1) they lay eggs; (2) they can breathe in water; (3) their bodies have scales.

The area where the circles overlap lists how they are similar. This might include: (1) they live in water; (2) their bodies have fins; (3) they are able to swim.

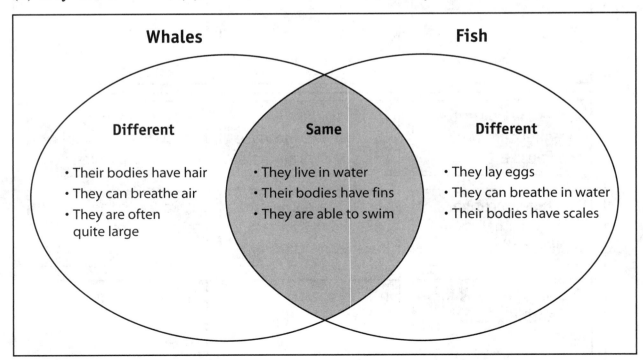

Name _____ Date _____

END-OF-YEAR ASSESSMENT QUESTIONS

72 A Venn diagram comparing the Ohio and U.S. Constitutions is shown.

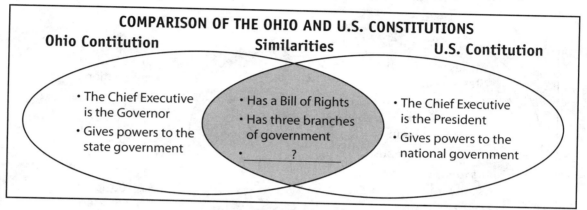

COMPARISON OF THE OHIO AND U.S. CONSTITUTIONS

Ohio Contitution — Similarities — U.S. Contitution

- The Chief Executive is the Governor
- Gives powers to the state government

- Has a Bill of Rights
- Has three branches of government
- _____ ?

- The Chief Executive is the President
- Gives powers to the national government

Which phrase belongs in place of the question mark?

Ⓐ Has the power to print money
Ⓑ Provides a framework for government
Ⓒ Lacks a Bill of Rights
Ⓓ Governs the same number of people

73 The diagram to the right illustrates an important concept of American government. Which concept is illustrated in this diagram?

Ⓐ The President is more important than the legislative branch.
Ⓑ All laws must be approved by the President and Supreme Court.
Ⓒ Power in the United States is separated among the three branches
Ⓓ The voters elect all three branches of the U.S. government.

PRESIDENTIAL FORM OF GOVERNMENT

VOTERS ELECT

Legislature (Congress)   Chief Executive (President)

appoints

Judiciary (Supreme Court)

74 How is Ohio's General Assembly similar to the United States Congress?

Ⓐ Both are government branches that enforce laws.
Ⓑ Both are made up of two houses.
Ⓒ Both are elected for a term of six years.
Ⓓ Both have the same number of members.

75 A Venn diagram comparing the legislative branches of the Ohio and United States government is shown.

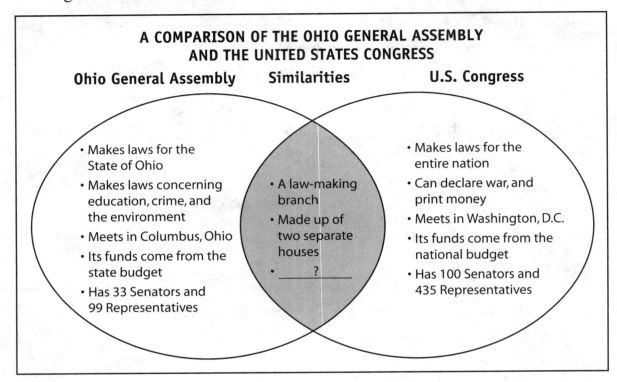

**A COMPARISON OF THE OHIO GENERAL ASSEMBLY
AND THE UNITED STATES CONGRESS**

Ohio General Assembly   **Similarities**   **U.S. Congress**

- Makes laws for the State of Ohio
- Makes laws concerning education, crime, and the environment
- Meets in Columbus, Ohio
- Its funds come from the state budget
- Has 33 Senators and 99 Representatives

- A law-making branch
- Made up of two separate houses
- _____?_____

- Makes laws for the entire nation
- Can declare war, and print money
- Meets in Washington, D.C.
- Its funds come from the national budget
- Has 100 Senators and 435 Representatives

Which item belongs in the "similarities" part of this Venn diagram?

Ⓐ   It meets in the U.S. Capitol building.
Ⓑ   The Governor is its most important member.
Ⓒ   Its authority comes from the Ohio Constitution.
Ⓓ   Its law-making powers are limited.

76 Three statements are shown.

- Its General Assembly has two houses.
- Its House of Representatives has 99 members.
- Its Senate has 33 members

Which organization do the statements in the box describe?

Ⓐ   The United States Congress
Ⓑ   The Ohio legislature
Ⓒ   Ohio's court system
Ⓓ   Ohio's executive branch

77 Each statement describes a branch of Ohio's government. Move the statement or draw a line to the correct column of the chart.

LEGISLATIVE BRANCH	EXECUTIVE BRANCH	JUDICIAL BRANCH
The role of Ohio's courts is to interpret and apply state laws.	The General Assembly passes laws concerning the state budget, education, and crime.	The Governor's main responsibility is to enforce the laws passed by the General Assembly.

78 Why did the authors of the U.S. Constitution create three separate branches of government?

Ⓐ   To allow the legislative branch to have the most power.
Ⓑ   To make sure all laws are approved by the Supreme Court.
Ⓒ   To permit the President to recommend policy to the legislature.
Ⓓ   To prevent any one branch of government from having too much power.

79 How does a person become a member of the U.S. Congress?

Ⓐ   By becoming a military leader.
Ⓑ   By being elected by voters.
Ⓒ   By being born into the position.
Ⓓ   By being appointed by the Supreme Court.

80 Which statement about Ohio's executive branch of government is accurate?

Ⓐ   Ohio's Governor is in charge of the executive branch.
Ⓑ   The leader of Ohio's executive branch is appointed for a term of six years.
Ⓒ   Ohio's executive branch is the law-making branch of government.
Ⓓ   Ohio's executive branch is in charge of the Ohio court system.

81 Which action can be taken only by our national government?

Ⓐ   Repairing potholes on local streets and roadways
Ⓑ   Charging automobiles tolls on roadways
Ⓒ   Electing a new mayor to govern a city
Ⓓ   Coining and printing money

1   A Venn diagram of national and state powers is shown.

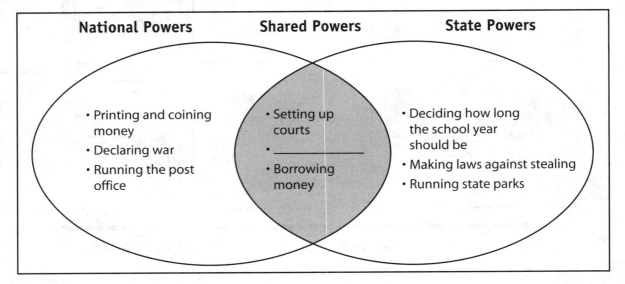

National Powers | **Shared Powers** | **State Powers**

- Printing and coining money
- Declaring war
- Running the post office

- Setting up courts
- _____
- Borrowing money

- Deciding how long the school year should be
- Making laws against stealing
- Running state parks

Which power belongs on the blank line above?

Ⓐ   deciding school subjects for high school students
Ⓑ   building interstate highways
Ⓒ   collecting taxes
Ⓓ   passing laws against theft

2   Based on the Venn diagram, which level of government has the power to declare war?

Ⓐ   The national government
Ⓑ   Ohio's state government
Ⓒ   Local town government
Ⓓ   County governments

3   A group of citizens holds a meeting outside Ohio's General Assembly. They discuss their concerns about a law being considered by the legislature. In holding this meeting, which right were these citizens exercising?

Ⓐ   right to have an attorney
Ⓑ   freedom of the press
Ⓒ   freedom of assembly
Ⓓ   freedom of religion

4   A concept map is shown.

What belongs on the top of the concept map? Write your answer in the space below.

```
┌────────────────────────────────────────────────────────┐
│                                                        │
└────────────────────────────────────────────────────────┘
```

5   A chart is shown.

?

- Pay taxes to support the costs of government.
- Serve on a jury if called upon.
- Testify in court if called upon.
- Attend school until at least 16 years old, and follow school rules.
- Obey the laws of local, state, and federal government.
- Help to defend the nation by serving in the armed forces if called upon.

What would be the best title for this chart?

Ⓐ   Local Government in Ohio
Ⓑ   Obligations of a Citizen
Ⓒ   Demands of U.S. Citizens
Ⓓ   First Amendment Freedoms

6   Which statement identifies a main idea of both the Ohio and U.S. Constitutions?

Ⓐ   There should be no limits to the power of the government.
Ⓑ   Americans should not be required to pay taxes on their incomes.
Ⓒ   The source of all government power comes from the people.
Ⓓ   People have a right to rebel against an unjust government.

7   A chart comparing the Ohio and U.S. Constitutions is shown.

	Constitution of Ohio	Constitution of the U.S.
Date First Adopted	February 1802	June 21, 1788
Legislative Houses	2 Houses	2 Houses
Names of the Legislative Houses	• House of Representatives • Senate	• House of Representatives • Senate
Chief Executive	Governor	President
Has a Bill of Rights?	Yes	Yes (added in 1791)
Its Highest Court	Ohio Supreme Court	U.S. Supreme Court

What conclusion can be drawn from this chart ?

Ⓐ   Both constitutions govern areas of about the same size.

Ⓑ   The United States has a chief executive but Ohio does not.

Ⓒ   The structures of the Ohio and U.S. governments are similar.

Ⓓ   Ohio's Constitution is more democratic than the U.S. Constitution.

---

8   The text of the First Amendment is shown.

> *Congress shall make no law respecting an establishment of religion, or prohibiting the free exercise thereof; or abridging the freedom of speech, or of the press; or the right of the people peaceably to assemble, and to petition the Government for a redress of grievances.*

Identify three freedoms in the First Amendment that protect the rights of individuals. Write your answers in the boxes below.

FIRST FREEDOM	SECOND FREEDOM	THIRD FREEDOM

9   A diagram dealing with the separation of powers is shown.

SEPARATION OF POWERS		
LEGISLATIVE BRANCH Power to make the laws	**EXECUTIVE BRANCH** Power to carry out the laws	**JUDICIAL BRANCH** Power to interpret the laws

	LEGISLATIVE BRANCH	EXECUTIVE BRANCH	JUDICIAL BRANCH
National Government	Congress	President	Supreme Court
State of Ohio	State Legislature	Governor	Supreme Court

Why were these powers separated among three independent branches for both the United States and Ohio? Write your answer in the space below.

---

10 An outline of the ways citizens influence government is shown.

> I. Ways in which citizens influence government
>   A. By voting in elections
>   B. By volunteering to help in an election campaign
>   C. By running for elective office
>   D. _____

Which statement best completes this outline ?

Ⓐ   By watching the news on evening television.
Ⓑ   By recycling used consumer goods.
Ⓒ   By attending a meeting to speak to a public official.
Ⓓ   By helping close relatives in need.

11 The U.S. Constitution and Ohio Constitution have similarities and some differences.

Each box below describes a characteristic of either the U.S. Constitution, the Ohio Constitution, or both documents. Move or draw a line from each characteristic to the correct column in the chart.

U.S. CONSTITUTION	BOTH	OHIO CONSTITUTION
Its chief executive is the Governor.	Its original document prohibited slavery.	Its chief executive is the President.
It divided the powers of government into three separate branches.	Its law-making body is called the General Assembly.	It was first approved and went into effect in 1803.
Its law-making body can declare war and print money.	Its law-making body is the U.S. Congress.	Its power to govern come from the people it governs.

12 An outline is shown.

> I. _____
>   A. Vote in elections
>   B. Volunteer to work in an election campaign
>   C. Run for elective office
>   D. Meet with elected officials

Which heading best completes the outline?

Ⓐ Election Day Comes in November
Ⓑ Voting is a Basic Right in a Democracy
Ⓒ Ways Citizens Can Influence their Government
Ⓓ Elections Permit Voters to Decide Issues Directly

13 A diagram of the responsibilities of the national government is shown.

Complete the chart by writing in the missing name on the blank line of each box.

Branch of Government:

_____

- Makes the laws
- Controls government spending
- Declares war
- Raises and supports armies

Branch of Government:

_____

- Carries out the laws
- Directs the nation's foreign policy
- Negotiates treaties
- Commands the nation's armed forces

RESPONSIBILITIES OF THE NATIONAL GOVERNMENT

Branch of Government:

_____

- Interprets the Constitution
- Rules on the constitutionality of laws
- Decides cases between states
- Reviews lower court decisions

14 A proposed amendment to the U.S. Constitution is shown.

No national, state, or local government may pass any law that prevents the publication of newspapers.

What would be the main benefit of adopting this amendment?

Ⓐ People would have better information to make informed decisions.
Ⓑ Newspapers would become more profitable businesses.
Ⓒ Journalists would earn more money for the stories they write.
Ⓓ Newspapers would become more powerful than the government.

Name _Anya Brown_   Date _4/9/15_

UNIT 4

ECONOMICS

*In this unit, you will learn about
money and how to budget it.*

*"Economics" is all around you, such as in
every place you or your parents shop.*

Economics is the study of how people choose to use resources. It also deals with how people make and spend money to meet their needs. In this unit, you will learn about the resources that are needed to make goods and to provide services. You will also learn why countries specialize in making some things and trade with other countries to obtain other things.

The following three topics will be examined in this unit:

1. **ECONOMIC DECISION MAKING AND SKILLS**

2. **PRODUCTION AND CONSUMPTION**

3. **FINANCIAL LITERACY**

Name _____ Date _____

ECONOMICS PRE-TEST

1 What money is left after a business pays its workers and all its bills?

- Ⓐ taxes
- Ⓑ profit
- Ⓒ debt
- Ⓓ supplies

2 A line graph is shown.

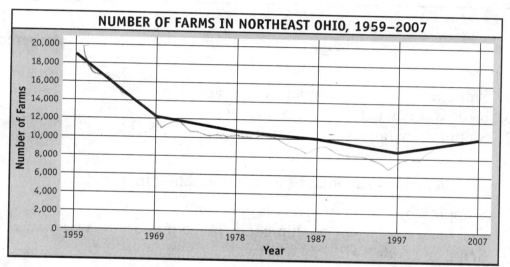

Source: USDA National Agricultural Statistics Service

Based on the line graph, in which time period did the number of farms in Northeast Ohio increase?

- Ⓐ 1959 to 1969
- Ⓑ 1969 to 1978
- Ⓒ 1978 to 1987
- Ⓓ 1997 to 2007

3 Based on this graph, which statement is accurate?

- Ⓐ The number of farms in Northeast Ohio has reached all time highs in the 21st century.
- Ⓑ The number of farms in Northeast Ohio has remained the same since 1959.
- Ⓒ The sizes of farms in Northeast Ohio are growing larger
- Ⓓ The number of farms in Northeast Ohio was almost the same in 1987 as it was in 2007.

4 A chart about transportation is shown.

METHODS OF TRANSPORTATION IN THE MID-1800s

Transportation Method	Average Speed Traveled	Costs of Shipping
Roads	2 miles per hour by wagon; 6–8 miles per hour by stagecoach	15 cents a ton for each mile
Canals	2 to 5 miles per hour	1.1 cents a ton for each mile
Railroads	10–20 miles per hour	3.4 cents a ton for each mile

Source: *The Transportation Revolution* by George R. Taylor

Based on the chart, what was one advantage of railroads compared to other methods of transportation in the mid-1800s?

Ⓐ Shipping goods by railroad was cheaper.
Ⓑ Railroads carried larger amounts of goods.
Ⓒ Shipping by railroad was much faster.
Ⓓ Railroads broke down less frequently.

5 Which statement is supported by the information in this chart?

Ⓐ Shipping by stagecoach was faster than by railroads.
Ⓑ The most costly way to ship goods in the mid-1800s was by canals.
Ⓒ Sending goods by canals was twice as expensive as by wagon.
Ⓓ Shipping goods by canal was the least expensive way to ship goods.

6 What type of resource is coal and iron ore when they are used to make goods?

Ⓐ Human resources
Ⓑ Natural resources
Ⓒ Labor resources
Ⓓ Capital resources

7 Entrepreneurs start a business for a variety of reasons. What is the primary reason for most entrepreneurs to start a new business?

Ⓐ To meet new people
Ⓑ To pass the time of day
Ⓒ To earn a profit
Ⓓ To purchase goods and services

Name _____ Date _____

8   A circle graph is shown.

The Jones family has decided to create a budget. They started by creating a circle graph that shows how each dollar of their money is currently spent.

On which item does the Jones family spend most of their money?

Ⓐ   Taxes
Ⓑ   Housing
Ⓒ   Food
Ⓓ   Transportation

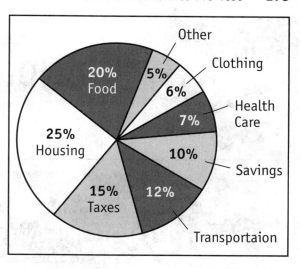

9   Three pictures are shown.

#1

#2

#3

Which of these pictures shows an item that is considered a capital good?

Ⓐ   Pictures #1 and #2
Ⓑ   Pictures #1 and #3
Ⓒ   Pictures #2 and #3
Ⓓ   Picture #3 only

10   What do natural resources and human resources have in common?

Ⓐ   They are both capital goods.
Ⓑ   They are both used to produce goods.
Ⓒ   They are both constantly rising in price.
Ⓓ   They are both examples of factory workers

END OF PRE-TEST IN ECONOMICS

CHAPTER 22

UNDERSTANDING DATA

TOPIC: ECONOMIC DECISION-MAKING AND SKILLS

Economic decision-making requires us to be able to think logically about key economic issues that affect our lives as consumers, producers, savers, investors and citizens. We need to be able to analyze costs and benefits, collect and organize economic evidence, and come up with alternatives to economic problems.

Economics 1	*Tables and charts help people to understand information and issues. Tables organize information in columns and rows. Charts organize information in a variety of visual formats (pictures, diagrams, graphs).*

After reading this chapter, you should be able to:

★ Define the following terms: • Table • Chart • Photograph • Circle graph	★ Explain how tables and charts help people to understand information and issues. ★ Interpret various forms of data, such as pictographs, diagrams, and circle graphs.

MAIN IDEAS OF THIS CONTENT STATEMENT

Economics explains how people make and spend money to meet their needs. Economists often present information in various formats, such as tables, charts, and graphs. These formats make this information easier to understand. "**Data**" (*information*) presented in this way also makes it easier to see a general pattern or trend. Lastly, it allows a large group of numbers to be presented in an organized manner.

TABLES AND CHARTS

In previous chapters, you have already learned about **tables** and **charts**. You learned that tables present information in columns and rows. The top row usually provides the titles of the columns. The column on the left usually identifies the rows.

THE AVERAGE INCOME OF OHIOANS, 2007–2012

Year	Average Income in Ohio (Per Person)
2007	$35,183
2008	$36,401
2009	$35,001
2010	$35,931
2011	$37,836
2012	$39,289

In this table, each row represents a different year. The right column shows the average income of a person in Ohio in that year.

Charts use a variety of formats to organize information. They may use pictures or photographs to illustrate a point. They may also use diagrams. As you learned in the previous unit, **diagrams** are drawings that show how something is organized or how it works. Arrows or lines often represent important relationships.

INTERPRETING PHOTOGRAPHS AND ILLUSTRATIONS

Photographs and **illustrations** can be especially useful in helping us to understand the past. They show how people looked, dressed and lived. A photograph or illustration can give us a "feeling" for an earlier time period. Since photographs only came into being in the mid-1800s, we often rely on drawings and paintings to get a glimpse of what life was like before that time.

Examine the two illustrations on the following page. They show two different types of homes from the same time period. Although these illustrations are from over 175 years ago, we can still learn a great deal from how some people lived in the South in the 1840s.

Louisiana Slave Quarters, 1840s

A Louisiana Plantation Home, 1842

What can you learn about the lifestyles of slaves and plantation owners by examining these illustrations?

_____

_____

_____

_____

_____

_____

TYPES OF GRAPHS

A **graph** presents numerical information in visual form. A **bar graph** shows numbers as bars. A **line graph** is made up of a series of points connected by a line. You should recall that you learned about these two types of graphs in an earlier chapter of this book. Another type of graph is a **circle graph** or pie chart.

INTERPRETING CIRCLE GRAPHS

SKILL BUILDER

A **circle graph** is a circle divided into sections of different sizes. Circle graphs are used to show relationships between a whole and its parts. The entire circle represents the whole. Circle graphs are often used to make generalizations and draw comparisons.

Source: *Historical Statistics of the United States*

The title of a circle graph identifies the information the graph presents. Here, the title indicates that these graphs show about trade between Britain and her colonies in 1770. The first circle shows goods shipped from Britain to the colonies. The second one shows goods shipped from the colonies to Britain. Each circle is divided into different slices. Each slice represents one of the three regions of the colonies.

The first graph shows which region British goods went to. The largest share of British goods went to the South. If you add the slices together, they will total 100% of the trade from Great Britain to its colonies.

LOCATING INFORMATION ON A CIRCLE GRAPH

To find specific information, you must examine each slice and see how it relates to the entire circle graph. For example, if you want to determine if the New England colonies shipped more goods to Britain than the Southern Colonies, you need to:

- Examine the second circle graph.

- Locate the slices that represent the New England and Southern Colonies. Then, compare these two slices.

- You should be able to see that 11% of the goods shipped to Britain came from New England, while 67% came from the Southern Colonies.

- Therefore, more goods were shipped to Britain from the Southern Colonies than from New England.

CONTENT-AREA VOCABULARY

Directions. Categorize the terms and phrases by moving or writing each one in one of the columns below. Some of the terms may be used more than once.

TERMS AND PHRASES

Columns	Rows	Horizontal axis
Percents	Lines	Bars
Circles	Diagrams	Vertical axis
Slices	Legend	Title

Tables	Charts	Line and Bar Graphs	Circle Graphs

Name _____ Date _____

STUDY CARDS

The Benefits of Using Graphs

1. What is a graph? _____
_____

2. What are three different types of graphs? _____
_____
_____

3. How does showing information in different formats help us to understand it better?
_____
_____
_____
_____

Circle Graphs

1. What is a circle graph? _____
_____

2. What are the main parts of a circle graph? _____
_____
_____

3. How is a circle graph a useful way to show information?
_____
_____
_____
_____

STUDY CARD PROMPTS

The Benefits of Using Graphs

1. **What is a graphs?**

2. **What are three different types of graphs?**

3. **How does showing information in different formats help us to understand it better?**

To check your answers to these questions, turn the card over and review the information you have written on the other side.

Circle Graphs

1. **What is a circle graph?**

2. **What are the main parts of a circle graph?**

3. **How is a circle graph a useful way to show information?**

To check your answers to these questions, turn the card over and review the information you have written on the other side.

PERFORMANCE-BASED ASSESSMENT QUESTIONS

1 Each year John F. Kennedy Elementary School receives money to run its educational program. This year the school's budget included an extra $10,000. The school board now must decide how this additional money is to be spent.

Part A.

A community newspaper conducted an opinion poll to see how local residents felt the additional $10,000 should be spent. To the right are the results of that opinion poll.

How did most community residents want the money to be spent? Write your answer on the line below.

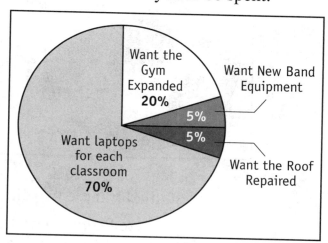

_____

Part B.

The following budget was finally approved by the school board.

Budget	Cost
Purchase a new computer lab	$4,000
Enlarge the gymnasium	$6,000

Which items did the school board *reject* spending money on that some members of the community favored? Write your answers on the lines below.

A. _____

_____

_____

B. _____

_____

_____

END-OF-YEAR ASSESSMENT QUESTIONS

2   Two circle graphs are shown.

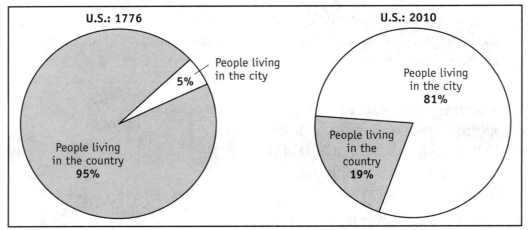

Source: U.S. Bureau of the Census

What is the best title for these two circle graphs?

Ⓐ   Comparing Where People Once Lived in the United States
Ⓑ   Comparing Types of Communities in the United States
Ⓒ   Where People Lived in the U.S. in 1776
Ⓓ   Where People Once Lived in the U.S. in 1776 and 2010

3   Based on the information in these two circle graphs, which statement can made about changes in where people live since 1776?

Ⓐ   Today, Americans still live mostly in country areas.
Ⓑ   The Urban Population of the United State has remained the same since 1776.
Ⓒ   Since 1776, Americans have been moving from the country into cities.
Ⓓ   In 1776, more people lived in cities than they do today.

4   Based on the information in the graphs, what conclusion can be reached?

Ⓐ   The current trend now shows that most people prefer living in cities.
Ⓑ   Where people live has changed little since 1776.
Ⓒ   Most people prefer living in the country.
Ⓓ   The current trend shows people are leaving cities for the countryside.

Name _____ Date _____

5   A pictograph of Ohio's population is shown.

THE POPULATION OF OHIO, 1900–2013

Each 👤 = 1 million people

Source: U.S. Bureau of the Census

What does each symbol on the pictograph represent?

Ⓐ   Ohio's current population
Ⓑ   100,000 people
Ⓒ   1 million people
Ⓓ   it cannot be determined

6   Since 1900, Ohio's population has changed. During which period did the population change the most?

Ⓐ   From 1900 to 1920
Ⓑ   From 1940 to 1960
Ⓒ   From 1960 to 1980
Ⓓ   From 2000 to 2013

7   Based on the pictograph, which statement is most accurate?

Ⓐ   Ohio's population has remained constant since 1900.
Ⓑ   The state's population has increased in every time period.
Ⓒ   More people are moving to Ohio than ever before.
Ⓓ   Ohio's population is lower now than in 1900.

8 A pictograph of Ohio's trade with foreign countries is shown.

SALES OF GOODS FROM OHIO TO FOREIGN COUNTRIES, 2013	
Canada	🚢🚢🚢🚢🚢🚢🚢🚢🚢🚢 🚢🚢🚢🚢🚢🚢🚢🚢🚢🚢
Mexico	🚢🚢🚢🚢🚢
China	🚢🚢🚢🚢
France	🚢🚢
United Kingdom	🚢🚢

Each 🚢 = $1 Billion

Source: *State of Ohio International Trade Division, Annual Report*

Based on the pictograph, what is the value of one 🚢?

- Ⓐ $1 Billion
- Ⓑ $3 Billion
- Ⓒ $5 Billion
- Ⓓ It cannot be determined

9 Based on the pictograph, what is the value of goods sent from Ohio to Mexico in 2013?

- Ⓐ $2.1 Billion
- Ⓑ $3.4 Billion
- Ⓒ $5.1 Billion
- Ⓓ $21 Billion

10 Based on the pictograph, which of these countries traded the least with Ohio in 2013?

- Ⓐ Mexico
- Ⓑ China
- Ⓒ France
- Ⓓ United Kingdom

11 What statement is most accurate from this pictograph?

- Ⓐ Ohio does not sell goods to foreign nations.
- Ⓑ Ohio mainly sells agricultural crops.
- Ⓒ Goods sold to foreign nations by Ohio is slowing.
- Ⓓ Canada is Ohio's best trading partner.

Name _____ Date _____

CHAPTER 23

ENTREPRENEURS: TAKING RISKS AND MAKING PROFITS

TOPIC: PRODUCTION AND CONSUMPTION

Production is the act of combining natural resources, human resources, capital goods, and entrepreneurship to make goods and services. Consumption is the use of goods and services.

Economics 2	*Entrepreneurs in Ohio and the United States organize productive resources and take risks to make a profit and compete with other producers.*

After reading this chapter, you should be able to:

★ Define the following terms: • Free market economy • Entrepreneurs • Profit • Productive resources • Human resources • Capital goods	★ Describe how entrepreneurs in Ohio and the United States organize productive resources. ★ Explain why entrepreneurs are willing to risk their money and compete with other producers.

MAIN IDEAS OF THIS CONTENT STATEMENT

The United States has a **free market economy**. That means that people can invest their money as they like. To **invest** is to put money into something in the hope of getting more money back later.

People who decide to invest their money in their own businesses are known as **entrepreneurs**. Entrepreneurs are people who invest their time and money in a business to make a profit. A **profit** is the amount of money that a business earns after it pays all of its expenses.

In order to make a profit, an entrepreneur must identify a need. The entrepreneur must then provide a **good** or **service** that meets that need, and which consumers are willing to buy.

An entrepreneur must organize various productive resources in order to make any good or service. **Productive resources** are all the things that go into making a good or service. They include natural resources, human resources, and capital goods.

Cotton is a raw material needed to make thread and clothing.

- **Natural resources** are resources that are found in nature, such as metals, water, plants and soil. Cotton, for example, is a plant. Farmers grow cotton, which they sell to factories making cotton thread and cloth. Raw cotton is the main natural resource needed to make cotton cloth. Natural resources used to make goods, such as raw cotton, are also known as **raw materials**.

- **Human resources** refer to the human labor that goes into making a good or providing a service. Examples would include a factory workers, a farmer who harvests his crop, or a cook in a restaurant. Skilled workers add value to raw materials by putting them together or processing them in order to make a product that is useful to consumers. An engineer might design a factory for turning raw cotton into cotton cloth. Skilled workers help to bring the raw cotton into the factory and oversee the production of the cotton cloth.

- **Capital goods** refer to the tools, equipment, and machines needed to produce other goods and services. Examples of capital goods include hammers, computers, and delivery vans. A factory that can turn raw cotton into cotton cloth is an example of a capital good. The roads and other facilities that help to produce and ship goods like cotton cloth are also capital goods.

A factory with machines that turn raw cotton into cotton cloth.

An entrepreneur is the person who brings these different productive resources together. The entrepreneur then sets the price of the finished good above what it costs to produce it in order to make a profit. However, the entrepreneur also competes with other producers.

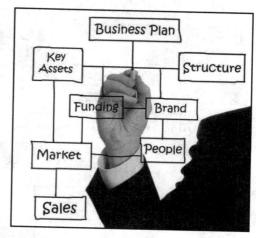

Consumers will usually buy the least expensive good or service if it is of the same quality. If an entrepreneur makes his or her goods or services too expensive, consumers will not buy them. Then the entrepreneur will go out of business. So, the entrepreneur must keep prices low enough to compete with other producers, but high enough to make a profit.

Since there is a chance the entrepreneur will not make a profit, or will lose money, economists say that the entrepreneur is taking a **risk**.

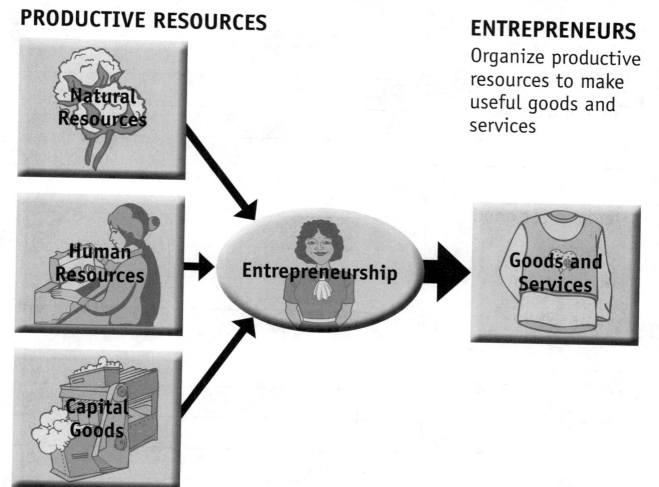

PRODUCTIVE RESOURCES

Natural Resources

Human Resources

Capital Goods

Entrepreneurship

ENTREPRENEURS
Organize productive resources to make useful goods and services

Goods and Services

CONTENT-AREA VOCABULARY

Directions. Which phrase or term does *not* belong with the other names and terms in the same box? Write your answer on the lines to the right of the box. Then use the same name or term in a sentence.

Human resources
Profits
Natural resources
Capital goods

_____

_____

_____

_____

Entrepreneur
Profit
Consumption
Risk

_____

_____

_____

_____

Demand for goods
Consumer
Consumption
Capital goods

_____

_____

_____

_____

Free market system
Entrepreneur
Natural resources
Profit

_____

_____

_____

_____

Name _____ Date _____

STUDY CARDS

Free Market Economy

1. What role does an entrepreneur play in a free market economy?

_____

_____

_____

_____

2. Why are entrepreneurs willing to risk their money?

_____

_____

_____

3. What can happen to an entrepreneur who fails to make a profit?

_____

_____

_____

Productive Resources

List three types of productive resources and provide an example of each.

1. _____

_____

Example: _____

2. _____

_____

Example: _____

3. _____

_____

Example: _____

STUDY CARD PROMPTS

Free Market Economy

1. **What role does an entrepreneur play in a free market economy?**

2. **Why are entrepreneurs willing to risk their money?**

3. **What can happen to an entrepreneur who fails to make a profit?**

To check your answers to these questions, turn the card over and review the information you have written on the other side.

Productive Resources

List three types of productive resources and provide an example of each.

1.

   Example:

2.

   Example:

3.

   Example:

To check your answers to these questions, turn the card over and review the information you have written on the other side.

PERFORMANCE-BASED ASSESSMENT QUESTIONS

> **ACCORDING TO THE OHIO DEPARTMENT OF EDUCATION, THERE WILL BE NO PERFORMANCE-BASED ASSESSMENT QUESTIONS ON THIS LEARNING STANDARD.**

END-OF-YEAR ASSESSMENT QUESTIONS

10 Three pictures are shown.

A

B

C

Which of these pictures show a person providing a good?

Ⓐ Pictures A and B
Ⓑ Pictures A, B, and C
Ⓒ Picture A only
Ⓓ Pictures B and C

11 Three examples are shown.

> ● Iron in the production of automobiles
> ● Aluminum in the production of coffee cans
> ● Rubber in the production of automobile tires

Which type of productive resource is illustrated by these examples?

Ⓐ natural resources
Ⓑ capital goods
Ⓒ human resources
Ⓓ entrepreneurship

12 Which is an example of a natural resource?

Ⓐ television
Ⓑ camera
Ⓒ coal
Ⓓ automobile

13 Which person helps to provide a good rather than a service?

Ⓐ teacher
Ⓑ mechanic
Ⓒ farmer
Ⓓ waitress

14 What are productive resources?

Ⓐ Things used to make goods and services
Ⓑ How people spend their earnings
Ⓒ Ways in which society creates jobs
Ⓓ Ways in which the government gets money

15 A person invests money to build a house, hoping that it will sell and provide a profit when it is finished. What is this person called?

Ⓐ a government official
Ⓑ an entrepreneur
Ⓒ a factory worker
Ⓓ an employee

16 Each of the statements below describes a characteristic of an entrepreneur. Some of these characteristics are inaccurate. Rewrite or draw a line from the statement to the correct column in the chart.

ACCURATE STATEMENT ABOUT AN ENTREPRENEUR	INACCURATE STATEMENT ABOUT AN ENTREPRENEUR

A person who starts a business and is responsible for its success or failure	A person who organizes workers to demand higher wages for fellow employees.	A person who can be dismissed by the boss or manager at the work place.
A person who works in a factory and is paid a wage.	A person who is willing to take risks.	A person who hopes to make a profit.

17 What are coal, water, and soil examples of?

Ⓐ natural resources
Ⓑ capital goods
Ⓒ human resources
Ⓓ entrepreneurship

18 Which of the following is an example of an entrepreneur?

Ⓐ a typist working in an office
Ⓑ an owner of a dry-cleaning store
Ⓒ a worker in a shoe factory
Ⓓ a model showing a designer's dress

19 Why are capital goods considered an important productive resource?

Ⓐ They allow workers to produce more goods.
Ⓑ They permit the government to control what products are made.
Ⓒ They always allow workers to share their labor.
Ⓓ They are provided to entrepreneurs for free.

20 A picture of six different workers is shown.

fireman   hairdresser   postman   teacher   waitress

Which conclusion can be drawn from this illustration?

Ⓐ Most workers have similar working hours.
Ⓑ Most workers perform similar tasks.
Ⓒ Workers in service jobs perform a variety of different tasks.
Ⓓ Service industry jobs pay less than factory jobs.

21 Each of the examples below identifies a productive resource. Rewrite or draw a line from each resource to the correct column in the chart showing its type.

NATURAL RESOURCE	HUMAN RESOURCE	CAPITAL GOODS

Aluminum	A carpenter	Coal
A hammer	A backhoe	An electrician
Nails	A plumber	Iron ore

Name _____ Date _____

CHAPTER 24

ACHIEVING FINANCIAL WELL-BEING

TOPIC: FINANCIAL LITERACY

"Financial literacy" is the knowledge and skills individuals need to manage limited financial resources effectively for a lifetime of financial security.

> **Economics 3** *Saving a portion of income contributes to an individual's financial well-being. Individuals can reduce spending to save more of their income.*

After reading this chapter, you should be able to:

★ Define the following terms: • Financial literacy • Financial well-being • Income • Budget • Saving	★ Explain how saving a part of your income can contribute to your financial well-being. ★ Show how an individual's reduction in spending can lead to money being saved.

MAIN IDEAS OF THIS CONTENT STATEMENT

Most Americans work for a living. They receive income from their work. **Income** is money a person or business receives for providing a good or service. Then they **spend** or payout their income to meet expenses. They buy food and clothes, pay taxes, and pay rent or make mortgage payments. They also pay for health insurance, life insurance, entertainment and vacations. All of this spending on goods and services is paid for out of their incomes.

When individuals can also put some of their income aside, this contributes to their financial well-being and security. **Financial well-being** means having enough money to meet one's needs, including extra money for emergencies, unexpected expenses, and future retirement. Money that is **saved**, income that is not spent, can also be invested. **Investing** is using money in the hope it will increase in the future.

A Budget. To save more of their income, individuals and families must often reduce their spending. To reduce spending, it often helps to have a budget. A **budget** is an estimate of the money that will be earned and spent by a person or business. Think of a budget as a financial plan. A budget helps a person or group to decide what to

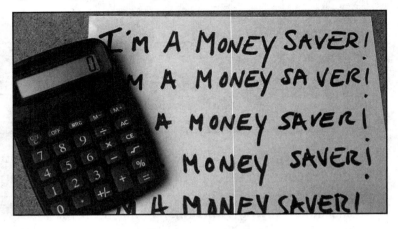

spend money on. A budget may also reveal that less money should be spent on some things in order to spend more on others.

Goal of a Budget. The goal of any budget is to have your income be equal to or greater than your expenses. To make your own budget, you must calculate all the money you expect to receive in a given time period, such as a month. Then you must estimate all the expenses you will need to pay in that same period. What is left over can be saved. By reviewing your expenses, you can often see some expenses that are unnecessary or that can be reduced. By reducing your spending, you can save more of your income.

THE BENEFITS OF SAVING

Why should you save your money? There are a number of good reasons for not spending everything you earn. Most people think it's a good idea to put some money aside for a "rainy day" — some future emergency or special need. Saving is also helpful when you wish to buy an expensive item. Saving money regularly is the simplest way to pay for costly goods. People who save their money make a short-term sacrifice by not spending.

It can be difficult to save money. Saving money teaches you to be disciplined in your financial affairs. The simplest way to save money is to reduce the amount of money you spend. By finding ways to lower your everyday spending, you will learn to build positive financial habits that will help you in the future.

STUDY CARDS

Financial Well-Being

1. **What is "financial well-being?"** _____

_____

_____

_____

2. **What is a budget?** _____

_____

_____

3. **What is the goal of most budgets?** _____

_____

_____

The Benefits of Saving

List three benefits a person enjoys from saving money.

1. _____

_____

_____

2. _____

_____

_____

3. _____

_____

_____

STUDY CARD PROMPTS

Financial Well-Being

1. **What is "financial well-being?"**

2. **What is a budget?**

3. **What is the goal of most budgets?**

To check your answers to these questions, turn the card over and review the information you have written on the other side.

The Benefits of Saving

List three benefits a person enjoys from saving money.

1.

2.

3.

To check your answers to these questions, turn the card over and review the information you have written on the other side.

Name _____ Date _____

CONTENT-AREA VOCABULARY

Directions. Write a sentence on the lines provided for each term and phrase below.

Income	Spending	Investment
Budget	Savings	Financial well-being

1. _____

2. _____

3. _____

4. _____

5. _____

6. _____

Directions. Now find a sentence in the chapter that defines each of the same terms. Write it below and the page on which the sentence appears.

Sentence from the Chapter	Page
1.	
2.	
3.	
4.	
5.	
6.	

PERFORMANCE–BASED ASSESSMENT QUESTIONS

ACCORDING TO THE OHIO DEPARTMENT OF EDUCATION, THERE WILL BE NO PERFORMANCE-BASED ASSESSMENT QUESTIONS ON THIS LEARNING STANDARD.

END–OF–YEAR ASSESSMENT QUESTIONS

22 A concept map is shown.

It is a good idea to put aside money for a future emergency.	It is a smart idea to put aside money if you wish to buy an expensive item.	It is a short-term sacrifice for most people to not spend all their money.

What concept should replace the question mark in the oval? Write your answer in the space below.

23 Why is it useful for people to prepare a budget?

   Ⓐ People usually enjoy creating columns with numbers.

   Ⓑ People are anxious to go shopping and spend their money.

   Ⓒ People can review expenses to find which ones are unnecessary.

   Ⓓ People do not want others to know how they are spending their money.

ECONOMICS UNIT TEST

1   A pictograph of the populations of the British colonies in 1730 is shown.

COLONIAL POPULATIONS, 1730*

Massachusetts	🧍 🧍 🧍 🧍 🧍 🧍 🧍 🧍 🧍 🧍 🧍 ▪	New Jersey	🧍 🧍 🧍 🧍
Virginia	🧍 🧍 🧍 🧍 🧍 🧍 🧍 🧍 🧍 🧍 🧍 ▪	North Carolina	🧍 🧍 🧍
Maryland	🧍 🧍 🧍 🧍 🧍 🧍 🧍 🧍 •	South Carolina	🧍 🧍 🧍
Connecticut	🧍 🧍 🧍 🧍 🧍 🧍 ▪	Rhode Island	🧍 🧍
Pennsylvania	🧍 🧍 🧍 🧍 🧍	New Hampshire	🧍 •
New York	🧍 🧍 🧍 🧍 🧍	Delaware	🧍

Key: 🧍 = 10,000 persons   🧍 = 8,000 persons   🧍 = 6,000 persons   ▪ = 4,000 persons   • = 2,000 persons   *Georgia not yet founded

Source: *Historical Statistics of the United States*

What does the 🧍 symbol in the pictograph represent?

Ⓐ 10,000 persons
Ⓑ 8,000 persons
Ⓒ 6,000 persons
Ⓓ 4,000 persons

2   Which conclusion about the British colonies in 1730 can be drawn from this pictograph?

Ⓐ The four most heavily populated colonies were in the South.
Ⓑ Large differences in population existed between the colonies.
Ⓒ The first colony established in America was Massachusetts.
Ⓓ Colonial populations grew slowly after 1730.

3   Which best describes the role of an entrepreneur in producing goods?

Ⓐ The entrepreneur organizes productive resources to make goods.
Ⓑ The entrepreneur buys whatever is produced.
Ⓒ The entrepreneur works in a factory making goods.
Ⓓ The entrepreneur sells the natural resources needed to make goods.

4   A bar graph of imports to the 13 colonies is shown.

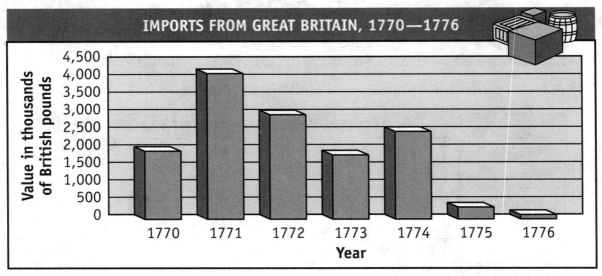

Source: *Historical Statistics of the United States*

What was the value, in British pounds, of imports to the colones from Great Britain in 1771?

Ⓐ   Less than 4,000 British pounds
Ⓑ   Just over 4,000 British pounds
Ⓒ   Just over 3 million British pounds
Ⓓ   Just over 4 million British pounds

5   Which conclusion about British imports can be drawn from this graph?

Ⓐ   Trade with Great Britain decreased sharply after 1774.
Ⓑ   Trade with Great Britain changed little year to year.
Ⓒ   Most imports from Great Britain were for manufactured products.
Ⓓ   The American colonies were Great Britain's best trading partners.

6   Which information can be found in this graph?

Ⓐ   The amount of goods sent to Great Britain from the British colonies, 1770 to 1776.
Ⓑ   The value of goods from Great Britain to the British colonies in U.S. dollars.
Ⓒ   The value of goods from Great Britain to the British colonies, 1770 to 1776.
Ⓓ   The total value of goods sent to the British colonies from countries in Europe, 1770 to 1776.

7 A picture of logs is shown.

Which productive resource is illustrated by this picture?

Ⓐ   a natural resource
Ⓑ   a capital good
Ⓒ   a human resources
Ⓓ   an entrepreneur

8 What is the main objective of an individual who creates a budget?

Ⓐ   to monitor spending so it is equal to or less than income
Ⓑ   to estimate all of your expenses on a daily basis
Ⓒ   to spend more money than you are earning
Ⓓ   to ensure that one has enough money for an expensive item

9 Which action can help an individual achieve financial well-being?

Ⓐ   Using up all of ones's money in order to start fresh.
Ⓑ   Thinking about how much one has and reducing expenses.
Ⓒ   Giving up a low-paying job to collect unemployment insurance.
Ⓓ   Spending money instead of saving it.

10 What is the main goal of an entrepreneur?

Ⓐ   to hire different kinds of people
Ⓑ   to make a profit
Ⓒ   to sell products more expensively than other business
Ⓓ   to spend more money than they take in

11 A concept map is shown.

In the space below, write the term that belongs in place of the question mark in the oval.

_____

12 Each box below describes a type of person. Rewrite or draw a line from each statement to the correct column in the chart.

AN ENTREPRENEUR	NOT AN ENTREPRENEUR

A person who works and must be paid overtime.

A person who can be fired for doing something wrong.

A person who starts a business in order to make a profit.

A person who works at a machine in a factory for wages.

A person who starts a business and runs it.

A person who sees an opportunity and makes a plan.

13 An outline is shown.

> I. Productive Resources
>   A. Natural Resources
>
>   B. _____
>   C. Human Resources
>   D. Entrepreneurship

Which type of productive resource is missing from the outline?

Ⓐ Capital Goods
Ⓑ Profits and Resources
Ⓒ Production Goals
Ⓓ Consumer Demands

14 How can the term "financial well-being" best be defined?

Ⓐ Investing money in stocks and bonds.
Ⓑ Having enough money to meet one's needs, including emergencies.
Ⓒ Spending more money each week than you earn.
Ⓓ Opening a bank account to put away money for gifts.

15 Which statement about the free market system is the most accurate?

Ⓐ It is the money left over after a business pays all its expenses.
Ⓑ It guarantees every business that it will make a profit.
Ⓒ It gives anyone with resources the freedom to create his or her own business.
Ⓓ It is the productive resources that go into making a product.

16 What would a discussion on natural resources, human resources, and capital goods most likely be about?

Ⓐ consumer spending
Ⓑ producing goods and services
Ⓒ factory workers
Ⓓ making a budget

17 Three descriptions are shown.

A person who starts a business and is responsible for its success or failure.	A person who is determined to make a profit.	A person who is willing to take risks and to organize resources.

What is the person called who displays all three of these characteristics?

Ⓐ a laborer
Ⓑ an entrepreneur
Ⓒ a worker
Ⓓ an employee

18 What phrase best describes the knowledge and skills individuals need to manage their monetary resources for a lifetime of financial security? Write your answer in the space below.

A PRACTICE GRADE 4
TEST IN SOCIAL STUDIES

This chapter consists of a complete practice test in two parts. This practice test should be taken on two different days. On one day, you should take the Performance-Based Assessment (PBA). On a different day, take the End-of-Year Test (EOY).

Before you take these practice tests, let's review a few test-taking hints.

★ **Answer All the Questions.** These tests have a variety of different questions. Try your best not to leave any questions unanswered. There is no penalty for guessing. A blank answer is always counted as wrong.

★ **Read Each Question Carefully.** Be sure you are aware of what the question asks. Make sure you understand each question fully before you answer it.

★ **Use the Process of Elimination.** When answering a multiple-choice question, some choices are obviously wrong. They are irrelevant, lack a connection to the question, or are inaccurate. First, try to eliminate any obviously wrong choices. Then, select the best choice that remains. Often your first guess is correct.

★ **Revisit Difficult Questions.** If you come across a difficult question, do not be discouraged. Circle the number or put a check mark (✓) next to any question you are not sure how to answer. Answer these questions as best you can. Then move to the next question. If time permits at the end of the test, go back and reread the questions you circled or checked. Sometimes an answer to a question might come to you after a second reading of the question.

★ **For Short-Answer and Constructive-Response Questions.** Make sure to answer all parts of the question. If time permits, re-read your answer and correct any errors.

★ **When You Finish.** If you finish, start to review your answers from the beginning. Be sure you answered all the questions. Don't disturb others.

Good luck on these practice tests!

Name _____ Date _____

PERFORMANCE-BASED ASSESSMENT

1 Laws are rules made by governments. Laws can protect rights, provide benefits and create responsibilities. Classify each of the laws below by placing it in its proper column.

You can rewrite the answers in the blank boxes of the chart, or indicate where the answers belong by drawing arrows.

PROTECTING RIGHTS	PROVIDING BENEFITS	CREATING RESPONSIBILITIES

Congress shall not limit free speech.	Retired persons shall receive social security payments.
A citizen receiving a jury summons must report to court.	18-year old males must register with Selective Service.
Workers must pay income taxes and file tax returns.	Citizens 18-years of age and older can vote in federal elections.

2   This question has two parts. First answer part A. Then answer part B.

LARGEST OHIO CITIES BY POPULATION

City	Population in 2010
Akron	199,110
Canton	73,007
Cleveland	396,815
Dayton	141,527
Cincinnati	296,943
Columbus	787,033
Parma	81,601
Toledo	287,208
Youngstown	66,982

Part A.

Based on the chart, which city in Ohio had the second largest population in 2010?

Write your answer in the space provided.

Part B.

Based on the chart, which two Ohio cities had populations between 100,000 and 200,000 in 2010?

Write your answers in the space provided

City 1:

City 2:

3   A map of Ohio is shown.

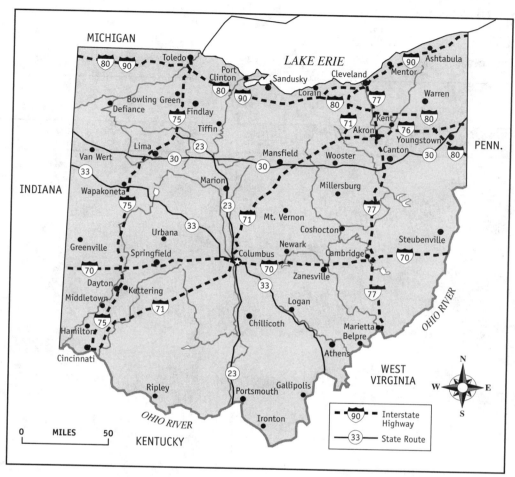

Using the map scale above, how many miles would someone have to travel on a trip from Columbus to Cambridge, and then from Cambridge to Cleveland?

Write your answers in the space provided.

- Columbus to Cambridge: _____ miles
- Cambridge to Cleveland: _____ miles

4 The United States was changed by the War of 1812. Complete the chart by selecting **two** effects of the War of 1812.

You can rewrite the answers in the blank boxes of the chart, or indicate where the answers belong by drawing arrows.

EFFECTS OF THE WAR OF 1812

Effect 1	Effect 2

New England increased its role as a manufacturing center.

Americans resisted British attempts to seize American sailors.

France lost its colonial empire in North America.

The British gained complete control of the Great Lakes.

5 People have modified their physical environment ever since prehistoric times. Complete the chart below by classifying the positive and negative effects of **two** ways of modifying the environment.

You can rewrite the answers in the blank boxes of the chart, or indicate where the answers belong by drawing arrows.

CONSEQUENCES OF MODIFYING THE ENVIRONMENT

Modification	Positive Consequences	Negative Consequences
Draining Wetlands		
Using Fertilizers and Pesticides		

Eliminates a natural filter that cleans fresh water.	Increases harmful chemicals that invade our foods.
Increases the land available for farming and other purposes.	Helps farmers to enrich the soil, kill insects, and grow more food.

6   The following question has two parts. First answer part A. Then answer part B.

BACKGROUND INFORMATION

The town of Smithfield has a budget surplus of $400,000. The town council is trying decide between two choices. They must decide whether to use this budget surplus money to build a skate park or to run an after-school program.

Skate Park

For $400,000, the town of Smithfield can build a concrete skate park of 10,000 square feet. This skate park would provide recreation for a town of 35,000 people. It is estimated that the skate park would last 10 years before there would be a need for any repairs or to re-surface the concrete. Without the skate park, residents of Smithfield will not have a safe place for youngsters to skate or skateboard.

After-School Program

The town of Smithfield could also open a community-run program at the local high school. The program would last two hours after school, and would operate from Monday to Friday. Such a program would provide for 50 students. The cost of the program would be $100,000 each year. For $400,000, Smithfield would be able to run the program for four years. Without such a program, these 50 students will have nowhere to go after school.

Part A.

Select how you believe Smithfield should spend its money. Check your selection below.

☐ Skate Park

☐ After-school program

Part B.

Explain how your selection in Part A is based on the information provided above. Write your answer on the lines provided.

_____

_____

_____

_____

_____

_____

Name _____ Date _____

7   The following question has two parts. First, answer part A. Then, answer part B.

Part A.

There are many ways that Ohioans are able to influence their state government.

Identify **one** way in which an individual citizen can influence Ohio's state government. Write your answer on the lines provided.

_____

_____

_____

_____

_____

_____

Part B.

Explain how the method that you identified in Part A influences government. Write your answer on the lines provided.

_____

_____

_____

_____

_____

_____

_____

_____

_____

_____

_____

8   The parents of Hamburger County are unhappy with conditions in the town's public schools. They have taken several actions that are protected by the First Amendment. Match each of the freedoms guaranteed by the First Amendment with the parents' action it protects.

You can rewrite the answers in the blank boxes of the chart, or indicate where the answers belong by drawing arrows.

FIRST AMENDMENT FREEDOMS

Freedom of Speech	
Freedom of the Press	
Right to Petition	
Freedom of Religion	
Freedom of Assembly	

PARENTS' ACTIONS

The parents hold a public meeting.

The parents criticize school officials in their public discussions.

The parents print a report in the community newspaper.

The parents want people to worship God in their own way outside of school.

The parents write school officials demanding that their children be given more homework.

9   The Woodlands Indians — the Fort Ancient, Hopewell and Adena peoples — lived in Ohio thousands of years ago. Members of these prehistoric Indian groups cooperated in various ways. One way they cooperated was by building mounds. Archaeologists (*people who study ancient cultures*) believe they built these mounds for different purposes. Some buried their dead under these mounds. Others built the mounds to hold religious ceremonies. Some of the mounds cover the remains of wooden buildings.

SOURCE 1

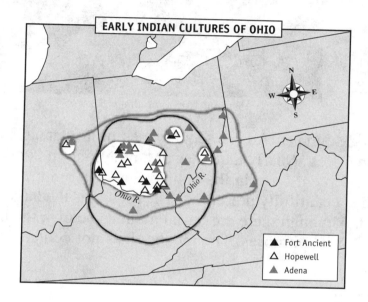

SOURCE 2

The Miamisburg Mound is located in the southeast part of the state. It is the largest cone-shaped earthwork in Ohio and possibly in the United States. The shapes of the mounds and the types of burials found here indicate that the Miamisburg Mound was the work of the Adena Indians. Once an ancient Indian burial ground, today it is the most well-known historical site in Miamisburg.

Miamisburg Mound

SOURCE 3

Serpant Mound in Adams County

The Serpent Mound in Adams County lies on a plateau overlooking the valley of Brush Creek. Nearly a quarter of a mile long, it is the largest example of an uncoiling serpent form in the United States. It stretches 1,348 feet over the ground, and is beautifully preserved. The mound is the largest mound of its kind in the world. Although there are burial mounds nearby, the mound was not constructed for burial purposes. The mound does not contain any human bones or remains.

SOURCE 4

Archaeologists dig for artifacts in a village of mound builders near Chillicothe.

Name _____ Date _____

The following question has two parts. First, answer part A. Then, answer part B.

Part A.

Using the sources above, explain **two** ways in which prehistoric Indian groups may have cooperated to build these mounds. Write your answer in the space provided.

_____

_____

_____

_____

_____

_____

_____

Part B.

Explain why European settlers and later Indian groups came into conflict. Write your answer in the space provided.

_____

_____

_____

_____

_____

_____

_____

_____

_____

_____

_____

END-OF-YEAR ASSESSMENT

Directions. For the multiple-choice questions, darken the circle next to the correct answer.

1 Which timeline shows events in the correct sequence?

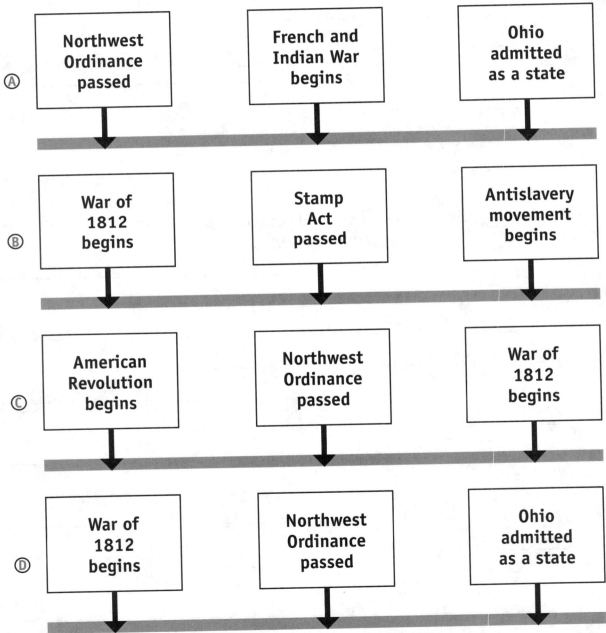

Ⓐ Northwest Ordinance passed → French and Indian War begins → Ohio admitted as a state

Ⓑ War of 1812 begins → Stamp Act passed → Antislavery movement begins

Ⓒ American Revolution begins → Northwest Ordinance passed → War of 1812 begins

Ⓓ War of 1812 begins → Northwest Ordinance passed → Ohio admitted as a state

2   The Smith family cannot decide what to do this weekend. Sam would like to have a family barbecue in their backyard. His sister, Shakira, wants the family to go out to dinner at their favorite restaurant.

Which action shows a compromise?

Ⓐ   They take a trip to their uncle's house since they cannot agree.
Ⓑ   They go to the restaurant because Shakira is older than Sam.
Ⓒ   They have a barbecue because Sam had better grades this month.
Ⓓ   They have a barbecue on Saturday and go to the restaurant on Sunday.

3   The names of two documents are shown.

Constitution of the State of Ohio

Constitution of the United States

In what way are these two documents similar?

Ⓐ   They both define the requirements for a high school diploma.
Ⓑ   They both grant the government the power to print money.
Ⓒ   They both establish a legislature known as Congress.
Ⓓ   They both divide government responsibilities among three branches.

4   Which of the following items is a primary source?

Ⓐ   a map showing where various Indian tribes once lived in Ohio
Ⓑ   a description of Ohio's Historic Indians in a recent textbook
Ⓒ   a diary of a pioneer who lived among the Shawnee Indians in 1790
Ⓓ   a painting by a modern artist showing how Ohio looked 200 years ago

5   Describe **two** negative consequences that come from the use of chemical fertilizers, herbicides or pesticides.

Write your answer in the space provided.

6   A table on the populations of the thirteen colonies is shown.

ESTIMATED AFRICAN-AMERICAN POPULATION IN THE THIRTEEN BRITISH COLONIES, 1690–1740

Year	New England Colonies	Middle Atlantic Colonies	Southern Colonies
1690	905	2,472	13,307
1700	1,680	5,361	22,476
1710	2,585	6,218	36,063
1720	3,956	10,825	54,058
1730	6,118	11,683	73,220
1740	8,541	16,452	125,031

Source: *Historical Statistics of the United States*

Which question can be answered from this table?

Ⓐ   Why did more slaves live in the Middle Atlantic than in New England?
Ⓑ   By 1720, were more slaves born in the colonies or in Africa?
Ⓒ   By 1740, how many colonial leaders opposed slavery?
Ⓓ   In which group of colonies was the African-American population largest?

7   An excerpt from the Northwest Ordinance is shown.

> **Article 6.** There shall be neither slavery nor involuntary servitude in the territory, otherwise than in the punishment of crimes where the person shall have been convicted …

Which democratic ideal is expressed in this excerpt?

Ⓐ   Right to personal liberty
Ⓑ   Right to employment
Ⓒ   Right to a free education
Ⓓ   Right to free land

8   Many Ohio innovations have benefited the United States. Which of these innovations was by a famous inventor born in Ohio?

Ⓐ   cotton gin
Ⓑ   steamship
Ⓒ   telegraph
Ⓓ   light bulb

9 In the early 1800s, each region of the United States had its own unique economic characteristics. Place each of the four characteristics in its region.

You can rewrite the answers in the blank boxes of the chart, or indicate where the answers belong by drawing arrows.

NORTH	SOUTH	WEST

Slaves did much of the work in this region.	This region's plantations grew cotton, rice, sugar and tobacco.
This region had the most cities, factories, and railroads.	This region sent timber and grain to distant cities.

10 Which action shows a duty of citizenship?

    Ⓐ Serve on a jury when called upon.
    Ⓑ Travel to a foreign country.
    Ⓒ Buy a home that is affordable.
    Ⓓ Take care of an elderly parent.

11 A bar graph of data is shown.

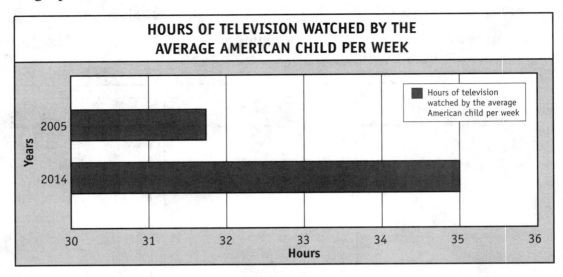

Which conclusion can be drawn from this graph?

Ⓐ The amount of television children watch is increasing.
Ⓑ The amount of television children watch has remained the same.
Ⓒ The amount of television children watch is decreasing.
Ⓓ The amount of television children watch now includes more educational programs.

12 A diagram of the branches of the federal government is shown.

BRANCHES OF THE FEDERAL GOVERNMENT

Legislative	Executive	Judicial
Senate House of Representatives	President	Supreme Court
		Lower Federal Courts

Which concept is illustrated by the information in this chart? Write your answer in the space provided.

13 Which two rights are guaranteed by the First Amendment?

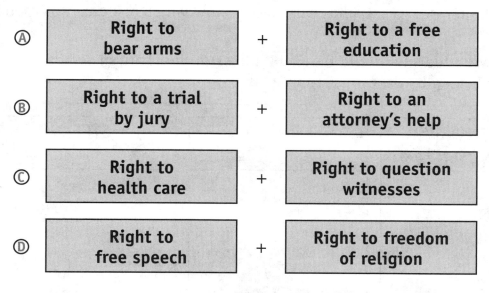

Ⓐ Right to bear arms + Right to a free education

Ⓑ Right to a trial by jury + Right to an attorney's help

Ⓒ Right to health care + Right to question witnesses

Ⓓ Right to free speech + Right to freedom of religion

14 What was the significance of the Battle of Fallen Timbers?

Ⓐ It encouraged French fur traders to return to Ohio.
Ⓑ It banned slavery throughout Ohio.
Ⓒ It opened Ohio to settlement by U.S. citizens.
Ⓓ It showed that American Indians could defeat the U.S. Army.

15 By 1775, why were so many colonists unhappy with British rule?

Ⓐ The British had taken the first steps towards ending slavery.
Ⓑ The British had been unable to win the French and Indian War.
Ⓒ The British had taxed the colonists without their consent.
Ⓓ The British had failed to develop much trade with the colonists.

16 What was the main result of the Battle of Lake Erie?

Ⓐ Americans gained control of the Great Lakes.
Ⓑ Americans were able to conquer Canada.
Ⓒ Americans lost the War of 1812 to Great Britain.
Ⓓ Americans defeated Tecumseh and the Shawnee Indians.

17 Which two bodies of water made Ohio's location important for national transportation in the early 1800s?

Ⓐ Mississippi River and the Gulf of Mexico
Ⓑ Ohio River and Lake Erie
Ⓒ Rio Grande and the Pacific Ocean
Ⓓ Hudson River and the Atlantic Ocean

18 In the mid-1800s, the growth of Ohio's industries was encourged by the state's plentiful natural resources. In the chart below, show which resource was used by each industry.

You can rewrite the answers in the blank boxes of the chart, or indicate where the answers belong by drawing arrows.

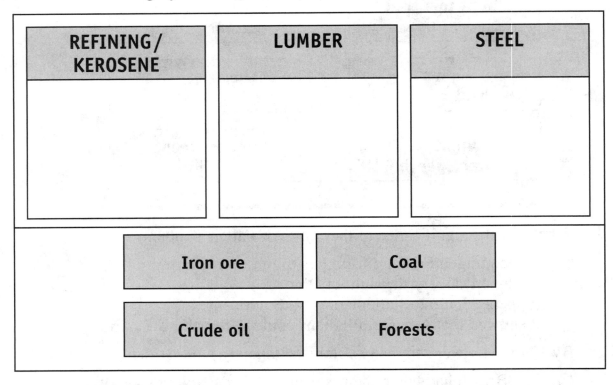

19 Which action was taken by abolitionists in Ohio in the decades before the Civil War?

Ⓐ They organized in opposition to the Stamp Act.
Ⓑ They declared American independence from Great Britain.
Ⓒ They helped slaves to escape along the Underground Railroad.
Ⓓ They called on Southern slaves to attack their owners.

20 Which branch of government decides if a law has been correctly applied to a specific situation?

Ⓐ executive branch
Ⓑ legislative branch
Ⓒ judicial branch
Ⓓ popular branch

21 A pair of circle graphs is shown.

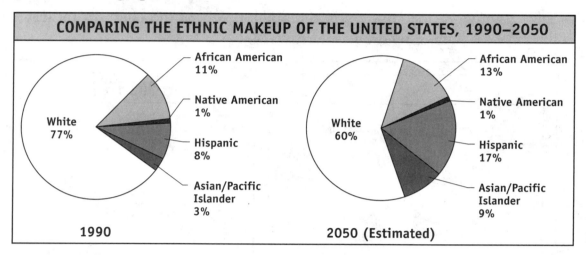

COMPARING THE ETHNIC MAKEUP OF THE UNITED STATES, 1990–2050

African American 11%
Native American 1%
White 77%
Hispanic 8%
Asian/Pacific Islander 3%
1990

African American 13%
Native American 1%
White 60%
Hispanic 17%
Asian/Pacific Islander 9%
2050 (Estimated)

Which conclusion can be drawn from these graphs?

Ⓐ   America is becoming more culturally diverse.

Ⓑ   America's Hispanic population is decreasing.

Ⓒ   America has fewer ethnic minorities now than in the past.

Ⓓ   American culture is not influenced by cultural diversity.

22 The steps necessary for a territory to become a state under the Northwest Ordinance of 1787 are listed in random order.

Arrange these steps in their correct sequence by placing a (1) (2) or (3) in the box under each statement.

When the territory's population reaches 60,000 people, the territory can apply for admission as a state.	A group of leaders will be appointed by Congress to govern the territory.	When the territory's population reaches 5,000 adults, citizens will elect representatives to govern them.
☐	☐	☐

23 Classify each of the statements below as a fact or an opinion.

You can rewrite the answers in the blank boxes of the chart, or indicate where the answers belong by drawing arrows.

FACTS	OPINIONS

Ohio is a great state for raising a family.	The next election for President will likely have a candidate from Ohio.
The Middle East poses the most serious threat to world peace.	The President of the United States lives in the White House.
The Bill of Rights consists of the first ten amendments.	American citizens have the right to vote when they reach 18 years old.

24 Which goal is an important aim of a democratic constitution?

Ⓐ to help the government collect more money
Ⓑ to protect an individual's right of expression
Ⓒ to help the country win foreign allies
Ⓓ to provide benefits to elected leaders

25 What is a constitution? Write your answer in the space provided.

26 A map of Ohio is shown.

OHIO'S MAJOR RIVERS AND CITIES

Based on the map, which phrase describes the relative location of Akron?

- Ⓐ North of Lake Erie and east of Youngstown
- Ⓑ Southeast of Cleveland and northwest of Canton
- Ⓒ Between Dayton and Columbus
- Ⓓ South of the Ohio River and southwest of Columbus

27 What is a positive consequence of building a dam?

- Ⓐ Dams act as natural sponges to absorb pollutants.
- Ⓑ Dams allow water to be stored for later use.
- Ⓒ Dams often require the flooding of some areas.
- Ⓓ Dams can sometimes lead to soil erosion.

28 Ohio has a law that requires citizens receiving a jury summons to appear in court. What is the main benefit provided by this law?

- Ⓐ People find temporary work as jurors.
- Ⓑ The courts are able to save money.
- Ⓒ Citizens have the right to a trial by jury
- Ⓓ Jurors sometimes learn about trials in the news.

29 A painting from the early 1800s is shown.

This painting shows slaves who have escaped from the South. They have made their way north guided by the North Star. They are being directed to a place where they can hide, rest, and be fed before traveling farther north to freedom.

What name was given to the network of secret routes and safe houses that helped these slaves to escape to freedom? Write your answer in the space provided.

---

30 Which person organizes resources to produce goods and make profits?

Ⓐ a laborer
Ⓑ an entrepreneur
Ⓒ a professional
Ⓓ an employee

31 One of the achievements of the Confederation Congress was passing the Northwest Ordinance in 1787. Below are four boxes with statements describing the Northwest Ordinance. Some of these statements are true. Others are false. Complete the chart by indicating in which column each statement belongs.

You can rewrite the answers in the blank boxes of the chart, or indicate where the answers belong by drawing arrows.

CHARACTERISTICS OF THE NORTHWEST ORDINANCE (1787)

True	False

It established three steps for a territory to become admitted as a new state.

New states would never receive all the same rights as the original thirteen states.

It abolished slavery throughout the Northwest Territory.

It was accompanied by a law that set aside a portion of the sale of land to establish schools.

It guaranteed freedom of religion and banned cruel punishments throughout the Northwest Territory.

It prohibited settlers from moving west of the Appalachian Mountains in order to protect Indian tribal rights.

32 The chart below shows some of the resources used by an entrepreneur to run a pizza shop. Complete the chart by classifying each resource by its type.

You can rewrite the answers in the blank boxes of the chart, or indicate where the answers belong by drawing arrows.

TYPES OF PRODUCTIVE RESOURCES

Natural Resources	Human Resources	Capital Goods

Wheat flour
(from ground wheat)

Fresh tomatoes
(to make tomato sauce)

Water

Hydroelectricity
(electricity made from rapidly moving water)

Pizza oven

Skilled workers
(that make and bake the pizza)

33 A map of the Northeastern United States is shown.

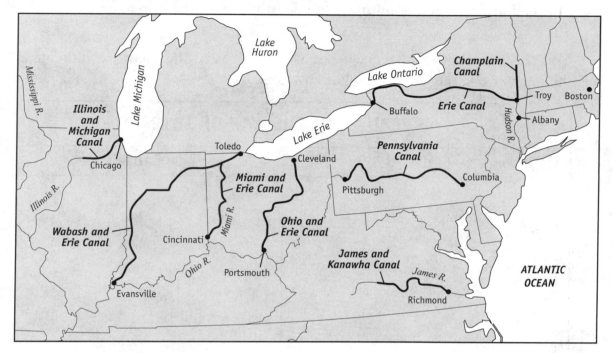

Why were the canals on this map so important to the nation?

Ⓐ They made it easier to reach California during the Gold Rush.
Ⓑ They provided the best escape routes for slaves.
Ⓒ They permitted farmers and manufacturers to ship goods more cheaply.
Ⓓ They helped to prevent the flooding of farmland during heavy rains.

---

34 How did Ohio's natural resources influence the economic development of the United States?

Ⓐ With its long growing season, Ohio became a major source of raw cotton for factories.
Ⓑ With its rich soil, Ohio became a major supplier of fruits and vegetables to Northeastern cities.
Ⓒ With its coal and iron ore resources, Ohio became a major center of heavy industry.
Ⓓ With its many forests, Ohio became a major center of shipbuilding.

35 In the War of 1812, Americans and British fought each other for the second time in less than 30 years. Complete the chart by selecting two causes of the War of 1812.

You can rewrite the answers in the blank boxes of the chart, or indicate where the answers belong by drawing arrows.

CAUSES OF THE WAR OF 1812

Cause 1	Cause 2

Sailors were being taken from American ships by the British navy.	Americans refused to pay taxes without representation in Parliament.
Britain and France both claimed ownership of the Ohio River Valley.	British officials were encouraging Indian tribes to attack settlers in Ohio.

36 The following question has two parts. First, answer part A. Then, answer part B.

Many constitutions begin with a special introduction. This introduction is known as a preamble. The authors of both the U.S. Constitution and the Ohio Constitution included a preamble.

The sources below are two examples of preambles.

SOURCE 1

Preamble to the Constitution of the United States of America, 1787
"We the people of the United States, in order to form a more perfect union,* establish justice, … provide for the common defense, promote the general welfare,* and secure the blessings of liberty* … do … establish this Constitution for the United States of America."

SOURCE 2

Preamble to the Constitution of the State of Ohio, 1851
"We, the people of the State of Ohio, grateful to Almighty God for our freedom, to secure its blessings and promote our common welfare,* do establish this Constitution."

* **To form a more perfect union** = to create a closer association of states than the one that existed
* **Promote the general welfare** = to contribute to the citizens' well-being and prosperity
* **Secure the blessings of liberty** = to protect and maintain personal freedom

Part A.
Which conclusion can be drawn from these sources?

Ⓐ   All constitutions have a preamble at the beginning.
Ⓑ   The U.S. and Ohio Constitutions have similar aims.
Ⓒ   All constitutions establish democratic governments.
Ⓓ   The U.S. and Ohio Constitutions are exactly the same.

Part B.

You have been asked to write a report on constitutions. Choose two main ideas that could be supported by the two sources on the previous page.

Write the answers in the blank boxes of the chart, or indicate where the answers belong by drawing arrows.

MAIN IDEA #1	MAIN IDEA #2

The U.S. and Ohio Constitutions both provide frameworks for government.	Some governments fail to follow the rules found in their own constitutions.
Most state constitutions are similar to Ohio's constitution.	The people are the final source of government power in both Ohio and the United States.

PERFORMANCE-BASED QUESTIONS

Number	Question Type	Points
1	Graphic Response	2
2	Short Consructed-Response	2
3	Short Constructed-Response	2
4	Graphic Response	2
5	Graphic Response	2
6	Short Constructed-Response	2
7	Short Constructed-Response	2
8	Graphic Response	2
9	Extended Constructed-Response	4

END-OF-YEAR QUESTIONS

Number	Question Type	Points
1	Multiple Choice	1
2	Multiple Choice	1
3	Multiple Choice	1
4	Multiple Choice	1
5	Short Answer	1
6	Multiple Choice	1
7	Multiple Choice	1
8	Multiple Choice	1
9	Graphic Response	2
10	Multiple Choice	1
11	Multiple Choice	1
12	Short Answer	1
13	Multiple Choice	1
14	Multiple Choice	1
15	Multiple Choice	1
16	Multiple Choice	1
17	Multiple Choice	1
18	Graphic Response	2
19	Multiple Choice	1
20	Multiple Choice	1
21	Multiple Choice	1
22	Graphic Response	2
23	Graphic Response	2
24	Multiple Choice	1
25	Short Answer	1
26	Multiple Choice	1
27	Multiple Choice	1
28	Multiple Choice	1
29	Short Answer	1
30	Multiple Choice	1
31	Graphic Response	2
32	Graphic Response	2
33	Multiple Choice	1
34	Multiple Choice	1
35	Graphic Response	2
36	Simulation	2

LABORATORY MANUAL
TO ACCOMPANY
PUNTOS
DE PARTIDA

LABORATORY MANUAL

TO ACCOMPANY

PUNTOS

DE PARTIDA

AN INVITATION TO SPANISH

María Sabló-Yates
Delta College

Listening Passages contributed by
Ana María Pérez-Gironés
Wesleyan University

THE McGRAW-HILL COMPANIES, INC.

New York St. Louis San Francisco Auckland Bogotá Caracas
Lisbon London Madrid Mexico City Milan Montreal New Delhi
San Juan Singapore Sydney Tokyo Toronto

5 EDITION

McGraw-Hill

A Division of The **McGraw·Hill** *Companies*

This is an EBI book

Laboratory Manual to accompany
Puntos de partida:
An Invitation to Spanish

4567890 BBC BBC 90032198

ISBN 0-07-038229-8

This book was set in Palatino on a Macintosh computer by Fog Press.
The editors were Thalia Dorwick, Scott Tinetti, and Kristin Swanson.
The production supervisor was Michelle Lyon.
Illustrations were by Wayne Clark, David Bohn, Axelle Fortier, Lori Heckelman,
Judith Macdonald, Stephanie O'Shaughnessy, Barbara Reinertson, Katherine
Tillotson, Stan Tusan, and Joe Veno.
This book was printed and bound by Braceland.

http://www.mhcollege.com

Contents

To the Student

The purpose of the tape program that accompanies *Puntos de partida* is to give you as much practice as possible in listening to and speaking, reading, and writing, and, above all, understanding the Spanish language in a variety of contexts. This edition of the Laboratory Manual contains a variety of exercises to help you accomplish that goal. To get the most out of the tape program, you should listen to the tapes after your instructor covers the corresponding material in class, and you should listen as often as possible. You will need the Laboratory Manual much of the time when you listen to the tapes, since many of the exercises are based on visuals, realia (real things—such as advertisements, classified ads, and so on—that you would encounter in a Spanish-speaking country), and written cues.

The tape program follows the format of chapters in the main text. Each chapter begins with a section (**Vocabulario: Preparación**) in which you can practice vocabulary in a variety of contexts. This preliminary vocabulary study is followed by pronunciation exercises (**Pronunciación y ortografía**). The minidialogues from the text are followed by exercises and activities on the grammatical concepts of the chapters (**Minidiálogos y gramática**), and by functional dialogue practice (**Situaciones**). Each chapter ends with a section that combines grammar points and vocabulary introduced in the chapter (**Un poco de todo: Para entregar**). This final section is to be handed in to your instructor for correction; no answers are provided on the tape or in the Answers appendix at the back of the manual. In addition, some exercises give you the option of answering in writing. Since writing the answers to these exercises is an option only, you should ask your instructor how she or he would prefer these to be handled.

You will find additional review sections (**Repasos**) after Chapters 3, 6, 9, 12, 15, and 18. Each **Repaso** contains a number of exercises labeled **Para entregar** that are to be handed in to your instructor. We have made an effort to reintroduce vocabulary and grammar from previous chapters in these review sections, and throughout the Laboratory Manual, so that you have the opportunity to use the grammatical structures and the vocabulary you have learned in a variety of contexts and situations.

The exercises and activities in most sections progress from controlled to more open-ended and personalized or interactive, to give you a chance to be more creative in Spanish while practicing the skills you have learned. With the exception of the **Para entregar** portions of the Laboratory Manual, the **Dictados,** and other writing-based activities, you will hear the answers to most exercises on the tape immediately after the item or at the end of a series of items. You will find the answers to most written exercises (except those called **Para entregar**) in the Answers appendix.

Although the tape program includes some material taken directly from *Puntos de partida*, it also contains many new exercises: surveys (**Encuestas**); dictations; personalized questions and interviews; visually based listening comprehension exercises; cultural listening passages, some based on survey questions answered by native speakers; activities based on realia; and brief interactive dialogues. Whenever possible, the exercises are presented in a context.

The following types of exercises are a regular feature of the *Puntos de partida* tape program and are found in most chapters.

- **Definiciones, Situaciones,** and **Asociaciones** use a multiple choice or matching format in order to test listening comprehension and vocabulary.
- **Identificaciones** and **Descripción,** as their names imply, will ask you to generate responses based on visuals, with or without written or oral cues. Although these are more controlled in nature, they are contextualized and related to the theme of the current or a previous chapter. You will find these types of exercises throughout the Laboratory Manual.
- **Encuestas** are personalized surveys in which you need only check an answer that is true for you. These surveys are offered for listening comprehension and are related to the theme of the chapter or to specific grammar points. You will find these at the beginning of both the vocabulary and the grammar sections.
- **Los hispanos hablan** is found after **Vocabulario: Preparación,** and presents comments from native speakers on a variety of topics: clothing, pastimes, favorite foods, and so on. Each section of **Los hispanos hablan** is tied to the theme and/or the vocabulary of the chapter in which it is

found. The passages offer listening comprehension that is based on cultural information. The follow-up activities include taking notes, evaluating true or false statements, making comparisons, completing charts, and answering questions.

- The **Minidiálogos** offer examples of real-life situations and often convey cultural information. Most of them are the same ones that appear in *Puntos de partida*. Although the text for the minidialogues does not appear in the Laboratory Manual (unless they are **Dictados**), the corresponding exercises generally do. The follow-up exercises include cloze dictations, true or false statements, summarizing statements, identifying the person who made a statement, inferring information from the dialogue, and writing information about the dialogue (in **¿Qué recuerdas?**). The minidialogues appear at the beginning of each grammar section.

- There are two types of question and answer sequences. The first will offer you an oral or written cue, and you will hear the correct answer on the tape after each item. **Entrevista** activities, in contrast, offer no cues or answers. The questions are more open-ended and personalized, and you will be able to stop the tape to write your answers. The **Entrevista** is a regular feature of the **Un poco de todo** section that is for handing in to your instructor.

- The **Situaciones** dialogues are taken from the textbook and video to accompany *Puntos de partida*. Like the minidialogues, they offer examples of real-life conversations and situations, as well as some cultural information. After they are read on tape, you will usually have the opportunity to participate in a similar conversation, interactive in nature, in which you use the cues that are provided. In some instances, you may have the option of writing your answers. You will always hear a correct answer on the tape. In earlier chapters, you will have the opportunity to repeat portions of the dialogue.

- **Conversación** is another type of interactive dialogue, and it is found in the **Repaso** sections. **Conversación** differs from the **Situaciones** follow-up exercises in that it is more open-ended and there are no cues given. The **Conversación** exercises are labeled **Para entregar**.

- Listening passages appear in the **Un poco de todo** section. These passages are cultural in nature and contain information on a variety of topics related to the Hispanic world. Their themes are related to the theme of each chapter. The passages are usually preceded by a section called **Antes de escuchar** in which you will practice listening strategies: guessing content, gisting, making inferences about the passage, and so on. Following each passage is a **Después de escuchar** section that offers a variety of comprehension or follow-up exercises.

- The Laboratory Manual also includes many types of dictations (**Dictados**) and other writing activities. You will be asked to listen for and write down specific information: letters, words, phrases, or entire sentences. In some instances, you will be asked to jot down notes about the content of brief passages. Answers are generally provided in the appendix.

Sound effects are used throughout the tape program, when appropriate. You will hear a variety of native speakers, so that you can get used to different accents and voice types found in the Spanish-speaking world, but no accent will be so pronounced as to be difficult for you to understand. In approximately the first third of the tape program, the speakers will speak at a slower rate. The rate of speech will increase gradually until it reaches natural or close to natural speed in the final third of the tape program.

Learning another language requires hard work and patience, as well as an open mind. We hope that the variety of exercises and the cultural information in the Laboratory Manual will provide a natural and stimulating context within which you will begin to communicate in Spanish!

We offer our sincere thanks to the following individuals: to Ana María Pérez-Gironés (Wesleyan University), who wrote the listening passages in **Un poco de todo**; to Manuela González-Bueno, who made many helpful suggestions for improving the **Pronunciación y ortografía** sections; to the Hispanic exchange students whose answers were the bases of the passages in the **Los hispanos hablan**; to William R. Glass (Pennsylvania State University), whose reading of previous editions of the manual provided welcome suggestions and advice; to Thalia Dorwick and Scott Tinetti, whose comments, suggestions, and superior editing made this Laboratory Manual and tape program possible; and to my family for their support and understanding throughout the writing process.

María Sabló-Yates

Primera parte

▼▼▼▼▼▼▼▼▼▼▼▼▼▼▼▼▼▼▼▼▼▼▼▼▼▼▼▼▼▼▼▼▼▼▼▼

Saludos y expresiones de cortesía

A. Diálogos. In the following dialogues, you will practice greeting others appropriately in Spanish. The dialogues will be read with pauses for repetition. After each dialogue, you will hear two summarizing statements. Circle the letter of the statement that best describes each dialogue. First, listen.

1. MANOLO: ¡Hola, Maricarmen!
    MARICARMEN: ¿Qué tal, Manolo? ¿Cómo estás?
    MANOLO: Muy bien. ¿Y tú?
    MARICARMEN: Regular. Nos vemos, ¿eh?
    MANOLO: Hasta mañana.

Comprensión: a.   b.

2. ELISA VELASCO: Buenas tardes, señor Gómez.
    MARTÍN GÓMEZ: Muy buenas, señora Velasco.
                  ¿Cómo está?
    ELISA VELASCO: Bien, gracias. ¿Y usted?
    MARTÍN GÓMEZ: Muy bien, gracias. Hasta luego
    ELISA VELASCO: Adiós.

Comprensión   a.   b.

3. LUPE: Buenos días, profesor.
    PROFESOR: Buenos días. ¿Cómo te llamas?
    LUPE: Me llamo Lupe Carrasco.
    PROFESOR: Mucho gusto, Lupe.
    LUPE: Igualmente

Comprensión: a.   b.

B. ¿Formal o informal? You will hear a series of expressions. Indicate whether each expression would be used in a formal or in an informal situation.

1. a.   formal   b.   informal
2. a.   formal   b.   informal
3. a.   formal   b.   informal
4. a.   formal   b.   informal

C. Situaciones

Paso 1. You will hear a series of questions or statements. Each will be said twice. Circle the letter of the best response or reaction to each.

1. a. Me llamo Ricardo Barrios.   b. Bien, gracias.
2. a. Encantada, Eduardo.   b. Muchas gracias, Eduardo.
3. a. Regular. ¿Y tú?   b. Mucho gusto, señorita Paz.
4. a. Con permiso, señor.   b. No hay de qué.
5. a. De nada, señora Colón.   b. Buenas noches, señora Colón.

Paso 2. Now, listen to the questions and statements again and read the correct answers in the pauses provided. You will hear each item only once. Be sure to repeat the correct answer after you hear it.

1. ...   2. ...   3. ...   4. ...   5. ...

D. ¿Qué dicen estas personas? (*What are these people saying*?) Circle the letter of the drawing that is best described by the sentences you hear. Each will be said twice.

1. a.   b.

2. a.   b.

3. a.   b.

4. a.   b.

Pronunciación y ortografía • El alfabeto español

A. El alfabeto español. You will hear the names of the letters of the Spanish alphabet, along with a list of place names. Listen and repeat, imitating the speaker. Notice that most Spanish consonants are pronounced differently than in English. In future chapters, you will have the opportunity to practice the pronunciation of most of these letters individually.

a	a	la Argentina	ñ	eñe	España
b	be	Bolivia	o	o	Oviedo
c	ce	Cáceres	p	pe	Panamá
d	de	Durango	q	cu	Quito
e	e	el Ecuador	r	ere	el Perú
f	efe	Florida	rr	erre	Monterrey
g	ge	Guatemala	s	ese	San Juan
h	hache	Honduras	t	te	Toledo
i	i	Ibiza	u	u	el Uruguay
j	jota	Jalisco	v	ve	Venezuela
k	ca	(*Kansas*)	w	doble ve	(*Washington*)
l	ele	Lima	x	equis	Extremadura
m	eme	México	y	i griega	el Paraguay
n	ene	Nicaragua	z	zeta	Zaragoza

B. Repeat the following words, phrases, and sentences. Imitate the speaker and pay close attention to the difference in pronunciation between Spanish and English.

1.	c/ch	Colón	Cecilia	Muchas gracias.	Buenas noches.
2.	g/gu	Geraldo	gusto	Miguel	guitarra
3.	h	la Habana	Héctor	hotel	historia
4.	j	Jamaica	Jiménez	José	Julio
5.	l/ll	Lupe	Manolo	Sevilla	me llamo
6.	y	Yolanda	yate	Paraguay	y
7.	r/rr	Mario	arte	Roberto	carro
8.	ñ	Begoña	Toño	señorita	Hasta mañana.

C. En el hotel. Imagine that you work as a hotel receptionist in Miami. Listen to how some Hispanic guests spell out their last names for you. Write down the names as you hear them.

1. _____   3. _____

2. _____   4. _____

Los cognados

A. Características. Repeat the following cognates, imitating the speaker.

1.	cruel	4.	liberal	7.	religiosa
2.	idealista	5.	terrible	8.	emocional
3.	flexible	6.	serio	9.	generoso

B. Dictado:* ¿Cómo son? (*What are they like?*) You will hear five sentences. Each will be said twice. Listen carefully and write the missing words.

1. Nicolás es _____.   4. Maite es muy _____.

2. La profesora Díaz es _____.   5. Íñigo no es _____.

3. Juan no es _____.

_____
*Answers to all **Dictado** exercises are given in the Appendix.

¿Cómo es usted?

A. Encuesta (*Survey*). You will hear a series of questions. For each question, check the appropriate answer. No answers will be given on the tape. The answers you choose should be correct for you!

1. ☐ Sí, soy independiente.
   ☐ No, no soy independiente.
2. ☐ Sí, soy impulsivo/a.
   ☐ No, no soy impulsivo/a.

3. ☐ Sí, soy eficiente.
   ☐ No, no soy eficiente.
4. ☐ Sí, soy materialista.
   ☐ No, no soy materialista.

B. Preguntas (*Questions*). Ask the following persons about their personalities, using **¿Eres... ?** or **¿Es usted... ?** as appropriate, and the cues you will hear. Follow the model. (Remember to repeat the correct question. If you prefer, stop the tape and write the questions.) You will hear answers to your questions.

MODELO: (*you see*) Marta (*you hear*) tímida →
(*you say*) Marta, ¿eres tímida? (*you hear*) Sí, soy tímida.

1. Ramón, _____.

2. Señora Alba, _____.

3. Señor Castán, _____.

4. Anita, _____.

Segunda parte

▼▼▼▼▼▼▼▼▼▼▼▼▼▼▼▼▼▼▼▼▼▼▼▼▼▼▼▼▼▼▼▼▼▼▼▼▼▼

Más cognados

A. Descripción. In this exercise, you will practice gisting, that is, getting the main idea—an important skill in language learning. Although some of the vocabulary you hear will not be familiar to you, concentrate on the words that you *do* know. After the exercise, stop the tape and choose the statement that best describes the passage.

1. ☐ This person is describing her country and the sports that are played there.
2. ☐ This person is describing herself, her studies, and her outside interests.

Now turn on the tape.

B. Categorías y asociaciones

Paso 1. You will hear a series of words. Check the category to which each belongs. In this exercise you will practice listening for specific information.

1. ☐ un instrumento musical
2. ☐ una nación
3. ☐ un lugar (*a place*)
4. ☐ un animal
5. ☐ una comida (*a food*)

☐ un concepto
☐ un concepto
☐ una cosa (*a thing*)
☐ una bebida (*a drink*)
☐ una persona

Paso 2. Now, practice telling in which categories the following cognates belong. Each will be said twice. Follow the model. (Remember to repeat the correct answer.) First, listen to the list of categories. ¡OJO! Not all categories will be used.

un lugar	un animal
un deporte (*a sport*)	un concepto
una persona	un instrumento musical

MODELO: (*you hear*) ¿Qué es un restaurante? → (*you say*) Es un lugar.

1. ...   2. ...   3. ...   4. ...   5. ...

Pronunciación y ortografía •Las vocales: **a, e, i, o, u**

A. Repeticiones. Repeat the following Spanish syllables, imitating the speaker. Try to pronounce each vowel with a short, tense sound.

1.	ma	fa	la	ta	pa
2.	me	fe	le	te	pe
3.	mi	fi	li	ti	pi
4.	mo	fo	lo	to	po
5.	mu	fu	lu	tu	pu
6.	sa	se	si	so	su

B. Las vocales. Compare the pronunciation of the following words in both English and Spanish. Listen for the schwa, the *uh* sound in English, and notice its absence in Spanish.

English:	*banana*	Spanish:	**banana**
	capital		**capital**

Now, repeat the following words, imitating the speaker. Be careful to avoid the English schwa. Remember to pronounce each vowel with a short and tense sound.

1.	hasta	tal	nada	mañana	natural
2.	me	qué	Pérez	usted	rebelde
3.	sí	señorita	permiso	imposible	tímido
4.	yo	con	cómo	noches	profesor
5.	tú	uno	mucho	Perú	Lupe

C. ¿Español o inglés? You will hear a series of words. Each will be said twice. Circle the letter of the word you hear, either a Spanish word (**español**) or an English word (**inglés**). Note that Spanish vowels are short and tense; they are never drawn out with a *u* or *i* glide as in English.

ESPAÑOL	INGLÉS		ESPAÑOL	INGLÉS
1. a. mi	b. me	4. a. con	b. cone
2. a. fe	b. Fay	5. a. ti	b. tea
3. a. es	b. ace	6. a. lo	b. low

D. Dictado. You will hear a series of words that are probably unfamiliar to you. Each will be said twice. Listen carefully, concentrating on the vowel sounds, and write in the missing vowels.

1. r____d____ll____   4. s____lv____v____d____s

2. M____r____b____l   5. ____lv____d____d____z____

3. ____n____l____t____r____l

Los números 0–30; **hay**

A. ¿Cuánto es? (*How much does it cost?*) You will hear the price of three different brands of items you want to purchase in pesos (the unit of currency in many Hispanic countries). Repeat the price of the *least* expensive brand. In this exercise, you will practice listening for specific information. (Remember to repeat the correct answer.)

    1. ...   2. ...   3. ...   4. ...

B. ¿Cuántos hay? (*How many are there?*) Read the following phrases when you hear the corresponding numbers. (Remember to repeat the correct answer.)

1. 21 personas (*f.*)
2. 18 profesores
3. 1 señora (*f.*)
4. 21 días (*m.*)
5. 30 cafés

C. ¿Qué hay en la sala de clase? (*What is in the classroom?*) You will hear a series of questions. Each will be said twice. Answer based on the following drawing. (Remember to repeat the correct answer.)

    1. ...   2. ...   3. ...   4. ...

Gustos y preferencias

A. ¿Qué te gusta? (*What do you like?*)

Paso 1. Encuesta (*Survey*). You will hear a series of questions. For each question, check the appropriate answer. No answers will be given on the tape.

The answers you choose should be correct for you.

1. ☐ ¡Sí, me gusta!   ☐ ¡No, no me gusta!
2. ☐ ¡Sí, creo que (*I think*) es fantástico!   ☐ ¡No, no me gusta!
3. ☐ Sí, me gusta.   ☐ No, no me gusta.
4. ☐ Sí, me gusta.   ☐ No, no me gusta.

Paso 2. Entrevista (*Interview*). Interview Professor Morales about his likes and dislikes using the oral cues. Remember to use **¿Le gusta... ?** and to repeat the correct question. You will hear his answer.

MODELO: (*you hear*) la universidad →
(*you say*) ¿Le gusta la universidad? (*you hear*) Sí, me gusta mucho.

1. ... 2. ... 3. ... 4. ...

B. Gustos y preferencias.
You will hear a series of questions. Each will be said twice. Answer using the written cues. Follow the model. Remember to repeat the correct answer.

MODELO: (*you hear*) ¿Te gusta el golf? (*you see*) Sí,... vólibol →
(*you say*) Sí, pero (*but*) me gusta más (*more*) el vólibol.

1. Sí,... / Gloria Estefan   3. Sí,... / el tenis
2. Sí,... / la música country   4. Sí,... / beber té

Los hispanos hablan: ¿Qué tipo de música te gusta más?

> In this section of the Laboratory Manual, you will hear authentic passages from Hispanics about a variety of subjects, including their school experiences, food preferences, hobbies, and so on. As you listen, try not to be distracted by unfamiliar vocabulary. Concentrate instead on what you *do* know and understand.*

In addition to the types of music that most young people listen to here in the United States (soft rock, heavy metal, and so on), Hispanic students also listen to music that is typical of their own country or region. Have you heard of **la salsa, el merengue,** or **el tango**? These are all types of music from different regions of Spanish America. Note that the word **conjunto** means *musical group*.

You will hear a passage in which a student tells about her likes and dislikes in music. First, listen to get a general idea of the content. Then, rewind the tape and listen again for specific information. Then you will hear a series of statements. Circle **C** (**cierto**) if the statement is true or **F** (**falso**) if it is false.

Habla Teresa: Me gusta más el rock en inglés y en español. Mis cantantes favoritos son Sting y Whitney Houston. Mis conjuntos favoritos son Metálica y Hombres G, un conjunto que canta en español. Me gusta la música instrumental y me encanta la música latina por su ritmo y su sabor... y porque es nuestra. Me gustan la salsa y el merengue. Me gusta la música en inglés y español. ¡Amo toda la música!

1. C F   2. C F   3. C F

---

*The listening text for the **Los hispanos hablan** sections will appear in the Laboratory Manual through **Capítulo 2**.

Tercera parte

▼▼▼▼▼▼▼▼▼▼▼▼▼▼▼▼▼▼▼▼▼▼▼▼▼▼▼▼▼▼▼▼

¿Qué hora es?

A. ¿Qué hora es? You will hear a series of times. Each will be said twice. Circle the letter of the clock face that indicates the time you hear.

MODELO: (*you hear*) Son las diez de la mañana. → (*you circle the letter a*)

(a.)

b.

1. a.

b.

2. a.

b.

3. a.

b.

4. a.

b.

8   *Ante todo*

B. **¿A qué hora es... ?** You will hear a series of questions about Marisol's schedule. Answer based on her schedule. (Remember to repeat the correct answer.) First, stop the tape and look at the schedule.

MODELO: (*you hear*) ¿A qué hora es la clase de español? →
(*you say*) Es a las ocho y media de la mañana.

Horario escolar*

Nombre: Marisol Abad
Dirección: Calle Alfaro, 16
Teléfono: 72-45-86

8:30	Español
9:40	Ciencias
11:00	Matemáticas
12:25	Inglés
2:15	Arte

*Horario... School schedule

1. ...   2. ...   3. ...   4. ...

Palabras interrogativas

A. **Preguntas y respuestas** (*Questions and answers*). Imagine that your friend Marisa has just made some statements that you didn't quite understand. You will hear each statement twice. Circle the letter of the interrogative word or phrase you would use to obtain information about what she said.

1. a. ¿a qué hora?   b. ¿cómo es?
2. a. ¿quién?   b. ¿dónde?
3. a. ¿cuál?   b. ¿dónde está?
4. a. ¿cuántas?   b. ¿cuándo?
5. a. ¿qué es?   b. ¿cómo es?
6. a. ¿cómo está?   b. ¿qué es?

B. Dictado. You will hear five questions. Each will be said twice. Write each question next to the appropriate drawing. First, stop the tape and look at the drawings.

1. _____

2. _____

3. _____

4. _____

5. _____

Situaciones

Paso 1. Saludos y expresiones de cortesía. In the following conversation, Diego González introduces himself to professor Salazar. Diego's lines will be read with pauses for repetition. But first, listen.

DIEGO:	Perdón. ¿Es usted el profesor Salazar?
PROFESOR:	Sí, yo soy.
DIEGO:	Buenas tardes. Me llamo Diego González. Soy el estudiante de la Universidad de California.
PROFESOR:	Ah, sí. El estudiante de Los Ángeles. Mucho gusto.
DIEGO:	Igualmente.
PROFESOR:	¡Bienvenido a México! Él es Antonio Sifuentes. Es estudiante posgraduado en la facultad.
ANTONIO:	¿Qué tal, Diego?
DIEGO:	Muy bien, gracias. ¿Y tú?
ANTONIO:	Muy bien. Mucho gusto.
DIEGO:	Igualmente, Antonio.

Paso 2. Aplicación. Now you will participate in a similar conversation, partially printed in your manual, in which you will play the role of Mariana, an exchange student in Mexico. Complete the conversation using the written cues. (Remember to repeat the correct answer. If you wish, stop the tape and write the answers.) Here are the cues for your conversation.

> mucho gusto, Gabriel   muchas gracias   es fantástica

PABLO: Mariana, te presento a (*I'd like to introduce you to*) Gabriel Herrera, un estudiante posgraduado de la facultad.

MARIANA: _____.

GABRIEL: El gusto es mío (*mine*). Bienvenida a México, Mariana.

MARIANA: _____.

GABRIEL: ¿Qué tal te gusta la universidad?

MARIANA: Pues, ¡creo que (*I think that*) _____!

Repaso (Para entregar)*

A. En el periódico (*newspaper*). You will hear a series of headlines from a Spanish newspaper. Each will be said twice. Write the number of the headline next to the section of the newspaper in which it most likely appears. Try not to be distracted by unfamiliar vocabulary; concentrate instead on the key words in the headline. First, listen to the list of sections.

_____ Política

_____ Libros (*Books*)

_____ Espectáculos (*Entertainment*)

_____ Deportes (*Sports*)

_____ Economía

B. *Listening Passage*: ¿Qué idiomas se hablan en Latinoamérica?†

> The first listening passage, as well as the passages in other chapters of the Laboratory Manual, will be preceded by prelistening exercises (**Antes de escuchar**). They will involve strategies such as predicting and guessing content before you listen, reading the true/false statements before listening, and so on. You should always do the prelistening section *before* you listen to the passage. Don't be distracted by unfamiliar vocabulary. Focus on what you *do* know. In most cases, you will be asked to listen for specific information.

Antes de escuchar (*Before listening*). Before you listen to the passage, *stop the tape* and do the following prelistening exercises.

Paso 1. Read the true/false statements. As you read them, try to infer the information you will hear in the passage, as well as listen for specific information.

1. Julia es de México.
2. Tegucigalpa es la capital de Honduras.
3. Julia habla guaraní.
4. No se habla portugués en Latinoamérica.
5. Las palabras (*words*) **español** y **castellano** son sinónimas.
6. El español es la única (*only*) lengua que se habla en Latinoamérica.

Paso 2. What can you infer from the true/false statements? Check all that apply.

☐ Julia will probably tell us where she is from and what language she speaks.

☐ There may be more than one word to describe the Spanish language.

☐ It is possible that more than one language is spoken throughout Latin America.

Now turn on the tape.

Listening Passage. Now, you will hear a passage about the Spanish language and where it is spoken. First, listen to get a general idea of the content. Then rewind the tape and listen again for specific information.

---

*No answers are given for **Para entregar** activities.
†The text for the Listening Passages will apear in the Laboratory Manual through **Capítulo 2.**

¡Hola! Me llamo Julia y soy de Tegucigalpa. ¡Sí! Tegucigalpa. ¿Es un nombre difícil? Tegucigalpa es la capital de Honduras. Honduras está en Centroamérica. En mi país se habla el castellano o español. **Español** y **castellano** son palabras sinónimas para hablar del mismo idioma. El castellano también se habla en España y en toda Latinoamérica. Bueno, no en toda Latinoamérica, porque en el Brasil se habla portugués y en Belice se habla inglés. Además del castellano, en el mundo hispánico se hablan otros idiomas también. Por ejemplo, en el Paraguay hay dos lenguas oficiales, el español y el guaraní. El guaraní es una lengua indígena original de la región. Mi amiga Susana es paraguaya y habla español y guaraní.

El español es una lengua muy importante en el mundo, porque lo hablan muchas personas. ¿Se habla español en tu estado?

Now stop the tape, and do the exercises in **Después de escuchar.**

Después de escuchar (*After listening*).

Paso 1. Here are the true/false statements. Circle **C** (**cierto**) if the statement is true or **F** (**falso**) if it is false. Then correct the statements that are false, according to the passage.

1. C   F   Julia es de México.

    _____

2. C   F   Tegucigalpa es la capital de Honduras.

    _____

3. C   F   Julia habla guaraní.

    _____

4. C   F   No se habla portugués en Latinoamérica.

    _____

5. C   F   Las palabras (*words*) **español** y **castellano** son sinónimas.

    _____

6. C   F   El español es la única (*only*) lengua que se habla en Latinoamérica.

    _____

Paso 2. Rewind the tape and listen to the passage again. Then, stop the tape and complete the following sentences with words chosen from the list.

inglés   español
lengua   paraguaya
castellano

1. La palabra **idioma** es sinónimo de _____.

2. Julia es de Honduras: es **hondureña**. Susana es de Paraguay: es _____.

3. Susana habla guaraní y _____ (o _____).

4. En Belice se habla _____.

Now turn on the tape.

C. Dictado. You will hear a radio announcement that tells the times of this afternoon's programs. Listen carefully and, while listening, write the time of each program next to the name of the program. After you listen to the radio announcement, stop the tape and write the type of program you think each is in English. First, listen to the names of the programs.

HORA	PROGRAMA	TIPO DE PROGRAMA
_____	Radionovela	_____
_____	Informe meteorológico	_____
_____	Visita con el veterinario	_____
_____	Tarde musical	_____
_____	Radionoticias	_____
_____	Programa del Dr. Rodríguez	_____

Now turn on the tape.

D. Y para terminar... Entrevista. You will hear a series of questions. Each will be said twice. Answer based on your own experience. Stop the tape and write the answers.

1. _____

2. _____

3. _____

4. _____

5. _____

6. _____

Vocabulario: Preparación

▼▼▼▼▼▼▼▼▼▼▼▼▼▼▼▼▼▼▼▼▼▼▼▼▼▼▼▼▼▼▼▼▼▼▼▼▼

A. ¿Qué necesita? (*What does she need?*) Luisa is making a list of things that she will need for her classes this semester. Listen carefully to her list and check the items that she needs. If she mentions a number, write it in the space provided. Don't be distracted by unfamiliar vocabulary; concentrate instead on the words that you *do* know. **¡OJO!** Not all items will be mentioned. First, listen to the list of possible items.

COSAS	SÍ	NO	¿CUÁNTOS O CUÁNTAS?
mochila(s)			
lápiz (lápices)			
bolígrafo(s)			
libro(s) de texto			
cuaderno(s)			
diccionario(s)			
calculadora(s)			
papel			
pizarra(s)			

B. Identificaciones. Identify the following items when you hear the corresponding number. Begin each sentence with **Es el...** or **Es la...** (Remember to repeat the correct answer.)

1. ... 2. ... 3. ... 4. ... 5. ... 6. ... 7. ... 8. ... 9. ... 10. ...

Los hispanos hablan: ¿Qué materias te gusta estudiar?

You will hear three Hispanic students describe the courses they like or don't like. As you listen to each one, complete the following chart with **sí** or **no**. Use **sí** to indicate that the student likes a given subject, and **no** to indicate that he or she does not. You will hear the students in the order given in the chart. ¡OJO! The students may mention subjects other than those listed in the chart. Check your answers in the Appendix.

MATERIAS	1. JOSÉ	2. RAÚL	3. JULIA
Historia			
Matemáticas			
Sicología			
Química			
Física			
Biología			
Idiomas			
Ciencias			

Pronunciación y ortografía:
Diphthongs and Linking

▼▼▼▼▼▼▼▼▼▼▼▼▼▼▼▼▼▼▼▼▼▼▼▼▼▼▼▼▼▼▼▼▼▼▼▼▼

A. Repaso: Las vocales. Repeat the following words, imitating the speaker. Pay close attention to the pronunciation of the indicated vowels.

WEAK VOWELS

(i, y)	Pili	silla	soy	y
(u)	gusto	lugar	uno	mujer

STRONG VOWELS

(a)	calculadora	Ana	banana	lápiz
(e)	trece	papel	clase	general
(o)	profesor	hombre	Lola	bolígrafo

B. Diptongos. Diphthongs are formed by two successive weak vowels (**i** or **y, u**) or by a combination of a weak vowel and a strong vowel (**a, e, o**). The two vowels are pronounced as a single syllable. Repeat the following words, imitating the speaker. Pay close attention to the pronunciation of the indicated diphthongs.

1. (ia) me**dia** gra**cia**s
2. (ie) b**ie**n s**ie**te
3. (io) Jul**io** edific**io**
4. (iu) c**iu**dad (*city*) v**iu**da (*widow*)

5.	(ua)	**cuaderno**	Mana**gua**
6.	(ue)	**bue**nos	**nue**ve
7.	(ui)	**muy**	**fui** (*I was/I went*)
8.	(uo)	**cuo**ta	ard**uo**
9.	(ai)	**aire**	h**ay**
10.	(ei)	**vei**nte	tr**ei**nta
11.	(oi)	**soy**	est**oy**
12.	(au)	**au**to	p**au**sa
13.	(eu)	**deu**da (*debt*)	C**eu**ta

C. Más sobre (*about*) **los diptongos**

Paso 1. Diphthongs can occur within a word or between words, causing the words to be "linked" and pronounced as one long word. Repeat the following phrases and sentences, imitating the speaker. Pay close attention to how the words are linked.

1. (oi/ia)   Armando‿y‿Alicia
               las letras o‿y‿hache
2. (ei/ie)   el tigre‿y‿el chimpancé
               Vicente‿y‿Elena
3. (oi/ie/ai/io) Soy‿extrovertida‿y‿optimista.
4. (ai/iu)   Elena‿y‿Humberto necesitan una mochila‿y‿unos libros

Paso 2. Linking also occurs naturally between many word boundaries in Spanish. Repeat the following sentences, imitating the speaker. Try to say each without pause, as if it were one long word.

1. ¿Es usted eficiente?
2. ¿Dónde hay un escritorio?
3. Tomás y Alicia están en la oficina.
4. Están en la Argentina y en el Uruguay.
5. No hay estudiantes en el edificio a estas horas (*at these hours*).

D. Dictado. You will hear a series of words containing diphthongs. Each will be said twice. Listen carefully and write the missing vowels.

1. c_____nc_____s   4. b_____nos

2. Patric_____   5. _____to

3. s_____s   6. s_____

Minidiálogos y gramática

▼▼

1. Identifying People, Places, and Things • Singular Nouns: Gender and Articles

A. Minidiálogo: En la clase del profesor Durán: El primer día

Paso 1. Dictado. The dialogue on the following page will be read twice. Listen carefully the first time; the second time, write in the missing words.

PROFESOR DURÁN: Aquí está _____

_____ del curso.

Son necesarios _____

_____ de texto y

_____ diccionario. También hay

_____ _____

de _____ y libros

de poesía.

ESTUDIANTE 1: ¡Es una lista infinita!

ESTUDIANTE 2: Sí, y los libros cuestan demasiado.

ESTUDIANTE 1: No, _____ _____ no es el precio de los libros. ¡Es

_____ _____ para leer los libros!

Paso 2. ¿Cierto o falso? Now stop the tape and read the following statements about the dialogue. Circle **C** (**cierto**) if the statement is true or **F** (**falso**) if it is false.

1. C   F   En la clase del profesor Durán es necesario leer muchos libros.

2. C   F   Para los estudiantes, el problema es el tiempo para leer los libros.

3. C   F   Los estudiantes necesitan una calculadora para la clase.

Now turn on the tape.

B. ¿Qué te gusta? Tell a friend what you like, using the oral cues and the correct definite article. (Remember to repeat the correct answer.)

MODELO: (*you hear*) profesora → (*you say*) Me gusta la profesora.

1. ...   2. ...   3. ...   4. ...   5. ...

C. ¿Qué hay en estos (*these*) **lugares?** Identify the items in each drawing after you hear the corresponding number. Begin each sentence with **Hay un...** or **Hay una...** (Remember to repeat the correct answer.)

MODELO: (*you see*) diccionario → (*you say*) Hay un diccionario en la mesa.

1.

silla

2.

bolígrafo

3.

estudiante

4.

consejero

2. Identifying People, Places, and Things • Nouns and Articles: Plural Forms

A. Descripción: El cuarto de Ignacio. You will hear Ignacio describe his room. As you listen, circle the number of the drawing that best matches his description. First, stop the tape and look at the drawings.

1.   2.   3.

B. Cambios (*Changes*). You will hear a series of nouns and articles. Give the plural forms of the first four nouns and articles and the singular forms of the next four. (Remember to repeat the correct answer.)

SINGULAR → PLURAL   PLURAL → SINGULAR

1. ...   2. ...   3. ...   4. ...   5. ...   6. ...   7. ...   8. ...

C. Los errores de Inés. You will hear some statements that your friend Inés makes about the following drawing. She is wrong and you must correct her. (Remember to repeat the correct answer.)

MODELO: (*you hear*) Hay dos libros. → (*you say*) No. Hay tres libros.

1. ...   2. ...   3. ...   4. ...   5. ...   6. ...

D. Dictado. You will hear a series of sentences. Each will be said twice. Listen carefully and write the missing words. You will be listening for words that are either singular or plural.

1. Hay _____ _____ en _____ _____.

2. _____ _____ están en _____ _____.

3. No hay _____ en _____ _____.

4. ¿Hay _____ _____ en _____ _____?

3. Expressing Actions • Subject Pronouns; Present Tense of **-ar** Verbs; Negation

A. Minidiálogo: Escuchando furtivamente. You will hear a dialogue followed by a series of statements about the dialogue. Stop the tape and on the following page circle **C** (**cierto**) if the statement is true or **F** (**falso**) if it is false. If the information is not contained in or cannot be inferred from the dialogue, circle **ND** (**No lo dice** [*It doesn't say*]). In this exercise you will be listening for specific information.

1. C F ND Diego vive (*lives*) en casa con su (*his*) familia.

2. C F ND A Diego le gusta la música.

3. C F ND Diego y Lupe trabajan porque necesitan dinero.

4. C F ND Diego enseña inglés.

Now turn on the tape.

B. ¿Quién habla? You will hear a series of sentences. Each will be said twice. Listen carefully and circle the letter of the *subject* of each sentence. In this exercise you will practice listening for specific information.

1. a. yo   b. ella
2. a. él   b. tú
3. a. Ana y yo   b. los estudiantes
4. a. Alberto   b. Alberto y tú
5. a. ustedes   b nosotras

C. ¿Quién... ? Answer the following questions using the oral cues. (Remember to repeat the correct answer.)

1. ¿Quién canta bien?

   MODELO: (*you hear*) Juan → (*you say*) Juan canta bien.

   a. ...   b. ...   c. ...   d. ...

2. ¿Quién practica deportes (*sports*)?

   MODELO: (*you hear*) yo → (*you say*) Yo practico deportes.

   a. ...   b. ...   c. ...   d. ...

D. Mis compañeros y yo. Form complete sentences about yourself and others, using the oral and written cues. (Remember to repeat the correct answer.)

> MODELO: (*you see and hear*) yo   (*you hear*) pagar la matrícula →
> (*you say*) Pago la matrícula.

1. Ana y yo
2. Chela y Roberto

3. el estudiante de Chile
4. Jaime, tú...

5. profesor, Ud....

E. ¿Dónde están? Look at the drawings on the following page. Tell where the people might be when you hear the corresponding question. (Remember to repeat the correct answer.)

> MODELO: (*you see and hear*) Dónde está Alicia? →
> (*you say*) Está en la clase.

1.

2.

3.

4.

4. Getting Information • Asking Yes/No Questions

A. Minidiálogo: En una universidad: La oficina de matrícula. You will hear a dialogue followed by a series of statements. Circle the letter of the person who might have made each statement. In this exercise, you will practice listening for specific information.

        a. la estudiante   b. el consejero

1. a b No deseo tomar una clase por la noche.

2. a b ¿Qué tal el Francés 10?

3. a b ¿Hay sitio en la clase de Sicología 2?

Now turn on the tape.

B. ¿Es una pregunta? You will hear a series of statements or questions. Listen carefully and circle the appropriate letter. Pay close attention to intonation.

1. a. statement   b. question
2. a. statement   b. question
3. a. statement   b. question
4. a. statement   b. question
5. a. statement   b. question

C. Entrevista con la profesora Villegas

Paso 1. Interview Professor Villegas for your school newspaper, using the following cues. Use the **Ud.** form of the verbs. Use the subject pronoun **Ud.** in your first question only. Professor Villegas will answer your questions. (Remember to repeat the correct question.)

    MODELO: (*you see and hear*) enseñar / inglés →
                    (*you say*) ¿Enseña Ud. inglés?   (*you hear*) No, enseño español.

1. enseñar / cuatro clases
2. enseñar / francés
3. trabajar / por la noche
4. hablar / con los estudiantes
5. le gusta / la universidad

Paso 2. ¿Qué recuerdas? (*What do you remember*?) Now stop the tape and report what professor Villegas said about herself. Use **La profesora Villegas...** in your first sentence only.

MODELO: La profesora Villegas enseña español.

1. _____

2. _____

3. _____

4. _____

5. _____

Now turn on the tape.

Situaciones

▼▼▼▼▼▼▼▼▼▼▼▼▼▼▼▼▼▼▼▼▼▼▼▼▼▼▼▼▼▼▼▼▼▼▼▼▼▼▼

Paso 1. Gustos y preferencias. In the following conversation, Diego and Lupe discover that they have certain things in common. Lupe's lines will be read with pauses for repetition. But first, listen.

DIEGO: ¡Ay, perdón!
LUPE: No hay por qué. ¡Ay, Diego!
DIEGO: ¡Lupe! ¿Qué haces?
LUPE: Busco un libro para la clase de antropología.
DIEGO: ¿Te gusta la antropología?
LUPE: Sí, me gusta mucho. Sobre todo, me gusta la antropología precolombina.
DIEGO: ¿En serio? Es mi materia favorita. ¿Qué clase tomas?
LUPE: Tomo la clase del profesor Salazar. Es una clase fascinante.
DIEGO: Yo también tomo esa clase. Así que somos compañeros... Bueno, Lupe, nos vemos en clase.
LUPE: Sí, nos vemos.

Paso 2. Aplicación. Now you will participate in a similar conversation, partially printed in your manual, in which you play the role of Héctor. Complete the conversation using the written cues. (Remember to repeat the correct answer. If you wish, stop the tape and write the answers.) Here are the cues for your conversation.

hola, Laura   dos libros más   profesor Serrano   a las 8:30 de la noche

HÉCTOR: ¡_____!

LAURA: ¿Qué tal, Héctor? ¿Qué buscas?

HÉCTOR: Pues, necesito _____ para la clase del

_____.

LAURA: Ah, sí... Es una clase fascinante, pero es necesario comprar muchos libros. A propósito (*By the way*), ¿a qué hora deseas estudiar en la biblioteca?

HÉCTOR: ¿Qué tal _____?

LAURA: ¡De acuerdo!

Un poco de todo (Para entregar)*

▼▼▼▼▼▼▼▼▼▼▼▼▼▼▼▼▼▼▼▼▼▼▼▼▼▼▼▼▼▼▼▼▼

A. Un día en la vida (*life*) de Armando

Paso 1. You will hear a series of sentences that describe a typical day in Armando's life. Each will be said twice. Listen carefully and circle the letter of the drawing that best matches each sentence. First, stop the tape and look at the drawings.

1. a.

   b.

2. a.

   b.

3. a.

   b.

4. a.

   b.

---

*No answers are given for **Para entregar** activities.

Paso 2. ¿Qué recuerdas? (*What do you remember?*) Now stop the tape and write sentences that describe the actions in the drawings you chose.

1. _____

2. _____

3. _____

4. _____

Now turn on the tape.

B. *Listening Passage*: **¿Cómo son las universidades hispánicas?**

Antes de escuchar. Before you listen to the passage, *stop the tape* and do the following prelistening exercises.

Paso 1. The passage contains some general information about Hispanic universities and how they differ from universities in the United States. Check the specific information that you expect to find in the passage.

☐ how the academic year is divided (that is, into semesters, quarters, and so on)

☐ the number of courses or credits that students are required to take

☐ the length of the academic year

☐ how much professors are paid

☐ how soon students need to declare their major

☐ whether or not foreign students attend Hispanic universities

Paso 2. The passage also contains information about Julia's course of studies. What information do you think she will give you?

☐ her major   ☐ which courses she has to take for her major

☐ which professors she likes best   ☐ the name of the university she attends

Now turn on the tape.

Listening Passage. Now you will hear a passage about Hispanic universities. In this passage, Julia talks about her major, **su especialización,** and some of the differences between Hispanic and U.S. universities.

¡Hola! ¿Qué tal? Soy tu amiga Julia, la hondureña. Estudio en la Universidad de Salamanca, en España. Mi carrera es ciencias políticas. La carrera es la especialización académica, como *major* o concentración.

En el mundo hispánico las universidades son muy diferentes de las de los Estados Unidos. Por lo general, no hay semestres. El año académico dura nueve meses. Los estudiantes toman de cuatro a siete cursos en un año. Además, los estudiantes no esperan dos años para declarar su carrera o especialización.

Yo tomo muchos cursos en relación con las ciencias políticas. ¿Cuáles? Pues, cursos de historia, filosofía, economía, estadística, etcétera. También tomo inglés. Estudio mucho, porque, como en todas las universidades, es necesario estudiar mucho en las universidades de España para pasar los cursos.

A pesar de eso, me gusta la vida universitaria. En Salamanca hay muchos estudiantes extranjeros, y muchos son de los Estados Unidos, como mi amiga Heather, que es de Carolina del Norte. Nosotras practicamos el español y el inglés muchas tardes después de las clases. ¿Con quién practicas tú el español?

Después de escuchar. Rewind the tape and listen to the passage again. Then, stop the tape and complete the following sentences with words chosen from the list.

extranjeros	semestres	el inglés	el alemán
ciencias políticas	carrera	especialización	ciencias naturales

1. Para expresar el concepto de *major*, se usa la palabra _____

   (o _____) en español.

2. Por lo general, no hay _____ en el año académico hispánico.

3. Julia toma cursos en relación con las _____.

4. También toma una lengua extranjera: _____.

5. En Salamanca, hay muchos estudiantes _____.

Now turn on the tape.

C. Y para terminar... Entrevista. You will hear a series of questions about your classes and your life at the university. Each will be said twice. Answer, based on your own experience. Stop the tape and write the answers.

Note: the word **tu** means *your*, and **mi** means *my*.

1. _____

2. _____

3. _____

4. _____

5. _____

6. _____

CAPÍTULO **2**

Vocabulario: Preparación

▼▼▼▼▼▼▼▼▼▼▼▼▼▼▼▼▼▼▼▼▼▼▼▼▼▼▼▼▼▼▼▼

A. Definiciones. You will hear a series of definitions of family relationships. Each will be said twice. Listen carefully and write the number of the definition next to the word defined. First, listen to the list of words.

_____ mi (*my*) abuelo

_____ mi tía

_____ mi hermano

_____ mi prima

_____ mi tío

_____ mi abuela

B. La familia Muñoz. You will hear a brief description of Sarita Muñoz's family. Listen carefully and complete the following family tree according to the description. First, stop the tape and look at the family tree.

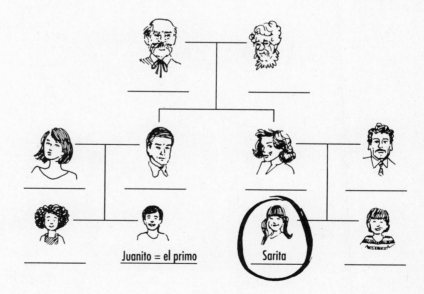

Juanito = el primo   Sarita

C. ¿Cuál es? You will hear a series of descriptions. Each will be said twice. Circle the letter of the item or person described.

1. a.   b.   2. a.   b.

3. a.   b.   4. a.   b.

5. a.   b.

D. Descripciones: ¿Cómo son? You will hear a series of sentences about the following fathers and their sons. Each will be said twice. Circle **C** (**cierto**) if the statement is true or **F** (**falso**) if it is false. First, stop the tape and look at the drawing.

Miguel   Alberto   Benito

Miguelito

1. C F   2. C F   3. C F   4. C F

E. Dictado: El inventario. Imagine that you and a friend, Isabel, are taking inventory at the university bookstore where you work. Write out the numerals as she dictates the list to you. She will say each number twice. ¡OJO! Items are given in random order. First, listen to the list of words.

_____ mochilas

_____ lápices

_____ cuadernos

_____ novelas

_____ calculadoras

_____ libros de español

Los hispanos hablan: Dinos algo acerca de (*Tell us something about*) tu familia*

▼▼

You will hear the following passage in which a student tells you about his family. Then you will hear a series of statements. Circle **C** (**cierto**) if the statement is true or **F** (**falso**) if it is false. If the information is not contained in the passage, circle **ND** (**No lo dice**).

Habla Antonio: Me llamo Antonio y soy de España. Ahora estudio en los Estados Unidos. Tengo tres hermanos que estudian aquí también, dos hermanos y una hermana. Tengo diecisiete años. En cuanto a los gustos, los cuatro somos un poco diferentes. A mí me gusta practicar deportes; a mi hermana le gusta cantar; a uno de mis hermanos le encanta escuchar música y al otro hermano le gusta mucho mirar deportes en la televisión. Físicamente somos muy similares, aunque creo que algunos vamos a ser más altos que otros. En cuanto a la personalidad, somos muy diferentes. Por ejemplo, yo soy una persona muy introvertida y pacífica. Sin embargo, mi hermana es muy extrovertida y gregaria.

1. C F ND   2. C F ND   3. C F ND   4. C F ND

Pronunciación y ortografía:
Stress and Written Accent Marks (Part 1)

▼▼

A. Repeticiones. Repeat the following words, imitating the speaker. The highlighted syllable receives the stress in pronunciation.

1. If a word ends in a vowel, **n**, or **s**, stress normally falls on the next-to-the-last syllable.

   sincera   interesante   cuadernos   examen

2. If a word ends in any other consonant, stress normally falls on the last syllable.

   estar   liberal   profesor   papel

B. Más repeticiones. Repeat the following words, imitating the speaker. The words have been divided into syllables for you. Pay close attention to which syllable receives the spoken stress.

1. Stress on the next-to-the-last syllable

li-bro	si-lla	cla-se	me-sa	Car-men
con-se-je-ra	li-te-ra-tu-ra	o-ri-gen	com-pu-ta-do-ra	cien-cias

_____

*This is the last **Los hispanos hablan** section to include a transcript of the spoken text in the student manual.

2. Stress on the last syllable

se-ñor   mu-jer   fa-vor   ac-tor   co-lor
po-pu-lar   li-ber-tad   ge-ne-ral   sen-ti-men-tal   u-ni-ver-si-dad

C. Dictado. You will hear the following words. Each will be said twice. Listen carefully and circle the syllable that receives the spoken stress.

1. con-trol
2. e-le-fan-te
3. mo-nu-men-tal

4. com-pa-ñe-ra
5. bue-nos
6. us-ted

Minidiálogos y gramática

▼▼▼▼▼▼▼▼▼▼▼▼▼▼▼▼▼▼▼▼▼▼▼▼▼▼▼▼▼

5. Expressing *To Be* • Present tense of **ser**; Summary of Uses

A. Presentaciones

Paso 1. You will hear a brief passage about a Spanish family. As you listen, try not to be distracted by unfamiliar vocabulary. Concentrate instead on what you *do* know and understand. You may want to take notes on the information in the passage.

_____

_____

_____

Paso 2. ¿Qué recuerdas? (*What do you remember*?) Now stop the tape and complete the following sentences based on the passage and your notes. ¡OJO! Use a form of the verb **ser** in the first blank of each sentence.

1. Marta _____ la _____ de Lola y Manolo.

2. Lola _____ profesora de _____.

3. Lola y Manolo _____ de _____.

4. Lola _____ rubia y _____; Manolo es _____ y moreno.

Now turn on the tape.

B. ¿De dónde son? Practice telling where you and your imaginary family and friends are from, using the written cues. (Remember to repeat the correct answer.)

> MODELO: (*you see and hear*) mi amigo Aristides / Colombia →
> (*you say*) Mi amigo Aristides es de Colombia.

1. mi amigo Lorenzo / la Argentina
2. tú / Costa Rica
3. mis abuelos / Cuba
4. mi hermano y yo / Chile

C. ¿De quién son estas cosas? Imagine that your friend wants to know to whom certain items belong. Answer her questions using the written cues. ¡OJO! Don't forget that **de** + **el** form the contraction **del**. (Remember to repeat the correct answer.)

> MODELO: (*you hear*) ¿De quién es el escritorio? (*you see*) el cliente →
> (*you say*) Es del cliente.

1. el estudiante 2. la profesora 3. las secretarias 4. el señor Costas

D. ¿Para quién son los regalos? Imagine that you need to give gifts to several of your friends and relatives, and money is no object! You will hear the name and a brief description of each person. Each statement will be said twice. Select appropriate gifts for them from the following list. First, listen to the list. (Remember to repeat the correct answer.)

> la calculadora   el coche nuevo
> los libros de filosofía   las novelas románticas
> las cintas (*tapes*) de Boyz II Men

Use the phrases **para ella, para él,** and **para ellos,** as in the model.

> MODELO: (*you hear*) Tu (*Your*) hermano Juan es estudiante universitario. →
> (*you say*) Los libros de filosofía son para él.

1. ... 2. ... 3. ... 4. ...

6. Describing • Adjectives: Gender, Number, and Position

A. Hablando (*Speaking*) **de la familia.** Imagine that your friend Graciela is decribing her family. Listen to her description and check the adjectives that apply to each member of her family. ¡OJO! Not all the adjectives will be used, and not all adjectives in the description appear in the chart. In this excercise, you will practice listening for specific information.

	ACTIVOS	BAJO	ALTAS	JÓVENES	SOLTERO	CASADA
su (*her*) tío						
los abuelos						
sus (*her*) primos						
su hermana						
su padre						

B. ¿Cómo son? Practice describing various people, using the oral and written cues. Remember to change the endings of the adjectives if necessary. (Remember to repeat the correct answer.)

> MODELO: (*you see and hear*) mis (*my*) profesores (*you hear*) listo →
> (*you say*) Mis profesores son listos.

1. mi (*my*) compañero de cuarto
2. la profesora de español
3. Bernardo
4. Amanda
5. yo (*f.*)

C. ¿De dónde son y qué idioma hablan? Imagine that your friend Carmen is asking you about some of the exchange students on campus. You will hear each of her questions twice. Answer according to the model, giving the nationality of the persons she mentions and the language they might speak. First, listen to the list of nationalities. You will need to change the endings in some cases. (Remember to repeat the correct answer.)

> italiano   alemán   francés   inglés   portugués   español

> MODELO: (*you hear*) ¿Evaristo es de Portugal? → (*you say*) Sí, es portugués y habla portugués.

1. ... 2. ... 3. ... 4. ... 5. ...

D. ¿Qué dicen (*are saying*) estas personas? When you hear the corresponding number, tell what these people are saying. Use definite articles and appropriate adjectives from the list to modify the nouns in the drawings. First, listen to the list of adjectives. (Remember to repeat the correct answer.)

> moreno   grande   corto   pequeño   alto

1.

libro

2.

edificio

3.

lápices

4.

niñas

5.

silla

7. Expressing Actions • Present Tense of **-er** and **-ir** Verbs; More About Subject Pronouns

A. Minidiálogo: Diego se presenta.

Paso 1. Dictado. You will hear the following paragraph in which Diego introduces himself. Listen carefully and write in the missing words.

Hola. Me llamo Diego González. Soy estudiante de UCLA, pero este año _____ a la

Universidad Nacional Autónoma de México. _____ con mi tía Matilde en la Ciudad

de México. _____ pizza con frecuencia y _____ cerveza en las fiestas.

Me gusta la ropa de moda; por eso _____ varios catálogos. _____

muchos libros de antropología para mi especialización. También _____ muchas car-

tas a mi familia. _____ que una educación universitaria es muy importante. Por eso

estudio y _____ mucho. ¡Pero _____ también que es muy importante

estar con los amigos y con la familia!

Paso 2. ¿Qué recuerdas? (*What do you remember?*) Now stop the tape and complete the following sentences based on the information in the passage. Remember to check your answers to **Paso 1** in the Appendix before beginning **Paso 2.**

1. Diego _____ a la Universidad Nacional Autónoma de México.

2. Él _____ en la casa de su (*his*) tía Matilde.

3. Diego _____ pizza con frecuencia y _____ cerveza en las fiestas.

4. Él _____ muchos libros de antropología.

Now turn on the tape.

B. ¿Qué hacen? (*What are they doing?*) You will hear a series of statements describing actions. Each will be said twice. Write the number of the statement next to the drawing that matches the action described in each statement. First, stop the tape and look at the drawings.

a. _____   b. _____

c. _____

Rosita

Pablito

d. _____

yo

Laura

e. _____

el Sr. Ramos

la Sra. Ramos

f. _____

Enrique

yo

C. ¿Quién... ? Answer the following questions using the oral cues. Use subject pronouns only if necessary. (Remember to repeat the correct answer.)

1. ¿Quién come en la cafetería?

   MODELO: (*you hear*) Evita → (*you say*) Evita come en la cafetería.

   a. ...   b. ...   c. ...   d. ...

2. ¿Quién vive en una residencia?

   MODELO: (*you hear*) yo → (*you say*) Vivo en una residencia.

   a. ...   b. ...   c. ...   d. ...

D. Un sábado típico de la familia Robles. Describe what happens on a typical Saturday at the Robles household, using the written and oral cues. Remember that subject pronouns are not always used in Spanish. (Remember to repeat the correct answer.)

   MODELO: (*you hear*) nosotros   (*you see*) estar en casa →
   (*you say*) Estamos en casa.

   1. leer el periódico
   2. escribir cartas
   3. asistir a un partido (*game*) de fútbol
   4. abrir una carta de mi prima
   5. comer a las seis

Situaciones

▼▼▼▼▼▼▼▼▼▼▼▼▼▼▼▼▼▼▼▼▼▼▼▼▼▼▼▼▼▼▼▼▼▼▼▼▼

Paso 1. Presentaciones (*Introductions*). In the following conversation, Paloma introduces her boyfriend, Gustavo, to her aunt. Paloma's lines will be read with pauses for repetition. But first, listen.

PALOMA:	¡Buenas tardes, tía Elisa!
ELISA:	¡Hola! ¡Adelante!
PALOMA:	Tía, quiero presentarte a mi novio, Gustavo. Gustavo, esta es mi tía, Elisa Velasco.
GUSTAVO:	Mucho gusto en conocerla, señora.
ELISA:	El gusto es mío, Gustavo.
PALOMA:	Y ya conoces a mi primo José Miguel.
JOSÉ MIGUEL:	¿Qué tal?
GUSTAVO:	¡Hola!

Paso 2. Aplicación. Now you will participate in a similar conversation, partially printed in your manual, in which you play the role of Gema. Complete the conversation, using the written cues. (Remember to repeat the correct answer. If you wish, you may stop the tape and write the answers.) Here are the cues for your conversation.

bien, gracias   quiero presentarte   es estudiante en la facultad

PAULA: ¡Hola, Gema! ¿Cómo estás?

GEMA: _____. Tía, _____ a mi amiga Margarita. Ella

_____. Margarita, esta es mi tía Paula Valverde.

PAULA: Mucho gusto, Margarita.

MARGARITA: El gusto es mío, señora Valverde.

Un poco de todo (Para entregar)

▼▼▼▼▼▼▼▼▼▼▼▼▼▼▼▼▼▼▼▼▼▼▼▼▼▼▼▼▼▼▼▼▼▼▼▼▼

A.   ¿Cuál es la foto? You will hear a description of a photograph. Listen carefully and choose the photograph that is described. First, listen to the following new words that you will hear in the description.

el pelo	*hair*
negro	*black*
el jardín	*garden*
blanco	*white*
prefiere	*he/she prefers*

Now stop the tape and look at the photos on the following page.

1.

2.

3.

B. *Listening Passage*: **Las familias hispanas***

Antes de escuchar. Before you listen to the passage, *stop the tape* and do the following prelistening exercises.

Paso 1. Read the following true/false statements. As you read them, try to infer the information the passage will give you, as well as the specific information for which you need to listen.

1. En las familias hispanas, más de (*more than*) dos generaciones viven en una sola casa.
2. Los abuelos no participan activamente en el cuidado (*care*) de los nietos.
3. Por lo general, las personas viejas viven en asilos (*nursing homes*).
4. Los abuelos cuidan (*care for*) a los nietos mientras (*while*) los padres trabajan.
5. Los hijos y los nietos cuidan a sus padres o a sus abuelos cuando estos (*the latter*) están viejos o enfermos.

Paso 2. The passage contains information about Julia's family and about Hispanic families in general. Which statements do you think apply to the Hispanic family in general?

☐ The Hispanic family is typically smaller than a U.S. family.

☐ Many Hispanic families are extended families; that is, more than one generation lives in the same household.

☐ The elderly and the sick are often sent to nursing homes.

☐ Grandparents are important in the daily lives of families.

☐ Many young couples live with their in-laws until they can become independent.

---

*This is the last Listening Passage section to include a transcript of the spoken text in the student manual.

Now turn on the tape.

Listening Passage. Now you will hear a passage about Hispanic families. In this passage, Julia talks about Hispanic families in general and about her own family in particular. The following words and phrases appear in the passage.

estadounidenses	de los Estados Unidos
No sólo... sino que además	*Not only . . . but also*
las ventajas	*advantages*
se ayudan	*they help each other*
el cuidado	*care*
enfermas	*sick*
murió	*he died*
la cuidamos	*we take care of her*

Here is the passage. First, listen to it to get a general idea of the content. Then rewind the tape and listen again for specific information.

Las familias hispanas son más grandes que las familias estadounidenses, por lo general. No sólo es normal tener más hijos, sino que además, con frecuencia los abuelos viven con la familia.

En español existe un nombre específico para los padres del esposo o esposa. Son los **suegros**, el suegro y la suegra. A veces si un matrimonio joven no tiene mucho dinero, los nuevos esposos viven con los padres de uno de ellos, (o sea, los suegros).

Para muchos norteamericanos esta es una situación extraña, ¿no? Pero es una situación que tiene sus ventajas también. Las familias hispanas conservan un contacto muy fuerte entre varias generaciones. Los miembros de la familia se visitan mucho y se ayudan constantemente con el cuidado de los niños y el de las personas viejas o enfermas.

Como ejemplo, yo puedo hablar de mi familia. Mi abuela materna vive con mi familia, porque su esposo, mi abuelo Rafael, murió joven. Sólo tenía 60 años. Mi abuela siempre ayudó a mi mamá con nosotros, sus nietos. Y ahora que mi abuela está vieja, mi mamá y nosotros la cuidamos. Es ley de la vida, ¿no? Mi abuela está contenta porque ahora también puede pasar tiempo con sus bisnietos, los hijos de mi hermano.

Now stop the tape and do the **Después de escuchar** exercises.

Después de escuchar

Paso 1. Here are the true/false statements. Circle **C** (**cierto**) if the statement is true or **F** (**falso**) if it is false. Then correct the statements that are false, according to the passage.

1. C F En las familias hispanas, más de dos generaciones viven en una sola casa.

   _____

2. C F Los abuelos no participan activamente en el cuidado de los nietos.

   _____

3. C F Por lo general, las personas viejas viven en asilos.

   _____

4. C F Los abuelos cuidan a los nietos mientras los padres trabajan.

   _____

5. C F Los hijos y los nietos cuidan a sus padres o a sus abuelos cuando estos están viejos o enfermos.

   _____

Paso 2. Rewind the tape and listen to the passage again. Then, stop the tape and complete the following sentences with words chosen from the list.

grandes   suegros   bisnietos   materna

1. La madre de mi madre es mi abuela _____.

2. Mis _____ son los padres de mi esposo/a.

3. Los _____ son los hijos de los nietos.

4. Por lo general, las familias hispanas son más _____ que las familias estadounidenses.

Now turn on the tape.

C. Y para terminar... Entrevista. You will hear a series of questions. Each will be said twice. Answer based on your experience. Stop the tape and write the answers.

1. _____

2. _____

3. _____

4. _____

5. _____

CAPÍTULO **3**

Vocabulario: Preparación

▼▼▼▼▼▼▼▼▼▼▼▼▼▼▼▼▼▼▼▼▼▼▼▼▼▼▼▼▼▼▼▼▼▼▼▼

A. Hablando (*Speaking*) **de la de moda**

Paso 1. Listen to the description of the clothing that a group of classmates wore to a popular nightclub last Friday evening. As you listen, check the clothing worn by each person.

	ZAPATOS DE TENIS	CALCETINES	CAMISA	PANTALONES	CINTURÓN	CAMISETA	CORBATA
Ana							
Juan							
Luis							

Paso 2. Dictado. Rewind the tape and listen again. As you listen, write the colors mentioned for each article of clothing. **¡OJO!** The clothes are not listed in order.

ARTÍCULOS	COLOR(ES)
corbata	
camisa	
cinturón	
pantalones	
camiseta	
zapatos de tenis	
calcetines	

B. Identificaciones. Identify the items on the following page after you hear the corresponding number. Begin each sentence with **Es un...** , **Es una...** , or **Son...**

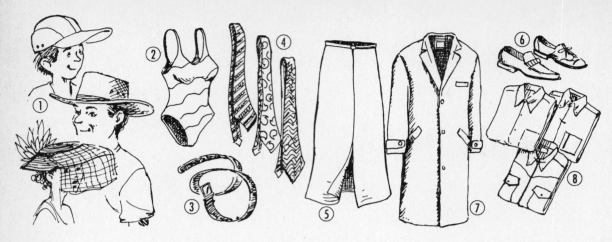

1. ...   2. ...   3. ...   4. ...   5. ...   6. ...   7. ...   8. ...

C. Dictado: El inventario del Almacén Robles. Imagine that you and a coworker are doing a partial inventory for a department store. Listen to what your coworker says, and write the numbers in numerals next to the correct items. You will hear each number twice. ¡OJO! The items are not listed in sequence. First, listen to the list of items.

ARTÍCULOS	NÚMERO (CANTIDAD)
pares de medias de nilón	
camisas blancas	
suéteres rojos	
pares de zapatos de tenis	
blusas azules	
faldas negras	

Los hispanos hablan: ¿Qué importancia tiene la ropa para ti y tus amigos?

You will hear a student, Teresa, give an answer to the preceding question. After listening, stop the tape and check all the statements that are true according to the passage. The following expressions appear in the passage.

una persona vale por lo que es	*a person's worth is determined by who he/she is*
aunque	*even though*
los harapos	*rags*

1. ☐ Teresa piensa que (*thinks that*) las modas son muy importantes.

2. ☐ Para ella, la persona es más importante que la ropa que usa.

3. ☐ La mayoría (*majority*) de sus amigos están de acuerdo con Teresa.

Pronunciación y ortografía:
Stress and Written Accent Marks (Part 2)

▼▼▼▼▼▼▼▼▼▼▼▼▼▼▼▼▼▼▼▼▼▼▼▼▼▼▼▼▼▼▼▼▼

A. Sílabas acentuadas. In Spanish, a written accent is required when a word does not follow the two basic rules.

1. The following words end in a vowel, **n**, or **s**. However, native speakers of Spanish do not pronounce these words according to the first basic rule. Repeat the following words, imitating the speaker.

ac-**ción**	fran-**cés**	a-le-**mán**	es-**tás**
sim-**pá**-ti-ca	me-**nú**	be-**bé**	te-**lé**-fo-no

2. These words break the second basic rule because they end in a consonant other than **n** or **s** and are not stressed on the last syllable. Repeat the following words, imitating the speaker.

lá-piz	**dó**-lar	**ál**-bum
Pé-rez	**Cá**-diz	**Gó**-mez

B. Más sílabas acentuadas. Here are other instances in which a Spanish word requires a written accent.

1. When a combinatin of two weak vowels or a weak and a strong vowel does not form a diphthong, the vowel that receives the spoken stress will have a written accent mark. This is very common in words ending in **-ía**. Compare the pronunciation of these pairs of words. Repeat each word, imitating the speaker.

A-li-cia	po-li-cí-a
Cle-men-cia	bio-lo-gí-a
cien-cias	dí-a
a-gua	grú-a (*construction crane*)

2. Some one-syllable words have accents to distinguish them from other words that sound like them. This accent is called a diacritical accent and it has no effect on the pronunciation of the word. Repeat each word, imitating the speaker.

él (*he*) / el (*the*)	tú (*you*) / tu (*your*)
sí (*yes*) / si (*if*)	mí (*me*) / mi (*my*)

3. Interrogative and exclamatory words require a written accent on the stressed vowel. Repeat each sentence, imitating the speaker.

¿Qué estudias?	¿Cómo te llamas?
¿Quién es tu profesora?	¡Qué bueno! (*How great!*)
¿Dónde está Venezuela?	

C. Palabras divididas. The following words have been divided into syllables for you. Read them when you hear the corresponding number. (Remember to repeat the correct answer.) ¡OJO! Some of the words will be unfamiliar to you. This should not be a problem because you have pronunciation rules to guide you.

1. nor-mal	4. a-na-to-mí-a	7. ter-mó-me-tro
2. prác-ti-co	5. cu-le-bra	8. co-li-brí
3. á-ni-mo	6. con-ver-ti-bles	9. con-di-cio-nal

D. Dictado. You will hear the following words. Each will be said twice. Listen carefully and write in a written accent where required. ¡OJO! Some of the words will be unfamiliar to you. This should not be a problem because you have the rules and the speaker's pronunciation to guide you.

1. metrica
2. distribuidor
3. anoche

4. Rosalia
5. actitud
6. sabiduria

7. jovenes
8. magico
9. esquema

Minidiálogos y gramática

▼▼▼▼▼▼▼▼▼▼▼▼▼▼▼▼▼▼▼▼▼▼▼▼▼▼▼▼▼▼▼▼▼▼▼

8. Expressing Possession • Possessive Adjectives (Unstressed)

A. Minidiálogo: Los gustos de Guillermo y Gloria. You will hear a brief paragraph followed by a series of statements. Circle **C (cierto)** if the statement is true or **F (falso)** if it is false. If the information is not contained in the passage, Circle **ND (No lo dice)**.

1. C F ND
2. C F ND
3. C F ND

4. C F ND
5. C F ND

B. ¿Cómo es la ropa de Vicente? Tell what Vicente's clothing is like, using the oral and written cues. ¡OJO! Watch for singular or plural forms of the verb **ser**. Remember to change the endings on adjectives, if necessary.

MODELO: (*you hear*) zapatos (*you see*) negro → (*you say*) Sus zapatos son negros.

1. viejo
2. rojo

3. amarillo
4. nuevo

5. azul

C. ¿Cómo es su universidad? Describe your university to an exchange student who has recently arrived on campus. You will be using an appropriate form of **nuestro** and the verb **ser**. Remember to change the endings on adjectives, if necessary.

MODELO: (*you see*) universidad (*you hear*) viejo →
(*you say*) Nuestra universidad es vieja.

1. profesores
2. clases

3. biblioteca
4. consejeros

9. Expressing Actions and States • **Tener, venir, preferir, querer,** and **poder**; Some Idioms with **tener**

A. Dictado: Minidiálogo. Una gorra para José Miguel, después de mirar en tres tiendas. You will hear the following dialogue. It will be read twice. Listen carefully and write in the missing words.

ELISA: ¿Qué gorra _____, José Miguel?

JOSÉ MIGUEL: _____ la gris.

ELISA: ¡Pero ya _____ una gris, y es prácticamente idéntica!

JOSÉ MIGUEL: Pues, no _____ estas otras gorras. ¿Podemos mirar en la tienda anterior

otra vez?

ELISA: ¿Otra vez? Bueno, si realmente insistes...

B. Es la semana de exámenes. Practice telling about what you and your friends do during exam week, using the written and oral cues. ¡OJO! Remember that subject pronouns are not always used in Spanish.

MODELO: (*you hear*) nosotros   (*you see*) tener muchos exámenes →
(*you say*) Tenemos muchos exámenes.

1.   estar en la biblioteca
2.   siempre venir conmigo (*with me*)
3.   leer cien páginas
4.   ¡ya no poder leer más!
5.   querer regresar a la residencia
6.   ...pero no poder

C. Situaciones y reacciones. You will hear a series of partial conversations. Each will be said twice. Listen carefully and circle the letter of the reaction or response that best completes each one.

1.   a.   Ay, ¡tú siempre tienes prisa!   b.   Tienes razón, ¿verdad?
2.   a.   ¿Por qué tienes sueño?   b.   Sí, tienes razón, pero tienes que estudiar más.
3.   a.   ¿Tienes que comer en un restaurante?   b.   ¿Tienes ganas de ir (*go*) a un restaurante?
4.   a.   ¿Cuántos años tienes?   b.   La verdad es que tienes miedo, ¿no?
5.   a.   No, no tengo ganas de comprar ropa.   b.   ¿Cuántos años tiene la niña ahora?

10. Expressing Destination and Future Actions •
Ir, ir + a + Infinitive; the Contraction al

A. ¿Qué va a hacer Gilberto este fin de semana?

Paso 1. You will hear a brief passage in which Gilberto tells what his plans are for this weekend. As you listen, number the following drawings so that they match the order in which Gilberto narrates his plans. Write the number in the smaller of the two blanks.

a. _____ _____

b. _____ _____

c. _____ _____

d. _____ _____

Paso 2. Now stop the tape and, in the larger blanks, write a sentence that decribes Gilberto's future actions. Use **ir + a +** infinitive. Check your answers in the Appendix.

Now turn on the tape.

B. ¿Adónde vas? You will hear a series of questions about what you like to do or want to do. Using the words and phrases listed below, tell where you would go to do these activities. First, listen to the list.

universidad	discoteca El Ciclón	Restaurante Gallego
Almacén Robles	biblioteca	mercado

MODELO: (*you hear*) Te gusta estudiar y aprender cosas nuevas. →
(*you say*) Por eso voy a la universidad.

1. ... 2. ... 3. ... 4. ... 5. ...

C. Preguntas. You will hear a series of questions. Each will be said twice. Answer, using **ir** + **a** + infinitive and the written cues.

> MODELO: (*you hear*) ¿Qué vas a comprar en la librería? (*you see*) unos cuadernos →
> (*you say*) Voy a comprar unos cuadernos.

1. tres horas
2. a casa de un amigo
3. en McDonald's
4. pantalones grises / un suéter rojo

Situaciones

▼▼▼▼▼▼▼▼▼▼▼▼▼▼▼▼▼▼▼▼▼▼▼▼▼▼▼▼▼▼▼▼▼▼▼▼▼▼▼

Paso 1. José Miguel va de compras. In the following conversation, José Miguel is talking to an employee in a clothing store. José Miguel's lines will be read with pauses for repetition. But first, listen.

EMPLEADA:	Buenos días. ¿En qué puedo servirle?
JOSÉ MIGUEL:	¿Qué precio tienen estas camisas?
EMPLEADA:	Están en rebaja. Cuestan 40.000 sucres cada una.
JOSÉ MIGUEL:	Es un precio excelente.
EMPLEADA:	Sí. Las camisas son de puro algodón, y las tenemos de muchos colores. Aquí tiene una verde, otra roja, otra amarilla y otra azul. ¿Qué talla usa?
JOSÉ MIGUEL:	La 38, por lo general.
EMPLEADA:	Mire. Estos pantalones son perfectos para esta camisa. Con este pantalón negro y esta camisa azul, Ud. está a la última moda.
JOSÉ MIGUEL:	Me gustan mucho los pantalones. Y la camisa también. ¿Me los puedo probar?
EMPLEADA:	Sí, cómo no. Por allí están los probadores.

Paso 2. Aplicación. Now you will participate in a similar conversation, partially printed in your manual, in which you play the role of the customer. Complete the conversation using the written cues. (Remember to repeat the correct answer. If you wish, stop the tape and write the correct answers.) Here are the cues for your conversation.

> zapatos de tenis   39   última moda

EMPLEADA:	Buenas tardes. ¿En qué puedo servirle?
UD.:	Busco un par de _____.
EMPLEADA:	Pues, aquí tenemos de todo. ¿Qué número usa?
UD.:	El _____, por lo general.
EMPLEADA:	Tenemos varios estilos y colores...
UD.:	Pues, quiero zapatos de _____.
EMPLEADA:	Cómo no. Siéntese (*Sit down*) aquí, por favor. Le voy a traer (*I'm going to bring you*) varios estilos para probar.

Un poco de todo (Para entregar)

▼▼▼▼▼▼▼▼▼▼▼▼▼▼▼▼▼▼▼▼▼▼▼▼▼▼▼▼▼▼▼▼▼▼▼▼

A. Buscando regalos para papá. Listen to a conversation between a brother and sister, José and Ana, who are looking for gifts for their father. Do not be distracted by unfamiliar vocabulary. As you listen, circle only the items that they decide to buy.

B. *Listening Passage*: El Rastro

Antes de escuchar. Before you listen to the passage, *stop the tape* and do the following prelistening exercise.

It is sometimes helpful to answer questions about yourself that are related to a passage that you will listen to or read. Answering the following questions will give you an idea of the information the passage might contain.

1. ¿Hay un mercado al aire libre en la ciudad donde tú vives?
2. Por lo general, ¿qué venden en los mercados al aire libre?
3. ¿Cómo crees que son los precios en un mercado al aire libre?
4. ¿Te gusta ir de compras?
5. ¿Te gusta regatear?
6. ¿Coleccionas algo? ¿Sellos (*Stamps*), monedas (*coins*), libros viejos, trenes (*trains*), muñecas (*dolls*)?

Now turn on the tape.

Listening Passage. Now, you will hear a passage about El Rastro, an open-air market in Madrid. The narrator is from Spain. The following words and phrases appear in the passage.

los sellos	*stamps*
las monedas	*coins*
los domingos	*on Sundays*
los puestos	*stalls*

Después de escuchar. Circle the letter of the phrase that best completes each sentence.

1. El Rastro es...
   a. una gran tienda.
   b. un centro comercial.
   c. un mercado con muchos puestos

2. El Rastro está abierto (*open*)...
   a. todo el fin de semana.
   b. el domingo por la mañana.
   c. el domingo por la tarde.
3. En el Rastro venden...
   a. sólo ropa y zapatos.
   b. sólo cosas para coleccionistas (*collectors*).
   c. muchas cosas de todo tipo.
4. El Rastro está...
   a. en Madrid y es muy famoso.
   b. en España y es nuevo.
   c. en todas las ciudades de España.

Now turn on the tape.

C. Y para terminar... Entrevista. You will hear a series of questions. Each will be said twice. Answer based on your own experience. Stop the tape and write the answers.

1. _____
2. _____
3. _____
4. _____
5. _____
6. _____
7. _____

A. ¿Dónde están?

Paso 1. You will hear four brief conversations or parts of conversations. Listen carefully and, next to the number of the conversation, write the location in which each conversation is taking place. Not all the locations will be used. First, listen to the list of possible locations.

> una tienda de ropa
> una librería
> la oficina del consejero
> una casa
> un mercado

1. _____   3. _____

2. _____   4. _____

Paso 2 (Para entregar). Now, stop the tape and write a brief conversation, or part of a conversation, that takes place in the one location not used in **Paso 1.**

_____

_____

_____

_____

_____

Now turn on the tape.

B. *Los hispanos hablan*: **Dinos algo acerca de** (*Tell us something about*) **tu familia.** You will hear the following passage in which a student tells you about her family. After the passage, you will hear a series of statements. Circle **C** (**cierto**) if the statement is true or **F** (**falso**) if it is false. The following words appear in the passage. Listen to them before the passage is read.

el contador público	*public accountant*
el gerente de finanzas	*manager of finances*
dirige y organiza	*she directs (manages) and organizes*
se encargan de diseñar	*they are in charge of designing*
de pocos recursos	*of little (financial) means*
la mayor	*the oldest*
más chica	*younger*
parecidas	*similares*
la gente nos confunde	*people mistake us for each other*
en cuanto	*as for, as far as* _____ *is concerned*
probar cosas distintas	*to try different things*

1. C F   2. C F   3. C F   4. C F   5. C F

C. Cosas de todos los días. Practice talking about yourself and others, using the written cues. When you hear the corresponding number, form sentences using the words provided in the order given, making any necessary changes and additions. You will hear the correct answer on the tape.

> MODELO: (*you see*) (yo) llegar / universidad / 7:00 →
> (*you say*) Llego a la universidad a las siete.

1. profesores / llegar / 7:00 / también
2. mi amiga y yo / estudiar / biblioteca / todos los días
3. nuestro / profesores / ser / amable
4. (nosotras) aprender / mucho / universidad
5. fines de semana / (yo) trabajar / restaurante
6. cuando / (yo) regresar / residencia, / (yo) estar / cansado (*f.*)

D. Conversación: En la facultad (Para entregar). You will hear a conversation, partially printed in your manual, between two friends who pass each other on campus. Then you will participate in a similar conversation, playing Luisa's role. Answer, based on your own experience. Stop the tape and write the answers.

ALFREDO: Hola, Luisa. ¿Qué tal?

LUISA: _____

ALFREDO: Regular. ¿Cuándo es el examen en tu clase de geografía?

LUISA: _____

ALFREDO: Buena suerte (*luck*), ¿eh? ¿Trabajas en la biblioteca hoy?

LUISA: _____

ALFREDO: Bueno, hasta luego, Luisa.

LUISA: _____

E. Dictado. You will hear a brief paragraph about Isabel and what she likes to do on weekends. Listen carefully and, while listening, write the information requested. Write out all numbers. First, listen to the information requested.

La especialización (*major*) de Isabel: _____.

El lugar donde trabaja Isabel: _____.

La hora a la cual (*at which*) llegan al centro comercial Isabel y sus amigos: _____.

Tres de las prendas de vestir (*articles of clothing*) que quiere comprar Isabel: _____,
_____ y _____.

El precio del abrigo que le gusta: _____.

F. Y para terminar... Entrevista (Para entregar). You will hear a series of questions about yourself. Each will be said twice. Answer, based on your own experience. Stop the tape and write the answers.

1. _____
2. _____
3. _____
4. _____
5. _____
6. _____
7. _____
8. _____
9. _____

CAPÍTULO **4**

Vocabulario: Preparación

▼▼▼▼▼▼▼▼▼▼▼▼▼▼▼▼▼▼▼▼▼▼▼▼▼▼▼▼▼▼▼▼▼▼

A. El horario (*schedule*) **de la profesora Velásquez**

Paso 1. Dictado. Imagine that you are Professor Velásquez's secretary and that you are filling in her weekly calendar. Listen carefully as she tells you her schedule for this week, and fill in the blanks in the calendar. Some of the entries have already been made. First, stop the tape and look at the calendar.

lunes	martes	miércoles	jueves	viernes
mañana 10:45 AM : Clase de conversación	mañana _____ : dentista	mañana _____ :	mañana _____ :	mañana _____ :
tarde _____ :	tarde _____ :	tarde _____ :	tarde 3:00 PM : clase de español	tarde _____ :

Paso 2. Preguntas. Now you will hear a series of questions. Each will be said twice. Answer based on the information in **Paso 1.** Be sure to check your answers to **Paso 1** in the Appendix before beginning **Paso 2.** Follow the model.

> MODELO: (*you hear*) ¿Qué días enseña la profesora una clase de conversación? →
> (*you say*) El lunes y el viernes.

1. ... 2. ... 3. ... 4. ...

B. Identificación: ¿Qué hay en estos cuartos? Identify the following items when you hear the corresponding number. Begin each sentence with **Es un...** or **Es una...** .

En la sala

1. ...   2. ...   3. ...   4. ...   5. ...   6. ...   7. ...

En la alcoba

8. ...   9. ...   10. ...

C. Mis compañeros y yo. Form complete sentences about yourself and others, using the oral and written cues. The last two sentences will be negative.

MODELO: (*you see*) Adela   (*you hear*) hacer ejercicio →
(*you say*) Adela hace ejercicio.

1. yo
2. Tito y yo
3. tú
4. ellos
5. Marta

Los hispanos hablan: Dictado: ¿Qué cosas tienes en tu alcoba?

This question is answered by Xiomara. As you listen to the passage, jot down some of the things that she has in her room. The following words appear in the passage.

el abanico	*fan*
el tocador	*dressing table*
los cuadros	pinturas
la gata de peluche	*stuffed toy cat*
me regaló	*he gave me (as a gift)*

Lo que Xiomara tiene en su alcoba

_____

_____

_____

_____

_____

Pronunciación y ortografía: b and v

▼▼▼▼▼▼▼▼▼▼▼▼▼▼▼▼▼▼▼▼▼▼▼▼▼▼▼▼▼▼▼▼▼

Spanish **b** and **v** are pronounced exactly the same way. At the beginning of a phrase, or after **m** or **n**, **b** and **v** are pronounced like the English *b*, as a stop; that is, no air is allowed to escape through the lips. In all other positions, **b** and **v** are fricatives; that is, they are produced by allowing some air to escape through the lips. There is no equivalent for this sound in English.

A. Repeat the following words and phrases, imitating the speaker. Note that the type of *b* sound you will hear is indicated at the beginning of the series.

1. [b]   bueno   viejo   barato   baño   hombre
2. [ƀ]   llevar   libro   pobre   abrigo   universidad
3. [b/ƀ]   bueno / es bueno   busca / Ud. busca   bien / muy bien   en Venezuela / de Venezuela   visita / él visita
4. [b/ƀ]   beber   bebida   vivir   biblioteca   vívido

B. Dictado. You will hear five sentences. Each will be said twice. Listen carefully and write what you hear.

1. _____
2. _____
3. _____
4. _____
5. _____

Minidiálogos y gramática

▼▼▼▼▼▼▼▼▼▼▼▼▼▼▼▼▼▼▼▼▼▼▼▼▼▼▼▼▼▼▼▼▼

11. Expressing Actions • Present Tense of Stem-Changing Verbs

A. Minidiálogo: ¡Nunca más! You will hear a conversation between a husband and wife, Armando and Alicia, who are talking about a stationery store. It will be followed by a series of statements. Circle **C** (**cierto**) if the statement is true or **F** (**falso**) if it is false. In this exercise you will practice listening for specific information.

1. C   F   En la papelería Franco piden precios muy caros.

2. C   F   A Armando no le gusta la papelería Franco.

3. C   F   Alicia dice (*says*) que va a volver a la papelería.

B. Encuesta. You will hear a series of statements about your habits. For each statement, check the appropriate response. No answers will be given on the tape. The answers you choose should be correct for you!

	SIEMPRE	CON FRECUENCIA	A VECES	¡NUNCA!
1.	☐	☐	☐	☐
2.	☐	☐	☐	☐
3.	☐	☐	☐	☐
4.	☐	☐	☐	☐
5.	☐	☐	☐	☐
6.	☐	☐	☐	☐

C. Un sábado típico en mi casa. Tell about the activities of your fictitious family on a typical Saturday. Use the written and oral cues.

1. yo
2. mis padres
3. mi hermana y yo
4. tú

D. Entrevista con los Sres. Ruiz. Interview Mr. and Mrs. Ruiz about some of the things they like to do. Use the written cues. You will hear an answer to each of your questions on the tape.

MODELO: (*you hear*) jugar al tenis →
(*you say*) ¿Juegan al tenis?   (*you hear*) No, no jugamos al tenis.

1. ...   2. ...   3. ...   4. ...

12. Expressing *-self/-selves* • Reflexive Pronouns

A. Minidiálogo: La rutina diaria de Diego. You will hear a brief description of Diego's daily routine. Then you will hear the following statements. Circle **C** (**cierto**) if the statement is true or **F** (**falso**) if it is false. If the information is not given in the description, circle **ND** (**No lo dice**).

1. C   F   ND   Diego se levanta a las nueve de la mañana.

2. C   F   ND   Él se acuesta muy tarde.

3. C   F   ND   Se viste en el baño.

4. C   F   ND   Por lo general, Diego tiene prisa por la mañana.

B. Encuesta. You will hear a series of statements about your habits. For each statement, check the appropriate response. No answers will be given on the tape. The answers you choose should be correct for you!

	SIEMPRE	CON FRECUENCIA	A VECES	¡NUNCA!
1.	☐	☐	☐	☐
2.	☐	☐	☐	☐
3.	☐	☐	☐	☐
4.	☐	☐	☐	☐
5.	☐	☐	☐	☐
6.	☐	☐	☐	☐

C. Hábitos y costumbres. Practice telling about some of the habits of the members of your fictitious family. Use the oral and written cues.

1. yo
2. mi primo y yo

3. mi hermanito
4. mis abuelos

D. ¿Qué van a hacer estas personas? When you hear the corresponding number, tell what the people in each drawing are going to do. ¡OJO! You will be using the **ir** + **a** + infinitive construction, and you will attach the reflexive pronouns to the infinitives. First, listen to the list of verbs.

acostarse   afeitarse   ducharse   quitarse   sentarse

13. Pointing Out People and Things • Demonstrative Adjectives

A. En la mueblería (*furniture store*) **González.** Imagine that you are a salesperson at the **mueblería González** and you are pointing out various items to a customer. Write the letter of the item you are describing next to the number of the description you hear. Remember that the items are being described from your point of view. First, stop the tape and look at the drawing.

1. _____   2. _____   3. _____   4. _____

B. ¿Cómo son estas cosas? Answer, using the oral cues and an appropriate form of the indicated demonstrative adjective. Remember to change the endings of the adjectives, and use **es** or **son**, as appropriate.

> MODELO: (*you see*) ese / sofás (*you hear*) verde → (*you say*) Esos sofás son verdes.

1. ese / armario
2. este / pantalones
3. aquel / cómoda
4. este / faldas
5. ese / sillones

C. Recuerdos de su viaje a México. Your friends want to know all about your trip to Mexico. Answer their questions, using an appropriate form of the demonstrative adjective **aquel** and the oral cues.

> MODELO: (*you hear and see*) ¿Qué tal el restaurante El Charro? (*you hear*) excelente →
> (*you say*) ¡Aquel restaurante es excelente!

1. ¿Qué tal el Hotel Libertad?
2. ¿Y los dependientes del hotel?
3. ¿Qué tal la ropa en el Mercado de la Merced?
4. ¿Y los parques de la capital?

Situaciones

▼▼▼

Paso 1. La rutina diaria. In this conversation, Diego and Antonio talk about their daily routine. Diego's lines will be read with pauses for repetition. But first, listen.

DIEGO: Dime, Antonio, ¿cómo es el horario de Uds.?

ANTONIO: Normalmente, yo me levanto a las siete y Juan se levanta a las seis y media. ¿A qué horas te levantas tú?

DIEGO: Si tengo clases, me levanto a las siete y media.

ANTONIO: ¡Perfecto! Primero Juan se baña y se afeita, después yo y por último tú.

DIEGO: ¿Y vuelven Uds. a casa para almorzar?

ANTONIO: Bueno, los lunes, miércoles y viernes sí vuelvo a casa para almorzar, porque no tengo clases por la tarde. Pero los martes y jueves almuerzo en la cafetería de la universidad. Juan no vuelve a casa para almorzar. Come en casa de su novia.

DIEGO: Muy bien. Entonces, los lunes, miércoles y viernes podemos almorzar aquí tú y yo. Antonio, creo que sí me va a gustar mucho vivir aquí.

Paso 2. Aplicación. Now you will participate in a similar conversation, partially printed in your manual, in which you play the role of Alfonso. Complete the conversation using the written cues. If you wish, stop the tape and write the correct answers. Here are the cues for your conversation.

gracias
quién prepara la comida

el viernes por la tarde
especial

MARCOS: Bienvenido a nuestro apartamento, Alfonso.

ALFONSO: _____[1], Marcos.

MARCOS: ¿Tienes alguna pregunta acerca del (*about the*) horario?

ALFONSO: Pues, sí. ¿_____[2] esta noche?

MARCOS: Bueno, Lucas prepara la comida esta noche, yo cocino (*cook*) el jueves y tú vas a cocinar el viernes.

ALFONSO: Perfecto. No tengo clases _____[3] y puedo preparar una cena (*dinner*) _____[4].

MARCOS: ¡Eso es magnífico!

Un poco de todo (Para entregar)

▼▼▼

A. ¿Cuál es su casa? You will hear a description of Raquel and Arturo's house, read by Raquel. Listen to the description and circle the number of the drawing on the next page that matches the description.

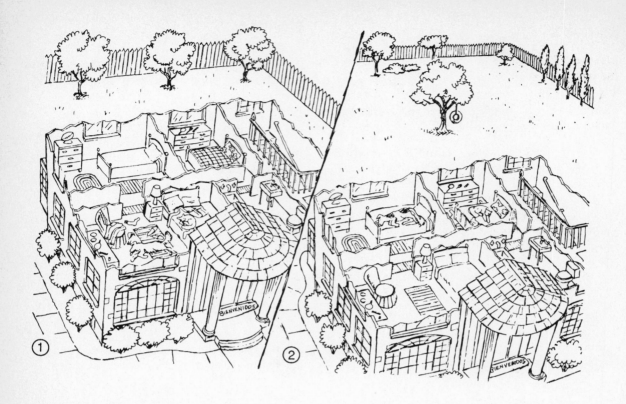

B. *Listening passage*: **Una casa hispana.**

Antes de escuchar. Before you listen to the passage, *stop the tape* and do the following prelistening exercises.

Paso 1. This passage will contain information about a house found in a Hispanic country. Check the specific information that you might expect to find in the passage.

☐ The speaker might talk about the different rooms in the house.

☐ The speaker might mention how many people are in his or her family.

☐ He or she might discuss the different architectural styles found in the Hispanic world.

Paso 2. Now complete the paragraph below with information that is true for your house or apartment. When a choice given, circle the choice that is true for you.

1. Mi (casa/apartamento) tiene _____ alcoba(s) y _____ baño(s).

2. (Tiene / No tiene) sala.

3. (Tiene / No tiene) comedor.

4. Vivo allí con (mi familia / mis amigos/as). (Vivo sola/a [*alone*].)

5. Mi (casa/apartamento) (es / no es) típico/a de esta región o ciudad.

6. En la región donde vivo, (es necesario / no es necesario) tener calefacción (*heating*) en el invierno (*winter*).

7. Algo que (*Something that*) me gusta mucho de mi (casa/apartamento) es

_____.

8. Algo que no me gusta es _____.

Now turn on the tape.

Listening Passage. Now you will hear a passage about Alma's house. The following words appear in the passage.

afueras	*outskirts*
el vecindario	*neighborhood*
recámaras	*bedrooms*
juntos	*together*
árboles	*trees*
el clima	*climate*
calefacción	*heating*

Después de escuchar. Read the following true/false statements. Circle **C** (**cierto**) if the statement is true or **F** (**falso**) if it is false. If the information is not given in the passage, circle **ND** (**No lo dice**). Correct the statements that are false.

1. C   F   ND   Todos los edificios en Panamá son de estilo colonial.

_____

2. C   F   ND   Alma vive en el centro de la Ciudad de Panamá.

_____

3. C   F   ND   Su casa es pequeña.

_____

4. C   F   ND   Alma y su familia almuerzan en el comedor.

_____

5. C   F   ND   La casa de Alma no tiene patio.

_____

Now turn on the tape.

C.   Y para terminar... Entrevista. You will hear a series of questions. Each will be said twice. Answer, based on your own experience. Stop the tape and write the answers.

1. _____
2. _____
3. _____
4. _____
5. _____
6. _____
7. _____
8. _____

CAPÍTULO **5**

Vocabulario: Preparación

▼▼▼▼▼▼▼▼▼▼▼▼▼▼▼▼▼▼▼▼▼▼▼▼▼▼▼▼▼▼▼▼▼▼▼▼▼

A. **¿Qué tiempo hace?** You will hear a series of weather conditions. Each will be said twice. Give the number of the drawing to which each corresponds, then repeat the description. First, stop the tape and look at the drawings.

1.

2.

3.

4.

5.

6.

B. **¿Cuándo es... ?** Your Peruvian friend Evangelina wants to know when certain events take place, including a birth date (**una fecha de nacimiento**), an anniversary (**un aniversario**), and a national holiday (**una fiesta nacional**). Answer, using the written cues.

> MODELO: (*you hear*) ¿Cuándo es el cumpleaños de Nicolás? (*you see*) Sunday, May 4 →
> (*you say*) Es el domingo, cuatro de mayo.

1. Saturday, November 22
2. Wednesday, April 14

3. February 11, 1899
4. July 4, 1776

C. ¿Dónde está? You will hear a series of descriptions. Listen carefully and name the country, location, or item described. You will be listening for specific information about the location of the place or item.

1. ...   2. ...   3. ...

4. ...   5. ...   6. ...

7. ...   8. ...   9. ...

Los hispanos hablan: ¿De dónde eres?

You will hear three brief answers to this question. As you listen, write the information in the spaces provided. First, stop the tape and look at the information for which you need to listen.

Habla José.

Ciudad: _____ País: _____

El clima: _____

La gente (*people*): _____

¿Hay una universidad en la ciudad?   Sí   No

Habla Clara.

Ciudad: _____ País: _____

El clima: _____

La gente: _____

¿Hay una universidad en la ciudad?   Sí   No

Habla Diana.

Ciudad: _____ País: _____

El clima: _____

La gente: _____

¿Hay una universidad en la ciudad?   Sí   No

Pronunciación y ortografía: r and rr

▼▼▼▼▼▼▼▼▼▼▼▼▼▼▼▼▼▼▼▼▼▼▼▼▼▼▼▼▼▼▼▼

The letter **r** has two pronunciations in Spanish: the trilled **r** (written as **rr** between vowels or as **r** at the beginning of a word), and the flap **r**, which appears in all other positions. Because mispronunciations can alter the meaning of a word, it is important to distinguish between these two pronunciations of the Spanish **r**. For example: **coro** (*chorus*) and **corro** (*I run*).

The flap **r** is similar to the sound produced by the rapid pronunciation of *tt* and *dd* in the English words *Betty* and *ladder*.

A. Listen to these word pairs. Then repeat them.

> *Petty* / pero   *sadder* / Sara   *motor* / moro

B. Repeat the following words, phrases, and sentences, imitating the speaker.

1. arte   gracias   para   vender   triste
2. ruso   Roberto   real   reportero   rebelde
3. burro   corral   carro   barra   corro
4. el extranjero   el precio del cuaderno   el nombre correcto   Enrique, Carlos y Rosita
   las residencias   una mujer refinada   Puerto Rico   El perro está en el corral.
   Soy el primo de Roberto Ramírez.   Estos errores son raros.

C. **¿R o rr?** You will hear a series of words. Each will be said twice. Circle the letter of the word you hear.

1. a. ahora   b. ahorra
2. a. caro   b. carro
3. a. coro   b. corro
4. a. coral   b. corral
5. a. pero   b. perro

Minidiálogos y gramática

▼▼▼▼▼▼▼▼▼▼▼▼▼▼▼▼▼▼▼▼▼▼▼▼▼▼▼▼▼▼▼▼

14. ¿Qué estás haciendo? • Present Progressive: estar + -ndo

A. **¿Qué están haciendo?** You will hear a series of sentences. Each will be said twice. Write the number of each statement next to the item that corresponds to the activity mentioned. First, listen to the list of items.

a. _____ el restaurante

b. _____ las bicicletas y la pelota (*ball*)

c. _____ el libro

d. _____ la computadora

e. _____ la música

B. Descripción: ¿Qué están haciendo en este momento? Using the present progressive of the following verbs, tell what each person in the Hernández family is doing at the moment. For the exercise, don't attach the reflexive pronouns to the present participle. First, listen to the list of verbs.

ponerse   afeitarse   jugar   vestirse   dormir   bañarse

① el bebé   ② los niños   ③ la Sra. Hernández   ④ el Sr. Hernández   ⑤ la abuela   ⑥ Susanita

MODELO: (*you hear*) 1. → (*you say*) El bebé está durmiendo.

2. ...   3. ...   4. ...   5. ...   6. ...

C. ¡Sé lo que (*I know what*) **estás haciendo!** Your friend Amalia will say where she is and you will guess what she might be doing there. You will hear each of her statements twice. You will hear a possible answer on the tape. First, listen to the list of possible actions.

estudiar   leer   trabajar
mirar la tele   preparar el almuerzo

MODELO: (*you hear*) Estoy en mi alcoba. → (*you say*) Estás estudiando, ¿verdad?

1. ...   2. ...   3. ...   4. ...

15. ¿**Ser** o **estar?** • Summary of the Uses of **ser** and **estar**

A. Minidiálogo: Un viaje de negocios (*business trip*). You will hear one side of a telephone conversation between a husband and his wife who is on a business trip. Then you will hear a series of questions from the dialogue. Circle the letter of the best response to each.

1. a. Estoy en Nueva York.   b. Estoy cansada, pero estoy bien.
2. a. Es el señor Miró.   b. Es muy moderno.
3. a. Estoy trabajando.   b. Hace buen tiempo.
4. a. Hace buen tiempo.   b. Son las once y media.

B. ¿Qué pregunta hiciste? (*What question did you ask?*) You will hear a series of statements that contain **ser** or **estar**. Each will be said twice. Circle the letter of the question that corresponds to each.

1. a. ¿Cómo estás?   b. ¿Cómo eres?
2. a. ¿Cómo están?   b. ¿Cómo son?
3. a. ¿Dónde estás?   b. ¿De dónde eres?
4. a. ¿Dónde está el consejero?   b. ¿De dónde es el consejero?
5. a. ¿De quién es la blusa?   b. ¿De qué es la blusa?

C. Marcos, ¿qué tal? When you hear the corresponding number, tell how your friend Marcos seems to be feeling on these different occasions. Use one of the following adjectives. Use Marcos's name only in the first sentence. First, listen to the list of adjectives.

     nervioso   furioso   triste   contento   preocupado

1.   2.   3.

4.   5.

1. ...   2. ...   3. ...   4. ...   5. ...

D. ¿Quiénes son? Imagine that the people in this photograph are your relatives. Tell who they are and describe them, using the oral cues and the appropriate forms of **ser** or **estar**. All the cues are about the couple on the right. Begin your first answer with **Son...**

1. ...   2. ...   3. ...   4. ...   5. ...   6. ...

16. Describing • Comparisons

A. Comparando dos ciudades

Paso 1. La comparación. Listen as Uncle
Ricardo compares Mexico City (**el Distrito
Federal [D.F.]**) and Sevilla.

Paso 2. ¿Qué recuerdas? Stop the tape and complete the following sentences based on Ricardo's
comparison.

Según (*According to*) Ricardo...

1. Sevilla es _____ bonita _____ la Ciudad de México.

2. Sevilla tiene _____ edificios altos _____ el D.F.

3. En el D.F. no hace _____ calor _____ en Sevilla.

4. Sevilla no tiene _____ habitantes _____ el D.F.

Now turn on the tape.

B. La rutina de Alicia. The following chart shows Alicia's routine for weekdays and weekends. You
will hear a series of statements about the chart. Each will be said twice. Circle **C** if the statement is true
or **F** if it is false, according to the chart. First stop the tape and read the chart.

ACCIÓN	DE LUNES A VIERNES	SÁBADO Y DOMINGO
levantarse	6:30	9:30
bañarse	7:15	10:00
trabajar	8 horas	1 hora
almorzar	20 minutos	30 minutos
divertirse	1 hora	8 horas
acostarse	11:00	11:00

1. C F   2. C F   3. C F   4. C F   5. C F

C. Un desacuerdo. Imagine that you and your friend Lourdes don't agree on anything! React to her
statements negatively, following the model and using the oral cues.

MODELO: (*you hear and see*) Los amigos son más importantes que la familia.
          (*you hear*) tan → (*you say*) No, los amigos son tan importantes como la familia.

1. El invierno es más bonito que el verano.
2. Hace tanto calor en Florida como en Alaska.
3. La clase de cálculo es menos difícil que la clase de física.
4. Los niños juegan más videojuegos (*videogames*) que los adultos.

Situaciones

▼▼▼▼▼▼▼▼▼▼▼▼▼▼▼▼▼▼▼▼▼▼▼▼▼▼▼▼▼▼▼▼

Paso 1. Hablando por teléfono. In this conversation, Carolina Díaz calls her friend Marta Durán Benítez. Marta's father, Manolo Durán, takes a phone message for his daughter. Carolina's lines will be read with pauses for repetition. But first, listen.

MANOLO:	¿Diga?
CAROLINA:	Buenos días. Habla Carolina Díaz. ¿Está Marta?
MANOLO:	No, Carolina. Marta no está en este momento. Está en el parque con su tío abuelo. ¿Quieres dejarle un recado?
CAROLINA:	Sí, muchas gracias. Me gustaría decirle que si quiere venir esta tarde a jugar conmigo. Hace buen tiempo y podríamos ir a jugar afuera.
MANOLO:	Muy bien, Carolina. Yo le doy el recado. Saluda a tus padres de mi parte, por favor.
CAROLINA:	Sí. Adiós.
MANOLO:	Adiós.

Paso 2. Aplicación. Now you will participate in a similar conversation, partially printed in your manual, in which you play the role of Susanita. Complete the conversation using the written cues. Here are the cues for your conversation:

Habla Susanita Márquez.   Muchas gracias. Adiós.
Hola. ¿Está Elena?   No, gracias. Puedo llamar más tarde.

EDUARDO: ¿Bueno? (*Hello?*)

SUSANITA: _____¹. ¿_____²?

EDUARDO: ¿De parte de quién, por favor? (*Who's calling, please?*)

SUSANITA: _____³.

EDUARDO: Hola, Susanita. Lo siento, pero Elena está en casa de su tía. ¿Quieres dejar un recado?

SUSANITA: _____⁴. _____⁵.

EDUARDO: Está bien. Elena va a regresar dentro de (*within*) una hora.

SUSANITA: _____⁶. _____⁷.

EDUARDO: Adiós.

Un poco de todo (Para entregar)

▼▼▼▼▼▼▼▼▼▼▼▼▼▼▼▼▼▼▼▼▼▼▼▼▼▼▼▼▼▼▼▼

A. En la plaza Santa Ana

Paso 1. ¿Qué pasa? You will hear a series of statements about the following drawing. Each will be said twice. Circle **C** if the statement is true or **F** if it is false. First, stop the tape and look at the drawing on the following page.

1. C F   2. C F   3. C F   4. C F   5. C F

Paso 2. Descripción. Now stop the tape and write five sentences that describe the drawing. You can talk about the weather, what the people are doing, how they seem to be feeling, their clothing, and so on. You can also make comparisons.

1. _____
2. _____
3. _____
4. _____
5. _____

Now turn on the tape.

B. *Listening Passage*: Hablando del clima

Antes de escuchar. Before you listen to the passage, *stop the tape* and do the following prelistening exercises.

Paso 1. Read the following true/false statements. As you read them, try to infer the information the passage will give you, as well as the specific information for which you need to listen.

1. En las regiones tropicales, por lo general, hay una estación seca (*dry*) y una lluviosa (*rainy*).
2. En Latinoamérica, no hace frío en ninguna (*any*) región.
3. Hay climas muy variados en el mundo hispánico.
4. En Sudamérica, las estaciones del año son opuestas a las (*opposite to those*) de los países del Hemisferio Norte.

Paso 2. You probably do know quite a bit about the climate in most of Latin America. That information will be fairly easy for you to recognize in the listening passage. Read the next set of true/false statements, and try to infer what type of information you need to listen for regarding the person who will narrate the passage.

La persona que habla...

1. es de Vermont.
2. prefiere el frío del invierno.
3. no sabe (*doesn't know how to*) esquiar.
4. quiere vivir en los Andes.

A la persona que habla...

5. no le gustan las estaciones lluviosas en los países tropicales.

Now turn on the tape.

Listening Passage. Now, you will hear a passage about the climate in different regions of the Hispanic world. This passage is read by Nicanor, a friend of Susana's. The following words appear in the passage.

seca	*dry*
lluviosa	*rainy*
molestan	*bother*
yo lo tengo claro	*it's clear to me*

Después de escuchar. Here is another version of the true/false statements you did in **Antes de escuchar.** Circle **C** if the statement is true or **F** if it is false. Then correct the statements that are false, according to the passage.

1. C F Nicanor es de Vermont.

_____

2. C F A Nicanor no le gusta el frío.

_____

3. C F En el mundo hispánico, hay climas muy variados.

_____

4. C F En Sudamérica no hace frío en ninguna región.

_____

5. C F A Nicanor le gustaría (*would like*) vivir en los Andes.

_____

6. C F Cuando es verano en el Hemisferio Norte, también es verano en el Hemisferio Sur.

_____

Now turn on the tape.

C. Y para terminar... Entrevista. You will hear a series of questions. Each will be said twice. Answer, based on your own experience. Write out all numbers. Stop the tape and write the answers.

1. _____
2. _____
3. _____
4. _____
5. _____
6. _____

Vocabulario: Preparación

▼▼▼▼▼▼▼▼▼▼▼▼▼▼▼▼▼▼▼▼▼▼▼▼▼▼▼▼▼

A. Definiciones. You will hear a series of definitions. Each will be said twice. Circle the letter of the word defined by each.

1. a. la zanahoria   b. los huevos
2. a. la lechuga   b. la langosta
3. a. la leche   b. el vino blanco
4. a. un postre   b. un sándwich
5. a. el almuerzo   b. la cena

B. Identificaciones. Identify the following foods when you hear the corresponding number. Use the definite article in your answer.

1.
2.
3.
4.

5.
6.
7.
8.

C. Categorías. You will hear a series of words. Repeat each word, telling in what category it belongs: **un tipo de carne, un marisco, una fruta, una verdura, un postre,** or **una bebida.**

> MODELO: (*you hear*) el té → (*you say*) El té es una bebida.

1. ...   2. ...   3. ...   4. ...   5. ...

D. ¿Qué sabes y a quién conoces?

Paso 1. Mis amigos. You will hear a brief paragraph about some of the things your friends know and whom they know. Listen and write either **sí** or **no** under the corresponding item. Two items have been done for you.

NOMBRE	BAILAR	A JUAN	JUGAR AL TENIS	A MIS PADRES	ESTA CIUDAD
Enrique	*sí*	*no*			
Roberto					
Susana					

Paso 2. ¿Qué recuerdas? Now stop the tape and complete the following statements with information from the completed chart. Check the answers to **Paso 1** in the appendix before you begin **Paso 2.**

1. Roberto y Susana _____ jugar al tenis.

2. Susana _____ bailar.

3. Nadie (*No one*) _____ a Juan.

4. Roberto y Enrique _____ bien la ciudad.

Now turn on the tape.

Los hispanos hablan: ¿Qué no te gusta nada comer?

You will hear answers to this question from Clara, Xiomara, and Teresa. As they describe the foods that they do not like, check the appropriate boxes. Rewind the tape and listen again, if necessary. First, listen to the list of foods.

		CLARA	XIOMARA	TERESA
1.	huevos	☐	☐	☐
2.	verduras	☐	☐	☐
3.	oreja de cerdo (*pig's ear*)	☐	☐	☐
4.	mondongo (*tripe soup*)	☐	☐	☐
5.	hamburguesas con pepinillos (*pickles*)	☐	☐	☐
6.	caracoles (*snails*)	☐	☐	☐
7.	comida rápida	☐	☐	☐
8.	mantequilla	☐	☐	☐
9.	platos sofisticados	☐	☐	☐

Pronunciación y ortografía: d

▼▼▼▼▼▼▼▼▼▼▼▼▼▼▼▼▼▼▼▼▼▼▼▼▼▼▼▼▼▼

A. Spanish **d** has two pronunciations. At the beginning of a phrase or sentence and after **n** or **l**, it is pronounced similarly to English *d* as in *dog*: [d], that is, as a stop. Listen to these words and repeat them after the speaker.

> [d]   diez   ¿dónde?   venden   condición   falda   el doctor

In all other cases, **d** is pronounced like the English sound *th* in ano*th*er but softer: [đ], that is, as a fricative. Listen and repeat the following words.

> [đ]   adiós   seda   ciudad   usted   cuadros   la doctora

B. Entonación. Repeat the following sentences, imitating the speaker. Pay close attention to the intonation.

> ¿Dónde está el dinero?   ¿Qué estudia usted?
> Dos y diez son doce.   Venden de todo, ¿verdad?

C. You will hear a series of words containing the letter **d**. Each will be said twice. Circle the letter of the **d** sound you hear.

1. a. [d]   b. [đ]
2. a. [d]   b. [đ]
3. a. [d]   b. [đ]

4. a. [d]   b. [đ]
5. a. [d]   b. [đ]

Minidiálogos y gramática

▼▼▼▼▼▼▼▼▼▼▼▼▼▼▼▼▼▼▼▼▼▼▼▼▼▼▼▼▼▼

17. Expressing *what* or *whom* • Direct Object Pronouns

A. Encuesta: ¿Qué te gusta comer? You will hear the names of various foods. Each will be said twice. Write in the blank the name of the food mentioned, then check the appropriate answer. No answers will be given on the tape. The answers you choose should be correct for you!

1. _____

☐ Siempre las como.

☐ Las como a veces.

☐ Nunca las como.

2. _____

☐ Siempre lo como.

☐ Lo como a veces.

☐ Nunca lo como.

3. _____

☐ Siempre la tomo.

☐ La tomo a veces.

☐ Nunca la tomo.

4. _____

☐ Siempre los como.

☐ Los como a veces.

☐ Nunca los como.

B. En la cocina. Imagine that you are preparing a meal, and your friend Pablo is in the kitchen helping you. Answer his questions, using object pronouns and the written cues. You will hear each question twice.

> MODELO: (*you hear*) ¿Necesitas la olla (*pot*) ahora?
> (*you see*) sí → (*you say*) ¿La olla? Sí, la necesito.
> (*you see*) no → (*you say*) ¿La olla? No, no la necesito todavía.

1. no 2. sí 3. sí 4. no

C. Entre amigos... Imagine that your friend Manuel, who hasn't seen you for a while, wants to know when you can get together again. Answer his questions, using the written cues. You will hear each question twice.

1. esta noche 2. para mañana 3. 4:00 4. café La Rioja

D. Hablando de los estudios. You will hear a series of questions about things you have already done. Each will be said twice. Answer, using **acabo de** and a direct object pronoun. Attach the direct object pronoun to the infinitive when you answer.

> MODELO: (*you hear*) ¿Por qué no escribes la composición? → (*you say*) Acabo de escribirla.

1. ... 2. ... 3. ... 4. ...

18. Expressing Negation • Indefinite and Negative Words

A. Minidiálogo: En la cocina de Diego y Antonio. You will hear the following dialogue, followed by a series of statements. Circle **C** if the statement is true or **F** if it is false. If the statement refers to information that is not in the dialogue, circle **ND** (**No lo dice**).

1. C F ND
2. C F ND
3. C F ND
4. C F ND

B. Descripción. You will hear a series of questions. Answer, according to the drawings.

> MODELO: (*you hear*) ¿Hay algo en la pizarra? →
> (*you say*) Sí, hay algo en la pizarra. Hay unas palabras.

1.

2.

3.

4.

5.

C. ¡Por eso no come nadie allí! You will hear a series of questions about a very unpopular restaurant. Each will be said twice. Answer, using the double negative.

MODELO: (*you hear*) ¿Sirven algunos postres especiales? →
(*you say*) No, no sirven ningún postre especial.

1. ...   2. ...   3. ...   4. ...

19. Influencing Others • Formal Commands; Introduction to the Subjunctive (For Recognition)

A. ¿Qué acaban de decir? You will hear a series of commands. Write the number of the command you hear next to the corresponding drawing. You will hear each statement twice. ¡OJO! There is an extra drawing.

a. _____

b. _____

c. _____

d. _____

e. _____

B. Profesora por un día... Imagine that you are the Spanish professor for the day. Practice telling your students what they should do, using the oral cues. Use **Uds.** commands.

1. ... 2. ... 3. ... 4. ... 5. ...

C. La dieta del señor Casiano. Mr. Casiano is on a diet and you are his doctor. He will ask you whether or not he can eat certain things. Answer his questions, using affirmative or negative commands and direct object pronouns.

> MODELO: (*you hear*) ¿Puedo comer chocolate? (*you see*) No, ... →
> (*you say*) No, no lo coma.

1. No, ... 2. No, ... 3. No, ... 4. Sí, ... 5. Sí, ...

D. Un nuevo restaurante

Paso 1. You will hear an ad for a new restaurant that is opening soon. Listen carefully and check the appropriate boxes based on the information you hear in the ad. First, listen to the list of actions.

	SÍ	NO
hacer reservaciones	☐	☐
vestirse formalmente	☐	☐
pedir el pescado	☐	☐
pedir una hamburguesa	☐	☐
llegar temprano	☐	☐
pagar con tarjeta de crédito	☐	☐
pagar al contado (*in cash*)	☐	☐

Paso 2. Now stop the tape and read the following recommendations. Check the recommendations that you would give a friend who wants to visit this restaurant. Remember to check your answers to **Paso 1** in the Appendix before beginning **Paso 2.**

1. ☐ No recomiendo que hagas reservaciones antes de ir a El Caribe.

2. ☐ Recomiendo que llegues temprano.

3. ☐ Recomiendo que vayas a El Caribe si te gusta mucho la carne.

4. ☐ Recomiendo que te vistas con ropa informal.

5. ☐ No recomiendo que lleves a toda tu familia.

6. ☐ Recomiendo que pagues con tarjeta de crédito o al contado.

Now turn on the tape.

Situaciones

▼▼

Paso 1. En el restaurante. In this conversation, Manolo Durán and his wife, Lola Benítez, have dinner in a restaurant. Manolo's lines will be read with pauses for repetition. But first, listen.

CAMARERO:	¿Ya saben lo que desean de comer los señores?
MANOLO:	Creo que sí, pero, ¿qué recomienda Ud.?
CAMARERO:	Hoy tenemos un plato especial: gambas al limón con arroz, un plato ligero y delicioso. Y también tenemos un salmón buenísimo que acaba de llegar esta tarde.
LOLA:	¡Qué rico! Yo quiero las gambas, por favor.
MANOLO:	Eh, para mí, el bistec estilo argentino, poco asado. Y una ensalada mixta para dos.
CAMARERO:	¿Y para empezar? Tenemos una sopa de ajo muy rica.
LOLA:	Para mí, una sopa, por favor.
MANOLO:	Y para mí también. Y le dice al chef que por favor le ponga un poco de atún a la ensalada.
CAMARERO:	Muy bien, señor.

Paso 2. Aplicación. Now you will participate in a similar conversation, partially printed in your manual, in which you play the role of the **cliente** in a restaurant. Complete the conversation using the written cues. Here are the cues for your conversation. **¡OJO!** The cues are not in order.

el flan de naranja   un coctel de camarones
los tacos de pollo   un vino blanco

CAMARERA: ¿Sabe ya lo que desea de comer?

CLIENTE: Sí. Favor de traerme _____¹.

CAMARERA: Sí, cómo no. ¿Y para empezar? Tenemos una gran variedad de antojitos (*appetizers*) que

seguramente le van a gustar.

CLIENTE: Bueno, tráigame _____², por favor.

CAMARERA: ¿Algo de postre?

CLIENTE: Sí, quiero _____³, por favor.

CAMARERA: Muy bien. ¿Y para beber?

CLIENTE: ¿Me puede traer _____⁴?

CAMARERA: Sí. Se lo traigo en seguida (*I'll bring it to you right away*).

Un poco de todo (Para entregar)

▼▼

A. ¿Qué va a pedir Juan? Juan and his friend Marta are in a restaurant. Listen to their conversation and circle the items that Juan is going to order. In this exercise, you will practice listening for specific information. First, stop the tape and look at the drawing.

B. *Listening passage*: **La vida social en los bares de España**

Antes de escuchar. Before you listen to the passage, *stop the tape* and do the following prelistening exercises.

Many aspects of social life and nightlife in Spain are different from those of the United States. Check the ones that you think apply *only* to Spain.

☐ Hay muchos bares. ¡A veces hay dos en cada calle (*street*)!

☐ La familia entera, padres e hijos pequeños, va al bar.

☐ Por lo general, no se sirve comida.

☐ Es costumbre pedir tapas: pequeños platos de comidas diversas.

Now turn on the tape.

Listening Passage. Now you will hear a passage about the many types of bars that are part of Spanish social life. The following words and phrases appear in the passage.

no tienen nada que ver con	*they have nothing to do with*
casero	*homemade, home-style*
sevillanos	personas de Sevilla
el ambiente	*atmosphere*

Después de escuchar. Rewind the tape and listen to the passage again. Then stop the tape, and complete the following sentences with words chosen from the list.

Sevilla   amigos   tarde   tapas   café   frío   bar   Madrid

1. En España, los españoles van con frecuencia a un _____ o a un _____

   para pasar el tiempo con los _____ y los compañeros.

2. En los bares, sirven _____, que son pequeños platos de comidas diversas.

3. Julia dice que prefiere la ciudad de _____ para divertirse. Allí no hace

   _____ en el invierno y la gente puede salir muy _____ todo el año.

Now turn on the tape.

C. Y para terminar... Entrevista. You will hear a series of questions. Each will be said twice. Answer based on your own experience. Use direct object pronouns in your answers, if possible. Stop the tape and write the answers.

1. _____

2. _____

3. _____

4. _____

5. _____

6. _____

7. _____

REPASO 2

A. ¿Dónde están estas personas?

Paso 1. You will hear four brief conversations or parts of conversations. Listen carefully and write the number of the conversation next to the location in which each conversation is taking place. Not all the locations will be used. First, listen to the list of possible locations.

_____ en una clase de geografía

_____ en una cocina

_____ en una playa, en primavera

_____ en una playa, en verano

_____ en un restaurante

Paso 2 (Para entregar). Now, stop the tape and write a brief conversation, or part of a conversation, that takes place in the one location not used in **Paso 1.**

_____

_____

_____

_____

_____

_____

Now turn on the tape.

B. *Los hispanos hablan*: ¿Qué te gusta mucho comer?

In this passage, Clara tells about two dishes typical of Spain: **el cocido** and **el gazpacho**. Then you will hear a series of statements. Circle **C** if the statement is true or **F** if it is false. The following words appear in the passage.

el hueso de codillo	*leg bone (as in ham)*
la morcilla	*blood sausage*
el pepino	*cucumber*
el pimiento	*pepper*
el ajo	*garlic*
el aceite de oliva	*olive oil*
el vinagre	*vinegar*
echarle por encima	*to sprinkle on top of it*
trocitos	*little bits (pieces)*

1. C F   2. C F   3. C F   4. C F

C. Conversación: En un restaurante (Para entregar). You will hear a conversation, partially printed in your manual, between a restaurant patron and a waiter. Then you will participate in a similar conversation, playing the role of the patron. Answer, based on your own preferences. Stop the tape and write the answers. First, stop the tape and read the menu on the following page.

Entremeses:
Jamón serrano
Champiñones al ajillo (mushrooms sautéed in garlic)
Calamares fritos (fried squid)

Entradas:
Gazpacho andaluz (cold tomato soup served with condiments)
Ensalada mixta (mixed green salad)
Alcachofas salteadas con jamón (artichokes sautéed with ham)

Platos fuertes:
Solomillo a la parrilla (beef cooked over a grill)
Paella valenciana (rice dish with seafood, chicken, pork & saffron)
Cordero al chilindrón (lamb and red pepper stew)

Postres:
Flan de naranja (orange flan)
Tarta de manzana (apple tart)
Peras al vino (pears in wine)

Bebidas:
Jerez (sherry)   Vino tinto
Té   Vino blanco
Café   Agua mineral

CAMARERO: ¿Desea un entremés?

UD.: _____.

CAMARERO: Muy bien. ¿Y de entrada?

UD.: _____.

CAMARERO: De plato fuerte, le recomiendo la paella valenciana. Es nuestra especialidad.

UD.: _____.

CAMARERO: ¿Desea algo de postre?

UD.: _____.

CAMARERO: Bueno. ¿Le traigo algo para tomar?

UD.: _____.

CAMARERO: Perfecto. Vuelvo en seguida (*right away*).

UD.: _____.

Now turn on the tape.

D. Cosas de todos los días. Practice telling about yourself and others, using the written cues. When you hear the corresponding number, form sentences using the words provided in the order given, making any necessary changes and additions. When you are given a choice between verbs, choose the correct one.

1. mi esposo y yo / (ser/estar) / profesores
2. (yo) levantarse / 6:45 / mañana
3. mi esposo / levantarse / más temprano / yo
4. él / (saber/conocer) / que yo (*f.*) / siempre / (ser/estar) / cansado
5. él / ducharse / vestirse / preparar / desayuno
6. (nosotros) salir / para / universidad / 7:50
7. las clases / empezar / 8:30

E. Dictado. You will hear a brief paragraph that tells about a house for sale. Listen carefully and, while listening, write in the information requested. Write all numbers as numerals. First, listen to the new vocabulary and the requested information.

mide	*measures*
el metro	*meter*
por	*by (as in 3 meters by 2 meters)*
el vecindario	*neighborhood*

El número de alcobas: _____

El número de baños: _____

¿Cuántos metros mide la sala? _____

Esta casa está cerca de _____ y enfrente de _____

La dirección (*address*) de la casa: _____

F. Y para terminar... Entrevista (Para entregar). You will hear a series of questions. Each will be said twice. Answer based on your own experience. Stop the tape and write the answers.

1. _____
2. _____
3. _____
4. _____
5. _____
6. _____
7. _____
8. _____
9. _____
10. _____

CAPÍTULO **7**

Vocabulario: Preparación

▼▼▼▼▼▼▼▼▼▼▼▼▼▼▼▼▼▼▼▼▼▼▼▼▼▼▼▼▼▼▼▼▼

A. Definiciones. You will hear a series of definitions. Each will be said twice. Circle the letter of the word that is defined by each. ¡OJO! There may be more than one answer in some cases.

1. a. el avión b. la playa c. el océano
2. a. el billete b. la estación de trenes c. el aeropuerto
3. a. el hotel b. el restaurante c. la llegada
4. a. el puerto b. el mar c. las montañas

B. Identificaciones. Identify the items after you hear the corresponding number. Begin each sentence with **Es un... , Es una... , or Son... .**

1. ... 2. ... 3. ... 4. ... 5. ...

C. Hablando de viajes... Using the oral and written cues, tell your friend Benito, who has never traveled by plane, the steps he should follow to make an airplane trip.

MODELO: (*you see*) Primero... (*you hear*) llamar a la agencia de viajes →
(*you say*) Primero llamas a la agencia de viajes.

1. pedir
2. El día del viaje, ...
3. facturar
4. Después...
5. Cuando anuncian la salida del vuelo, ...
6. Por fin...

Los hispanos hablan: Unas vacaciones inolvidables (*unforgettable*)

You will hear Cecilia's description of an unforgettable vacation. Then you will hear a series of statements. Circle **C** if the statement is true or **F** if it is false. The following words appear in the description.

hace un año	*one year ago*
veranear	pasar el verano
partimos	*we left*
el colectivo	*type of taxi shared by several passengers*
hacernos cargo de	*take care of*
la aduana	*customs*
las valijas	las maletas
armamos la carpa	*we set up the tent*

1. C F Cecilia y su amiga pasaron (*spent*) el verano en las montañas.

2. C F Los padres de las muchachas pagaron (*paid for*) el viaje.

3. C F Cecilia y su amiga pasaron un mes en el Uruguay.

4. C F Había (*There were*) otra gente joven en la playa donde se quedaron Cecilia y su amiga.

Pronunciación y ortografía: g, gu, and j

▼▼▼▼▼▼▼▼▼▼▼▼▼▼▼▼▼▼▼▼▼▼▼▼▼▼▼▼▼▼▼▼

A. In Spanish, the letter **g** followed by **e** or **i** has the same sound as the letter **j** followed by any vowel. This sound [x] is similar to the English *h*. The pronunciation of this sound varies, depending on the region or country of origin of the speaker. Note the difference in the pronunciation of these words.

España:	Jorge	jueves	general	álgebra
el Caribe:	Jorge	jueves	general	álgebra

Repeat the following words, imitating the speaker.

1. [x] general gigante geranio
2. [x] jamón Juan pasaje

Now, say the following words when you hear the corresponding number. Repeat the correct pronunciation after the speaker.

3. gimnasio
4. giralda
5. rojo
6. jipijapa

B. When the letter **g** is followed by the vowels **a, o,** or **u** or by the combination **ue** or **ui**, its pronunciation is very similar to the letter *g* in the English word *get*: [g]. It is also pronounced this way at the beginning of a word, after a pause, or after the letter **n**.

Repeat the following words, imitating the speaker.

[g] ángulo gusto gato Miguel guitarra

Now, say the following words when you hear the corresponding number. Repeat the correct pronunciation after the speaker.

1. gorila 2. grande 3. guerrilla 4. Guevara

C. In all other positions, the Spanish **g** is a fricative [g̶]. It has a softer sound produced by allowing some air to escape when it is pronounced. There is no exact equivalent for this variant in English.

Repeat the following words, imitating the speaker.

1. [g] abrigo   algodón   el gato   el gusto   los gorilas
2. [g] / g̶] un grupo   el grupo   gracias   las gracias   un gato   el gato
3. [x / g̶] gigante   jugos   juguete

Now, read the following sentences when you hear the corresponding numbers. Repeat the correct pronunciation after the speaker.

4. ¡Qué ganga!
5. Domingo es guapo y delgado.
6. Tengo algunas amigas guatemaltecas.
7. La guitarra de Guillermo es de Gijón.

D. Dictado. You will hear four sentences. Each will be said twice. Listen carefully and write what you hear.

1. _____
2. _____
3. _____
4. _____

Minidiálogos y gramática

▼▼▼▼▼▼▼▼▼▼▼▼▼▼▼▼▼▼▼▼▼▼▼▼▼▼▼▼▼▼▼

20. Expressing *to whom* or *for whom* • Indirect Object Pronouns; **dar** and **decir**

A. Encuesta. You will hear a series of statements. Indicate what is true for you by checking the appropriate answer. No answers will be given on the tape. The answers you choose should be correct for you!

	SIEMPRE	A VECES	¡NUNCA!
1.	☐	☐	☐
2.	☐	☐	☐
3.	☐	☐	☐
4.	☐	☐	☐
5.	☐	☐	☐
6.	☐	☐	☐
7.	☐	☐	☐
8.	☐	☐	☐

B. En casa, durante la cena. Practice telling for whom the following things are being done, according to the model.

> MODELO: (*you see*) Mi padre sirve el guacamole.   (*you hear*) a nosotros →
> (*you say*) Mi padre *nos* sirve el guacamole.

1. Mi madre sirve la sopa.
2. Ahora ella prepara la ensalada.
3. Mi hermano trae el café.
4. Rosalinda da postre.

C. Descripción. When you hear the corresponding number, tell what the following people are doing, using the written cues with indirect object pronouns.

En la fiesta de aniversario de los Sres. Moreno

1. Susana: regalar
2. Miguel: mandar
3. Tito: regalar

En casa, durante el desayuno

4. Pedro: dar
5. Marta: dar
6. Luis: servir / todos

21. Expressing Likes and Dislikes • gustar

A. Los gustos de nuestra familia. You will hear the father of the following family make some statements about the family's likes and dislikes. Circle **C** if a statement is true or **F** if it is false, based on the drawing. First, stop the tape and look at the drawing.

1. C F   2. C F   3. C F   4. C F   5. C F

B. ¡Vamos de vacaciones! Pero... ¿adónde? You and your family can't decide where to go on vacation. You will hear what each person likes. Then decide where each person would like to go, using a location from the following list. There may be more than one answer in some cases. First, listen to the list. You will hear a possible answer on the tape.

Disneylandia   Nueva York
Florida   quedarse en casa
las playas de México   Roma

MODELO: (*you hear*) A mi padre le gusta mucho jugar al golf. →
(*you say*) Le gustaría ir a Florida.

1. ...   2. ...   3. ...   4. ...   5. ...

C. ¿Qué le gusta? ¿Qué no le gusta? Using the written cues, tell what you like or dislike about the following situations or locations. You will hear a possible answer on the tape.

MODELO: (*you see and hear*) ¿En la universidad?   (*you see*) fiestas / exámenes →
(*you say*) Me gustan las fiestas. No me gustan los exámenes.

1. ¿En la playa?   jugar al vólibol / sol
2. ¿En un restaurante?   comida / música
3. ¿En un parque?   flores / insectos
4. ¿En la cafetería?   hablar con mis amigos / comida

22. Talking About the Past •
Preterite of Regular Verbs
and of **dar, hacer, ir**, and **ser**

A. Minidiálogo: Elisa habla de su viaje a Puerto Rico.

You will hear Elisa tell about a recent trip she
took to Puerto Rico. The passage is narrated in the past

Now turn off the tape and read the following statements. Circle C if the statement is true or F if it is
false. Correct the false statements.

1.   C   F   Elisa viajó a Puerto Rico en barco.

_____

2.   C   F   El viaje a Puerto Rico fue corto.

_____

3.   C   F   Elisa visitó muchos lugares interesantes de la isla.

_____

4.   C   F   Elisa habló con muchas personas en Puerto Rico.

_____

5.   C   F   A Elisa no le gustó su viaje.

_____

Now turn on the tape.

B.   ¿Qué hizo Nadia anoche? You will hear a series of statements. Each will be said twice. Write the
number of each statement next to the drawing that is described by that statement. First, stop the tape
and look at the drawings. Nadia's friend is Guadalupe.

a. _____

b. _____

c. _____

d. _____

e. _____

f. _____

g. _____

h. _____

i. _____

C. **¿Qué pasó ayer?** Practice telling what the following people did yesterday, using the oral and written cues. Do not say the subject pronouns in parentheses.

Antes de la fiesta

1. (yo)

2. mi compañero

3. (nosotros)

Antes del examen de química

4. Nati y yo

5. (tú)

6. todos

D. **¿Quién hizo... ?** You will hear a series of questions about what you and your friends did last night (**anoche**). Answer according to the drawings. First, stop the tape and look at the drawings.

MODELO: (*you hear*) ¿Quién habló por teléfono? → (*you say*) Alicia habló por teléfono.

Situaciones

▼▼▼▼▼▼▼▼▼▼▼▼▼▼▼▼▼▼▼▼▼▼▼▼▼▼▼▼▼▼▼▼▼

Paso 1. En la agencia de viajes. In this conversation, you will hear Elisa Velasco making arrangements for a trip to the Galápagos Islands. Listen and read along with the speakers.

SR. GÓMEZ:	¿Cuánto tiempo piensa quedarse en las islas?
ELISA:	Me gustaría pasar una semana allí. Quiero viajar en avión desde Quito. ¿Cuánto cuesta un boleto de ida y vuelta?
SR. GÓMEZ:	Cuesta 615.000 sucres si Ud. viaja el sábado en la mañana.
ELISA:	Está bien.
SR. GÓMEZ:	¿Desea que le haga una reservación de hotel también?
ELISA:	Sí, por favor.
SR. GÓMEZ:	Entonces, le hago las siguientes reservaciones: el avión sale de Quito a las islas el sábado 13 y seis noches de reservación en el hotel de la isla Santa Cruz.
ELISA:	Perfecto. Muchas gracias.
SR. GÓMEZ:	No hay por qué. ¿Cómo le gustaría pagar? ¿Lo de siempre?
ELISA:	Sí, con tarjeta de crédito... ¡la del periódico, por supuesto!

Paso 2. Aplicación. Now you will participate in a similar conversation, partially printed in your manual, in which you play the role of a client who wishes to purchase train tickets. Complete the conversation using the written cues. Here are the cues for your conversation. ¡OJO! The cues are not in order.

gracias / aquí / tenerlos   a qué hora / salir / tren / para Colón
darme (*command*) / billete de ida y vuelta

CLIENTE: ¿ _____?[1]

AGENTE: A las ocho y media de la mañana.

CLIENTE: _____,[2] por favor.

AGENTE: Son veinte balboas (*monetary unit of Panama*).

CLIENTE: _____.[3]

Un poco de todo (Para entregar)

▼▼▼▼▼▼▼▼▼▼▼▼▼▼▼▼▼▼▼▼▼▼▼▼▼▼▼▼▼▼▼▼▼

A. En el periódico: Anuncios. You will hear an ad for a Mexican airline company. Then you will hear a series of statements. Circle **C** if the statement is true or **F** if it is false, based on the information contained in the ad and the following chart of departures. First, listen to the following phrases you will hear in this activity.

un viaje de negocios   *a business trip*   un viaje de placer   *a trip for pleasure*

MIAMI 10 vuelos semanales

SALIDAS	LUNES	MARTES	MIERCOLES	JUEVES	VIERNES	SABADO	DOMINGO
	11:50 Y 15:05	16:10	11:50 Y 16:10	15:15	11:50 Y 11:05	15:15	15:05

1. C F   2. C F   3. C F   4. C F

B. *Listening Passage*: Un anuncio turístico

Antes de escuchar. *Stop the tape* and do the following prelistening exercises.

Paso 1. Find out how much you know about Mexico's tourist attractions by answering the following questions. As you read the questions, try to infer the information the passage will give you, as well as the specific information for which you need to listen.

1. ¿Conoce Ud. México? ¿Sabe que la Ciudad de México es una de las ciudades más grandes del mundo, más grande aun (*even*) que Nueva York? ¡Tiene más de 25.000.000 de habitantes!
2. ¿Sabe Ud. el nombre de algunos de los pueblos indígenas (*native*) de México? Los olmecas y los toltecas son menos famosos que otros. ¿Cuáles son los más famosos?

Paso 2. Empareje (*Match*) el nombre de la ciudad mexicana con la atracción turística por la cual (*by which*) se conoce.

1. _____ la Ciudad de México		a.	ruinas mayas y playas bonitas
2. _____ Teotihuacán		b.	objetos de plata (*silver*) y artesanías (*crafts*)
3. _____ Acapulco		c.	las Pirámides del Sol y de la Luna (*Moon*)
4. _____ Taxco		d.	playas
5. _____ Cancún		e.	el mejor museo antropológico del mundo

Now turn on the tape.

Listening Passage. Now, you will hear a travel ad about an excursion to Mexico. The following words appear in the passage.

mezclar	*to mix*
la plata	*silver*
relajarse	*to relax*
broncearse	*to get a tan*
el submarinismo	*snorkeling*
saborear	*to taste*
tentadora	*tempting*
las plazas	*spaces (on the tour)*

Después de escuchar. Indicate the things that the tourists can do on this trip.

1. ☐ Pueden broncearse.
2. ☐ Hacen submarinismo.
3. ☐ Escalan (*They climb*) unas montañas muy altas.
4. ☐ Compran objetos de plata.
5. ☐ Pueden nadar en dos playas, por lo menos (*at least*).
6. ☐ Ven las ruinas de Machu Picchu.
7. ☐ Visitan un museo antropológico.

Now turn on the tape.

C. Y para terminar... Entrevista. You will hear a series of questions. Each will be said twice. Answer, based on your own experience. Stop the tape and write the answers.

1. _____

2. _____

3. _____

4. _____

5. _____

6. _____

Vocabulario: Preparación

▼▼▼▼▼▼▼▼▼▼▼▼▼▼▼▼▼▼▼▼▼▼▼▼▼▼▼▼▼▼▼▼▼▼▼

A. ¿Una fiesta familiar típica? You will hear a description of Sara's last family gathering. Then you will hear a series of statements. Circle **C** if the statement is true or **F** if it is false. If the information is not given, circle **ND** (**No lo dice**).

1. C   F   ND   Según lo que dice Sara, las fiestas familiares normalmente son muy divertidas.

2. C   F   ND   A la tía Eustacia le gusta discutir (*argue*) con el padre de Sara.

3. C   F   ND   Normalmente, los primos de Sara se portan mal (*behave poorly*) en las fiestas familiares.

4. C   F   ND   Sara no lo pasa bien nunca en las fiestas familiares.

5. C   F   ND   Los hermanos de Sara discuten mucho con sus padres.

B. Asociaciones. With which of the following celebrations do you associate the descriptions that you hear on the tape? Each will be said twice. ¡OJO! There might be more than one possible answer in some cases.

1. a. La Navidad   b. el Día de la Raza   c. el cumpleaños
2. a. el día de los enamorados   b. la Pascua   c. el Cuatro de Julio
3. a. el Día de los Reyes Magos   b. el Día de Gracias   c. el Día de los Muertos
4. a. la quinceañera   b. el Día de los Reyes Magos   c. el día del santo

C. ¿Cómo reacciona Ud.? Practice telling how you react to these situations, using the oral and written cues. Use the word **cuando** in each sentence.

> MODELO: (*you see*) Me olvido del cumpleaños de mi madre.   (*you hear*) ponerme triste →
> (*you say*) Me pongo triste cuando me olvido del cumpleaños de mi madre.

1. Mis padre me quitan (*take away*) el coche.
2. Veo una película triste.
3. Saco buenas notas (*grades*).
4. Tengo que hacer cola.

Los hispanos hablan: Una fiesta inolvidable (*unforgettable*)

You will hear Karen and Xiomara talk about two unforgettable parties. The following words appear in the descriptions.

las damas	*ladies (maids of honor)*	orgulloso	*proud*
el vals	*waltz*	el brindis	*toast*
duró	*lasted*	he pasado	*I have spent*
estuvo presente	*were there*		

Now, stop the tape and indicate the statements that can be inferred from the information in the two descriptions.

1. ☐ La quinceañera (fiesta de los quince años) es una fiesta importante para Karen y Xiomara.

2. ☐ Hay muchos invitados en estas fiestas.

3. ☐ La quinceañera es una fiesta que dura (*lasts*) hasta muy tarde.

4. ☐ Karen y Xiomara celebraron su quinceañea en los Estados Unidos.

5. ☐ En estas fiestas hay música.

Now turn on the tape.

Pronunciación y ortografía: c and qu

▼▼▼▼▼▼▼▼▼▼▼▼▼▼▼▼▼▼▼▼▼▼▼▼▼▼▼▼▼▼▼▼▼▼▼▼

A. The [k] sound in Spanish can be written two ways: before the vowels **a, o,** and **u** it is written as **c**; before **i** and **e**, it is written as **qu**. The letter **k** itself appears only in words that are borrowed from other languages. Unlike the English [k] sound, the Spanish sound is not aspirated; that is, no air is allowed to escape when it is pronounced. Compare the following pairs of English words in which the first [k] sound is aspirated and the second is not.

can / scan   cold / scold   kit / skit

B. Repeat the following words, imitating the speaker. Remember to pronounce the [k] sound without aspiration.

1. casa   cosa   rico   loca   roca
2. ¿quién?   Quito   aquí   ¿qué?   pequeño
3. kilo   kilogramo   kerosén   kilómetro   karate

Now, when you hear the corresponding number, read the following words. Repeat the correct pronunciation after the speaker.

4. paquete   6. química   8. camarones
5. quinceañera 7. comida   9. ¿por qué?

C. Dictado. You will hear a series of words. Each will be said twice. Listen carefully and write what you hear. ¡OJO! Some of the words may be unfamiliar to you. Concentrate on the sounds.

1. _____

2. _____

3. _____

4. _____

5. _____

6. _____

Minidiálogos y gramática

▼▼▼▼▼▼▼▼▼▼▼▼▼▼▼▼▼▼▼▼▼▼▼▼▼▼▼▼▼▼▼▼▼

23. Talking About the Past (2) • Irregular Preterites

A. Encuesta: Hablando de lo que pasó ayer. You will hear a series of statements about what happened to you yesterday. For each statement, check the appropriate answer. No answers will be given on the tape. The answers you choose should be correct for you!

1. ☐ Sí ☐ No   5. ☐ Sí ☐ No

2. ☐ Sí ☐ No   6. ☐ Sí ☐ No

3. ☐ Sí ☐ No   7. ☐ Sí ☐ No

4. ☐ Sí ☐ No   8. ☐ Sí ☐ No

B. Una fiesta de cumpleaños. Tell what happened at the party, using the written and oral cues.

MODELO: (*you see*) estar en casa de Mario (*you hear*) todos →
(*you say*) Todos estuvimos en casa de Mario.

1. tener que preparar la comida   3. hacer mucho ruido
2. venir con regalos   4. ¡estar estupenda!

C. Preguntas: ¿Qué hiciste la Navidad pasada? You will hear a series of questions. Each will be said twice. Answer, using the written cues. Use object pronouns when possible.

1. en mi casa   4. debajo del árbol (*tree*)
2. sí: venir todos mis tíos y primos   5. los niños
3. a su novia

24. Talking About the Past (3) • Preterite of Stem-Changing Verbs

A. La fiesta de sorpresa

Paso 1. You will hear a brief paragraph, narrated by Ernesto, about a surprise party. Listen carefully and check the appropriate actions for each person. First, stop the tape and look at the chart.

PERSONA	VESTIRSE ELEGANTEMENTE	SENTIRSE MAL	DORMIR TODA LA TARDE	PREFERIR QUEDARSE EN CASA
Julia				
Verónica				
Tomás				
Ernesto (el narrador)				

Paso 2. You will hear a series of statements about the preceding paragraph. Each will be said twice. Circle **C** if the statement is true or **F** if it is false. If the information is not given, circle **ND** (**No lo dice**).

1. C   F   ND   4. C   F   ND

2. C   F   ND   5. C   F   ND

3. C   F   ND

B. ¿Qué le pasó a Antonio? Tell what happened to Antonio when you hear the corresponding number. First, listen to the beginning of Antonio's story.

Raquel Morales invitó a Antonio a una fiesta en su casa. Antonio le dijo a Raquel que él asistiría (*would attend*), pero todo le salió mal. En primer lugar...

1. no recordar llevar refrescos
2. perder la dirección de la Srta. Morales
3. llegar muy tarde a la fiesta
4. no divertirse
5. sentirse enfermo después de la fiesta

6. acostarse muy tarde
7. dormir mal esa noche
8. despertarse a las cinco de la mañana
9. tener que ir a clases de todas formas (*anyway*)

25. Expressing Direct and Indirect Objects Together • Double Object Pronouns

A. Dictado: Una fiesta de sorpresa para Lupita. You will hear a passage narrated by Olivia about a surprise party she gave recently. As you listen, write the missing words.

El viernes pasado, mis amigos y yo dimos una fiesta de sorpresa para una de nuestras amigas,

Lupita. Yo escribí las invitaciones y _____ _____ mandé a todos. Carmen hizo un pastel y

_____ _____ dio antes de la fiesta. Anita preparó una comida elegante y _____ _____

sirvió en el comedor. Arturo y Patricio sacaron muchas fotos y _____ _____ regalaron a

Lupita. Todos llevamos regalos y _____ _____ presentamos a Lupita al final de la fiesta.

¡Lupita nos dijo que fue una fiesta maravillosa!

B. En casa, durante la cena. During dinner, your brother asks about the different foods that might be left. He will say each question twice. Listen carefully and circle the items to which he is referring.

MODELO: (*you hear*) ¿Hay más? ¿Me la pasas, por favor? →
(*you see and circle*) (la sopa)   el pan   el pescado

1. las galletas   la fruta   el helado
2. la carne   el postre   los camarones
3. la leche   el vino   las arvejas
4. las papas fritas   la cerveza   el pastel

C. ¿Dónde está? Carolina would like to borrow some things from you. Tell her to whom you gave each item, basing your answer on the written cues on the following page and selecting the correct pronouns. You will hear each of Carolina's questions twice.

MODELO: (*you hear*) Oye, ¿dónde está tu diccionario?
(*you see*) Se (lo/la) presté a Nicolás. Él (lo/la) necesita para un examen. →
(*you say*) Se lo presté a Nicolás. Él lo necesita para un examen.

1. Se (lo/la) presté a Nicolás. Él (lo/la) necesita para un viaje.
2. Se (los/las) presté a Teresa. Ella (los/las) necesita para su fiesta.
3. Se (lo/las) presté a Juan. Él (la/las) necesita para escribir un trabajo.
4. Se (lo/la) presté a Nina. Ella (lo/la) necesita para ir al parque.

Situaciones

▼▼▼▼▼▼▼▼▼▼▼▼▼▼▼▼▼▼▼▼▼▼▼▼▼▼▼▼▼▼▼▼▼▼▼

Paso 1. La despedida. In the following conversation, Manolo Durán and his family are saying good-bye to other family members after a celebration. Listen and read along with the speakers.

JAIME:	Bueno, hasta otro, hermano.
MANOLO:	¡Y que sea pronto!
ELENA:	Hasta luego. Nos divertimos mucho, ¿eh?
ANA:	Que tengáis buen viaje.
PEDRO:	Nos mandaréis copias de las fotos, ¿no?
JAIME:	Por supuesto que sí. Ha sido maravilloso veros. ¡Que haya suerte!

Paso 2. Aplicación. In the preceding conversation, Manolo and his family were saying good-bye. It is also important to greet your guests. You will hear a series of conversations. Listen carefully and indicate when each conversation might take place: at the beginning of a party, during the party, or at the end of the party.

1. a. a la llegada   b. durante la fiesta   c. a la despedida
2. a. a la llegada   b. durante la fiesta   c. a la despedida
3. a. a la llegada   b. durante la fiesta   c. a la despedida
4. a. a la llegada   b. durante la fiesta   c. a la despedida

Un poco de todo (Para entregar)

▼▼▼▼▼▼▼▼▼▼▼▼▼▼▼▼▼▼▼▼▼▼▼▼▼▼▼▼▼▼▼▼▼▼▼

A. Un día típico. You will hear a description of a day in Ángela's life, narrated in the past. Then you will hear a series of statements. Circle **C** if the statement is true or **F** if it is false. If the information is not given, circle **ND** (**No lo dice**).

1. C F ND   Ángela se acostó tarde ayer.

2. C F ND   Ángela se levantó a las seis y media.

3. C F ND   Ángela se puso furiosa cuando llegó a la oficina.

4. C F ND   El jefe (*boss*) le dio mucho trabajo.

5. C F ND   Los padres de Ángela viven lejos de ella.

6. C F ND   Cuando Ángela se acostó, se durmió inmediatamente.

B. _Listening Passage_: El carnaval

Antes de escuchar. You will hear a passage about carnival celebrations. The following words appear in the passage.

pagano	_pagan, not religious_
la Cuaresma	_Lent_
las máscaras	_masks_
los disfraces	_costumes_
caricaturesco	_cartoonish, satirical_
se mezclan	_are blended_
inolvidable	_unforgettable_

Listening Passage. Here is the passage. First, listen to it to get a general idea of the content. Then rewind the tape and listen again for specific information.

Después de escuchar. Indicate the statements that contain information that you _cannot_ infer from the listening passage.

1. ☐ El Carnaval es una tradición exclusivamente europea.

2. ☐ A pesar de (_In spite of_) las diferencias, las celebraciones de Carnaval tienen muchas semejanzas (_similarities_).

3. ☐ El Carnaval celebra la llegada del buen tiempo.

4. ☐ Los mejores Carnavales se celebran en Europa.

5. ☐ La gran diferencia entre el Carnaval de Río y los otros Carnavales es que el de Río se celebra en un mes distinto (diferente).

6. ☐ La persona que habla tuvo gran dificultad con el idioma en Río de Janeiro.

7. ☐ La persona que habla quiere ir al _Mardi Gras_ de Nueva Orléans el próximo año.

Now turn on the tape.

C. Y para terminar... Entrevista. You will hear a series of questions. Each will be said twice. Answer, based on your own experience. Stop the tape and write the answers.

1. _____

2. _____

3. _____

4. _____

5. _____

6. _____

7. _____

CAPÍTULO **9**

Vocabulario: Preparación

▼▼▼▼▼▼▼▼▼▼▼▼▼▼▼▼▼▼▼▼▼▼▼▼▼▼▼▼▼▼▼▼▼▼▼

A. Gustos y preferencias. You will hear a series of descriptions of what people like to do. Each will be said twice. Listen carefully, and circle the letter of the activity or activities that are best suited to each person.

1.	a. nadar	b. jugar al ajedrez	c. tomar el sol
2.	a. dar fiestas	b. ir al teatro	c. ir a un bar
3.	a. ir a un museo	b. hacer *camping*	c. hacer un *picnic*
4.	a. pasear en bicicleta	b. esquiar	c. correr
5.	a. jugar al fútbol	b. ir a un museo	c. ir al cine

B. Las actividades y el tiempo. You will hear a series of descriptions of weather and activities. Write the number of the description next to the corresponding picture. ¡OJO! Listen carefully. There is an extra description.

a. _____

b. _____

c. _____

d. _____

C. Mandatos para el nuevo robot. Imagine that your family has been chosen to test a model robot in your home. Tell the robot what to do in each of the following situations, using the oral cues. ¡OJO! You will be using **Ud.** command forms.

MODELO: (*you hear*) 1. (*you see*) →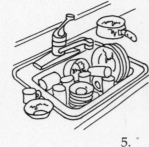
(*you say*) Lave los platos.

2.  3.  4. 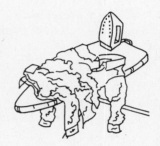 5.

D. ¿Qué están haciendo estas personas? Tell what each person is doing when you hear the corrsponding name. Use the present progressive in your answers.

MODELO: (*you hear*) 1. (*you see*) →
(*you say*) Jorge está lavando las ventanas.

2.  3.

4.  5.

Los hispanos hablan: ¿Cuál es tu pasatiempo favorito?

Paso 1. You will hear two answers to this question. Listen carefully and jot down notes about what each person says. The following words appear in the answers.

los aparadores	*display windows*
las sodas	*soda fountains*
los bancos	*benches*

Xiomara

_____

_____

_____

Gabriel

_____

_____

_____

Paso 2. Now, stop the tape and answer these questions.

1. ¿Qué actividades tienen en común las dos jóvenes?

_____

2. ¿Qué pasatiempos no tienen en común Gabriela y Xiomara?

_____

Now turn on the tape.

Pronunciación y ortografía: p and t

▼▼▼▼▼▼▼▼▼▼▼▼▼▼▼▼▼▼▼▼▼▼▼▼▼▼▼▼▼▼▼▼▼▼▼▼

A. Like the [k] sound, Spanish **p** and **t** are not aspirated as they are in English. Compare the following pairs of aspirated and nonaspirated English sounds.

pin / spin   pan / span   tan / Stan   top / stop

Repeat the following words, imitating the speaker.

1. pasar   patinar   programa   puerta   esperar
2. tienda   todos   traje   estar   usted

Now, read the following phrases and sentences after you hear the corresponding number. Repeat the correct pronunciation after the speaker.

3. una tía trabajadora   5. Tomás, toma tu té.
4. unos pantalones pardos   6. Pablo paga el periódico.

B. Repaso: [p], [t], [k]. You will hear a series of words. Each will be said twice. Circle the letter of the word you hear.

1. a. pata   b. bata
2. a. van   b. pan
3. a. coma   b. goma

4. a. dos   b. tos
5. a. de   b. té
6. a. callo   b. gallo

C. Dictado. You will hear four sentences. Each will be said twice. Listen carefully and write what you hear.

1. _____

2. _____

3. _____

4. _____

Minidiálogos y gramática

▼▼▼▼▼▼▼▼▼▼▼▼▼▼▼▼▼▼▼▼▼▼▼▼▼▼▼▼▼▼▼▼▼▼

26. Descriptions and Habitual Actions in the Past • Imperfect of Regular and Irregular Verbs

A. Minidiálogo: Diego habla de los aztecas.

Paso 1. Dictado. You will hear the following paragraph in which Diego describes some aspects of Aztec culture. Listen carefully and write the missing words.

Los aztecas construyeron grandes pirámides para sus dioses. En lo alto de cada pirámide

_____ un templo donde _____ lugar las ceremonias y se

_____ los sacrificios. Las pirámides _____ muchísimos escalones,

y _____ necesario subirlos todos para llegar a los templos.

Cerca de muchas pirámides _____ un terreno como el de una cancha de

basquetbol. Allí se _____ partidos que _____ parte de una

ceremonia. Los participantes _____ con una pelota de goma dura, que sólo

_____ mover con las caderas y las rodillas...

Paso 2. ¿Qué recuerdas? Now stop the tape and complete the following sentences with words chosen from the list.

ceremonia	religiosa
dioses	sacrificios
pirámides	

1. Los aztecas ofrecían _____ a sus _____ .

2. El juego de pelota que se jugaba era parte de una _____ .

3. Las _____ eran estructuras altas que tenían una función

_____ .

Now turn on the tape.

B. Encuesta: ¿Qué hacías y cómo eras cuando eras joven? You will hear a series of statements about what you used to do or what you were like when you were younger. For each statement, check the appropriate answer. No answers will be given on the tape. The answers you choose should be correct for you!

1. ☐ Sí   ☐ No   5. ☐ Sí   ☐ No

2. ☐ Sí   ☐ No   6. ☐ Sí   ☐ No

3. ☐ Sí   ☐ No   7. ☐ Sí   ☐ No

4. ☐ Sí   ☐ No

C. En el aeropuerto: Una despedida

Paso 1. You will hear a description of a farewell between parents and their son, who is leaving home to attend medical school. Listen carefully, and indicate the appropriate actions for each person. First, stop the tape and look at the chart.

	ESTAR EN EL AEROPUERTO	IR A SAN JOSÉ	ESTAR MUY NERVIOSO/A	ESTAR PREOCUPADO/A	SENTIRSE TRISTE
Gustavo					
la madre de Gustavo					
el padre de Gustavo					

Paso 2. Now you will hear a series of statements about the passage. Each will be said twice. Circle **C** if the statement is true or **F** if it is false.

1. C F   2. C F   3. C F   4. C F   5. C F

Paso 3. Now answer the questions you hear, based on the information in your chart. Check the answers for **Paso 1** in the Appendix before you begin **Paso 3**. Each question will be said twice. Stop the tape and write the answers.

1. _____

2. _____

3. _____

4. _____

5. _____

D. Describiendo el pasado: En la primaria. Practice telling what you and others used to do in grade school, using the oral and written cues.

     MODELO: *(you see)* (yo) *(you hear)* jugar mucho → *(you say)* Jugaba mucho.

1. Rodolfo
2. (tú)

3. todos
4. (nosotros)

27. Expressing Extremes • Superlatives

A. Las opiniones de Margarita

Paso 1. Dictado. You will hear a brief paragraph in which Margarita gives her opinions about a variety of topics. Listen carefully and write down her opinions. First, listen to the list of topics.

la fiesta más divertida del año: _____

el peor mes del año: _____

la mejor película del mundo: _____

el quehacer doméstico más aburrido: _____

Paso 2. Now stop the tape and express your own opinion about the same topics. No answers will be given on the tape. The answers you choose should be correct for you!

En mi opinión...

1. La fiesta más divertida del año es _____.

2. El peor mes del año es _____.

3. La mejor película del mundo es _____.

4. El quehacer doméstico más aburrido es _____.

Now turn on the tape.

B. Sólo lo mejor... Imagine that your friend's **quinceañera** has the best of everything. Answer some questions about it, using the written cues.

     MODELO: *(you see and hear)* Los vestidos son elegantes, ¿no? *(you see)* fiesta →
            (you say) Sí, son los vestidos más elegantes de la fiesta.

1. Antonio es un chico guapo, ¿verdad? / fiesta
2. La música es buena, ¿no? / mundo

3. Y la comida, qué rica, ¿no? / mundo
4. La fiesta es divertida, ¿verdad? / año

28. Getting Information • Summary of Interrogative Words

A. Preguntas y respuestas. You will hear a series of questions. Each will be said twice. Circle the letter of the best answer to each.

1. a. Es de Juan.   b. Es negro.
2. a. Están en México.   b. Son de México.
3. a. Soy alto y delgado.   b. Bien, gracias. ¿Y Ud.?
4. a. Mañana.   b. Tengo cinco.
5. a. Es gris.   b. Tengo frío.
6. a. Con Elvira.   b. Elvira va a la tienda.
7. a. A las nueve.   b. Son las nueve.

B. ¿Qué dijiste? Your friend Eva has just made several statements, but you haven't understood everything she said. You will hear each statement only once. Choose either **¿Qué?** or **¿Cuál?** and form a question to elicit the information you need.

> MODELO: (*you hear*) La capital del Perú es Lima.
> (*you see*) a. ¿qué? b. ¿cuál? →
> (*you say*) b. ¿Cuál es la capital del Perú?

1. a. ¿qué?   b. ¿cuál?   4. a. ¿qué?   b. ¿cuál?
2. a. ¿qué?   b. ¿cuál?   5. a. ¿qué?   b. ¿cuál?
3. a. ¿qué?   b. ¿cuál?

C. Entrevista con la señorita Moreno. Interview Ms. Moreno, an exchange student, for your campus newspaper, using the written cues. Add any necessary words. You will hear the correct question, as well as her answer. Use her name only in the first question.

> MODELO: (*you hear*) 1. → (*you see*) ¿dónde? / ser
> (*you say*) Srta. Moreno, ¿de dónde es Ud.?   (*you hear*) Soy de Chile.

2. ¿dónde? / vivir   4. ¿qué? / idiomas / hablar
3. ¿dónde? / trabajar   5. ¿cuál? / ser / deporte favorito

Situaciones

▼▼

Paso 1. La invitación. In the following conversation, Lupe tells Antonio and Juan about a surprise party for Diego. Listen and read along with the speakers. Pay close attention to how Rocío rejects Lupe's invitation, and how Antonio and Juan accept it.

ANTONIO: ¡Hola, Lupe!
LUPE: Hola, Antonio. Oye, ¿está aquí Diego?
ANTONIO: No, no está. ¿Por qué?
LUPE: Ah, muy bien. Pues, el próximo fin de semana le quiero dar una fiesta sorpresa a Diego. Es su cumpleaños. Quiero invitar a todos Uds. a la fiesta.
ANTONIO: ¡Qué padre! ¿Y cuándo es la fiesta? ¿El viernes? ¿El sábado?
LUPE: El sábado. Rocío, ¿te gustaría venir?
ROCÍO: Ay, Lupe, me gustaría mucho, pero no puedo. Ya tengo planes para el sábado. Mis padres vienen al D.F. a visitarme y vamos a ir al Ballet Folklórico esa noche.
JUAN: ¡Qué pena! Pero yo sí voy.
ANTONIO: Y yo también. Gracias por la invitación. ¿Puedo invitar a Mónica y a José Luis también?

LUPE: ¡Claro que sí! ¡Muy bien! Entonces, ¿por qué no vienen a mi casa a las siete? Y por favor, no le vayan a decir nada a Diego.

JUAN: No te preocupes. Él va a estar muy sorprendido.

Paso 2. Aplicación. Now you will participate in two similar conversations, partially printed in your manual, in which you reject and accept invitations. Complete them using the written cues. Here are the cues for your first conversation. You will need to conjugate the verbs.

gracias / pero no poder / tener que estudiar

1. TEODORO: Oye, ¿te gustaría ir al cine el viernes? Dan (*They're showing*) una película buenísima.

    UD.:   _____¹._____².

    TEODORO: ¡Qué lástima! Tal vez podamos ir el próximo viernes.

Here are the cues for your second conversation. You will also need to conjugate the verbs.

ser una buena idea / a qué hora querer (tú) salir / sí, estar bien

2. CARIDAD: ¿Qué tal si vamos al parque esta tarde y hacemos un *picnic*?

    UD.:   ¡_____¹! ¿_____²?

    CARIDAD: A las tres, más o menos. ¿Vale? (*O.K.?*, *Sp.*)

    UD.:   _____³

Un poco de todo (Para entregar)

▼▼▼▼▼▼▼▼▼▼▼▼▼▼▼▼▼▼▼▼▼▼▼▼▼▼▼▼▼▼▼▼▼

A. Descripción. En casa de los Delibes. You will hear a series of statements about the following drawing. Each will be said twice. Circle **C** if the statement is true or **F** if it is false. First, stop the tape and look at the drawing.

1. C F   2. C F   3. C F   4. C F   5. C F   6. C F

B. *Listening Passage:* **¿Cómo se pasan los fines de semana y los días de fiesta?**

Antes de escuchar. *Stop the tape* and do the following prelistening exercise.

Before you listen to the passage, read the following statements about how some people spend weekends or holidays. Check those statements that are true for you and your family.

☐   Los fines de semana son ocasiones familiares.

☐   Pasamos los fines de semana o los días de fiesta en nuestra casa en el campo.

☐   Mi madre siempre prepara una comida especial los domingos.

☐   Paso el fin de semana con mis amigos y no con mi familia.

☐   Después de comer, toda la familia sale a dar un paseo por el parque.

☐   Paso el fin de semana con mis abuelos.

Now turn on the tape.

Listening Passage. Now you will hear a passage about how some Hispanics spend their weekends and holidays. The following words appear in the passage.

adinerados	personas que tienen mucho dinero
a mediodía	*at noon*
se casan	*get married*
el hogar	*home*
el descanso	*rest*
se suele	*it is the custom (to)*
elegir	*to choose, pick*
los columpios	*swings*
los críos	*young children*
charlando	hablando, conversando
relajados	*relaxed*

Después de escuchar. Read the following statements. Circle **C** if the statement is true or **F** if it is false. If the statement is false, according to the passage, correct it.

1.   C   F   Muchos hispanos tienen otra casa fuera de la ciudad.

_____

2.   C   F   Normalmente los abuelos no pasan tiempo con sus hijos y nietos.

_____

3.   C   F   Los domingos se almuerza rápidamente para poder ir al cine o al teatro.

_____

4.   C   F   Por lo general, los padres no pasan tiempo con sus hijos durante el fin de semana.

_____

Now turn on the tape.

C.   Y para terminar... Entrevista. You will hear a series of questions. Each will be said twice. Answer, based on your own experience. Stop the tape and write the answers.

1. _____

2. _____

3. _____

4. _____

5. _____

6. _____

REPASO **3**

A. ¿Dónde están estas personas?

Paso 1. You will hear five brief conversations or parts of conversations. Listen carefully and write the number of each conversation next to the location in which it is taking place. Not all the locations will be used. First, listen to the list of possible locations.

_____ en un avión   _____ en las montañas

_____ en una agencia de viajes   _____ en una fiesta

_____ en la alcoba   _____ en el aeropuerto

_____ en la cocina   _____ en una cancha (*court*) de tenis

Paso 2 (Para entregar). Now, stop the tape and write a brief conversation, or part of a conversation, that takes place in one of the locations not used in **Paso 1.**

_____

_____

_____

_____

_____

_____

Now turn on the tape.

B. Dictado (Para entregar). You will hear a conversation between a tourist who is interested in traveling to Cancún and a travel agent. Listen carefully and write down the requested information. First, listen to the list of information that is being requested.

el tipo de boleto que el turista quiere: _____

la fecha de salida: _____

la fecha de regreso (*return*): _____

la sección y la clase en que va a viajar: _____

la ciudad de la cual (*from which*) va a salir el avión: _____

el tipo de hotel que quiere: _____

el nombre del hotel en que se va a quedar: _____

C. Cosas de todos los días. Practice telling about yourself and others, using the written cues. When you hear the corresponding number, form sentences using the words provided in the order given, making any necessary changes and additions. You will be using the imperfect tense in all the sentences.

1. cuando / yo / ser / niña / (yo) vivir / Colombia
2. mi familia / tener / casa / bonito / cerca / Bogotá
3. mi hermano y yo / asistir / escuelas / público
4. todos los sábados / mi mamá y yo / ir de compras
5. a mis hermanos / gustar / ir / parque
6. domingos / (nosotros) reunirse con / nuestro / abuelos

D. Conversación (Para entregar). You will hear a conversation, partially printed in your manual, about weekend activities. Then you will participate in a similar conversation, playing the role of **Ud.** Answer, based on your own experience. Stop the tape and write the answers.

YOLANDA: ¿Qué tal el fin de semana? ¿Hiciste algo interesante el viernes o el sábado?

UD.: _____.

YOLANDA: Pues yo fui al teatro el viernes, y el sábado salí a cenar con unos amigos. No hice nada el domingo. ¿Y tú?

UD.: _____.

YOLANDA: Tengo ganas de tomar un café. ¿Quieres venir conmigo? Así podemos hablar más acerca del (*about the*) fin de semana.

UD.: _____.

Now turn on the tape.

E. Y para terminar... Entrevista (Para entregar). You will hear a series of questions. Each will be said twice. Answer, based on your own experience. Pay close attention to the verbal tense of each question. Stop the tape and write the answers.

1. _____
2. _____
3. _____
4. _____
5. _____
6. _____
7. _____
8. _____
9. _____

CAPÍTULO 10

Vocabulario: Preparación

▼▼▼▼▼▼▼▼▼▼▼▼▼▼▼▼▼▼▼▼▼▼▼▼▼▼▼▼▼▼▼▼▼▼

A. Asociaciones. You will hear a series of activities. Each will be said twice. Circle the body part that you associate with each. **¡OJO!** There may be more than one answer for each activity.

1. los pies   las piernas   los dientes   la garganta
2. los pulmones las manos   la nariz   los ojos
3. los pulmones la boca   las manos   las piernas
4. los dientes   la garganta   el corazón   la boca
5. los ojos   los pulmones   las piernas   el estómago
6. la nariz   los oídos   las orejas   la garganta

B. Algunas partes del cuerpo. Identify the following body parts when you hear the corresponding number. Use **Es...** or **Son...** and the appropriate definite article.

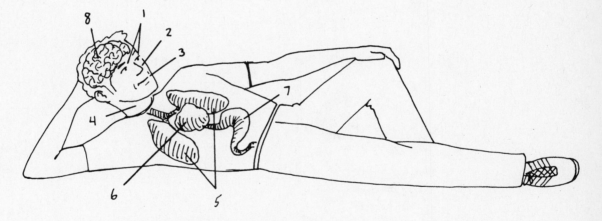

C. Para completar. You will hear a series of incomplete statements. Each will be said twice. Circle the letter of the word or phrase that best completes each statement.

1. a. ponerle una inyección   b. respirar bien
2. a. guardamos cama   b. nos sacan una muela
3. a. una tos   b. un jarabe
4. a. frío   b. un resfriado

D. Descripción: Hablando de problemas de salud

Paso 1. In each of the drawings on the following page, a person is suffering from some type of ailment. Stop the tape and write what the ailment is, based on the cues in the drawing. You should also tell where each person might be. The first one is partially done for you.

1. _____

Darío tiene dolor de _____.

(A Darío le duele el _____.)

Él está en _____.

2. _____

_____

_____

3. _____

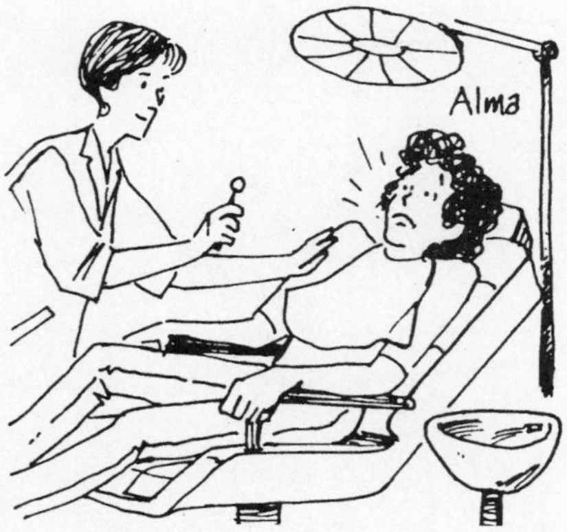

_____

_____

4. _____

_____

_____

Now turn on the tape.

Paso 2. Lo que dijo la médica. Now you will hear a doctor's recommendations. Each will be said twice. Write the letter of the recommendation next to the number of the corresponding drawing.

Los hispanos hablan: ¿Practicas un deporte? ¿Por qué?

Paso 1. You will hear several Hispanic students tell about the sports they play and why. The first time you listen, write the name of the sport or sports played by each student. Then, listen again and jot down each person's reasons for choosing the sport. The following words appear in the passages.

emocionante	*exciting*
entretenido	*entertaining, fun*
que uno se engorde	*that one get fat*
habilidad y destreza	*ability and skill*
mantenerse en forma	*to stay in shape*

	DEPORTE(S)	RAZÓN POR LA CUAL SE PRACTICA
Clara		
Antonio		
Gabriela		
Patricia		
Teresa		
José		
Xiomara		
Erick		

Paso 2. Now stop the tape and answer these questions, based on the chart. Check your answers to **Paso 1** in the Appendix before you begin **Paso 2**.

1. ¿Qué deporte es más popular entre los estudiantes que contestaron las preguntas?

   _____

2. ¿Cuántas personas mencionaron entre sus razones la salud o los beneficios para el cuerpo?

   _____

Now turn on the tape.

Pronunciación y ortografía:
s, z, ce, and ci

▼▼▼▼▼▼▼▼▼▼▼▼▼▼▼▼▼▼▼▼▼▼▼▼▼▼▼▼▼▼▼▼▼▼▼▼

A. The [s] sound in Spanish can be spelled several different ways and has several variants, depending on the country or region of origin of the speaker. Listen to the difference between these pronunciations of the [s] sound in two distinct Spanish-speaking areas of the world.*

Spain: Vamos a llamar a Susana este lunes.
Latin America: Vamos a llamar a Susana este lunes.

_____

*The Latin American variant of the [s] sound is used by most speakers in this tape program.

Spain: Cecilia siempre cena con Alicia.
Latin America: Cecilia siempre cena con Alicia.

Spain: Zaragoza   Zurbarán   zapatería
Latin America: Zaragoza   Zurbarán   zapatería

Notice also that in some parts of the Hispanic world, in rapid speech, the [s] sound becomes aspirated at the end of a syllable or word. Listen as the speaker pronounces these sentences.

¿Hasta cuándo vas a estar allí?   Les mandamos las cartas.

B. Repeat the following words, imitating the speaker.

1. sala   pastel   vaso   años
2. cerebro   ciencias   piscina   ciudad
3. corazón   azul   perezoso   zapatos
4. estación   solución   inyección   situación

Now read the following words, phrases, and sentences after you hear the corresponding number. Repeat the correct pronunciation.

5. los ojos
6. las orejas
7. unas médicas españolas
8. unas soluciones científicas
9. No conozco a Luz Mendoza de Pérez.
10. Los zapatos de Celia son azules.

C. Repaso. You will hear a series of words spelled with **c** or **qu**. Each will be said twice. Circle the letter or letters used to spell each word. **¡OJO!** Most of the words will be unfamiliar to you. Concentrate on the sounds you hear.

1. c qu   2. c qu   3. c qu   4. c qu   5. c qu   6. c qu

You should have circled the letters qu, c, c, qu, c, and qu.

Minidiálogos y gramática

▼▼▼▼▼▼▼▼▼▼▼▼▼▼▼▼▼▼▼▼▼▼▼▼▼▼▼▼▼▼▼▼▼

29. Narrating in the Past • Using the Preterite and the Imperfect

A. Dictado: Minidiálogo: En el consultorio de la Dra. Méndez.
You will hear the following dialogue between Lola and Dra. Méndez. Listen carefully and write the missing words. Then you will hear a series of statements about the dialogue. Circle **C, F,** or **ND (No lo dice).**

DRA. MÉNDEZ: ¿Cuándo _____ a sentirse mal su hija?

LOLA: Ayer por la tarde. _____ congestionada,

_____ mucho y se _____ de

que le _____ el cuerpo y la cabeza.

DRA. MÉNDEZ: ¿Y le _____ algo de fiebre?

LOLA:　Sí. Por la noche le _____ la temperatura y _____ treinta y ocho grados.

DRA. MÉNDEZ:　A ver... Tal vez necesito ponerle una inyección...

MARTA:　Eh... bueno... ¡Creo que ahora me encuentro un poco mejor!

1.　C　　F　　ND

2.　C　　F　　ND

3.　C　　F　　ND

4.　C　　F　　ND

B.　Condiciones y acciones: De viaje. You will hear a series of sentences describing conditions. Each will be said twice. Write the number of each condition next to the logical action. First, listen to the list of actions.

a.　_____　Por eso llegué tarde al aeropuerto.

b.　_____　Por eso pedí asiento en la sección de no fumar.

c.　_____　Por eso lo facturé.

d.　_____　Por eso pedí un vuelo directo.

e.　_____　Por eso compré un boleto de ida y vuelta.

C.　¿Un sábado típico? You will hear a series of sentences that describe Carlos's usual Saturday routine. Form new sentences using the oral cues to talk about what he did *last* Saturday. Begin each sentence with **El sábado pasado...**

MODELO:　(*you see and hear*) Todos los sábados, Carlos se despertaba a las siete.
(*you hear*) ocho → (*you say*) El sábado pasado, se despertó a las ocho.

1.　Todos los sábados, iba al centro comercial.
2.　Todos los sábados, tomaba té por la mañana.
3.　Todos los sábados, visitaba a su madre.
4.　Todos los sábados, se acostaba temprano.

D.　Descripción. Tell what the following people were doing when you hear the corresponding number. Follow the model. You will hear a possible answer on the tape.

MODELO:　(*you hear*) uno　(*you see*) cocinar / mientras / poner la mesa →
(*you say*) Luis cocinaba mientras Paula ponía la mesa.

1.　cocinar / mientras / poner la mesa

2. leer / cuando / entrar

3. cantar / mientras / tocar el piano

4. llorar / mientras / ponerle una inyección   5. jugar / cuando / pegarle

E. Una decisión difícil

Paso 1. You will hear the following sentences about Laura's decision to leave her hometown. Then, when you hear the cue in parentheses, restate the sentences, changing the italicized verbs to the preterite or imperfect, as appropriate. In each case, you will insert the cue at the beginning of the sentence. In this excercise, you will practice narrating in the past.

MODELO: (*you see and hear*) *Vivimos* en un pequeño pueblo en las montañas.   (de niños) →
(*you say*) De niños, vivíamos en un pequeño pueblo en las montañas.

1. Mi madre *trabaja* en una panadería (*bakery*).   (los martes y los jueves)
2. Mi padre *trabaja* en una tienda de comestibles (*food store*).   (todos los días)
3. *Vamos* a la ciudad y *compramos* cosas que no *podemos* encontrar en nuestro pueblo.   (con frecuencia)
4. *Consigo* trabajo permanente en la ciudad y *decido* dejar mi pueblo para siempre.   (un verano)
5. *Empiezo* a tomar clases de noche en la universidad y *dejo* mi puesto permanente por uno de tiempo parcial.   (al año siguiente)
6. Mis padres *están* tristes porque yo no *vivo* con ellos, pero ahora están contentos con mi decisión.   (antes)

Paso 2. Answer the questions you hear, based on the preceding story. Each question will be said twice.

1. ...   2. ...   3. ...   4. ...

30. Recognizing **que**, **quien(es)**, **lo que** • Relative Pronouns

En el consultorio

Paso 1. You will hear a brief paragraph describing a visit to the doctor's office. Listen carefully and take notes, if you wish.

Apuntes (*Notes*)

_____

_____

_____

_____

_____

_____

Paso 2. ¿Qué recuerdas? Now stop the tape and complete the following sentences based on the paragraph.

1. lo que tenía la narradora: _____

2. la persona con quien quería hablar: _____

3. lo que le dijo la recepcionista: _____

4. la persona a quien va a llamar la próxima vez que se enferme: _____

Now start the tape.

31. Expressing *Each Other* • Reciprocal Actions with Reflexive Pronouns

Descripción: ¿Qué hacen estas personas? Using the written cues, tell what the following pairs of people are doing when you hear the corresponding number. You will be describing reciprocal actions. You will hear a possible answer on the tape.

1. quererse mucho
2. escribirse con frecuencia
3. darse la mano (*to shake hands*)
4. hablarse por teléfono

Situaciones

▼▼▼▼▼▼▼▼▼▼▼▼▼▼▼▼▼▼▼▼▼▼▼▼▼▼▼▼▼▼▼▼▼▼▼▼

Paso 1. En el consultorio de la Dra. Méndez. In the following conversation, Marta is sick and is being examined by Dra. Méndez. Listen and read along with the speakers.

DRA. MÉNDEZ: ¿Así que no te sientes bien, Marta? Dime lo que te pasa.

MARTA: Anoche me dolió mucho el estómago. Y también la garganta.

LOLA: Sí, y ayer por la tarde estaba muy congestionada.

DRA. MÉNDEZ: ¿Sí? ¿Y cuándo comenzó a sentir estos síntomas?

LOLA: Fue unos días después de que se reunió con su amiga Carolina, quien ya estaba enferma.

DRA. MÉNDEZ: Ajá. Marta, saca la lengua, por favor. Di «ahhh».

MARTA: Ahhh...

DRA. MÉNDEZ: A ver... Respira. Más fuerte. Otra vez.

LOLA: ¿Qué pasa, doctora? ¿Es grave?

DRA. MÉNDEZ: No, no se preocupe. No es nada grave. Lo que tiene es un resfriado. Marta, debes guardar cama durante unos días y tomar muchos líquidos. Sra. Durán, voy a darle dos recetas. Las pastillas son para quitarle la congestión. Y el jarabe se lo puede dar cuando ella tosa.

LOLA: Muy bien, doctora.

DRA. MÉNDEZ: Y debe quedarse en casa algunos días.

MARTA: ¡Estupendo!

LOLA: Marta, por favor...

Paso 2. Aplicación. Now you will participate in a similar conversation, partially printed in your manual, in which you play the role of a patient. Complete the dialogue using the written cues. You will need to conjugate the verbs. Here are the cues for your conversation.

el lunes pasado   no tener fiebre
estar muy cansado/a   tener dolor de cabeza

DOCTORA: Siéntese, por favor. ¿Qué le ocurre?

UD: Bueno, _____¹ y

_____.²

DOCTORA: ¿Cuándo empezó a tener estos síntomas?

UD: _____.³

DOCTORA: Bueno, le voy a tomar la temperatura. Si tiene fiebre, le voy a recomendar que guarde cama por uno o dos días y que tome un antibiótico.

UD: Y, ¿si _____⁴?

DOCTORA: Entonces le voy a recomendar que tenga paciencia. Es posible que sólo sea un resfriado.

Un poco de todo (Para entregar)

▼▼▼▼▼▼▼▼▼▼▼▼▼▼▼▼▼▼▼▼▼▼▼▼▼▼▼▼▼▼▼▼▼▼▼▼▼

A. En el periódico: La salud

Paso 1. You will hear the following ads from Hispanic newspapers. Listen to them and circle the Spanish words or phrases that express the following. First, stop the tape and scan the list of English words.

DEJE DE FUMAR

1. killers   2. medical treatment   3. a vice

LENTES DE CONTACTO

4. a replacement pair   5. immediate replacement   6. soft or flexible

Now turn on the tape.

Paso 2. Now you will hear a series of statements about the ads. Each will be said twice. Circle **C**, **F**, or **ND** (**No lo dice**), according to the ads.

1. C F ND
2. C F ND
3. C F ND
4. C F ND

B. *Listening Passage*: **El sistema médico en los países hispánicos**

Antes de escuchar. Stop the tape and do the following prelistening exercise. Read the following statements about medical systems. Check those that you think apply only to the United States.

1. ☐ El sistema médico está controlado por el gobierno (*government*).

2. ☐ Hay una gran cantidad de compañías de seguro (*insurance companies*).

3. ☐ Hay menos compañías de seguro.

4. ☐ Cada persona paga los gastos médicos de acuerdo con (*according to*) su salario y no de acuerdo con el tipo de seguro que tiene.

5. ☐ Cualquier (*Any*) persona tiene derecho (*right*) al mejor tratamiento médico posible.

6. ☐ Hay muchas personas que no tienen acceso al tratamiento médico, ya sea (*be it*) por falta de dinero o porque no tienen seguro.

7. ☐ A veces, es necesario esperar mucho tiempo para ver al médico.

8. ☐ A veces hay mucha demanda, pero hay pocos servicios y personal disponibles (*available personnel*).

Now turn on the tape.

Listening Passage. Now you will hear a passage about the medical systems in most of the Hispanic world. The following words and phrases appear in the passage.

proveen	*they provide*
la cobertura	*coverage*
innegable	*undeniable*
la capacidad económica	*economic ability to pay*
el impuesto	*tax*
imprescindible	*indispensable*
tiende a disminuir	*tends to diminish or reduce*
el quebradero de cabeza	*problem, something that requires great thought*

Después de escuchar. Stop the tape, then indicate whether the following statements are true or false, according to the passage. Correct the false statements.

1. C F El sistema médico más común en los países hispanos es el privado.

   _____

2. C F El gobierno controla el sistema médico en los Estados Unidos.

   _____

3. C F En un sistema de medicina socializada, todos tienen derecho a recibir tratamiento médico.

   _____

4. C F Una desventaja de la medicina socializada, especialmente en países menos ricos, es que a veces no hay suficientes servicios médicos o suficientes doctores.

_____

5. C F El sistema de medicina socializada no diferencia entre los que pagan más y los que pagan menos.

_____

Now turn on the tape.

C. Y para terminar... Entrevista. You will hear a series of questions. Each will be said twice. Answer, based on your own experience. Stop the tape and write the answers.

Hablando de la última vez que estuviste enfermo o enferma

1. _____

2. _____

3. _____

Hablando de la salud en general

4. _____

5. _____

6. _____

CAPÍTULO **11**

Vocabulario: Preparación

▼▼▼▼▼▼▼▼▼▼▼▼▼▼▼▼▼▼▼▼▼▼▼▼▼▼▼▼▼▼▼▼

A. Descripción: ¡Qué día más terrible! You will hear a series of sentences. Each will be said twice. Write the letter of each sentence next to the appropriate drawing. First, stop the tape and look at the drawings.

1. _____

2. _____

3. _____

4. _____

5. _____

B. Más partes del cuerpo. Identify the following body parts when you hear the corresponding number. Begin each sentence with **Es...** or **Son...** and the appropriate definite article.

C. Presiones de los estudios. Imagine that you have been under a lot of pressure at school and it is affecting your judgment as well as other aspects of your life. Describe what has happened to you, using the oral and written cues.

> MODELO: (*you hear*) no pagar (*you see*) mis cuentas → (*you say*) No pagué mis cuentas.

1. apagar las luces
2. las escaleras
3. el escritorio
4. la pierna
5. un examen

D. Preguntas personales. You will hear a series of questions about how you do certain things. Answer, using the written cues or your own information. You will hear a possible answer on the tape. First, listen to the cues.

hablar español
jugar al béisbol
faltar a clase

hacer cola
escuchar el estéreo
tocar el piano

salir con mis amigos
limpiar la estufa

1. ...   2. ...   3. ...   4. ...

Los hispanos hablan: Describe una superstición común en tu país

Paso 1. You will hear three Hispanic students tell about common superstitions in their respective countries. Take notes as you listen, if you wish. Then check the statements that are true, based on what you heard. The following words appear in the students' answers.

evitan	*avoid*
la escalera	*ladder*
la maldición	*curse*
derramar	*to spill*
campanadas	*tolls (of a bell)*

Apuntes (*Notes*)

_____

_____

_____

_____

_____

1. ☐ En los tres países, el gato juega un papel (*plays a role*) en las supersticiones.

2. ☐ En Colombia, es buena suerte derramar sal para el Año Nuevo.

3. ☐ El martes trece es un día de mala suerte en uno de los países mencionados.

4. ☐ Muchas de estas supersticiones son semejantes (*similar*) a las supersticiones estadounidenses.

Now turn on the tape.

Pronunciación y ortografía:
ñ and ch

▼▼▼▼▼▼▼▼▼▼▼▼▼▼▼▼▼▼▼▼▼▼▼▼▼▼▼▼▼▼▼

A. The pronunciation of the letter **ñ** is similar to the sound [ny] in the English words *canyon* and *union*. However, in Spanish it is pronounced as one single sound.

Repeat the following words and sentences, imitating the speaker.

1. cana / caña   sonar / soñar   mono / moño   tino / tiño   cena / seña
2. año   señora   cañón   español   pequeña   compañero

Now read the following sentences when you hear the corresponding number. Repeat the correct pronunciation.

3. El señor Muñoz es de España.
4. Los niños pequeños no enseñan español.
5. La señorita Ordóñez tiene veinte años.
6. El cumpleaños de la señora Yáñez es mañana.

B. You will hear a series of words. Each will be said twice. Circle the letter of the word you hear.

1. a. pena   b. peña
2. a. una   b. uña
3. a. lena   b. leña
4. a. suena   b. sueña
5. a. mono   b. moño

C. In Spanish, when the letters **c** and **h** are combined, they are pronounced like the English **ch** in *church*. Read the following words when you hear the corresponding number, then repeat the correct pronunciation.

1. mucho
2. muchacho
3. Conchita
4. Chile
5. mochila
6. hache

D. Dictado. You will hear five sentences. Each will be said twice. Write what you hear.

1. _____
2. _____
3. _____
4. _____
5. _____

Minidiálogos y gramática

▼▼▼▼▼▼▼▼▼▼▼▼▼▼▼▼▼▼▼▼▼▼▼▼▼▼▼▼▼▼▼

32. Telling How Long Something Has Been Happening or How Long Ago Something Happened • Hace... que: Another Use of hacer

A.   ¿Cuánto tiempo hace... ? Each of the following drawings shows how long something has been going on. Stop the tape and look at the drawings. Then answer the questions. Each will be said twice.

1. ...   2. ...

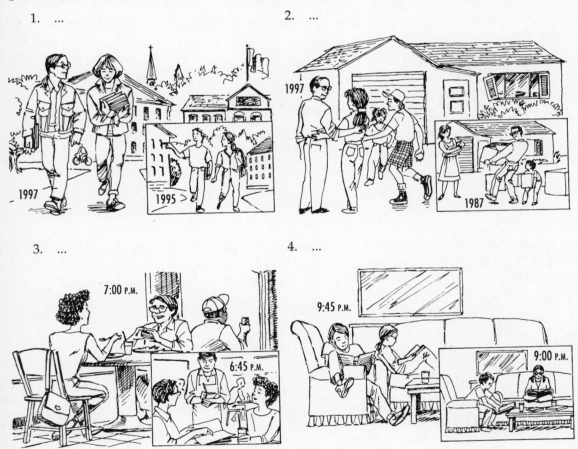

3. ...   4. ...

B.   ¡Felicidades Arturo y Matilde! You will hear a series of questions about a couple celebrating its 50th wedding anniversary. Answer, using the written cues.

1.   55 años   2.   50 años   3.   48 años   4.   10 años

33. Expressing Unplanned or Unexpected Events • Another Use of **se**

A. Encuesta: ¿Cómo eras en la escuela primaria? You will hear a series of questions about what you were like when you were in grade school. For each question, check the appropriate answer. No answers will be given on the tape. The answers you choose should be correct for you!

1. ☐ Sí ☐ No   3. ☐ Sí ☐ No   5. ☐ Sí ☐ No

2. ☐ Sí ☐ No   4. ☐ Sí ☐ No   6. ☐ Sí ☐ No

B. ¡Qué distraído! You will hear a description of Luis, followed by a series of statements about what he forgot to do this morning. Place the number of each statement next to its logical result. First, listen to the results.

a. _____ Va a llegar tarde al trabajo.

b. _____ No va a poder arrancar (*start*) el coche.

c. _____ Es posible que se le queme (*burn down*) el apartamento.

d. _____ Le van a robar la computadora.

e. _____ Lo van a echar (*evict*) de su apartamento.

C. Dictado. You will hear the following sentences. Each will be said twice. Listen carefully and write the missing words.

1. A ellos _____ _____ _____ el número de teléfono de Beatriz.

2. A Juan _____ _____ _____ las gafas.

3. Durante nuestro último viaje _____ _____ _____ el equipaje en la estación del tren.

4. A los niños _____ _____ _____ los juguetes (*toys*).

34. ¿Por o para? • A Summary of Their Uses

A. ¿Qué hacen estas personas? Using **por**, tell what the following people are doing when you hear the corresponding number.

MODELO: (*you hear*) uno   (*you see*) hablar / teléfono →
(*you say*) Marcos habla por teléfono.

Marcos

1. hablar / teléfono

2. viajar / barco

3. caminar / playa

4. correr / parque

5. pagar / 15 dólares / bolígrafos

6. nadar / mañana

B. ¿Para qué están Uds. aquí? Using the oral and written cues, tell why the people mentioned are in the locations you will hear on the tape. Each question will be said twice. First, listen to the list of reasons.

celebrar nuestro aniversario
descansar y divertirse
hablar con el médico

hacer reservaciones para un viaje a Acapulco
preparar la comida

MODELO: (*you see*) Armando: Está allí... (*you hear*) ¿Para qué está Armando en la cocina? →
(*you say*) Está allí para preparar la comida.

1. Diana: Está allí...
2. el Sr. Guerra: Está allí...
3. mi esposo/a y yo: Estamos aquí...
4. la familia Aragón: Está allí...

C. La vida diaria. You will hear the following sentences followed by an oral cue. Extend each sentence, using **por** or **para**, as appropriate.

MODELO: (*you see and hear*) Tengo que mandar los cheques. (*you hear*) el miércoles →
(*you say*) Tengo que mandar los cheques para el miércoles.

1. Salen el próximo mes.
2. Fueron al cine.
3. Estuvo en Honduras.
4. Habla muy bien el inglés.
5. A las ocho vamos a salir.
6. Vendieron su coche viejo.

Situaciones

▼▼

Paso 1. Un día fatal. In the following conversation, José Miguel, his mother, and his grandmother are in the dining room. Listen and read along with the speakers.

JOSÉ MIGUEL:	Bueno, mamá, aquí están las compras del mercado.
ELISA:	¡Ay! ¡José Miguel! ¡Se te cayó todo!
JOSÉ MIGUEL:	Lo siento, mamá. ¡Fue sin querer!
ELISA:	Debes tener más cuidado, hijo.
JOSÉ MIGUEL:	Perdóname. Parece que me levanté con el pie izquierdo hoy. ¡Qué lata!
ELISA:	Ay, no vale la pena molestarte.
MARÍA:	Bueno, pero hay algo bueno en todo esto...
ELISA:	¿Qué es?
MARÍA:	¡Que no llevamos una vida aburrida!

Paso 2. Aplicación. Now you will participate in two conversations, partially printed in your manual, in which you play the role of **Ud.** Complete each conversation using the written cues. Remember to repeat the correct answer. Here are the cues for your conversations. **¡OJO!** The cues are not in order.

> Discúlpeme.
> No se preocupe.
> ¡Lo siento! Fue sin querer.

1. En la farmacia: Ud. se da con una señora y a ella se la cae el frasco (*jar*) de medicina que llevaba.

    SRA.: ¡Ay, no!... ¡el frasco!

    UD.: _____.[1]

    SRA.: ¿Qué voy a hacer? Era una medicina para mi hijito, que está enfermo.

    UD.: _____.[2] Yo le compro otro frasco.

2. En el avión: Ud. se equivoca y toma el asiento de otro pasajero. Cuando la persona vuelve, quiere que Ud. le dé su puesto.

    SR.: Perdón, pero ese es mi asiento.

    UD.: _____.[3] Aquí lo tiene.

    SR.: Muchas gracias.

Un poco de todo (Para entregar)

▼▼

A. Situaciones delicadas. You will hear four situations. Choose the best response to each.

1. a. ¡Ay, me hice daño en la mano!
   b. ¡Qué mala suerte, Sr. Ramos! ¿Tiene otro vaso?
   c. Lo siento muchísimo, Sr. Ramos. Fue sin querer. ¿Puedo comprarle otro?

2. a. No me importa que no te guste el menú. Vamos a comer aquí.
   b. Lo siento mucho, pero pensé que te gustaría este restaurante. ¿Quieres ir a otro?
   c. Bueno, yo me quedo aquí, pero si tú quieres irte (*to leave*) a mí no me importa.
3. a. Lo siento, viejo, pero no tengo ganas de trabajar más hoy.
   b. Bueno, si Ud. insiste, me quedo a trabajar.
   c. Solamente voy a trabajar tarde si me da un aumento de sueldo.
4. a. No se preocupe. Estoy bien.
   b. Mire, señor, si sus niños no dejan de hacer tanto ruido, voy a llamar a la policía.
   c. Por favor, señor, dígales a sus niños que no hagan tanto ruido... ¡Tengo un dolor de cabeza tremendo!

B. *Listening Passage*: **Un accidente.** You will hear a conversation between a person who has just had an accident and a person who was on the scene. First, listen to get a general idea of the content. Then rewind the tape and listen again for specific information.

Después de escuchar. You will hear a series of questions. Each will be said twice. Not all the questions are based on details of the conversation; some will ask for your opinion. Stop the tape and write the answers. The following words and expressions appear in the questions.

perdió el conocimiento	*became unconscious*
el accidentado	la víctima del accidente
deprimido	*depressed*

1. _____
2. _____
3. _____
4. _____
5. _____

C. Y para terminar... Entrevista. You will hear a series of questions. Each will be said twice. Answer, based on your own experience. Stop the tape and write the answers.

1. _____
2. _____
3. _____
4. _____
5. _____
6. _____

CAPÍTULO **12**

Vocabulario: Preparación

▼▼▼▼▼▼▼▼▼▼▼▼▼▼▼▼▼▼▼▼▼▼▼▼▼▼▼▼▼▼▼

A. Hablando de «cositas» (*"a few small things"*). You will hear a brief dialogue between two friends, Lidia and Daniel. Listen carefully and circle the items that are mentioned in their conversation. Don't be distracted by unfamiliar vocabulary. First, stop the tape and look at the drawing.

B. Definiciones. You will hear a series of statements. Each will be said twice. Circle the letter of the word that is defined by each.

1.	a. la videocasetera	b.	el Walkman
2.	a. el inquilino	b.	el alquiler
3.	a. el vecindario	b.	la vecina
4.	a. la jefa	b.	el sueldo
5.	a. el contestador automático	b.	la motocicleta
6.	a. el control remoto	b.	la grabadora
7.	a. el primer piso	b.	la planta baja

C. Identificaciones. Identify the following items when you hear the corresponding number. Begin each sentence with **Es un...** or **Es una...** .

1. ... 2. ... 3. ... 4. ... 5. ...

Los hispanos hablan: Quiero...

Paso 1. Listen to Diana, José, and Karen describe what they want. As you listen to their descriptions, check the appropriate boxes. First, listen to the list of objects.

	DIANA	JOSÉ	KAREN		DIANA	JOSÉ	KAREN
ropa	☐	☐	☐	un radio portátil	☐	☐	☐
un estéreo	☐	☐	☐	un gran trabajo	☐	☐	☐
cosméticos	☐	☐	☐	un boleto de avión	☐	☐	☐
discos compactos	☐	☐	☐	una grabadora	☐	☐	☐
una guitarra	☐	☐	☐	una batería (*drum set*)	☐	☐	☐
aretes	☐	☐	☐	un ordenador	☐	☐	☐
un auto	☐	☐	☐	una bicicleta	☐	☐	☐

Paso 2. Now, stop the tape and answer the following questions about the descriptions and the chart you completed in **Paso 1.** Check your answers to **Paso 1** in the Appendix before you begin **Paso 2.**

1. De las tres personas, ¿quién quiere más cosas?

   _____

2. De las tres personas, ¿quién quiere viajar?

   _____

3. ¿Qué cosas desea más de una persona?

   _____

Now turn on the tape.

Pronunciación y ortografía: y and ll

▼▼▼▼▼▼▼▼▼▼▼▼▼▼▼▼▼▼▼▼▼▼▼▼▼▼▼▼▼▼▼▼

A. At the beginning of a word or syllable, the Spanish sound [y] is pronounced somewhat like the letter *y* in English *yo-yo* or *papaya*. However, there is no exact English equivalent for this sound. In addition, there are variants of the sound, depending on the country of origin of the speaker.

Listen to these diferences.

el Caribe:	Yolanda lleva una blusa amarilla. Yo no.
España:	Yolanda lleva una blusa amarilla. Yo no.
la Argentina:	Yolanda lleva una blusa amarilla. Yo no.

B. Although **y** and **ll** are pronounced exactly the same by most Spanish speakers, in some regions of Spain **ll** is pronounced like the [ly] sound in *million*, except that it is one single sound.

Listen to these differences.

España:	Guillermo es de Castilla.
Sudamérica:	Guillermo es de Castilla.

C. Repeat the following words, imitating the speaker.

1. llamo   llueve   yogurt   yate (*yacht*)   yanqui   yoga
2. ellas   tortilla   millón   mayo   destruyo (*I destroy*)   tuyo (*yours*)

D. ¿Ll o l? You will hear a series of words. Each will be said twice. Circle the letter used to spell each.

1. ll   l   3. ll   l   5. ll   l
2. ll   l   4. ll   l   6. ll   l

E. Repaso: ñ, l, ll, y: Dictado. You will hear three sentences. Each will be said twice. Write what you hear.

1. _____

2. _____

3. _____

Minidiálogos y gramática

▼▼▼▼▼▼▼▼▼▼▼▼▼▼▼▼▼▼▼▼▼▼▼▼▼▼▼▼▼▼▼▼▼▼▼▼

35. Influencing Others • tú Commands

A. Minidiálogo: «¡Marta, tu cuarto es un desastre!». You will
hear a brief paragraph in which Manolo complains to his
daughter Marta about her room. Then you will hear a series
of statements. Circle the letter of the person who might have
made each statement.

1. a. Manolo   b. Marta
2. a. Manolo   b. Marta
3. a. Manolo   b. Marta
4. a. Manolo   b. Marta

B. Encuesta: ¿Qué te decían tus padres? You will hear a series of commands that your parents may
or may not have given to you when you were a child. For each command, check the appropriate
answer. No answers will be given on the tape. The answers you choose should be correct for you!

Mandatos afirmativos

1. ☐ Sí   ☐ No   3. ☐ Sí   ☐ No

2. ☐ Sí   ☐ No   4. ☐ Sí   ☐ No

Mandatos negativos

5. ☐ Sí   ☐ No   7. ☐ Sí   ☐ No

6. ☐ Sí   ☐ No   8. ☐ Sí   ☐ No

C. **La vida doméstica de la Cenicienta** (*Cinderella*). Play the role of the stepmother and tell Cinderella what she has to do before she can go to the ball. Use affirmative informal commands for the infinitives you will hear.

1. ...   2. ...   3. ...   4. ...   5. ...

D. **¡No lo hagas!** Imagine that you are a parent of the child depicted in the drawings. When you hear the corresponding number, tell her *not* to do the things she is doing in each drawing. Use negative informal commands. You will hear a possible answer on the tape.

MODELO: (*you hear*) uno   (*you see*) pegar / Isabel →
(*you say*) No le pegues a Isabel.

1. pegar / Isabel

2. saltar (*to jump*) / cama

3. poner / mesa

4. pasear / calle

5. jugar / tantos videojuegos

6. escribir / pared

36. Expressing Subjective States and Actions • Present Subjunctive: An Introduction

A. Minidiálogo: Una decisión importante. You will hear a
dialogue in which José Miguel asks Gustavo for advice on
purchasing a computer. Then you will hear a series of statements
about the dialogue. Circle **C, F,** or **ND** (**No lo dice**).

1. C   F   ND
2. C   F   ND
3. C   F   ND

4. C   F   ND
5. C   F   ND

B. Encuesta: Hablando de la tecnología. You will hear a series of statements about technology. For
each statement, check the appropriate answer. No answers will be given on the tape. The answers you
choose should be correct for you!

1. ☐ Sí   ☐ No   ☐ No tengo opinión.

2. ☐ Sí   ☐ No   ☐ No tengo opinión.

3. ☐ Sí   ☐ No   ☐ No tengo opinión.

4. ☐ Sí   ☐ No   ☐ No tengo opinión.

5. ☐ Sí   ☐ No   ☐ No tengo opinión.

6. ☐ Sí   ☐ No   ☐ No tengo opinión.

C. ¿Qué quiere Arturo?

Paso 1. You will hear Arturo talk about what he wants his siblings to do. Listen to what he says, and
complete the following chart by checking the thing he wants each sibling to do or not to do.

PERSONA	NO JUGAR «NINTENDO»	NO USAR SU COCHE	PRESTARLE SU CÁMARA	BAJAR EL VOLUMEN DEL ESTÉREO
su hermana				
su hermano menor				
sus hermanitos				

Paso 2. Now answer the questions you hear, based on the completed chart. Each question will be said
twice. Check the answers to **Paso 1** in the Appendix before you begin **Paso 2.**

1. ...   2. ...   3. ...   4. ...

D. ¿Qué quieren? Answer the following questions using the oral cues.

1. ¿Qué quiere la jefa?

MODELO: (*you hear*) Sara → (*you say*) Quiere que Sara llegue a tiempo.

a. ...   b. ...   c. ...   d. ...

2. ¿Qué quieres que haga Juan?

MODELO: (*you hear*) comer ahora → (*you say*) Quiero que Juan coma ahora.

a. ...   b. ...   c. ...   d. ...

37. Expressing Desires and Requests • Use of the Subjunctive: Influence

A. Presiones de la vida moderna

Paso 1. You will hear a brief paragraph in which Margarita describes her job and what she doesn't like about it. Listen carefully and take notes.

Apuntes (*Notes*)

_____

_____

_____

_____

_____

_____

_____

_____

Paso 2. ¿Qué recuerdas? Now stop the tape and complete the following sentences based on the passage and your notes. Use phrases from the list. Be sure to use the correct present subjunctive form of the verbs.

equivocarse   tener teléfono celular
ser más flexible   trabajar los fines de semana
solucionar sus problemas

1. Los clientes quieren que Margarita _____ técnicos.

2. Su jefa no quiere que ella _____.

3. Margarita quiere que su horario _____.

4. A veces, es necesario que Margarita _____.

5. Margarita prefiere que su coche no _____.

Now turn on the tape.

B. ¿Qué recomienda el nuevo jefe? Imagine that you have a new boss in your office, and he is determined to make some changes. When you hear the corresponding numbers, tell what he recommends, using the written cues.

MODELO: (*you hear*) uno   (*you see*) El jefe recomienda... Ud. / buscar otro trabajo →
(*you say*) El jefe recomienda que Ud. busque otro trabajo.

2. El jefe recomienda... yo / no llegar tarde
3. El jefe insiste en... todos / trabajar hasta muy tarde
4. El jefe prohíbe... Federico / dormir en la oficina
5. El jefe prohíbe... tú / fumar en la oficina

C. Antes del viaje: ¿Qué quiere Ud. que hagan estas personas? Imagine that you are a tour leader, traveling with a large group of students. Using the oral and written cues, tell each person what you want him or her to do. Begin each sentence with **Quiero que...** , as in the model.

MODELO: (*you hear*) hacer las maletas   (*you see*) Uds. →
(*you say*) Quiero que Uds. hagan las maletas.

1. Toño   2. (tú)   3. Ana y Teresa   4. todos   5. todos

Situaciones

▼▼▼▼▼▼▼▼▼▼▼▼▼▼▼▼▼▼▼▼▼▼▼▼▼▼▼▼▼▼▼▼▼▼▼▼▼▼

Paso 1. Buscando una computadora. In the following conversation, José Miguel and Gustavo talk to a salesperson about computers. Listen and read along with the speakers.

VENDEDORA: Buenas tardes. ¿En qué les puedo atender?

JOSÉ MIGUEL: Buenas tardes. Leímos su anuncio en el periódico. Quisiéramos ver las computadoras.

VENDEDORA: ¿Qué modelo buscan? Tenemos varios aquí. Este es nuevo. Viene con monitor, ratón ergonómico y un módem interno.

JOSÉ MIGUEL: Pero, no tiene lector de CD-ROM interno, ¿verdad? Prefiero uno que lo tenga.

VENDEDORA: Ese modelo allí tiene lector de CD-ROM interno. Venga. Esta es la mejor de las que tienen CD-ROM.

JOSÉ MIGUEL: ¿Qué te parece, Gustavo?

GUSTAVO: No está mal... ¿Tiene suficiente memoria para navegar por el *Internet*?

VENDEDORA: Sí.

GUSTAVO: ¿Y se puede utilizar también un *browser* de páginas o programas de multimedia?

VENDEDORA: Este modelo es ideal para multimedia. Y lleva incluidos los programas necesarios para navegar la red.

JOSÉ MIGUEL: Ah, muy bien, porque pienso utilizar el *Internet* para ayudarme con mis trabajos en la universidad...

Paso 2. Aplicación. In the preceding conversation, José Miguel and Gustavo were shopping for a computer. It is also important to know how to arrange for repairs once you've bought one! Complete the following dialogue using the written cues. You will play the role of the client. Here are the cues for your conversation. ¡OJO! The cues are not in order.

va a estar lista (*ready*)
muy buenas
mi computadora no funciona
es una marca (*brand*) nacional

DEPENDIENTE: Buenas tardes. ¿En qué puedo servirle?

CLIENTE: _____¹ _____²

DEPENDIENTE: ¿La compró Ud. aquí?

CLIENTE: No, pero _____³

DEPENDIENTE: En ese caso no hay problema. Se la arreglamos en seguida.

CLIENTE: Muchas gracias. ¿Cuándo _____⁴?

DEPENDIENTE: Dentro de (*Within*) dos días.

Un poco de todo (Para entregar)

▼▼▼▼▼▼▼▼▼▼▼▼▼▼▼▼▼▼▼▼▼▼▼▼▼▼▼▼▼▼

A. Descripción: Una familia de la era de la tecnología

Paso 1. You will hear five brief descriptions. Write the letter of each description next to the drawing that it describes. ¡OJO! Not all the drawings will be described. First, stop the tape and look at the drawings.

1. _____

2. _____

3. _____

4. _____

5. _____

6. _____

Paso 2. Now stop the tape and write a description of the drawing for which there was no match.

_____

_____

_____

_____

_____

_____

_____

_____

Now turn on the tape.

B. *Listening Passage*: **Recuerdos de España**

Antes de escuchar. *Stop the tape* and do the following prelistening exercises.

Answer these questions about Spain to see how much you already know about this European country.

1. ¿Cómo piensas que es el nivel de vida (*standard of living*) en España?
2. ¿Crees que España ha cambiado (*has changed*) mucho en los últimos treinta años?
3. ¿Sabes lo que es la Unión Europea? España pertenece (*belongs*) a ella desde 1986.
4. ¿Cuántas semanas de vacaciones te dan al año si trabajas en los Estados Unidos? ¿Y en España?

Now turn on the tape.

Listening Passage. Now you will hear a passage in which a person from Spain tells us about his homeland. The following words appear in the passage.

a finales de	*at the end of*	occidental	*western*
en vías de desarrollo	*developing*	con eficacia	*efficiently*
a nivel	*at the level*	los medios	*means*
las cuestiones	*matters*	el ascenso	*promotion*
incluso	*even*	Me he americanizado.	*I have become Americanized.*

Después de escuchar. Stop the tape and check all the statements that, according to the speaker of the passage, describe present-day Spain.

1. ☐ España es un país en vías de desarrollo.

2. ☐ El nivel de vida en las ciudades grandes es bueno.

3. ☐ A los españoles no les gusta trabajar.

4. ☐ Es normal que los españoles tengan cuatro semanas de vacaciones al año.

5. ☐ Las universidades españolas tienen un mejor sistema de bibliotecas que las norteamericanas.

6. ☐ España es un país moderno y desarrollado.

7. ☐ La Unión Europea ha beneficiado (*has benefitted*) a España.

Now turn on the tape.

C. Y para terminar... Entrevista. You will hear a series of questions. Each will be said twice. Answer, based on your own experience. Stop the tape and write the answers.

1. _____

2. _____

3. _____

4. _____

5. _____

6. _____

A. ¿Dónde están estas personas?

Paso 1. You will hear four brief conversations or parts of conversations. Listen carefully and write the number of the conversation next to the location in which each conversation is taking place. Not all the locations will be used. First, listen to the list of possible locations.

_____ en una tienda de aparatos electrónicos   _____ en una oficina

_____ en un consultorio   _____ en un coche

_____ en una casa de apartamentos   _____ en casa, durante la cena

Paso 2 (Para entregar). Now, stop the tape and write a brief conversation, or part of a conversation, that takes place in one of the locations not used in **Paso 1.**

_____

_____

_____

_____

_____

_____

_____

Now turn on the tape.

B. _Los hispanos hablan:_ **Además de los estudios, ¿tienes un trabajo?**

Listen to the answers several Hispanic high school students gave to this question. Then stop the tape and indicate the statements that you can infer from the information given in the answers.

1. ☐ Es normal que los jóvenes hispánicos trabajen mientras asisten a la escuela o a la universidad.

2. ☐ En vez de (_Instead of_) trabajar, muchos jóvenes participan en actividades extraescolares.

3. ☐ Si un joven hispánico trabaja, es posible que sea porque no asiste a la universidad o a la escuela.

4. ☐ A los jóvenes hispánicos no les gusta trabajar.

Now turn on the tape.

C. Dictado. You will hear a brief paragraph that tells about a recent purchase. Listen carefully and, while listening, write the information requested. Write all numbers as numerals. First, listen to the requested information.

Lo que el narrador quería comprar en la tienda: _____

¿Cuánto pagó por el aparato? _____

Lo que tiene que pagar al mes: _____

¿Cuánto tiempo hace que tiene el aparato? _____

Tres de los aparatos que todavía quiere comprar: _____

_____

D. Cosas de todos los días. Practice telling about yourself and others, using the written cues. When you hear the corresponding number, form sentences using the words provided in the order given, making any necessary changes and additions. You will be using the preterite and the imperfect. Use the correct preterite form of the verb in the first sentence.

1. fiesta / empezar / nueve
2. Lisbet / traer / queso / vino
3. Rafael y yo / llegar / tarde / porque / no saber / dirección
4. Mateo / estar / contentísimo / porque / venir / su novia
5. todos / bailar / mientras / Tito / poner / discos compactos
6. durante la fiesta / Irene / darse con / mesa
7. y / a Roberto / caérsele / un vaso
8. ser / tres / cuando / por fin / terminar / fiesta
9. todos / volver / su / casa / cansadísimos

E. Conversación: Haciendo la limpieza (*cleaning*) **(Para entregar).** You will hear a conversation, partially printed in your manual, between a father and his son who are doing housework. Then you will participate in a similar conversation, playing the role of the father. Complete the conversation, based on your own preferences. Stop the tape and write the answers.

HIJO: ¿Qué quieres que haga con esta ropa?

PADRE: _____ .

HIJO: ¿Y la basura? ¿Dónde la pongo?

PADRE: _____ .

HIJO: Bueno, ya terminé con la basura y la ropa. ¿Qué quieres que haga con estas revistas?

PADRE: _____ .

HIJO: ¿Y los libros que están en el suelo?

PADRE: _____ .

HIJO: ¿Quieres que haga las camas?

PADRE: _____ . Bueno, ya terminamos. Gracias por tu ayuda.

HIJO: ¡De nada!

F.   Entrevista (Para entregar). You will hear a series of questions. Each will be said twice. Answer, based on your own experience. Stop the tape and write the answers.

1. _____

2. _____

3. _____

4. _____

5. _____

6. _____

7. _____

8. _____

9. _____

CAPÍTULO **13**

Vocabulario: Preparación

A. Encuesta. You will hear a series of questions. Check the appropriate boxes. No answers will be given on the tape. The answers you choose should be correct for you!

1. ☐ Sí   ☐ No   5. ☐ Sí   ☐ No
2. ☐ Sí   ☐ No   6. ☐ Sí   ☐ No
3. ☐ Sí   ☐ No   7. ☐ Sí   ☐ No
4. ☐ Sí   ☐ No   8. ☐ Sí   ☐ No

B. Identificaciones. You will hear a series of words. Write the number of each word next to the item the word describes. First, stop the tape and look at the drawings.

Now turn on the tape.

C. Definiciones. You will hear a series of definitions. Each will be said twice. Circle the letter of the word that is defined by each.

1. a. el bailarín   b. el cantante
2. a. la arquitecta   b. la artesanía
3. a. el músico   b. la ópera
4. a. la escultora   b. el dramaturgo
5. a. la compositora   b. el guía
6. a. el poeta   b. el artista

D. Descripción: ¿En qué piso? You will be asked to tell on what floor a number of families live or on which floor businesses are located. Each question will be said twice. Answer, based on the following drawing. First, stop the tape and look at the drawing.

1. ...
2. ...
3. ...
4. ...
5. ...

= 6

= 5

= 4

= 3

= 2

= 1

la planta baja

E. Poniendo las cosas en orden

Paso 1. You will hear a series of questions. Each will be said twice. Circle the correct answer.

1. febrero	enero	junio	abril
2. julio	agosto	octubre	diciembre
3. lunes	jueves	sábado	martes
4. Michael Jordan	Rosie O'Donnell	Neil Armstrong	Antonio Banderas

Paso 2. Now stop the tape and write a sentence, using ordinal numbers, about each of the answers you circled. Number four is done for you.

1. _____

2. _____

3. _____

4. _La primera persona que caminó en la luna fue Neil Armstrong._

Now turn on the tape.

Los hispanos hablan: Dinos algo acerca de la ciudad donde vives

Paso 1. First, stop the tape and check the statements that are true for the city or town in which you live.

1. ☐ Muchas personas viven en el centro de la ciudad.

2. ☐ Hay muchas partes antiguas (*old*).

3. ☐ La mayoría de los teatros, museos, tiendas, etcétera, se encuentran en el centro.

4. ☐ Es normal que la gente esté en las calles hasta muy tarde.

5. ☐ Hay metro (*subway*).

6. ☐ Hay mucha vida cultural.

7. ☐ Es normal que la gente camine en vez de (*instead of*) usar el coche.

Now turn on the tape.

Now listen to Clara's description of Madrid. As you listen, try not to be distracted by unfamiliar vocabulary. Concentrate instead on what you *do* know and understand.

Paso 2. Stop the tape and check the statements that are true, according to the passage.

1. ☐ Clara nació en Madrid.

2. ☐ Madrid es una ciudad cosmopolita.

3. ☐ Si uno vive en Madrid, es absolutamente necesario tener coche.

4. ☐ En Madrid, es normal que la gente esté en las calles hasta muy tarde.

5. ☐ Es común que mucha gente viva en el centro de la ciudad.

6. ☐ La mayoría de las actividades culturales se encuentran en el centro.

Now turn on the tape.

Pronunciación y ortografía: x and n

▼▼

A. The letter **x** is usually pronounced [ks], as in English. Before a consonant, however, it is often pronounced [s]. Repeat the following words, imitating the speaker.

1.	[ks]	léxico	sexo	axial	existen	examen
2.	[s]	explican	extraordinario	extremo	sexto	extraterrestre

Read the following sentences when you hear the corresponding numbers. Repeat the correct pronunciation.

3. ¿Piensas que existen los extraterrestres?
4. ¡Nos explican que es algo extraordinario!
5. No me gustan las temperaturas extremas.
6. La medicina no es una ciencia exacta.

B. Before the letters **p, b, v,** and **m,** the letter **n** is pronounced [m]. Before the sounds [k], [g], and [x], **n** is pronounced like the [ng] sound in the English word *sing*. In all other positions, **n** is pronounced as it is in English.

1. [m] convence un beso un peso con Manuel con Pablo
   en Venezuela
2. [ng] en casa en Castilla son generosos en Quito en Granada
   con Juan

Read the following words, phrases, and sentences when you hear the corresponding numbers. Repeat the correct pronunciation.

3. en Perú
4. son jóvenes
5. con Gloria
6. en México
7. En general, sus poemas son buenos.
8. Los museos están en Madrid.

Minidiálogos y gramática

38. Expressing Feelings • Use of the Subjunctive: Emotion

A. Minidiálogo: Diego y Lupe escuchan un grupo de mariachis.
You will hear a dialogue followed by a series of statements. Circle the letter of the person who might have made each statement.

1. a. Lupe   b. Diego   3. a. Lupe   b. Diego
2. a. Lupe   b. Diego   4. a. Lupe   b. Diego

B. El día de la función (*show*). Tell how the following people feel, using the oral and written cues.

MODELO: (*you hear*) el director   (*you see*) temer que / los actores / olvidar sus líneas →
          (*you say*) El director teme que los actores olviden sus líneas.

1. esperar que / los actores / no enfermarse
2. temer que / la actriz / estar muy nerviosa
3. temer que / los otros actores / no llegar a tiempo
4. esperar que / la obra / ser buena
5. tener miedo de que / la obra / ser muy larga

C. Descripción: Esperanzas (*Hopes*) **y temores** (*fears*). You will hear two questions about each drawing. Answer, based on the drawings and the written cues.

1. sacar (*to get*) malas notas (*grades*) / sacar una «A»

2. funcionar su computadora / no funcionar su computadora

3. haber regalos para él / no haber nada para él

39. Expressing Uncertainty • Use of the Subjunctive: Doubt and Denial

A. ¿Cierto o falso?

Paso 1. Encuesta. You will hear a series of statements about your likes and dislikes. Tell whether each statement is true or false. Answer, based on your own experience. No answers will be given on the tape. The answers you give should be correct for you!

1. ☐ No es cierto que me encante.   ☐ Es cierto que me encanta.

2. ☐ No es cierto que lo tenga.   ☐ Es cierto que lo tengo.

3. ☐ No es cierto que lo prefiera.   ☐ Es cierto que lo prefiero.

4. ☐ No es cierto que conozca a uno.   ☐ Es cierto que conozco a uno.

5. ☐ No es cierto que sea aficionado/a.   ☐ Es cierto que soy aficionado/a.

Paso 2. Now stop the tape and complete the following sentences based on your own preferences.

1. Es cierto que me encanta _____.

2. No es cierto que me encante _____.

3. Es cierto que tengo _____.

4. No es cierto que tenga _____.

5. Es cierto que soy aficionado/a al /a la _____.

6. No es cierto que sea aficionado/a al /a la _____.

Now turn on the tape.

B. ¿Qué piensa Ud.? Imagine that your friend Josefina has made a series of statements. Respond to each, using the written cues. You will hear each one twice. **¡OJO!** You will have to use the indicative in some cases.

> MODELO: (*you hear*) Anita va al teatro esta noche.   (*you see*) No creo que... →
> (*you say*) No creo que Anita vaya al teatro esta noche.

1. No creo que...
2. Dudo que...
3. Es imposible que...
4. Es verdad que...
5. Estoy seguro/a de que...

C. Observaciones. You will hear a series of statements about the following drawings. Each will be said twice. React to each statement, according to the model. Begin each answer with **Es verdad que...** or **No es verdad que... .**

> MODELO: (*you hear*) Amalia tiene un auto nuevo. →
> (*you say*) No es verdad que Amalia tenga un auto nuevo.

1.

2.

3.

4.

5.

40. Expressing Influence, Emotion, Doubt, and Denial • The Subjunctive: A Summary

A. Minidiálogo: Lola Benítez les habla a sus estudiantes norteamericanos. You will hear a brief paragraph in which Lola Benítez asks her students to write a composition about the art of Sevilla. Then you will hear a series of statements about the passage. Circle **C, F,** or **ND (No lo dice).**

1. C   F   ND

2. C   F   ND

3. C   F   ND

4. C   F   ND

5. C   F   ND

B. Se venden coches nuevos y usados. You will hear three ads for automobiles. Listen and complete the following sentences by writing the number of the ad in the appropriate space. First, stop the tape and read the incomplete statements.

Dudo que el coche del anuncio número _____ sea una ganga.

El auto del anuncio número _____ es un auto pequeño y económico.

Es probable que el coche del anuncio número _____ gaste mucha gasolina.

Now turn on the tape.

C. ¿Qué quieres que hagan estas personas? You will hear a series of questions. Answer, using an appropriate written cue.

MODELO: (*you hear*) ¿Qué quieres que haga el profesor? →
(*you say*) Quiero que no nos dé un examen.

explicarme las obras de arte   tomarme la temperatura
mostrarme las computadoras   traerme la ensalada
no darnos un examen

1. ...   2. ...   3. ...   4. ...

Situaciones

▼▼▼▼▼▼▼▼▼▼▼▼▼▼▼▼▼▼▼▼▼▼▼▼▼▼▼▼▼▼▼▼▼▼▼▼

Paso 1. Hablando del arte. In this conversation, Diego and Lupe are talking about art preferences. Listen and read along with the speakers.

DIEGO: ¿Ya sabes sobre qué vas a escribir tu trabajo para la clase de arte?

LUPE: Creo que sí. Me interesan mucho el arte y la vida de Frida Kahlo, así que voy a escribir algo sobre ella.

DIEGO: Kahlo pintó muchos autorretratos, ¿no?

LUPE: Sí, y sus autorretratos siempre tienen elementos simbólicos que representan sus emociones y su estado de ánimo. Sus cuadros me gustan muchísimo. Su esposo fue Diego Rivera, uno de los muralistas más famosos de México. Mira. Aquí ves uno de sus cuadros.

DIEGO: Conozco varios murales de Rivera. Los vi en el Palacio Nacional. Pero a mí me impresionan más los murales de José Clemente Orozco.

LUPE: Sí, Orozco fue un muralista excelente. Mira. Aquí ves uno de sus cuadros.

DIEGO: Así que vas a escribir sobre Frida Kahlo. ¿Qué más te interesa sobre ella?

LUPE: Bueno, me interesa mucho su arte, claro. Pero también me interesa porque llevó una vida muy difícil. Sufrió mucho, pero nunca dejó de apreciar la belleza de vivir...

Paso 2. Aplicación. Now you will participate in a similar conversation, partially printed in your manual, in which you play the role of **Ud.** Complete it using the written cues. You will need to conjugate the verbs. Here are the cues for your conversation. ¡OJO! The cues are not in order.

> haber entradas
> ir (nosotros) a un concierto de música clásica
> ser más emocionante

SU AMIGA: ¿Qué tal si vamos a un concierto este fin de semana? Hace tiempo que no vamos.

UD.: Está bien, pero esta vez prefiero que _____.¹

SU AMIGA: Bueno, si insistes. Pero, ¿por qué te gusta tanto ese tipo de música?

UD.: Me gusta porque creo que _____.²

SU AMIGA: Bueno, hay un concierto de Beethoven el sábado a las ocho. ¿Qué te parece?

UD.: ¡Perfecto! Ojalá que todavía _____.³

Un poco de todo (Para entregar)

▼▼▼▼▼▼▼▼▼▼▼▼▼▼▼▼▼▼▼▼▼▼▼▼▼▼▼▼▼▼▼▼▼▼▼▼▼▼▼

A. En un museo. You will hear a dialogue in which a museum guide explains Pablo Picasso's famous painting, *Guernica*, to some visitors. You will also hear two of the visitors' reactions to the painting. Then you will hear a series of statements. Circle **C, F,** or **ND** (**No lo dice**).

1. C F ND   2. C F ND   3. C F ND   4. C F ND

B. *Listening Passage*: **Primeras impresiones**

Antes de escuchar. You will hear a passage in which a person who is now living in this country tells about her first impressions of people in the United States. The following words and phrases appear in the passage.

las amistades	los amigos	echo de menos	*I miss*
aumentó	*increased*	el pueblo	*people*
judía	*Jewish*	demuestra	*shows*
para que yo pudiera	*so that I could*	nos besamos	*we kiss each other*
maravilloso	*marvelous, wonderful*	(nos) abrazamos	*we hug (each other)*
para que yo tuviera	*so that I would have*		

Listening Passage. Here is the passage. First, listen to it to get a general idea of the content. Then rewind the tape and listen again for specific information.

Después de escuchar. Circle the best answer to each of the following questions. ¡OJO! There may be more than one answer for some items.

1. Es probable que la persona que habla sea de...
   a. España.   b. los Estados Unidos.   c. Latinoamérica.   d. Nueva York.
2. Al principio (*beginning*), esta persona pensaba que los estadounidenses eran...
   a. abiertos.   b. perezosos.   c. fríos.   d. contentos.
3. La amiga que invitó a esta persona a su casa era...
   a. protestante.   b. judía.   c. ateísta.   d. católica.
4. Antes de visitar a la familia de Abi, la narradora...
   a. no conocía Nueva York.
   b. compró regalos.
   c. pasaba la Navidad con su familia.
   d. no sabía mucho de las tradiciones judías.
5. La familia de Abi no entendía...
   a. español.
   b. la tradición de Navidad.
   c. por qué se dan regalos el seis de enero.
   d. por qué la narradora no tenía muchos amigos.
6. Ahora, la estudiante hispánica piensa que...
   a. los estadounidenses son gente fría.
   b. los estadounidenses no se besan lo suficiente.
   c. los estadounidenses no saben nada de las tradiciones hispánicas.
   d. los estadounidenses demuestran el cariño de una manera distinta de la de los hispanos.

Now turn on the tape.

C. Y para terminar... Entrevista. You will hear a series of questions. Each will be said twice. Answer, based on your own experience. Stop the tape and write the answers.

1. _____
2. _____
3. _____
4. _____
5. _____
6. _____

CAPÍTULO **14**

Vocabulario: Preparación

▼▼▼▼▼▼▼▼▼▼▼▼▼▼▼▼▼▼▼▼▼▼▼▼▼▼▼▼▼▼

¿Qué opina sobre el medio ambiente? You will hear a series of statements about environmental concerns. Express your opinion about the issues by checking the appropriate boxes. No answers will be given on the tape. The answers you choose should be correct for you!

	SÍ ENFÁTICO	SÍ	NO TENGO OPINIÓN	NO	NO ENFÁTICO
1.	☐	☐	☐	☐	☐
2.	☐	☐	☐	☐	☐
3.	☐	☐	☐	☐	☐
4.	☐	☐	☐	☐	☐
5.	☐	☐	☐	☐	☐
6.	☐	☐	☐	☐	☐

B. Identificaciones. You will hear a series of words or phrases. Each will be said twice. Write the number of each phrase next to the appropriate drawing. ¡OJO! There is an extra drawing.

a. _____

b. _____

c. _____

d. _____

e. _____

f. _____

C. Definiciones: Hablando de coches. You will hear a series of statements. Each will be said twice. Circle the letter of the word that is best defined by each.

1. a. la batería   b. la gasolina   c. la licencia
2. a. la licencia   b. el camino   c. el taller
3. a. el parabrisas   b. los frenos   c. el semáforo
4. a. la esquina   b. la carretera   c. la llanta
5. a. el accidente   b. el aceite   c. el taller

D. Un accidente

Paso 1. Identificaciones. Identify the following items when you hear the corresponding number. Begin each sentence with **Es un... , Es una... ,** or **Son... .**

Paso 2. Descripción. Now you will hear a series of statements about the preceding drawing. Circle **C** or **F**.

1. C   F   2. C   F   3. C   F   4. C   F

E. Gustos y preferencias. You will hear descriptions of two people, Nicolás and Susana. Then you will hear a series of statements. Write the number of each statement next to the name of the person who might have made it.

Nicolás: _____

Susana: _____

Los hispanos hablan: En tu opinión, ¿cuáles son las semejanzas y diferencias más grandes entre las ciudades hispánicas y las norteamericanas?

You will hear excerpts from several answers to this question. After you listen, stop the tape and check the appropriate boxes to describe Hispanic and U.S. cities. The following words and phrases appear in the answers.

recorrer un gran trecho	*to travel a great distance*
no hace falta	no es necesario
las fuentes	*fountains*
como no sea	*unless it is* (*unless we are talking about*)
a la par de	al lado de
seguro	*safe*

	LAS CIUDADES HISPÁNICAS	LAS CIUDADES NORTEAMERICANAS
1. Son muy grandes.	☐	☐
2. Están contaminadas.	☐	☐
3. Tienen más vida.	☐	☐
4. Son menos seguras.	☐	☐
5. La gente vive en la ciudad misma (*proper*).	☐	☐
6. Las tiendas están en las vecindades.	☐	☐
7. Hay más árboles, vegetación y parques.	☐	☐

Now turn on the tape.

Pronunciación y ortografía:
More Cognate Practice

▼▼▼▼▼▼▼▼▼▼▼▼▼▼▼▼▼▼▼▼▼▼▼▼▼▼▼▼▼▼▼▼▼▼

A. You were introduced to cognates in the **Ante todo** sections of *Puntos de partida*. As you know, English and Spanish cognates do not always share the same pronunciation or spelling. Listen to the following pairs of cognates, paying close attention to the differences in spelling and pronunciation.

chemical / químico   affirm / afirmar   national / nacional

Read the following cognates when you hear the corresponding number. Remember to repeat the correct pronunciation.

1. correcto
2. anual
3. teoría
4. alianza
5. físico
6. teléfono
7. patético
8. intención

B. Dictado. You will hear the following words. Each will be said twice. Listen carefully and write the missing letters.

1. _____os_____ato

2. a_____ención

3. a_____oníaco

4 _____eología

5. o_____osición

6. _____otogra_____ía

7. co_____e_____ión

8. ar_____itecta

Minidiálogos y gramática

▼▼▼▼▼▼▼▼▼▼▼▼▼▼▼▼▼▼▼▼▼▼▼▼▼▼▼▼▼▼▼

41. Más descripciones • Past Participle Used as an Adjective

A. Descripción. Which picture is best described by the sentences you hear? You will hear each sentence twice.

VOCABULARIO ÚTIL: colgar   *to hang up*
                        enchufar   *to plug in*

1. a.

                        b.

2. a.

                        b.

3. a.

b.

4. a.

b.

5. a.

b.

6. a.

b.

B. Definiciones. You will hear a series of definitions. Each will be said twice. Circle the answer that best matches each definition. ¡OJO! There may be more than one answer for some items.

1. a. el agua   b. el aire   c. la batería
2. a. Stephen King   b. Descartes   c. Tom Clancy

3. a. la mano   b. los ojos   c. la ventana
4. a. el papel   b. el pie   c. la computadora

C. Consecuencias lógicas. You will hear a series of sentences that describe actions. Respond to each sentence, telling the probable outcome of the action.

> MODELO: (*you hear*) Escribí la composición. → (*you say*) Ahora la composición está escrita.

1. ... 2. ... 3. ... 4. ... 5. ...

42. ¿Qué has hecho? • Perfect Forms: Present Perfect Indicative and Present Perfect Subjunctive

A. Minidiálogo: Una llanta desinflada. You will hear a dialogue followed by a series of statements. Circle **C**, **F**, or **ND** (**No lo dice**).

1. C F ND   4. C F ND

2. C F ND   5. C F ND

3. C F ND

B. ¿Qué ha pasado ya? You will hear a series of sentences. Each will be said twice. Circle the letter of the subject of the verb in each sentence.

1. a. yo   b. ella   4. a. nosotros   b. yo
2. a. él   b. nosotros   5. a. ellos   b. él
3. a. nosotros b. tú

C. ¿Qué hemos hecho hoy? Form new sentences, using the oral and written cues. Use the present perfect indicative of the verbs.

1. despertarse   4. desayunar
2. hacer las camas   5. salir para la oficina
3. vestirse   6. llevar el auto a la gasolinera

D. ¿Te puedo ayudar? Imagine that you have a lot to do before a dinner party, and your friend Ernesto wants to know if he can help. You appreciate his offer, but you have already done the things he asks about. You will hear each of his questions twice. Answer them according to the model.

> MODELO: (*you hear*) ¿Quieres que llame a los Sres. Moreno? →
> (*you say*) No, gracias, ya los he llamado.

1. ... 2. ... 3. ... 4. ... 5. ...

E. Un caso de contaminación ambiental. Imagine that a case of environmental pollution was discovered earlier this year in your community. Using the oral and written cues, form sentences that express what the residents have said about the incident. Follow the model.

> MODELO: (*you see*) ya estudiar el problema (*you hear*) es probable →
> (*you say*) Es probable que ya hayan estudiado el problema.

1. todavía no avisar (*to notify*) a todos los habitantes de la ciudad
2. ya consultar con los expertos
3. encontrar la solución todavía
4. proteger los animales de la zona

Situaciones

▼▼▼▼▼▼▼▼▼▼▼▼▼▼▼▼▼▼▼▼▼▼▼▼▼▼▼▼▼▼▼▼▼▼▼▼▼

Paso 1. En busca de un taller. In the following conversation, Elisa and José Miguel help out a motorist in trouble. Listen and read along with the speakers.

CONDUCTORA: Buenos días. Disculpe, señora. ¿Podría decirme a cuánto queda el pueblo más cercano?

ELISA: Bueno, hay un pueblo no muy lejos de aquí, como a unos diez minutos. Pero es muy pequeño. ¿Qué busca?

CONDUCTORA: Es el carro. Temo que tenga algo serio. Ha comenzado a hacer un ruido muy extraño, y quiero que lo revise un mecánico. ¿Sabe Ud. si hay un taller en el pueblo?

ELISA: Ay, lo dudo mucho. Pero hay otro pueblo más grande no muy lejos, y es muy posible que haya un taller allí. Siga todo derecho unos cinco kilómetros, y luego doble a la izquierda en la carretera para Quito. ¿Sabe? Se me ocurre algo. Nosotros vamos en esa dirección. La podemos acompañar. No me gusta que se quede sola en este camino con un carro que no arranca.

CONDUCTORA: Eso es muy amable de su parte, pero no se molesten.

JOSÉ MIGUEL: De veras, no es ninguna molestia. Necesitamos encontrar una gasolinera. Tenemos que llenar el tanque.

CONDUCTORA: Muchas gracias. Uds. me han ayudado muchísimo.

ELISA: No hay de qué. ¿Vamos?

Paso 2. Aplicación. Now you will participate in a conversation, partially printed in your manual, in which you play the role of a motorist (*conductor*) who needs help. You are now at the repair shop. Complete it using the written cues. You will need to conjugate the verbs. Here are the cues for your conversation. **¡OJO!** The cues are not in order.

muchísimas gracias
revisarle las llantas y los frenos

ser el motor / ser un auto nuevo
tener algo serio / haber comenzado

CONDUCTOR: Temo que mi auto _____ ¹. _____ ²
a hacer un ruido extraño.

MECÁNICO: Es posible que sea el motor.

CONDUCTOR: Dudo que _____ ³... _____ ⁴.

MECÁNICO: En ese caso, le recomiendo que lo deje aquí para poder revisarlo con cuidado.

CONDUCTOR: Está bien. También quiero que _____ ⁵.

MECÁNICO: Por supuesto. Eso es parte de nuestro servicio normal. Puede venir a buscar su auto dentro de tres horas.

CONDUCTOR: _____ ⁶.

Un poco de todo (Para entregar)

▼▼▼▼▼▼▼▼▼▼▼▼▼▼▼▼▼▼▼▼▼▼▼▼▼▼▼▼▼▼▼▼▼▼▼▼

A. Descripciones. You will hear a series of descriptions. Each will be said twice. Write the number of each description next to the drawing described. ¡OJO! There is one extra drawing. First, stop the tape and look at the drawings.

a. _____

b. _____

c. _____

d. _____

e. _____

B. *Listening Passage*: **Los coches**

Antes de escuchar. You will hear a passage about the types of cars driven in the Hispanic world. The following words appear in the passage.

la molestia	*bother*
la ayuda	*something helpful*
la clase media-baja	*lower middle class*

Listening Passage. Here is the passage. First, listen to it to get a general idea of the content. Then rewind the tape and listen again for specific information.

Después de escuchar. Read the following statements. Circle **C** or **F**. Correct the statements that are false, according to the passage.

1. C   F   Las personas que viven en los países hispanos no están acostumbradas a conducir.

    _____

2. C   F   Hay muchos autos japoneses y estadounidenses en España.

    _____

3. C   F   No se venden marcas europeas en Latinoamérica.

    _____

4. C   F   El precio de la gasolina es comparable en España y en los Estados Unidos.

    _____

5. C   F   En México, es posible encontrar marcas que ya no se fabrican en otras partes del mundo.

    _____

Now turn on the tape.

C. Y para terminar... Entrevista. You will hear a series of questions. Each will be said twice. Answer, based on your own experience. Stop the tape and write the answers.

1. _____

2. _____

3. _____

4. _____

5. _____

6. _____

7. _____

CAPÍTULO **15**

Vocabulario: Preparación

▼▼▼▼▼▼▼▼▼▼▼▼▼▼▼▼▼▼▼▼▼▼▼▼▼▼▼▼▼▼▼▼▼

A. Encuesta: Hablando de las relaciones sentimentales. You will hear a series of statements about personal relationships. For each statement, check the appropriate answer. No answers will be given on the tape. The answers you choose should be correct for you!

1. ☐ Sí ☐ No			6. ☐ Sí ☐ No		
2. ☐ Sí ☐ No			7. ☐ Sí ☐ No		
3. ☐ Sí ☐ No			8. ☐ Sí ☐ No		
4. ☐ Sí ☐ No			9. ☐ Sí ☐ No		
5. ☐ Sí ☐ No			10. ☐ Sí ☐ No		

B. Definiciones. You will hear a series of definitions. Each will be said twice. Circle the letter of the word defined. ¡OJO! There is more than one answer for some items.

1. a. la amistad   b. el corazón   c. el amor
2. a. el noviazgo   b. el divorcio   c. una visita al consejero matrimonial
3. a. la luna de miel   b. la cita   c. la pareja
4. a. el noviazgo   b. la boda   c. la cita
5. a. la dueña   b. la consejera   c. la novia

C. Asociaciones. You will hear a series of phrases. Each will be said twice. Circle the letter of the word that you associate with each.

1. a. la infancia   b. la niñez   c. la adolescencia
2. a. la vejez   b. la juventud   c. el nacimiento
3. a. la madurez   b. la adolescencia   c. la infancia
4. a. la infancia   b. la vejez   c. la juventud

Los hispanos hablan: Las relaciones sociales

As you might expect, social relations differ from country to country. You will hear Eduardo's impressions of the differences in social relations between the United States and his native country, Uruguay. The passage has been divided into two parts. Remember to concentrate on the vocabulary you know. Don't be distracted by unfamiliar vocabulary.

Paso 1. Before you listen to the passage, stop the tape and indicate if the following statements are true for you. There are no right or wrong answers.

1. ☐ Sí ☐ No Me gusta que mis amigos vengan a visitarme sin avisar (*without letting me know ahead of time*).

2. ☐ Sí ☐ No   Por lo general, mi vida social es espontánea; es decir, generalmente, no planeo todas mis actividades.

3. ☐ Sí ☐ No   Participo en actividades sociales en las cuales (*in which*) hay personas de varias generaciones (niños, jóvenes, personas de mi edad, personas mayores o viejas).

4. ☐ Sí ☐ No   Para mí, la vida privada (*privacy*) es algo importante.

5. ☐ Sí ☐ No   Todavía vivo con mi familia.

Now turn on the tape.

La vida social: Parte 1. The following words appear in the first part of the passage.

extrañan	*they miss*
se dedica	*spend a lot of time on* (*something*)
sin avisar	*without letting one know ahead of time*
mal visto	*not looked upon favorably*

La vida social: Parte 2. The following words appear in the second part of the passage.

la vida privada	*privacy*
insólito	*unusual*

Paso 2. Now, stop the tape and write a brief paragraph that summarizes how Eduardo feels about social relations in the United States. It may help to look back at the statements you read before listening to the passage.

Eduardo piensa que... _____

_____

_____

_____

_____

_____

_____

_____

Now turn on the tape.

Pronunciación y ortografía:
More Cognate Practice

▼▼▼▼▼▼▼▼▼▼▼▼▼▼▼▼▼▼▼▼▼▼▼▼▼▼▼▼▼▼▼▼▼▼▼▼▼

A. False Cognates. Unlike true cognates, false cognates do not have the same meaning in English as they do in Spanish. Repeat the following words, some of which you have already seen and used actively, paying close attention to their pronunciation and true meaning in Spanish.

la carta (*letter*)	el pie (*foot*)
dime (*tell me*)	actual (*current, present-day*)

emocionante (*thrilling*)
asistir (*to attend*)
el pan (*bread*)
el éxito (*success*)
sin (*without*)

actualmente (*nowadays*)
embarazada (*pregnant*)
el pariente (*relative*)
dice (*he/she says*)
la red (*net*)

B. You will hear the following paragraphs from an article in a Spanish newspaper. Pay close attention to the pronunciation of the indicated cognates. Then you will practice reading the paragraphs.

El *ministro* de *Transportes* y *Comunicaciones*, Abel Caballero, ha *declarado* que el Gobierno está dando los primeros pasos para la *construcción* de un *satélite* español de *telecomunicaciones* que, de tomarse la *decisión final*, *comenzará* a ser *operativo* el año que viene.
   Muchos de los *componentes* del *satélite* tendrían que ser *importados*, pero al menos el treinta y seis por ciento los podría construir la *industria* española.

Now, turn off the tape and read the paragraphs. You may also wish to rewind the tape and read along with the speaker.

Now turn on the tape.

Minidiálogos y gramática

▼▼▼▼▼▼▼▼▼▼▼▼▼▼▼▼▼▼▼▼▼▼▼▼▼▼▼▼▼▼▼▼▼▼▼

43. ¿Hay alguien que... ? ¿Hay un lugar donde... ? • Subjunctive After Nonexistent and Indefinite Antecedents

A. Minidiálogo: La persona ideal. You will hear a dialogue followed by a series of statements. Each will be said twice. Circle **C**, **F**, or **ND** (**No lo dice**).

1. C F ND

2. C F ND

3. C F ND

4. C F ND

5. C F ND

B. En busca de una nueva casa. Form new sentences, using the oral cues.

1. (*you see and hear*) ¿Qué tipo de casa buscan Uds.? (*you hear*) estar en el campo →
   (*you say*) Buscamos una casa que esté en el campo.

   a. ... b. ... c. ...

2. (*you see and hear*) ¿Y cómo quieren Uds. que sean los vecinos? (*you hear*) jugar a las cartas
   (*you say*) Queremos vecinos que jueguen a las cartas.

   a. ... b. ... c. ...

C. Escenas de la vida. You will hear a series of statements. Each will be said twice. Respond to each statement, using the written cues.

MODELO: (*you hear*) Necesitamos un secretario que hable español.
(*you see*) Pues, yo conozco... →
(*you say*) Pues, yo conozco a un secretario que habla español.

1. Yo te puedo recomendar...
2. Lo siento, pero no hay nadie aquí...
3. Pues yo busco...
4. Pues yo también quiero...
5. Ellos van a ofrecerte un puesto...

D. ¿Qué quieren estas personas? You will hear what these people already have. Say what they want, using the written cues. If you prefer, stop the tape and write the answers.

MODELO: (*you see*) es viejo / ser nuevo →
(*you hear*) Arturo tiene un auto que es viejo.
(*you say*) Quiere un auto que sea nuevo.

1. no tiene vista / tener vista

_____

2.   es perezoso / ser trabajador

_____

3.   es muy grande / ser pequeño

_____

4.   hacen mucho ruido / no hacer tanto ruido

_____

44. **Lo hago para que tú...** • Subjunctive After Conjunctions of Contingency and Purpose

A. Minidiálogo: Antes del viaje. You will hear a dialogue between Francisco and Araceli about their upcoming trip. Then you will hear a series of statements. Circle **C, F,** or **ND** (**No lo dice**).

1. C   F   ND   4. C   F   ND

2. C   F   ND   5. C   F   ND

3. C   F   ND

B. Un viaje. You will hear the following pairs of sentences. Then you will hear a conjunction. Join each pair of sentences, using the conjunction and making any necessary changes.

> MODELO: (*you see and hear*) Hacemos el viaje. No cuesta mucho.   (*you hear*) con tal que →
> (*you say*) Hacemos el viaje con tal que no cueste mucho.

1. Tenemos que salir. Empieza a llover.
2. No queremos ir. Hace sol.
3. Pon las maletas en el coche. Podemos salir pronto.
4. Trae el mapa. Nos perdemos.

C. ¿Quién lo dijo? When you hear the number, read aloud each of the following statements, giving the present subjunctive form of the verb in parentheses. You will hear the correct answer on the tape. Then you will hear the names of two different people. Circle the letter of the person who might have made each statement.

1. a   b   No les doy los paquetes a los clientes antes de que me (*pagar*).

2. a   b   Voy a revisar las llantas en caso de que (*necesitar*) aire.

3. a   b   No compro esa computadora a menos que (*ser*) fácil de manejar.

4. a   b   Voy a tomarle la temperatura al paciente antes de que lo (*ver*) la doctora.

Situaciones

▼▼▼▼▼▼▼▼▼▼▼▼▼▼▼▼▼▼▼▼▼▼▼▼▼▼▼▼▼▼▼▼▼

Paso 1. Una invitación. In this conversation, Lola and her friend Eva make plans for the weekend. Listen and read along with the speakers.

LOLA: ¡Por fin es viernes! Qué semana más larga, ¿eh?

EVA: ¿Qué vais a hacer este fin de semana?

LOLA: Pues, nos vamos a pasar el día con mi hermano en Cádiz. Es el cumpleaños de mi sobrino. Y el domingo no tenemos planes. Y vosotros, ¿qué hacéis?

EVA: El domingo vamos a una boda aquí en Sevilla. Se casa una prima mía. ¿Tenéis planes para esta noche?

LOLA: Creo que no, a menos que Manolo haya hecho planes.

EVA: ¿Y por qué no salimos todos juntos? ¡Hace tanto tiempo que no lo hacemos!

LOLA: Por mí, encantada. Podemos ir a cenar o al cine. Hay dos o tres películas interesantes que a Manolo y a mí nos gustaría ver. También podemos llevar a las niñas. ¡Carolina y Marta ya son como hermanas! Se lo voy a preguntar a Manolo y te llamo después.

EVA: Muy bien. Yo también hablo con Jesús. Hablamos luego y entonces decidimos qué hacer, ¿vale?

LOLA: Estupendo.

Paso 2. Aplicación. Now you will participate in a similar conversation, partially printed in your manual, in which you play the role of **Ud.** Complete it using the written cues. You will need to conjugate the verbs. Here are the cues for your conversation. ¡OJO! Use the cues in the order given.

> estar libre / esta tarde
> venir conmigo / tomar un café

UD.: ¡Hola Yolanda! ¡Hace tiempo que no te veo! ¿_____¹?

YOLANDA: ¡Qué coincidencia! Te iba a llamar anoche. Resulta que no tengo que trabajar esta tarde.

UD.: ¡Magnífico! ¿Quieres _____²?

YOLANDA: Pues, ¡claro! Tengo un montón (*lot*) que contarte...

Un poco de todo (Para entregar)

▼▼▼▼▼▼▼▼▼▼▼▼▼▼▼▼▼▼▼▼▼▼▼▼▼▼▼▼▼▼

A. Identificaciones. You will hear six sentences. Each will be said twice. Write the number of each sentence next to the drawing that is described. ¡OJO! There are two extra drawings. First, stop the tape and look at the drawings.

a. _____

b. _____

c. _____

d. _____

e. _____

f. _____

g. _____

h. _____

B. *Listening Passage*: Semejanzas y diferencias

Antes de escuchar. You will hear a conversation, already in progress, between two students: One is from Spain and the other is from the United States. They are talking about the similarities and differences between people of their age group in the U.S. and Spain. Notice that the student from Spain uses the **vosotros** forms of verbs, pronouns, and possessive adjectives instead of the **ustedes** forms. Although the **vosotros** forms are not frequently used in *Puntos de partida*, you should be able to recognize them.

Listening Passage. The following words and phrases appear in the conversation.

independizarse	*to become independent*
me di cuenta que	*I realized*
no se ve tan mal	*it is not looked down upon (considered odd, viewed as bad)*
dura	*lasts*
el préstamo	*loan*
la beca	*scholarship, grant*
los ingresos	*earnings, assets*
estatal	*state run (adj.)*

Después de escuchar. Indicate the country to which the following sentences refer, based on the conversation that you just heard.

	ESPAÑA	LOS ESTADOS UNIDOS
1. La mayoría de las universidades son estatales.	☐	☐
2. Es normal obtener un préstamo para asistir a la universidad.	☐	☐
3. Es normal que una persona mayor de 18 años viva con sus padres.	☐	☐

	ESPAÑA	LOS ESTADOS UNIDOS
4. Se ve mal que los hijos vivan con la familia después de cumplir los dieciocho años.	☐	☐
5. La universidad dura cinco años, generalmente.	☐	☐
6. A los jóvenes les gusta la música rock y llevar *jeans*.	☐	☐

Now turn on the tape.

C. Y para terminar... Entrevista. You will hear a series of questions. Each will be said twice. Answer, based on your own experience. Stop the tape and write the answers. Write out all numbers as words.

1. _____

2. _____

3. _____

4. _____

5. _____

6. _____

A. ¿Dónde están estas personas?

Paso 1. You will hear four brief conversations or parts of conversations. Listen carefully and write the number of the conversation next to the location in which each conversation is taking place. Not all the locations will be used. First, listen to the list of possible locations.

_____ en el museo de bellas artes (*fine arts*)   _____ en el museo de arqueología

_____ en el coche   _____ en la gasolinera / el taller

_____ en una boda   _____ en una fiesta de aniversario

_____ en la ópera   _____ en el ballet

Paso 2 (Para entregar). Now, stop the tape and write a brief conversation, or part of a conversation, that takes place in one of the locations not used in **Paso 1**.

_____

_____

_____

_____

_____

_____

_____

_____

Now turn on the tape.

B. *Los hispanos hablan*: ¿Hay algún objeto que tenga mucha importancia en la vida diaria de tu familia?

Listen to the answers several students gave to this question. Take notes, if you wish, as you listen. Then check the statements that are true, based on what you heard. The following words appear in the students' answers.

desplazarse	ir
la pérdida	*loss*
cualquier inconveniente	*any inconvenience (small problem)*

Apuntes (*Notes*)

_____

_____

_____

_____

_____

1. ☐ De los estudiantes que respondieron a la pregunta, la mayoría dijo que el auto es el objeto más importante.

2. ☐ Para una de las personas, los libros eran muy importantes.

3. ☐ Según los estudiantes, la función del auto era principalmente para ir de paseo y para divertirse.

4. ☐ Muchos mencionaron que el teléfono también era importante.

Now turn on the tape.

C. Dictado. You will hear a brief paragraph that tells about a new museum that is opening soon. Listen carefully and, while listening, write the information requested. Write all numbers as numerals. First, listen to the requested information.

El nombre del museo: _____

El tipo de arte que se va a exhibir: _____

La fecha en que se va a abrir el museo: _____

El nombre del director del museo: _____

La hora de la recepción: _____

¿Es necesario hacer reservaciones? _____

¿Va a ser posible hablar con algunos de los artistas? _____

D. Cosas de todos los días. Use the written cues to tell about newlyweds Arturo and Lidia's search for a new apartment. When you hear the corresponding number, form sentences using the words provided in the order given, making any necessary changes and additions. You will be using the present indicative and the present subjunctive in your sentences.

1. Arturo y Lidia / buscar / nuevo / apartamento
2. (ellos) tratar / leer / periódico / todos los días
3. (ellos) querer / apartamento / que / estar / cerca / universidad
4. (ellos) preferir / que / apartamento / estar / primer piso
5. también / ser necesario / que / apartamento / tener vista
6. Lidia / insistir en/ que / aprtamento / ser / grande
7. Arturo / temer / que / alquiler / ser / muy alto
8. ¡ojalá / que / (ellos) poder / encontrar / algo pronto!

E. Conversación: Una cita para el fin de semana (Para entregar). You will hear a conversation, partially printed in your manual, between two friends who are making plans for the weekend. Then you will participate in a similar conversation, playing the role of **Ud.** Complete the conversation, based on your own preferences. Stop the tape and write the answers.

UD.: Hola, _____. ¿ _____?

YOLANDA: ¡Qué coincidencia! Te iba a llamar anoche. Claro que sí. Me gustaría muchísimo. ¿A qué hora debo estar lista (*ready*)?

UD.: _____.

YOLANDA: De acuerdo. Nos vemos, ¿eh?

UD.: _____.

F. Entrevista (Para entregar). You will hear a series of questions. Each will be said twice. Answer, based on your own experience. Stop the tape and write the answers.

1. _____
2. _____
3. _____
4. _____
5. _____
6. _____
7. _____
8. _____
9. _____

CAPÍTULO **16**

Vocabulario: Preparación

▼▼▼▼▼▼▼▼▼▼▼▼▼▼▼▼▼▼▼▼▼▼▼▼▼▼▼▼▼▼▼▼▼▼▼

A. ¿A quién necesitan en estas situaciones? You will hear a series of situations. Each will be said twice. Circle the letter of the person or professional who would best be able to help.

1. a. un arquitecto   b. un analista de sistemas
2. a. una dentista   b. una enfermera
3. a. una consejera matrimonial   b. un policía
4. a. una fotógrafa   b. un bibliotecario
5. a. un plomero   b. una electricista

B. ¿Quiénes son? Using the list of professions below, identify these people after you hear the corresponding number. Begin each sentence with **Es un...** or **Es una...** . First, listen to the list of professions.

obrero/a   cocinero/a
peluquero/a   fotógrafo/a
periodista   plomero/a
veterinario/a   hombre o mujer de negocios

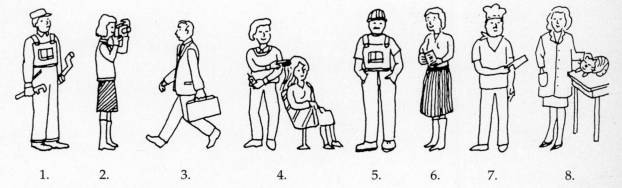

1.   2.   3.   4.   5.   6.   7.   8.

C. En busca de un puesto

Paso 1. Imagine that you are looking for a new job in a large corporation. Tell how you will go about getting the job, using phrases from the following list. First, listen to the list, then stop the tape and put the remaining items in order, from 3 to 6.

_____ tratar de caerle bien al entrevistador   _____ ir a la entrevista

_____ aceptar el puesto y renunciar a mi puesto actual   _____ llenar la solicitud

__2__ pedirle una solicitud de empleo   __1__ llamar a la directora de personal

Now turn on the tape.

Paso 2. Now tell what you will do to look for a job when you hear the numbers. Follow the model.

MODELO: (*you hear*) uno   (*you see*) llamar a la directora de personal →
(*you say*) Llamo a la directora de personal.

D. Descripción. You will hear a series of questions. Each will be said twice. Answer, based on the drawing. If you prefer, stop the tape and write the answers.

1. _____
2. _____
3. _____
4. _____
5. _____

Los hispanos hablan: ¿Cuáles son las profesiones de más prestigio (*prestige*) en su país? ¿Qué profesión es menos apreciada?

You will hear two answers to these questions. Then, after each answer, you will hear a series of statements about the answer. Circle **C** or **F**. The following words appear in the answers.

el agente de bolsa	*stockbroker*
la remuneración	el pago (el sueldo)
sea cual sea su profesión	no importa la profesión que tenga
la enseñanza	*teaching*
remunerado	pagado

Habla Tomás, un arquitecto español.   Habla Francisco, un científico español.

  1. C F   2. C F   3. C F   1. C F   2. C F   3. C F

Pronunciación y ortografía:
More on Stress and the Written Accent

▼▼▼▼▼▼▼▼▼▼▼▼▼▼▼▼▼▼▼▼▼▼▼▼▼▼▼▼▼▼▼▼▼

A. You have probably noticed that the written accent is an important factor in the spelling of some verbs. You know that in the case of the preterite, for example, a missing accent can change the meaning of the verb. Listen to the following pairs of words.

habló	(*he, she, or you spoke*)	/ hablo	(*I am speaking or I speak*)
hablé	(*I spoke*)	/ hable	(*that he, she, you, or I may speak—present subjunctive; speak [formal command]*)

When you hear the corresponding number, read the following pairs of words. Then repeat the correct pronunciation, imitating the speaker.

1. tomo / tomó
2. ahorro / ahorró
3. limpie / limpié

B. The written accent also is important in maintaining the original stress of a word to which syllables have been added. In the word **jóvenes**, for example, the written accent maintains the stress of the singular word **joven**, even though another syllable has been added. Sometimes, the reverse will be true. A word that has a written accent will lose the accent when a syllable is added. Compare **inglés** and **ingleses**. This happens because the new word receives the stress naturally; that is, it follows the rules of stress.

When you hear the corresponding number, read the following groups of words. Then repeat the correct pronunciation, imitating the speaker.

1. dígame / dígamelo
2. póngase / póngaselo
3. escriba / escríbanos
4. depositen / deposítenlos
5. almacén / almacenes
6. nación / naciones

C. Dictado. You will hear the following words. Each will be said twice. Write in an accent mark, if necessary.

1. cobro
2. cobro
3. toque
4. toque
5. describe
6. describemela
7. levantate
8. levanta
9. franceses
10. frances

D. You have probably noticed that when a pair of words is written the same but has different meanings, one of the words is accented. This accent is called a *diacritical* accent.

Listen to and repeat the following words, paying close attention to the meaning of each.

1. mi (*my*) / mí (*me*)
2. tu (*your*) / tú (*you*)
3. el (*the*) / él (*he*)
4. si (*if*) / sí (*yes*)
5. se (*oneself*) / sé (*I know; be* [informal command])
6. de (*of, from*) / dé (*give* [formal command]; *give* [present subjunctive])
7. te (*you, yourself*) / té (*tea*)
8. solo (*alone, sole* [adjective]) / sólo (*only* [adverb])
9. que (*that, which*) / ¿qué? (*what?*)

E. Dictado. Listen to the following sentences. Determine by context whether or not the meaning of the italicized words requires a written accent. If so, write it in. Each sentence will be said twice.

1. Creo *que* ese regalo es para *mi*.
2. Aquí *esta tu te*. ¿*Que* más quieres?
3. *El* dijo *que te* iba a llamar a las ocho.
4. *Si, mi* amigo *se* llama Antonio.

Minidiálogos y gramática

▼▼▼▼▼▼▼▼▼▼▼▼▼▼▼▼▼▼▼▼▼▼▼▼▼▼▼▼▼

45. Talking About the Future • Future Verb Forms

A. Un futuro perfecto

Paso 1. You will hear a brief paragraph in which Angélica talks about her future. Then you will hear a series of statements. Circle **C, F,** or **ND.**

1. C F ND

2. C F ND

3. C F ND

4. C F ND

5. C F ND

Paso 2. Now stop the tape and complete the following statements according to your own preferences.

1. Cuando yo me gradúe, _____.

2. Trabajaré para _____.

3. Viviré en _____.

4. Mi casa será _____.

5. Tendré un auto _____.

6. Pasaré mis vacaciones en _____.

7. Mi vida será _____.

Now turn on the tape.

B. El viernes por la tarde. Using the oral and written cues, tell what the following people will do with their paychecks.

1. Bernardo
2. Adela y yo

3. tú... ¿verdad?
4. yo

C. El cumpleaños de Jaime. Jaime's birthday is next week. Answer the questions about his birthday, using the written cues. Each question will be said twice.

> MODELO: (*you hear*) ¿Cuántos años va a *cumplir* Jaime?   (*you see*) dieciocho →
> (*you say*) Cumplirá dieciocho años.

1. sus amigos y sus parientes
2. una videocasetera
3. un pastel de chocolate
4. discos compactos
5. ¡Feliz cumpleaños!

46. Expressing Future or Pending Actions • Subjunctive and Indicative After Conjunctions of Time

A. Minidiálogo: Antes de la entrevista. You will hear a dialogue between Lupe and her mother, followed by a series of statements. Circle the letter of the person who might have made each statement.

1. a. Lupe   b. la Sra. Carrasco
2. a. Lupe   b. la Sra. Carrasco
3. a. Lupe   b. la Sra. Carrasco
4. a. Lupe   b. la Sra. Carrasco
5. a. Lupe   b. la Sra. Carrasco
6. a. Lupe   b. la Sra. Carrasco

B. Escenas de la vida cotidiana. You will hear the following pairs of sentences. Combine them to form one complete sentence, using the oral cues.

> MODELO: (*you see and hear*) Voy a decidirlo. Hablo con él.   (*you hear*) después de que →
> (*you say*) Voy a decidirlo después de que hable con él.

1. Amalia va a viajar. Consigue un poco de dinero.
2. No estaré contenta. Recibo un aumento.
3. Podrán ahorrar más. Sus hijos terminan sus estudios.
4. Tito, devuélveme el dinero. Se te olvida.

C. Asuntos económicos. You will hear a series of incomplete sentences. Circle the letter of the correct ending for each, then repeat the completed sentence. ¡OJO! In this exercise, you will be choosing between the present subjunctive and the present indicative.

> MODELO: (*you hear*) Voy a depositar mi cheque cuando... a. lo reciba   b. lo recibo →
> (*you say*) a.   Voy a depositar mi cheque cuando lo reciba.

1. a. las reciba   b. las recibo
2. a. tenga más dinero   b. tengo más dinero
3. a. consiga otro puesto   b. consigo otro puesto
4. a. lo firme   b. lo firmo

Situaciones

▼▼▼▼▼▼▼▼▼▼▼▼▼▼▼▼▼▼▼▼▼▼▼▼▼▼▼▼▼▼▼▼▼▼▼▼▼▼▼

Paso 1. Lupe solicita un puesto. In the following conversation, Lupe is being interviewed for a position as a receptionist in a bank. Read the conversation along with the speakers.

SRA. IBÁÑEZ: He hablado con varios aspirantes para el puesto de recepcionista, pero Ud. tiene el currículum más interesante. Veo que ha trabajado como recepcionista en la oficina de un abogado. ¿Por qué renunció a ese trabajo?

LUPE: Bueno, soy estudiante en la universidad. Me gustaba mucho el trabajo en la oficina del abogado, pero querían que trabajara la jornada completa. Desafortunadamente, no me era posible.

SRA. IBÁÑEZ: Y cuando trabajaba para el abogado, ¿cuáles eran sus responsabilidades?

LUPE: Contestaba el teléfono, hacía las citas con los clientes, organizaba el archivo... también le llevaba sus cuentas y pagaba los gastos básicos de la oficina. Eran las típicas responsabilidades de una recepcionista.

SRA. IBÁÑEZ: Ajá, entiendo. Srta. Carrasco, buscamos una persona que sea amable, que aprenda rápidamente, que sepa escribir a máquina y utilizar una computadora y que tenga paciencia con los clientes. Parece que Ud. cumple con estos requisitos. ¿Podrá asistir a un entrenamiento de seis horas la semana que viene?

LUPE: Sí, Sra. Ibáñez.

SRA. IBÁÑEZ: ¿Y podrá trabajar de vez en cuando en las otras sucursales del banco?

LUPE: ¡Claro que sí! No hay problema.

SRA. IBÁÑEZ: Muy bien.

Paso 2. Aplicación. Now you will participate in a similar conversation, partially printed in your manual, in which you play the role of **Ud.** and answer questions about your imaginary job. Complete it using the written cues. Here are the cues for your conversation. **¡OJO!** The cues are not in order.

es muy amable   ya encontraste trabajo
fantástico   tres semanas

AMIGA: ¡Hola! Hace tiempo que no te veo. ¿Qué tal te va en tu nuevo trabajo?

UD.: ¡_____¹! Es un puesto estupendo.

AMIGA: Y tu jefa, ¿cómo es?

UD.: _____.² Nos llevamos muy bien.

AMIGA: Espero que te den vacaciones este año.

UD.: Sí, sí... Fíjate que me dan _____.³ Y tú,

¿_____⁴?

AMIGA: ¡Qué va! Todavía ando buscando...

Un poco de todo (Para entregar)

▼▼▼▼▼▼▼▼▼▼▼▼▼▼▼▼▼▼▼▼▼▼▼▼▼▼▼▼▼▼▼▼▼▼▼▼

A. ¿Qué cree Ud. que van a hacer estas personas? You will hear three situations. Each will be said twice. Choose the most logical solution for each and repeat it.

1. a. Teresa comprará un coche barato y económico.
   b. Comprará un coche de lujo (*luxury*).
   c. No comprará ningún coche.
2. a. Basilio tendrá que conseguir otro trabajo para pagar el nuevo alquiler.
   b. Robará un banco.
   c. Compartirá (*He will share*) su apartamento con cuatro amigos.
3. a. Luisa empezará a poner el dinero que gasta en diversiones en su cuenta de ahorros.
   b. Ella comprará el regalo la próxima semana.
   c. Insistirá en que su jefe le dé un aumento de sueldo inmediatamente.

B. *Listening Passage*: **El sistema universitario hispánico**

Antes de escuchar. You will hear a passage about the differences between the university system in most of the Hispanic world and that of the United States. The following words appear in the passage.

la etapa	*stage*	una vez que	*once*
suele durar	*usually lasts*	el requisito	*requirement*
se matricula	*enrolls*	la profundidad	*depth*
por lo tanto	*therefore*		

Listening Passage. Here is the passage. First, listen to it to get a general idea of the content. Then rewind the tape and listen again for specific information.

Después de escuchar. Indicate whether the following statements refer to the Hispanic world or to the United States, according to the information in the passage.

	EL MUNDO HISPÁNICO	LOS ESTADOS UNIDOS
1. La mayoría de las carreras duran menos de cinco años.	☐	☐
2. Al entrar (*Upon entering*) en la universidad, un estudiante se matricula directamente en el área de su especialización.	☐	☐
	☐	☐
3. El estudiante tiene pocas opciones una vez que empieza sus estudios.	☐	☐
4. Hay requisitos «generales» como ciencias naturales, ciencias sociales o humanidades.	☐	☐
5. El currículum es bastante estricto.	☐	☐
6. Los estudios que se hacen para una licenciatura son bastante profundos y variados.	☐	☐
7. Por lo general, la especialización no se «declara» el primer año de estudios universitarios.	☐	☐

Now turn on the tape.

C. En el periódico: Empleos. The ads for jobs on this page and the next page appeared in a Mexican newspaper. Choose the ad you are most interested in, based on the profession, and scan it. Then, after you hear each question, answer it based on the ad. If the information requested is not in the ad, write **No lo dice.** First, stop the tape and look at the ads. Stop the tape and write the answers.

1. _____

2. _____

3. _____

4. _____

5. _____

D. Y para terminar... Entrevista. You will hear a series of questions. Each will be said twice. Answer, based on your own experience. Stop the tape and write the answers. Note that in number six, you will need to write a longer answer.

1. _____

2. _____

3. _____

4. _____

5. _____

6. _____

_____

_____

_____

_____

CAPÍTULO **17**

Vocabulario: Preparación

▼▼▼▼▼▼▼▼▼▼▼▼▼▼▼▼▼▼▼▼▼▼▼▼▼▼▼▼

A. Encuesta: ¿Con qué frecuencia... ? You will hear a series of statements about different ways of learning about what goes on in the world. For each statement, check the appropriate answer. No answers will be given on the tape. The answers you choose should be correct for you!

	TODOS LOS DÍAS	DE VEZ EN CUANDO	CASI NUNCA
1.	☐	☐	☐
2.	☐	☐	☐
3.	☐	☐	☐
4.	☐	☐	☐
5.	☐	☐	☐
6.	☐	☐	☐
7.	☐	☐	☐
8.	☐	☐	☐

B. El noticiero del Canal 10. You will hear a brief "newsbreak" from a television station. Then you will hear a series of statements about the newscast. Circle **C, F,** or **ND.**

1. C F ND   2. C F ND   3. C F ND   4. C F ND   5. C F ND

C. Definiciones. You will hear a series of statements. Each will be said twice. Place the number of the statements next to the word that is best defined by each. First, listen to the list of words.

_____ una guerra

_____ la prensa

_____ un dictador

_____ los terroristas

_____ la testigo

_____ el reportero

_____ la huelga

_____ el noticiero

D. Opiniones. You will hear a series of statements. Each will be said twice. React to each statement, using expressions chosen from the list. Be sure to express your own opinion. You will hear a possible answer on the tape. If you prefer, stop the tape and write the answers on the next page.

Dudo que...   Es verdad que...
Es cierto que...   No es cierto que...

1. _____

2. _____

3. _____

4. _____

5. _____

Los hispanos hablan: Más sobre las ciudades hispánicas

When asked about some of the differences between U.S. cities and the Hispanic city in which she lives, Cecilia mentioned that some of the laws were different. As you listen to her answer, write down the effect she thinks each law or situation has on the population.

LEY O SITUACIÓN	RESULTADO

1. Un horario para volver a casa _____
_____

2. Una edad permitida para tomar bebidas alcohólicas _____
_____

3. Los chicos mayores de dieciocho años están en la universidad _____
_____

Pronunciación y ortografía:
Intonation, Punctuation, and Rhythm (Review of Linking)

▼▼▼▼▼▼▼▼▼▼▼▼▼▼▼▼▼▼▼▼▼▼▼▼▼▼▼▼▼▼▼

A. As you have probably noticed throughout the entire tape program and from listening to your instructor in class, intonation plays an important role in Spanish. The meaning of a sentence can change according to its intonation and punctuation. Listen to the following sentences. The arrows indicate a falling or rising intonation.

Los reporteros están aquí. (*statement*)

¿Los reporteros están aquí? (*question*)

¡Los reporteros están aquí! (*exclamation*)

B. Repeat the following sentences, paying particular attention to punctuation, intonation, and rhythm.

1. ¿Ya destruyeron el edificio?

2. ¡Es imposible que construyan eso en la ciudad!

3. ¿Ya hablaste con la consejera?

4. Prepararon la cena, ¿verdad? Espero que ya esté lista (*ready*) porque ¡tengo mucha hambre!

5. Ojalá que no perdamos el vuelo... Tenemos que estar en Los Ángeles antes de las ocho de la noche.

C. When you hear the corresponding number, read the following sentences. Then repeat them, imitating the speaker. Write in arrows to indicate rising or falling intonation. Be sure to check your answers in the Appendix.

1. Enero es el primer mes del año.

2. ¡No entiendo lo que me estás diciendo!

3. ¿Trabajaba en una tienda?

4. No olvides el diccionario la próxima vez, ¿eh?

5. Nació el catorce de abril de mil novecientos sesenta y uno.

6. ¿Adónde crees que vas a ir a estas horas de la noche?

D. Dictado. You will hear the following sentences. Each will be said twice. Listen carefully for intonation. Repeat what you hear, then punctuate each sentence.

1. Cuál es tu profesión   Te pagan bien

2. Tú no la conoces verdad

3. Prefiere Ud. que le sirva la comida en el patio

4. Qué ejercicio más fácil

5. No sé dónde viven pero sí sé su número de teléfono

Minidiálogos y gramática

▼▼▼▼▼▼▼▼▼▼▼▼▼▼▼▼▼▼▼▼▼▼▼▼▼▼▼▼▼▼▼▼

47. ¡Ojalá que pudiéramos hacerlo! • Past Subjunctive

A. Minidiálogo: ¡Ojalá que no fuera así! You will hear a dialogue followed by a series of statements. Circle **C**, **F** or **ND**.

1. C   F   ND   4. C   F   ND

2. C   F   ND   5. C   F   ND

3. C   F   ND

B. Encuesta: Hablando de la escuela secundaria. You will hear a series of statements about what your life was like in high school. For each statement, circle **C** or **F**.

1. C F   4. C F   7. C F

2. C F   5. C F   8. C F

3. C F   6. C F   9. C F

C. ¿Qué esperabas? Answer the following questions using the oral cues.

1. ¿Qué esperabas que hiciera el robot antes de la fiesta?

     MODELO: (*you hear*) lavar las ventanas → (*you say*) Esperaba que lavara las ventanas.

     a. ...   b. ...   c. ...   d. ...

2. ¿Qué esperabas que hicieran los invitados durante la fiesta?

     MODELO: (*you hear*) bailar → (*you say*) Esperaba que bailaran.

     a. ...   b. ...   c. ...   d. ...

D. Recuerdos de un viaje. Imagine that you have recently returned from a trip abroad, and your friends want to know all the details. Tell them about some of the things you had to do, using the oral cues. Begin each sentence with **Fue necesario que... .** ¡OJO! You will be using the past subjunctive in your answers.

     1. ...   2. ...   3. ...   4. ...

E. ¿Qué quería Ud.? Imagine that you are never happy with your family's plans. What would you rather have done? Use the oral cues to tell what you preferred. Begin each sentence with **Yo quería que... .**

     MODELO: (*you see and hear*) Ayer cenamos en un restaurante. (*You hear*) en casa →
                 (*you say*) Yo quería que cenáramos en casa.

1. Ayer vimos una película.
2. El mes pasado fuimos a la playa.
3. Anoche miramos un programa de televisión.
4. Para mi cumpleaños, me regalaron un estéreo.
5. Esta noche mi madre sirvió patatas en la cena.

48. More About Expressing Possession • Stressed Possessives

A. Lo mío y lo tuyo

Paso 1. You will hear a brief conversation between Beto and Anita who are arguing about their bikes. Then you will hear a series of statements. Circle **C, F,** or **ND**.

1. C F ND   3. C F ND

2. C F ND   4. C F ND

Paso 2. Más comparaciones. Your friend will make a series of statements about things that she has or about members of her family. Each will be said twice. React to each statement using the written cues. You will need to conjugate the verbs.

> MODELO: (*you hear*) Mi auto es nuevo y económico.
> (*you see*) ser viejo y gasta mucha gasolina →
> (*you say*) Pues el mío es viejo y gasta mucha gasolina.

1. tener poca memoria
2. vivir en el campo
3. ser arquitecta
4. no funcionar
5. estar escritas a máquina (*typed*)

C. En el departamento de artículos perdidos y encontrados. You will hear a series of questions. Each will be said twice. Answer in the negative.

> MODELO: (*you hear*) ¿Es de Ud. esta maleta? → (*you say*) No, no es mía.

1. ...   2. ...   3. ...   4. ...   5. ...

Situaciones

▼▼▼▼▼▼▼▼▼▼▼▼▼▼▼▼▼▼▼▼▼▼▼▼▼▼▼▼▼▼▼▼▼▼▼▼

Paso 1. La tertulia. In the following conversation, Manolo, Maricarmen and Paco get together for a **tertulia,** an informal discussion of various topics. Today they are discussing politics. Read the conversation along with the speakers.

> MANOLO: Muy bien, ¿de qué hablamos hoy?
> MARICARMEN: Hablamos del partido político de Paco. Y este, como siempre, cree que los líderes políticos de su partido tienen el derecho de dictar cómo viven los demás. Y yo, claro, no estoy de acuerdo.
> PACO: Maricarmen, te equivocas. Es todo lo contrario. Mira. Mi partido ofrece soluciones razonables a los problemas más graves de hoy.
> MANOLO: Hasta cierto punto, estoy de acuerdo con Maricarmen. ¿Viste las noticias del Canal 2 anoche? Paco, tu querido partido quería votar cuanto antes la nueva legislación, para que nadie más pudiera protestar.
> PACO: ¡No, señor! No es así. ¿Siempre crees todo lo que dicen la prensa y la televisión? ¡Ojalá el asunto fuera tan sencillo!
> MARICARMEN: Pero Paco, no me parecen razonables las soluciones propuestas por tu partido. Es verdad que necesitamos nuevas leyes laborales, pero estas no resuelven nada.
> PACO: ¡Al contrario! Maricarmen, el anterior presidente no había hecho nada en los últimos años. Mira las noticias. Hay huelgas, desempleo, desastres económicos...
> MANOLO: ¡Paco! ¿Tú siempre crees todo lo que dicen la prensa y la televisión?
> PACO: Pues, ¡parece que lo único en que estamos de acuerdo es en que *no* estamos de acuerdo!

Paso 2. Aplicación. Now you will participate in a similar conversation, partially printed in your manual, in which you will express your own opinions. Use the following phrases to begin your statements. Stop the tape and write the answers. Answer, based on your own opinions. No answers will be given on the tape. First, listen to the phrases.

> Bueno, pero yo (no) creo que...   Lo siento, pero yo pienso que...
> Eso suena (*sounds*) bien, pero...   Sí, pero...
> Estoy de acuerdo...

PERSONA 1:   Creo que el actual presidente no ha hecho nada para mejorar las condiciones económicas del país.

UD.:   _____ ¹

PERSONA 2:   ¿Y qué tal su política exterior (*foreign policy*)? Creo que es un desastre.

UD.:   _____ ²

PERSONA 3:   Pues yo pienso que es el mejor presidente que hemos tenido en varios años. El problema es el Congreso. Siempre se opone a las reformas que propone el presidente.

UD.:   _____ ³

Un poco de todo (Para entregar)

▼▼▼▼▼▼▼▼▼▼▼▼▼▼▼▼▼▼▼▼▼▼▼▼▼▼▼▼▼▼▼▼▼▼

A. En el periódico. You will hear a series of headlines from a Hispanic newspaper. Each will be said twice. Listen and write the number of each headline next to the section of the newspaper to which it belongs. First, listen to the list of sections.

_____ Sociales   _____ Política   _____ Clasificados

_____ Deportes   _____ Negocios   _____ Espectáculos
                                                                     (*Entertainment*)

B. *Listening Passage*: Resumen de las noticias

Antes de escuchar. You will hear a news brief on the radio, just as it would be if you were listening to it in a Hispanic country. After you listen to the passage, you will be asked to complete the following statements about it. Stop the tape and scan them now to get a general idea of the information to look for.

Noticia 1:   Fuerte maremoto en _____, de más de _____ grados en

la escala Richter.

Noticia 2:   Tema: _____   Mes: _____

Noticia 3:   Visita de Juan Carlos I, _____ de _____. Duración de la

visita: _____

Noticia 4:   Propuesta del partido de oposición para _____ el precio de la

_____, el _____ y el _____, el primero en

un _____ por ciento y los dos últimos en un _____ por

ciento. El próximo noticiero de amplio reportaje será a las _____.

Now turn on the tape.

Listening Passage. The following words and phrases appear in the passage.

el mediodía	*noon*	el paro	*unemployment*
la redacción	*editorial desk*	la propuesta	*proposal*
el maremoto	*seaquake*	el apoyo	*support*
sin hogar	*homeless*	nos sintonicen	*you tune in to us* (*our broadcast*)

Después de escuchar. Now complete the statements in **Antes de escuchar.**

C. Descripción: Escenas actuales. You will hear the following cartoon caption. Then you will hear a series of questions. Each will be said twice. Answer, based on the cartoon and your own experience. Stop the tape and write the answers.

—Lo bueno de las campañas políticas es que no te las pueden repetir.

1. _____
2. _____
3. _____
4. _____

D. Y para terminar... Entrevista. You will hear a series of questions. Each will be said twice. Answer, based on your own experience. Stop the tape and write the answers.

1. _____
2. _____
3. _____
4. _____
5. _____
6. _____

CAPÍTULO **18**

Vocabulario: Preparación

▼▼▼▼▼▼▼▼▼▼▼▼▼▼▼▼▼▼▼▼▼▼▼▼▼▼▼▼▼▼▼

A. Encuesta: ¿Qué hiciste en tu último viaje? You will hear a series of questions about what you did on your last trip. For each question, check the appropriate answer. No answers will be given on the tape. The answers you choose should be correct for you!

1. ☐ Sí	☐ No		6. ☐ Sí	☐ No
2. ☐ Sí	☐ No		7. ☐ Sí	☐ No
3. ☐ Sí	☐ No		8. ☐ Sí	☐ No
4. ☐ Sí	☐ No		9. ☐ Sí	☐ No
5. ☐ Sí	☐ No		10. ☐ Sí	☐ No

B. Definiciones. You will hear a series of definitions. Each will be said twice. Write the number of the definition next to the word or phrase that is best defined by each. First, listen to the list of words and phrases.

_____ viajar a otro país   _____ una multa

_____ el formulario de inmigración   _____ la frontera

_____ la nacionalidad   _____ el pasaporte

C. Descripción. Identify the following items when you hear the corresponding number. Begin each sentence with **Es un... , Es una... ,** or **Son... .**

1. ...   2. ...   3. ...   4. ...   5. ...   6. ...   7. ...

D. Descripción. Describe what these people are doing, using the verbs you will hear for each segment of the drawing. You will hear a possible answer on the tape. Use present progressive forms (**estar + -ndo**).

1. ... 2. ... 3. ... 4. ... 5. ...

Los hispanos hablan: Una aventura en el extranjero

You will hear Clara's story of a trip to the city of Fez, which is in Morocco (**Marruecos**). The story is divided into two parts. The first time you listen to the story, try to get the gist of the narration. Then listen again, or as many times as necessary, for specific information. After you hear each part of the story, stop the tape and answer the true/false items.

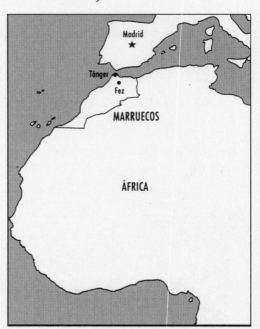

Parte 1. The following words and phrases appear in the first part of the story.

hacer transbordo	*to change planes*
Tánger	*Tangiers*
la plaza	el asiento
el croquis	*sketch*

1. C F Clara viajó a Marruecos para estudiar árabe.

2. C F Clara tomó un vuelo directo de Madrid a Fez.

3. C F El vuelo de Madrid a Tánger fue fácil.

4. C F El aeropuerto de Tánger era muy moderno.

Now turn on the tape.

Parte 2. The following words and phrases appear in the second part of the story.

el destino	*destination*	chapurreado	*poor*
se levantasen	*they got up*	el sello	*official stamp*
las hélices	*propellers*	a punto de estallar	*about to explode*

1. C F Clara usó el color de su tarjeta de embarque para saber qué vuelo tomar.

2. C F Todo —el avión, el aeropuerto, el pasajero que se sentó con ella— tenía aspecto de película.

3. C F Cuando llegó a Fez, Clara ya había pasado por la aduana.

4. C F El padre de Clara ya estaba en el aeropuerto de Fez cuando el avión de su hija aterrizó (*landed*).

Now turn on the tape.

Pronunciación y ortografía:
Nationalities

▼▼▼▼▼▼▼▼▼▼▼▼▼▼▼▼▼▼▼▼▼▼▼▼▼▼▼▼▼▼▼▼

A. Repeat the following names of countries and the nationalities of those who were born there.

1. Nicaragua, nicaragüense
   el Canadá, canadiense
   los Estados Unidos, estadounidense
   Costa Rica, costarricense
2. la Argentina, argentino/a
   el Perú, peruano/a
   Colombia, colombiano/a
   Bolivia, boliviano/a

3. el Uruguay, uruguayo/a
   el Paraguay, paraguayo/a
4. Honduras, hondureño/a
   Panamá, panameño/a
   el Brasil, brasileño/a
5. Guatemala, guatemalteco/a
   Portugal, portugués (portuguesa)
   Inglaterra, inglés (inglesa)

B. Now you will hear a series of nationalities. Each will be said twice. Repeat each and write the number of the nationality next to the country of origin. First, listen to the list of countries.

_____ Chile

_____ El Salvador

_____ Puerto Rico

_____ el Ecuador

_____ Venezuela

_____ Israel

C. Repaso general: Refranes

Paso 1. Stop the tape and match the number of the Hispanic proverb with its English equivalent. ¡OJO! There is no equivalent English proverb in some cases, just a literal translation.

a. _____ He who sleeps gets swept away.

b. _____ There is an exception to every rule.

c. _____ Every cloud has a silver lining.

d. _____ Everything has a purpose.

e. _____ Nothing is impossible.

f. _____ The early bird catches the worm.

g. _____ Tell it like it is.

1. Llamar al pan, pan y al vino, vino.

2. El agua para bañarse, el vino para beberse.

3. Quien mucho duerme, poco aprende.

4. No hay mal que por bien no venga.

5. No hay regla sin excepción.

6. No hay montaña tan alta que un asno cargado de oro no la suba.

7. Camarón que se duerme, se lo lleva la corriente.

Now turn on the tape.

Paso 2. When you hear the corresponding number, read the proverbs. Then listen to the correct pronunciation and repeat it.

1. Llamar al pan, pan y al vino, vino.
2. El agua para bañarse, el vino para beberse.
3. Quien mucho duerme, poco aprende.
4. No hay mal que por bien no venga.
5. No hay regla sin excepción.
6. No hay montaña tan alta que un asno cargado de oro no la suba.
7. Camarón que se duerme, se lo lleva la corriente.

D. Dictado. You will hear a series of sentences. Each will be said twice. Write what you hear. Pay close attention to punctuation.

1. _____

2. _____

3. _____
   _____

4. _____
   _____

5. _____

Minidiálogos y gramática

▼▼▼▼▼▼▼▼▼▼▼▼▼▼▼▼▼▼▼▼▼▼▼▼▼▼▼▼▼

49. Expressing What You Would Do • Conditional Verb Forms

A. Minidiálogo: La fantasía de la maestra de Mafalda. You will hear Mafalda's teacher describe how she would like her life to be. Then you will hear three statements. Circle the number of the statement that best summarizes the teacher's description.

1.   2.   3.

B. ¿Qué harían para mejorar las condiciones? Using the oral and written cues, tell what the following people would like to do to improve the world.

> MODELO: (*you hear*) Gema   (*you see*) eliminar las guerras →
> (*you say*) Gema eliminaría las guerras.

1. desarrollar otros tipos de energía
2. construir viviendas para todos
3. resolver los problemas domésticos
4. eliminar el hambre y las desigualdades sociales
5. protestar por el uso de las armas atómicas

C. ¿Qué harías en Madrid? When you hear the corresponding number, tell what you would do in Madrid. Use the written cues.

> MODELO: (*you hear*) uno   (*you see*) quedarse en un buen hotel →
> (*you say*) Me quedaría en un buen hotel.

2. comunicarse en español
3. ir al Museo del Prado
4. conocer la ciudad
5. comer paella

D. ¡Entendiste mal! Make statements about your plans, using the written cues when you hear the corresponding numbers. Make any necessary changes or additions. When your friend Alicia misunderstands your statements, correct her. Follow the model.

> MODELO: (*you see*) llegar / trece / junio →
> (*you say*) UD.: Llegaré el trece de junio.
> (*you hear*) ALICIA: ¿No dijiste que llegarías el tres?
> (*you say*) UD.: No, te dije que llegaría el trece. Entendiste mal.

1. estar / bar / doce
2. estudiar / Juan
3. ir / vacaciones / junio
4. verte / casa

50. Hypothetical Situations: *What if . . . ?* • **si** Clause Sentences

A. Los deseos de los amigos hispánicos

Paso 1. You will hear a series of statements. Each will be said twice. Write the number of the statement below the appropriate drawing. **¡OJO!** There is an extra statement.

a. _____   b. _____   c. _____

Paso 2. Mis deseos. Now stop the tape and complete the following sentences according to your own preferences. You will be using the conditional tense. No answers will be given on the tape.

1. Si tuviera dinero, _____.

2. Si pudiera, _____.

3. Si me dieran un aumento de sueldo, _____.

4. Si viviera en México, _____.

5. Si tuviera más tiempo, _____.

Now turn on the tape.

B. Descripción: ¿Qué haría Ud.? You will hear a series of statements. Each will be said twice. Write the number of each statement next to the appropriate drawing. First, stop the tape and look at the drawings.

a. _____

b. _____

c. _____

d. _____

e. _____

f. _____

C. Situaciones. You will hear three brief situations. Circle the letter of the best reaction to each.

1. a. ...regresaría a casa en autobús   b. ...llamaría a la policía
2. a. ...escribiría un cheque   b. ...me ofrecería a lavar los platos
3. a. ...trataría de negociar con el líder   b. ...despediría (*I would fire*) a todos los empleados
del sindicato (*union*) laboral

D. Consejos. Imagine that your friend Pablo has a problem with his roommates. What would you do in his place? Answer, using the oral cues.

MODELO: (*you hear*) llamar a mis padres → (*you say*) Si yo fuera Pablo, llamaría a mis padres.

1. ...   2. ...   3. ...   4. ...

E. Las finanzas. You will hear the following sentences. Restate each, using the conditional.

MODELO: (*you see and hear*) No le ofrecerán el puesto a menos que tenga buenas
recomendaciones. →
(*you say*) Le ofrecerían el puesto si tuviera buenas recomendaciones.

1. No le harán el préstamo a menos que esté trabajando.
2. No ahorraré más dinero a menos que controle mis gastos.
3. No pagaré las cuentas antes de que reciba el cheque semanal.
4. No te cobrarán el cheque hasta que lo firmes.

Situaciones

▼▼

Paso 1. En la agencia de viajes. In this conversation, Lupe and Diego visit a travel agency. Read the conversation along with the speakers.

AGENTE: ¿Ya tienen alojamiento en Mérida?

LUPE: No, todavía no. Buscamos un hotel que sea decente, pero que tampoco sea muy caro. No tenemos el dinero para pagar un hotel de lujo.

AGENTE: Entiendo. Muy pocos estudiantes tienen mucho dinero. Bueno, les puedo ofrecer habitaciones en varios hoteles a precios muy razonables. A ver... ¿Cuándo piensan hacer el viaje?

DIEGO: La última semana de mayo.

AGENTE: Ajá... Eso va a estar un poco difícil. Casi todos los hoteles estarán completamente ocupados durante esa semana. Si viajaran una semana más tarde, encontrarían más habitaciones desocupadas.

LUPE: Bueno, está bien. Entonces, la primera semana de junio.

AGENTE: Excelente. Les puedo ofrecer dos habitaciones individuales con baño privado en el hotel Estrella del Mar. No es un hotel de lujo, pero es bueno y muy lindo. El precio por cada habitación es de 150 pesos por noche.

LUPE: Perfecto.

AGENTE: Y, ¿cuántos días piensan quedarse?

DIEGO: Unos cuatros o cinco días, nada más. Yo soy de California, y debo regresar pronto.

AGENTE: Muy bien. Tienen habitaciones reservadas para la primera semana de junio. ¿Sus nombres, por favor?

DIEGO: Sí, cómo no. Yo me llamo Diego González y la señorita es Guadalupe Carrasco.

AGENTE: Muy bien.

DIEGO: Gracias.

Paso 2. Aplicación. Now you will hear a similar conversation, partially printed in your manual, in which you play the role of the **viajero**. First complete the conversation using the written cues. Then stop the tape and write the answers. Write out all numbers. First, listen to the cues for your conversation. ¡OJO! The cues are not in order.

muchas gracias	uno o dos meses
556	aquí lo tiene
la pensión María Cristina	

AGENTE: Pasaporte, por favor.

VIAJERO: _____.[1]

AGENTE: ¿En qué vuelo llegó?

VIAJERO: En el _____.[2]

AGENTE: Y, ¿cuánto tiempo piensa permanecer (*to remain*) en el país?

VIAJERO: Pienso quedarme _____.[3]

AGENTE: ¿Tiene una dirección aquí en la que se le pueda localizar?

VIAJERO: Sí, cómo no. Estaré en _____,[4] en la Calle del Prado, número 27.

AGENTE: Está bien. Puede pasar.

VIAJERO: _____.[5]

Un poco de todo (Para entregar)

▼▼▼▼▼▼▼▼▼▼▼▼▼▼▼▼▼▼▼▼▼▼▼▼▼▼▼▼▼▼▼▼▼▼▼▼

A. De vacaciones en el extranjero. You will hear a brief paragraph describing a series of actions and events. Number the actions listed below from one to ten in the order in which they occur in the paragraph.

First, listen to the list of actions.

_____ aterrizar (*to land*) en Madrid

_____ hacer las maletas

_____ recoger los boletos

_____ despegar (*to take off*) otra vez

__9__ pasar por la aduana

__1__ visitar la agencia de viajes

_____ ir al hotel

_____ sentarse en la sección de fumar

_____ bajar del avión

__5__ hacer escala en Londres (*London*)

Now turn on the tape.

B. *Listening Passage*: **La vida de los exiliados**

Antes de escuchar. Stop the tape and do the following prelistening exercise.

Entre las personas de diferentes nacionalidades hispánicas que viven en los Estados Unidos, los cubanos forman un grupo importante. Conteste las siguientes preguntas sobre la comunidad cubanoamericana.

1. ¿Dónde viven los cubanoamericanos, principalmente?

   _____

2. Muchos cubanos llegaron a los Estados Unidos dentro de un corto período de tiempo. ¿Por qué emigraron?

   _____

3. ¿Qué tipo de gobierno existe en Cuba hoy día? ¿Cómo se llama la persona que gobierna Cuba actualmente?

   _____

4. ¿Pueden los ciudadanos norteamericanos viajar libremente a Cuba?

   _____

Now turn on the tape.

Listening Passage. Now you will hear a passage about the immigration of a Cuban family to the United States. The following words appear in the passage.

por si fuera poco	*as if that were not bad enough*
el internado	*internship, residency*
el comercio	*business*
echar de menos	*to miss, long for*
que en paz descanse	*may she rest in peace*

Después de escuchar. Circle the letter of the phrase that best completes each statement, based on the listening passage.

1. Esta familia, como muchas otras familias cubanas, llegó a los Estados Unidos...
   a. a principio de los años ochenta
   b. hace poco
   c. a principio de los años sesenta
2. Emigraron porque...
   a. no estaban de acuerdo con el gobierno
   b. no tenían trabajo
   c. tenían problemas con la discriminación
3. Al llegar a Florida...
   a. todo fue fácil para ellos
   b. el esposo pudo encontrar trabajo como médico
   c. fue necesario que el esposo tuviera dos trabajos
4. Los padres todavía...
   a. echan de menos su país
   b. quisieran vivir en la Cuba de Fidel Castro
   c. piensan que fue un error salir de Cuba

Now turn on the tape.

C. En el periódico: Viajes. The following ad appeared in a Mexican newspaper. You will hear a series of statements about the ad. Circle **C** or **F**. First, stop the tape and scan the ad.

RIVIERA PAQUETES
¡OFERTA ESPECIAL!

VACACIONES...?

Venga con su familia al Hotel Riviera del Sol de Ixtapa y disfrute de un merecido descanso en las soleadas playas y tibias aguas del espléndido Pacífico Mexicano y ahorre con nuestros tradicionales:

RIVIERA PAQUETES...!!!

"RIVIERA PAQUETE DE PRIMAVERA"

3 NOCHES
4 DIAS

CON TRES DESAYUNOS

Precio por persona:
$ 80,000.00

Noche Extra:
$ 28,000.00

"PAQUETE MINI RIVIERA DE PRIMAVERA"

2 NOCHES
3 DIAS

CON DOS DESAYUNOS

Precio por persona:
$ 58,000.00

Noche Extra:
$ 28,000.00

1. C F 2. C F 3. C F 4. C F

D. Y para terminar... Entrevista. You will hear a series of questions. Each will be said twice. Answer, based on your own experience. Stop the tape and write the answers.

1. _____
2. _____
3. _____
4. _____
5. _____
6. _____

R E P A S O 6

A. ¿Dónde están estas personas?

Paso 1. You will hear five brief conversations or parts of conversations. Listen carefully and write the number of the conversation next to the location in which each conversation is taking place. Not all the locations will be used. First, listen to the list of possible locations.

_____ en un banco   _____ en la estación del metro

_____ en la aduana   _____ en el estanco

_____ en la oficina de redacción (*editorial office*)   _____ en la farmacia

Paso 2 (Para entregar). Now, stop the tape and write a brief conversation, or part of a conversation, that takes place in the location not used in **Paso 1**.

_____

_____

_____

_____

_____

_____

_____

_____

Now turn on the tape.

B. Dictado.

You will hear a brief paragraph that tells about a political campaign. Listen carefully and, while listening, write the information requested. Write all numbers as numerals. First, listen to the requested information.

el nombre de la candidata que perdió las elecciones: _____
el nombre del candidato que ganó las elecciones: _____
el porcentaje (*percentage*) de ciudadanos que votó por la candidata que perdió: _____
la cuestión (*issue*) principal de la campaña: _____

C. Cosas de todos los días.

Use the written cues to tell about an imaginary event that occurred yesterday. When you hear the corresponding number, form sentences using the words provided in the order given, making any necessary changes and additions. You will be using a variety of tenses and moods. Use the preterite in the first sentence.

1. ayer / (yo) ser / testigo / de / acontecimiento
2. (yo) estar / restaurante / cuando / un hombre / desmayarse (*to faint*)
3. ser necesario / que / dueño / de / restaurante / llamar / a / ambulancia
4. (yo) temer / que / hombre / estar / muerto
5. (yo) dudar / que / (yo) poder / ayudarlo
6. cuando / (yo) volver / a casa / (yo) poner / televisor
7. reportero / estar diciendo / que / hombre / estar / hospital / por / semana

D. Conversación (Para entregar). You will hear a conversation, partially printed in your manual, between an interviewer and a job applicant. Then you will participate in a similar conversation, playing the role of **Ud.** Complete the conversation, based on your own preferences. Stop the tape and write the answers.

ENTREVISTADOR: Buenas tardes. Siéntese, por favor.

UD.: _____.

ENTREVISTADOR: A ver... Dígame algo de sus estudios y de sus planes para el futuro.

UD.: _____
_____.

ENTREVISTADOR: Y, ¿cuándo piensa graduarse?

UD.: _____.

ENTREVISTADOR: Bueno, parece que Ud. no ha tenido mucha experiencia, pero sus notas (*grades*) son excelentes. En este puesto, la actitud y el deseo de aprender y entrenarse (*undergo training*) son más importantes que la experiencia. ¿Qué le parece el sueldo que ofrecemos?

UD.: _____.

ENTREVISTADOR: Muy bien. Le voy a ofrecer el puesto con tal de que continúe sacando buenas notas y pueda asistir a los cursos de entrenamiento que ofrecemos aquí una vez por semana. ¿Podrá asistir a los cursos?

UD.: _____.

E. Descripción: ¿Unos discos estupendos? (Para entregar) You will hear a series of questions. Each will be said twice. Answer, based on the cartoon on the next page. Stop the tape and write the answers. As you look at the cartoon and listen to the questions, keep in mind that the tourist in the drawing wants to go to Kiland, an imaginary country where Kiland is spoken. First, stop the tape and look at the cartoon.

1. _____
2. _____
3. _____
4. _____
5. _____
6. _____

F. Y para terminar... Entrevista final (Para entregar). You will hear a series of questions, or situations followed by questions. Each will be said twice. Answer, based on your own experience. Model answers will be given on the tape for the last two questions. Stop the tape and write the answers.

1. _____

2. _____

3. _____

4. _____

5. _____

_____

_____

_____

6. _____

_____

_____

_____

ANSWER KEY

Answers

Primera parte

Pronunciación y ortografía C. En el hotel   1. Muñoz 2. Robles 3. Casimira 4. Gamorro

Los cognados B. Dictado 1. Nicolás es *pesimista*. 2. La profesora Díaz es *reservada*. 3. Juan no es *elegante*. 4. Maite es muy *sincera*. 5. Íñigo no es *impulsivo*.

Segunda parte

Pronunciación y ortografía D. Dictado   1. *rodilla* 2. Ma*ribel* 3. *unilateral* 4. *salvavidas* 5. *olvidadizo*

Tercera parte

Palabras interrogativas B. Dictado   *You should have written the sentences next to the numbers of the following drawings.* 1. ¿Quién es? 2. ¿Qué es? 3. ¿Cuánto es el chocolate? 4. ¿A qué hora es? 5. ¿Dónde está?

CAPÍTULO 1

Vocabulario: Preparación

A. ¿Qué necesita?   *Here is the text of Luisa's list. Check your chart against it.* A ver... para este semestre necesito algunas cosas para mis clases. Necesito cinco cuadernos, siete libros de texto, tres bolígrafos y un lápiz. También debo comprar una mochila y una calculadora.

Los hispanos hablan: ¿Qué materias te gusta estudiar?

1. JOSÉ: *No:* matemáticas; *Sí:* química, física, biología, sicología, literatura. 2. RAUL: *No:* idiomas; *Sí:* ciencias. 3. JULIA: *No:* historia, química; *Sí:* matemáticas, sicología.

Pronunciación y ortografía

D. Dictado   1. *ciencias* 2. *Patricio* 3. *seis* 4. *buenos* 5. *auto* 6. *soy*

Grammar Section 1   A. Minidiálogo: En la clase del profesor Durán: El primer día

PROFESOR DURÁN: Aquí está *el programa* del curso. Son necesarios *el libro* de texto y *un* diccionario. También hay *una lista* de *novelas* y libros de poesía.

ESTUDIANTE 1: ¡Es una lista infinita!

ESTUDIANTE 2: Sí, y los libros cuestan demasiado.

ESTUDIANTE 1: No, *el problema* no es el precio de los libros. ¡Es *el tiempo* para leer los libros!

Grammar Section 2   D. Dictado   1. Hay *unos estudiantes* en *la oficina*. 2. *Los diccionarios* están en *la biblioteca*. 3. No hay *clientes* en *la clase*. 4. ¿Hay *una calculadora* en *la mochila*?

Grammar Section 4   C. Entrevista con la profesora Villegas. Paso 2: ¿Qué recuerdas?   *Answers will vary. Sample answers:* 1. La profesora Villegas enseña tres clases. La profesora Villegas no enseña cuatro clases. 2. (Ella) Enseña español. No enseña francés. 3. (Ella) Trabaja por la noche. 4. (Ella) Habla con los estudiantes. 5. Sí, le gusta la universidad.

CAPÍTULO 2

Vocabulario: Preparación

B. La familia Muñoz   Gregorio = el abuelo; Julia = la abuela; Marta = la tía; Juan = el tío; Sara = la madre; Manuel = el padre; Elena = la prima; Juanito = el primo; Manolito = el hermano

E. Dictado: El inventario   *45* mochilas; *99* lápices; *52* cuadernos; *74* novelas; *31* calculadoras; *100* libros de español

Pronunciación y ortografía

C. Dictado 1. con - *trol* 2. e - le - *fan* - te 3. mo - nu - men - *tal* 4. com - pa - *ñe* - ra 5. *bue* - nos 6. us - *ted*

Minidiálogos y gramática

Grammar Section 5 A. Presentaciones. Paso 2: ¿Qué recuerdas? 1. Marta *es* la *hija* de Lola y Manolo. 2. Lola *es* profesora de *español*. 3. Lola y Manolo *son* de *España*. 4. Lola *es* rubia y *delgada*; Manolo es *alto* y moreno.

Grammar Section 6 A. Hablando de la familia *For each person, you should have checked*: SU TÍO: bajo, soltero; LOS ABUELOS: viejos, activos; SUS PRIMOS: jóvenes, activos; SU HERMANA: casada; SU PADRE: bajo

Grammar Section 7 A. Diego se presenta. Paso 1: Dictado Hola. Me llamo Diego González. Soy estudiante de UCLA, pero este año *asisto* a la Universidad Nacional Autónoma de México. *Vivo* con mi tía Matilde en la Ciudad de México. *Como* pizza con frecuencia y *bebo* cerveza en las fiestas. Me gusta la ropa de moda; por eso *recibo* varios catálogos. *Leo* muchos libros de antropología para mi especialización. También *escribo* muchas cartas a mi familia. *Creo* que una educación universitaria es muy importante. Por eso estudio y *aprendo* mucho. ¡Pero *comprendo* también que es muy importante estar con los amigos y con la familia! **Paso 2: ¿Qué recuerdas?** 1. Diego *asiste* a la Universidad Nacional Autónoma de México. 2. Él *vive* en la casa de su tía Matilde. 3. Diego *come* pizza con frecuencia y *bebe* cerveza en las fiestas. 4. Él *lee* muchos libros de antropología.

CAPÍTULO 3

Vocabulario: Preparación

A. Hablando de la de moda. Paso 1 *For each person you should have checked*: ANA: zapatos de tenis, calcetines, pantalones, camiseta. JUAN: zapatos de tenis, pantalones, camiseta. LUIS: calcetines, camisa, pantalones, cinturón, corbata. **Paso 2. Dictado** corbata: amarilla; camisa: azul; cinturón: negro; pantalones: grises, negros, azules; camiseta: morada, blanca; zapatos de tenis: blancos; calcetines: grises, morados.

C. Dictado: El inventario del Almacén Robles pares de medias de nilón: 1.136; camisas blancas: 567; suéteres rojos: 9.081; pares de zapatos de tenis: 3.329; blusas azules: 111; faldas negras: 843

Pronunciación y ortografía

D. Dictado 1. métrica 2. distribuidor 3. anoche 4. Rosalía 5. actitud 6. sabiduría 7. jóvenes 8. mágico 9. esquema

Minidiálogos y gramática

Grammar Section 9 A. Dictado: Minidiálogo: Una gorra para José Miguel, después de mirar en tres tiendas

> ELISA: ¿Qué gorra *prefieres*, José Miguel?
> JOSÉ MIGUEL: *Prefiero* la gris.
> ELISA: ¡Pero ya *tienes* una gris, y es prácticamente idéntica!
> JOSÉ MIGUEL: Pues, no *quiero* estas otras gorras. ¿Podemos mirar en la tienda anterior otra vez?
> ELISA: ¿Otra vez? Bueno, si realmente insistes...

Grammar Section 10 A. ¿Qué va a hacer Gilberto este fin de semana? a. 2 b. 1 c. 4 d. 3 **Paso 2** *Answers may vary slightly.* 1. Gilberto va al centro comercial con sus amigos. 2. Gilberto va a jugar al basquetbol con su amigo David. 3. Gilberto va a cenar en un restaurante con su familia. 4. Gilberto va a estudiar para un examen de ciencias.

REPASO 1

E. Dictado la especialización de Isabel: *sociología*; el lugar donde trabaja Isabel: *en una librería*; la hora a la cual llegan al centro comercial Isabel y sus amigos: *a las nueve y media de la mañana*; tres de las prendas de vestir que quiere comprar Isabel: *un par de zapatos, calcetines y una falda negra* (also: *un par de pantalones grises, varios suéteres, un abrigo nuevo*); el precio del abrigo que le gusta: *doscientos cincuenta dólares*

CAPÍTULO 4

Vocabulario: Preparación

A. Dictado: El horario de la profesora Velásquez
lunes: mañana: 10:45, clase de conversación
martes: mañana: 8:30, dentista; 10:15, librería; tarde: 3:00, clase de español
miércoles: mañana: 9:00, profesora Díaz; tarde: 1:00, biblioteca
jueves: tarde: 3:00, clase de español
viernes: mañana: 10:45, clase de conversación; tarde: 7:30, fiesta

Los hispanos hablan: Dictado: ¿Qué cosas tienes en tu alcoba?

Equipo de estéreo, reloj despertador, biblioteca, televisor, abanico, lámpara para estudiar, escritorio, cama, tocador, dos *closets*, alfombras, cuadros, fotos, *posters*, una gata de peluche

Pronunciación y ortografía

B. Dictado 1. Alberto viene en veinte minutos. 2. ¿Trabajas el viernes o el sábado? 3. La abuela de Roberto es baja. 4. No hay un baile el jueves, ¿verdad? 5. ¿Vas a llevar esa corbata?

CAPÍTULO 5

Los hispanos hablan: ¿De dónde eres?

JOSÉ: Ciudad: *Río Segundo*, País: *Costa Rica*, El clima: *fresco y agradable*, La gente: *amable*, ¿Hay una universidad en la ciudad?: *No*; CLARA: Ciudad: *Granada*, País: *España*, El clima: *inviernos fríos y hay nieve*, La gente: *joven*, ¿Hay una universidad en la ciudad?: *Sí*; DIANA: Ciudad: *Cali*, País: *Colombia*, El clima: *hace mucho calor*, La gente: *alegre y amable*, ¿Hay una universidad en la ciudad?: *Sí*

Minidiálogos y gramática

Grammar Section 16 A. Comparando dos ciudades. Paso 2: ¿Qué recuerdas? 1. Sevilla es *tan* bonita *como* la Ciudad de México. 2. Sevilla tiene *menos* edificios altos *que* el D.F. 3. En el D.F. no hace *tanto* calor *como* en Sevilla. 4. Sevilla no tiene *tantos* habitantes *como* el D.F.

CAPÍTULO 6

Vocabulario: Preparación

D. ¿Qué sabes y a quién conoces? Paso 1 ENRIQUE: *Sí*: bailar, mis padres; *No*: a Juan, jugar al tenis, esta ciudad. ROBERTO: *Sí*: bailar, jugar al tenis, mis padres; *No*: a Juan, esta ciudad. SUSANA: *Sí*: jugar al tenis, mis padres, esta ciudad; *No*: bailar, a Juan. **Paso 2: ¿Qué recuerdas?** 1. Roberto y Susana *saben* jugar al tenis. 2. Susana *no sabe* bailar. 3. Nadie *conoce* a Juan. 4. Roberto y Enrique *no conocen* bien la ciudad.

Los hispanos hablan: ¿Qué no te gusta nada comer?

You should have checked the following boxes for each person: CLARA: oreja de cerdo, caracoles; XIOMARA: verduras, mondongo, platos sofisticados; TERESA: huevos, mondongo, hamburguesas con pepinillos, comida rápida, mantequilla

Minidiálogos y gramática

Grammar Section 17   A. Encuesta: ¿Qué te gusta comer?   *Here are the foods that were mentioned*: 1. las galletas 2. el atún 3. el agua mineral 4. los frijoles

Grammar Section 19   D. Un nuevo restaurante. Paso 1   *Sí*: hacer reservaciones, pedir el pescado, llegar temprano, pagar con tarjeta de crédito, pagar al contado; *No*: vestirse formalmente, pedir una hamburguesa

REPASO 2

E.   Dictado   el número de alcobas: *4;* el número de baños: *2; ¿*Cuántos metros mide la sala?: *4 metros por 5 metros;* Esta casa está cerca de *las escuelas* y enfrente de *un parque;* la dirección de la casa: *Calle Miraflores, número 246*

CAPÍTULO 7

Pronunciación y ortografía

D.   Dictado   1. Don Guillermo es viejo y generoso. 2. Por lo general, los jóvenes son inteligentes. 3. Juan estudia geografía y geología. 4. A mi amiga Gloria le gustan los gatos.

Minidiálogos y gramática

Grammar Section 22   A. Minidiálogo: Elisa habla de su viaje a Puerto Rico   1. F: Elisa viajó a Puerto Rico en avión. 2. F: El viaje a Puerto Rico fue largo. 3. C 4. C 5. F: A Elisa le gustó su viaje.

CAPÍTULO 8

Pronunciación y ortografía

C.   Dictado   1. quemar 2. quince 3. campaña 4. compras 5. coqueta 6. comedor

Minidiálogos y gramática

Grammar Section 24   A. La fiesta de sorpresa. Paso 1   *You should have checked the following actions for each person*: JULIA: vestirse elegantemente; VERÓNICA: vestirse elegantemente; TOMÁS: sentirse mal, dormir toda la tarde, preferir quedarse en casa; ERNESTO (el narrador): vestirse elegantemente

Grammar Section 25   A. Dictado: Una fiesta de sorpresa para Lupita   El viernes pasado, mis amigos y yo dimos una fiesta de sorpresa para una de nuestras amigas, Lupita. Yo escribí las invitaciones y *se las* mandé a todos. Carmen hizo un pastel y *me lo* dio antes de la fiesta. Anita preparó una comida elegante y *nos la* sirvió en el comedor. Arturo y Patricio sacaron muchas fotos y *se las* regalaron a Lupita. Todos llevamos regalos y *se los* presentamos a Lupita al final de la fiesta. ¡Lupita nos dijo que fue una fiesta maravillosa!

CAPÍTULO 9

Los hispanos hablan: ¿Cuál es tu pasatiempo favorito?
Paso 1   *Here is the text of Xiomara and Gabriela's answers. Compare it with the notes you took.*
XIOMARA: Mi pasatiempo favorito es salir con mis amigas a dar paseos por la ciudad o ir a la piscina

a nadar un rato. También me gusta muchísimo hacer aeróbicos en mi casa. Mi mejor amiga es Teresa y con ella es con quien salgo. Nos gusta ver los aparadores de las tiendas, ir de compras, hablar con nuestros novios, ir a buscar amigos o amigas, conversar en mi casa, tomar refrescos en las sodas, sentarnos en los bancos de los parques y ver películas.

GABRIELA: Bueno, no tengo sólo un pasatiempo favorito. En realidad son muchas las cosas que me gusta hacer en mi tiempo libre. Me gusta leer y escuchar música, me gusta ir a mi club y reunirme con mis amigos. Allí practicamos deportes —tenis, natación, *squash*. Algo que hacemos muy amenudo, generalmente los fines de semana, es organizar *picnics*, y más tarde, en la noche, nos reunimos en fiestas o vamos al cine o a algún café. **Paso 2** *Answers may vary. Answers*: 1. Las actividades que tienen en común las dos jóvenes son el salir o reunirse con sus amigos, nadar y ver películas. 2. Algunos de los pasatiempos que no tienen en común son el ir de compras, el leer, el escuchar música, el hacer aeróbicos, el conversar en casa, el ir al club, el jugar al tenis/*squash* y el organizar picnics.

Pronunciación y ortografía

C. Dictado   1. Paco toca el piano para sus parientes. 2. Los tíos de Tito son de Puerto Rico. 3. ¿Por qué pagas tanto por la ropa? 4. Tito trabaja para el padre de Pepe.

Minidiálogos y gramática

Grammar Section 26   A. Minidiálogo: Diego habla de los aztecas. Paso 1: Dictado   Los aztecas construyeron grandes pirámides para sus dioses. En lo alto de cada pirámide *había* un templo donde *tenían* lugar las ceremonias y se *ofrecían* los sacrificios. Las pirámides *tenían* muchísimos escalones y *era* necesario subirlos todos para llegar a los templos.

Cerca de muchas pirámides *había* un terreno como el de una cancha de basquetbol. Allí se *celebraban* partidos que *eran* parte de una ceremonia. Los participantes *jugaban* con una pelota de goma dura, que sólo *podían* mover con las caderas y las rodillas. **Paso 2: ¿Qué recuerdas?**   1. Los aztecas ofrecían *sacrificios* a sus *dioses*. 2. El juego de pelota que se jugaba era parte de una *ceremonia*. 3. Las *pirámides* eran estructuras altas que tenían una función *religiosa*.

C.   En el aeropuerto: Una despedida. Paso 1   *You should have checked the following actions for each person*: GUSTAVO: estar en el aeropuerto, ir a San José, sentirse triste. LA MADRE DE GUSTAVO: estar en el aeropuerto, estar muy nerviosa. EL PADRE DE GUSTAVO: estar en el aeropuerto, estar preocupado.

Grammar Section 27   A. Las opiniones de Margarita. Paso 1: Dictado
La fiesta más divertida del año es *el Carnaval*.
El peor mes del año es *mayo*.
Le mejor película del mundo es *Como agua para chocolate*.
El quehacer doméstico más aburrido es *pasar la aspiradora*.

REPASO 3

B.   Dictado   el tipo de boleto que el turista quiere: *un boleto de ida y vuelta*; la fecha de salida: *el doce de noviembre*; la fecha de regreso: *el veintisiete de noviembre*; la sección y la clase en que va a viajar: *la sección de no fumar, primera clase*; la ciudad de la cual va a salir el avión: *Chicago*; el tipo de hotel que quiere: *un hotel con aire acondicionado que esté cerca de la playa*; el nombre del hotel en que se va a quedar: *el Hotel Presidente*

CAPÍTULO 10

Vocabulario: Preparación

D.   Descripción. Hablando de problemas de salud   *Possible answers*: 1. Darío tiene dolor de estómago. (A Darío le duele el estómago.) Él está en un consultorio. 2. Toño tiene fiebre. (Toño tiene dolor de cabeza.) Está en casa (en su cama). 3. Alma tiene dolor de muela. (A Alma le duele la muela [una muela]). Está en el consultorio (la oficina) de la dentista. 4. Gabriela está muy enferma. Tiene dolor de cabeza, está mareada y congestionada. Ella está en una oficina (su oficina).

Los hispanos hablan: ¿Practicas un deporte? ¿Por qué?

Paso 1

	DEPORTE(S)	RAZÓN POR LA CUAL SE PRACTICA
Clara	correr	puedes practicarlo con amigos, es emocionante
Antonio	el tenis	le apasiona
Gabriela	*squash*	es entretenido y tiene mucha acción
Patricia	el tenis	es buenísimo para la salud
Teresa	caminar / nadar	son buenos para el cuerpo / no permiten que uno se engorde
José	el fútbol	es saludable, divertido, emocionante
Xiomara	la natación / los aeróbicos	es saludable, le gusta sentirse bien con su cuerpo y verse bonita
Erick	la natación	sirve de ejercicio físico y mental, ayuda a uno a mantenerse en forma

Paso 2   1. la natación 2. cinco

Minidiálogos y gramática

Grammar Section 29   A. Dictado: Minidiálogo: En el consultorio de la Dra. Méndez

DRA. MÉNDEZ: ¿Cuándo *empezó* a sentirse mal su hija?

LOLA: Ayer por la tarde. *Estaba* congestionada, *tosía* mucho y se *quejaba* de que le *dolían* el cuerpo y la cabeza.

DRA. MÉNDEZ: ¿Y le *notó* algo de fiebre?

LOLA: Sí. Por la noche le *tomé* la temperatura y *tenía* 38 grados.

DRA. MÉNDEZ: A ver... Tal vez necesito ponerle una inyección...

MARTA: Eh... bueno... ¡Creo que ahora me encuentro un poco mejor!

Grammar Section 30   En el consultorio. Paso 2: ¿Qué recuerdas?   lo que tenía la narradora: *una temperatura alta y tos;* la persona con quien quería hablar: *la doctora Blanco;* lo que le dijo la recepcionista: *dijo que la doctora estaba ocupada;* la persona a quien va a llamar la próxima vez que se enferme: *va a llamar a su madre*

CAPÍTULO 11

Pronunciación y ortografía

D. Dictado   1. El cumpleaños de Begoña es mañana. 2. La señorita (Srta.) Núñez estudia mucho. 3. Los señores (Sres.) Ibáñez son los dueños del Hotel España. 4. Esa muchacha es chilena. 5. Hay ocho mochilas en la clase.

Minidiálogos y gramática

Grammar Section 33   C. Dictado   1. A ellos *se les olvidó* el número de teléfono de Beatriz. 2. A Juan *se le perdieron* las gafas. 3. Durante nuestro último viaje, *se nos quedó* el equipaje en la estación del tren. 4. A los niños *se les rompieron* los juguetes.

Los hispanos hablan: Quiero...

Paso 1   *You should have checked the following items for each person*: DIANA: ropa, cosméticos, discos compactos, aretes, un radio portátil, una grabadora, un ordenador, una bicicleta. JOSÉ: ropa, un estéreo, una guitarra, un auto, un gran trabajo, una batería. KAREN: ropa, un estéreo, un auto (coche), un boleto de avión.

Paso 2   1. De las tres personas, ¿quién quiere más cosas? *Diana quiere más cosas.*
2. De las tres personas, ¿quién quiere viajar? *Karen quiere viajar.*
3. ¿Qué cosas desea más de una persona? *La ropa, el auto y el estéreo.*

Pronunciación y ortografía

E. Dictado   1. El señor Muñoz es de España y habla español. 2. Yolanda Carrillo es de Castilla.
3. ¿Llueve o no llueve allá en Yucatán?

Minidiálogos y gramática

Grammar Section 36   C. ¿Qué quiere Arturo? Paso 1   *You should have checked the following actions for each person*: SU HERMANA: no usar su coche, prestarle su cámara; SU HERMANO MENOR: bajar el volumen del estéreo; SUS HERMANITOS: no jugar «Nintendo»

Grammar Section 37   A. Presiones de la vida moderna. Paso 2: ¿Qué recuerdas?
1. Los clientes quieren que Margarita *solucione sus problemas* técnicos.
2. Su jefa no quiere que ella *se equivoque.*
3. Margarita quiere que su horario *sea más flexible.*
4. A veces, es necesario que Margarita *trabaje los fines de semana.*
5. Margarita prefiere que su coche no *tenga teléfono celular.*

REPASO 4

C. Dictado   lo que el narrador quería compra en la tienda: *un teléfono celular;* ¿Cuánto pagó por el aparato? *20 dólares;* lo que tiene que pagar al mes: *40 dólares;* ¿Cuánto tiempo hace que tiene el aparato?: *2 meses;* tres de los aparatos que todavía quiere comprar: *un contestador automático, una videocasetera, una cámara de video* (also: *una computadora portátil, un* fax)

CAPÍTULO 13

Vocabulario: Preparación

E.   Poniendo las cosas en orden. Paso 2   *Possible answers*: 1. Junio es el sexto mes del año. (El sexto mes del año es junio.) 2. Agosto es el octavo mes del año. (El octavo mes del año es agosto.) 3. El primer día de la semana en el calendario hispánico es lunes. (Lunes es el primer día de la semana en el calendario hispánico.)

Minidiálogos y gramática

Grammar Section 40   B. Se venden coches nuevos y usados   1. Dudo que el coche del anuncio número 3 sea una ganga. 2. El auto del anuncio número 2 es un auto pequeño y económico. 3. Es probable que el coche del anuncio número 1 gaste mucha gasolina.

CAPÍTULO 14

Pronunciación y ortografía

B. Dictado   1. *fosfato* 2. *atención* 3. *amoníaco* 4. *teología* 5. *oposición* 6. *fotografía* 7. *colección* 8. *arquitecta*

CAPÍTULO 15

Los hispanos hablan: Las relaciones sociales

Paso 2   *Here is a transcript of Eduardo's answer. Compare it to the summary that you wrote.*

Creo que una de las cosas más difíciles de aceptar al principio fue la falta de vida social. Generalmente, los latinoamericanos y los españoles dicen que extrañan el contacto social que hay en nuestros países. Aquí la gente se dedica mucho a su trabajo y usa el tiempo libre para estudiar o dedicarse a algún pasatiempo. Esto, naturalmente, casi no les deja tiempo libre para los amigos. Generalmente, la vida social en los países hispanos es más espontánea. Por ejemplo, es muy común que los amigos visiten sin avisar, lo cual aquí es mal visto por mucha gente.

Una diferencia grande que veo es la falta de contacto entre las generaciones. Generalmente, creo que hay mucha más interacción entre las diferentes generaciones en el mundo hispano. Por ejemplo, los niños participan en las actividades de la gente grande y van a todos lados, así también como los viejos.

También la necesidad de la vida privada de los estadounidenses es un concepto un poco incomprensible para nosotros. Cuando alguien de la familia de mi esposa viene a visitarnos de Europa, a veces se queda mucho tiempo en nuestra casa. A muchos amigos de los Estados Unidos, les parece insólito que no nos molesten estas largas visitas. En contraste, a nosotros los hispanos, nos parece insólito que estos amigos, a veces, pongan a sus propios padres en un hotel cuando estos los vienen a visitar.

Creo que, generalizando un poco, se puede decir que los estadounidenses son educados para ser independientes desde jóvenes. En contraste, los hispanos se mantienen más cerca de sus familias. Por ejemplo, no es nada raro que un hijo soltero de treinta años todavía viva con sus padres. Aquí en los Estados Unidos sólo conozco a una persona en esta situación.

REPASO 5

C. Dictado   el nombre del museo: *el Museo del Pueblo*; el tipo de arte que se va a exhibir: *tejidos y objetos de cerámica auténticos*; la fecha en que se va a abrir el museo: *el lunes, 31 de julio*; el nombre del director del museo: *Arturo Rosa*; la hora de la recepción: *las 6 de la tarde*; ¿Es necesario hacer reservaciones?: *no*; ¿Va a ser posible hablar con algunos de los artistas?: *sí*

CAPÍTULO 16

Vocabulario: Preparación

C. En busca de un puesto. Paso 1   5: tratar de caerle bien al entrevistador; 6: aceptar el puesto y renunciar a mi puesto actual; 2: pedirle una solicitud de empleo; 4: ir a la entrevista; 3: llenar la solicitud; 1: llamar a la directora de personal

Pronunciación y ortografía

C. Dictado   1. cobró 2. cobro 3. toque 4. toqué 5. describe 6. descríbemela 7. levántate 8. levanta 9. franceses 10. francés

E. Dictado   1. Creo *que* ese regalo es para *mí*. 2. Aquí *está tu té*. ¿*Qué* más quieres? 3. *Él* dijo *que te* iba a llamar a las ocho. 4. *Sí, mi* amigo *se* llama Antonio.

CAPÍTULO 17

Los hispanos hablan: Más sobre las ciudades hispanas

1. Hace que por la noche no haya nadie en las calles. 2. Hace que los adolescentes tomen más alcohol.
3. Por eso en las ciudades sólo hay menores de dieciocho (diez y ocho) años y mayores de veintisiete (veinte y siete).

Pronunciación y ortografía

C.   1. Enero es el primer mes del año. 2. ¡No entiendo lo que me estás diciendo! 3. ¿Trabajaba en una tienda? 4. No olvides el diccionario la próxima vez, ¿eh? 5. Nació el catorce de abril de mil novecientos sesenta y uno. 6. ¿Adónde crees que vas a ir a estas horas de la noche?

D. Dictado   1. ¿Cuál es tu profesión? ¿Te pagan bien? 2. Tú no la conoces, ¿verdad? 3. ¿Prefiere Ud. que le sirva la comida en el patio? 4. ¡Qué ejercicio más fácil! 5. No sé dónde viven, pero sí sé su número de teléfono.

CAPÍTULO 18

Pronunciación y ortografía

D. Dictado   1. Cuando viajes a Madrid, no olvides tu cámara. 2. Mandaré la carta en cuanto compre sellos y un sobre. 3. Perdón, señora, ¿pudiera decirme dónde está la estación del metro? 4. ¡Dios mío! ¡No sabía que iba a costar tanto para hablar con un abogado! 5. Oye, Julia, ¿oíste las últimas noticias?

REPASO 6

B. Dictado   el nombre de la candidata que perdió las elecciones: *Quejada;* el nombre del candidato que ganó las elecciones: *Sánchez;* el porcentaje de ciudadanos que votó por la candidata que perdió: *treinta (30) por ciento;* la cuestión principal de la campaña: *el medio ambiente*

About the Author

Maria Sabló-Yates is a native of Panama. She holds a B.A. and an M.A. from the University of Washington (Seattle). She has taught at the University of Washington and Central Michigan University (Mt. Pleasant, Michigan), and is currently an instructor at Delta College (University Center, Michigan). She is the author of previous editions of the *Puntos de partida* Laboratory Manual, and of the first through fourth editions of the Laboratory Manual to accompany *¿Qué tal? An Introductory Course*.